A GOOD MAN

A GOOD MAN

The Life of Sam J. Ervin

by

Dick Dabney

Illustrated with Photographs

Houghton Mifflin Company Boston

1976

LIBRARY OF CONGRESS CATALOGING IN PUBLICATION DATA
Dabney, Dick.   A good man.   Includes index.
1.   Ervin, Samuel James, 1896–   I.   Title.
E748.E93D32   973.924′092′4 [B]   75-42421
ISBN 0-395-20715-0

Printed in the United States of America

v 10 9 8 7 6 5 4 3 2 1

This book is dedicated to
Reba Lawson Dabney

Dr. Hu
speaks
twenty-three
   languages.

What loneliness.

— MAILER

Illustrations

following page 180

A GOOD MAN

Chapter 1

HE BEGAN LIFE like everybody else, not knowing very much, and most of his thinking was done at night — because in the daytime he was shuttled around with the other children and didn't have time to think; dominated by the other children, too. Being, at two and three years old, the youngest, or the youngest walking, and therefore the most susceptible to domination. So he did most of his thinking in the nights, which were darker than they ever were to be again. There was no street lamp out on the dirt road that ran by the big white house, and the leaves of the ancient oaks shut out the moon.

It was dark, and he would lie there, perhaps having been awakened by violent noises from the other bed, where his older brother, Ed, who maybe wasn't going to make it, lay wracked with whooping cough and later with asthma; who would wake up gasping, lurch out of bed, and stumble over the cool wood floor to the straightbacked chair to sit, erect and fragile, looking out to that dark world he knew no better than Sam did. Ed was two years older than Sam, the oldest son, and was expected to grow up to be a lawyer like his daddy. But Sam didn't know about that, and didn't know the father very well, either — that dapper, dry little man who was gone away to the mountain courts.

Sometimes the mother would come in, a tall woman who spoke gently to the boy in the chair, hugged him, and went out, leaving Ed

still sitting there, gasping, making it seem to Sam that the high-ceilinged room itself was out of breath, that he himself was out of breath.
Then the gasping would subside and the brother would go back to
bed, back to sleep, and it would be Sam lying there breathing heavily,
staring up at the darkened ceiling across which no trapezoids of light
yet slid.

No automobiles then, 1898, not in Morganton, North Carolina, and
no paved roads, no radio. What sounds you heard at night were
human sounds, sounds of people you knew. Or animal scuttlings,
wind sounds, all of which were human, too, or you feared they were.
Morganton, population 2000, was a half-mile away. Beyond the
house was the absolute countryside and the deep blue mountains,
deep blue by day. Sam didn't know what went on up there, either,
except that his father would saddle the horse, Nellie, and ride out in
that direction toward the mountain courts and whatever mighty
deeds were done up there.

There would be long spells when there was nothing to be heard, or
not much: dog-bark or horse-whicker, the wind nudging the leaves,
his mother pacing on the front porch below, waiting for his father to
come home. Perhaps she wasn't even pacing; maybe just sitting in the
chair down there, and Sam would hear the rockers creaking. She was
still a young woman, thirty-three, and her husband was passionately
in love with her. That showed up in the letters he wrote home from
the mountain courts, letters in which he would mention the other
children by name — Laura, Margaret, Catharine, Ed — but not Sam,
never Sam, yet. Sometimes, early in the night, there would come the
sounds of giggling from the room where the three sisters slept.

Sam, too, loved the woman down there on the porch, but she was
busy with the other children, especially busy with Ed, who was cross-
eyed as well as asthmatic, and whose chronic illnesses meant that the
expectations of the father might yet be visited on the next in line, on
Sam.

And so, at two or three, Sam was already something of a politician,
as most children in large families are; was beginning to learn that his
adoration of his mother would never be reciprocated in the way his
deepest heart desired, and that the good life, therefore, would consist
not of adoration but of mingling harmoniously with the dozen or so
family members who lived within a few roads of where he lay now in

his bed, in the dark and still expectancy of this North Carolina night, at the end of the nineteenth century. He was woven densely into a family, albeit about the fringe. So long as Ed's case was doubtful, about the fringe. He would wait for the train, and the train would take a long time to get there.

The pigs snorted, squealed, hustled thudding against the pen's sides — meaning, fox or coon or wild dog prowling; then silence. Which went on for so long that the house's smells reclaimed him, the pungency of turpentine, aroma of mustard plaster.

Those were the medicines used by his father's father, who slept down the hall, who was ill from pleurotonea and from cataracts and no doubt from other things besides, and who came upstairs shortly after the boys did and fell into a profound sleep. This old man, who was seventy-five, slept with his foot-long white beard outside the covers.

Whether Sam was to become senior son or not, he already belonged to the world of men, and he sensed that; was already part of an elite, poor though the family was, off to the side though the family was, then. He was a man and he was white and above all was healthy. Although he had it proven to him every night that health was a state from which one could be dis-elected at any moment.

He would listen for the train. Yes. Lingering under the medicine smells, blending into the smell of what came off the mint bed, was the sooty aroma of that train. You could not smell the outhouse as a general rule nor could you smell the pigs, because there was a Negro with a shovel, Uncle Settlemyre, who came once a week and took care of all that. Negroes took care of a lot of things in Morganton. Sam would concentrate on the train.

At first you couldn't tell whether it was coming. There would be a faint whisper, then nothing. Perhaps it had indeed been the train itself passing momentarily a declivity in the blue mountains, which were black by night. Or it might have been the same imagination that had you thinking you couldn't breathe, and you would go to sleep long minutes later, having heard no more. Or there would be another whisper, perhaps louder, then another, then no more intervals, but that one continuous marvelous unnamable whisk of steel wheels on steel rails knifing through the night, and then you were certain it was it, it, it, it, it, the train rattling toward the outskirts of town, the whistle shrieking more wildly than any wind night had ever torn down from those mountains. What made the engineer pull the cord, the townsmen said, was the madhouse. He had a relative there, they said, and the whistle's shriek was recognition of the place where shrieks were born.

Madness was the main industry of the town, because the Burke Tannery, the Dunavant Cotton Mills, and the Morganton Manufacturing and Trading Company were puny enterprises compared to the mammoth state hospital set up on the outer side of town. Sometimes you could see patients being marched in long platoons through the streets.

Sometimes the whistle's shriek would announce the return of his father, and, fifteen minutes later, there would be the halloo from down the dirt road and the answering halloo from the porch, his mother's soft voice, and the bootsteps down the flagstones and up the stairs, and the intense conference, lasting God knew how long, as the boy waited. Then those same bootsteps scraping on the stairs, and his father, smelling of leather, would be in the room, half-blinded by the kerosene lamp he had lit his way up the stairs with. And Sam, deep there in the darkness, and able to see better than the father, would watch as the man in the Prince Albert coat walked softly across the bare wood floor to stand looking down on the labored breathing of the eldest son. Then the father would come over to Sam's crib, and the arm would extend blackly down and Sam would reach his hand up and grasp the thing and the father would go out and Sam would lie there in the darkness, with his mouth full of the maple sugar candy, the one thing he knew for sure came down from the mountain courts.

More often than not, though, his father wouldn't come. There would be only the night smells and night sounds, and Sam would fall asleep to the hammering of rain on the tin roof. It rained a lot in those mountains then, as it does now. One night there were curses, a pistol shot, running feet.

No matter how early Sam got up in the morning, his grandfather had gone down before him, and was working in the garden. It was a large garden, almost an acre. The Negro, of course, came regularly to work it, and the father worked it, too, when he was home. And when he wasn't home, sent down instructions about what to plant, and when, and what nutrients to put in the soil. But the grandfather worked it more regularly than the father or even the Negro did, and was always to be found out there in the cool of the pine-smelling morning. When it began to warm up he would take the hoe to the toolshed, draw a bucket of water out of the well, wash up, and go into the parlor. The three sisters and Ed would follow him in there, the door would be shut, and Sam would be left alone. Lessons.

The house, which the grandfather had named Fern Hill, was a large, white-frame place with four bedrooms upstairs, a parlor, dining room and two bedrooms downstairs, and a narrow front porch. The kitchen was a little shack out back that had only recently been connected to the big house by a hallway. That was for the four-way ventilation, Sam's father having been taught that it was healthier that way. On rainy days, Sam would spend a lot of time in that hallway, alone, feeding the ants with pinches of white flour, thereby bringing down on himself the wrath of the big Negress, Betty, the cook. He didn't dare go down to the creek, which ran through the pine woods. There were Negroes living in tar-paper shacks along that creek, and not good Negroes, either; not like Betty.

He would follow his mother around the house, or sit with her out on the front porch, watching people pass by on the dirt road. She liked to laugh a lot. Her laughter was gentle, and sometimes she would be overcome by it. She had another kind of polite, forced laughter that she used when his father told the same stories over and over again. She called him by his full name, Samuel, and seemed to expect more out of him than she would out of someone named Sam.

In the afternoons, when the other children were playing out in the yard, the grandfather would sit alone in the parlor, with the door open, writing with a goose-quill pen on paper he ruled himself. He would call to Sam's sisters to come rule the paper for him but they wouldn't do it. So there he sat, writing in his secret journal, no one knew what. This old man, whose white hair once had been sandy, as Sam's was now, was a professional novelist, although it did not pay at all anymore, and had never paid much.

That had begun right after the War Between the States, down in Manning, South Carolina, where the Ervins had lived then, and where the old man, John Witherspoon Ervin, had been a school-teacher, serving the sons of planters, and receiving in return, more

often than not, their promissory notes to pay "later," which became
"never" when General Sherman gave Manning his special attention
on the way north from having done the same for Atlanta.

There had been no jobs and no money. His assets consisted of the
classical education he'd received at the University of South Carolina,
his lifelong interest in history and literature — and not much else.
Thus, learning how to write novels had seemed the practical thing to
do. He'd gone into his study each morning and locked the door,
locked the eight kids out, locked the wife out, locked out as far as
possible the charred stench of Sherman's passing, and would write all
day long on ledger paper left over from collecting the Confederate
taxes, with quill pens plucked from a neighbor's goose, with ink his
wife made out of roots.

He'd worked hard, sleeping in his study, speaking to no one,
and emerging only on Saturday nights. Sam (Sr.), the youngest child,
ten years old then, was already hired out, picking cotton with the
Negroes in the field, all day, every day, at a half-cent a pound, storing
up in his tough and sunbeaten mind the memory of the tall, pale man
who stayed in where it was cool.

One of John Witherspoon Ervin's novels, *The Eutaw Cadet,* brought
in $500, a year's good wages in those times. But his other novels and
stories fetched as little as $20. So that, in the decade after the War
Between the States, when the father was writing *Silver Shot, The Bride
of St. David's, The Unexpected Letter, The Belle of the Ball-Room, A
Mysterious Disappearance,* and things like that, the work-hardened little
son was brooding on his own servitude; and out of his sun-fried
resentment the character of Sam Jr., a child more than twenty years
away from being born, was being formed in the long hot silences of
the South Carolina cotton fields.

By 1877 the Ervins were so poor they had to move, and when they
made the trek up to Morganton, North Carolina, it was the bitter little
son who was in charge. The novelist tried to found a school for boys
in Morganton, failed at it, and, of course, kept on writing. Like most
Southern writers of his era, he was unwilling to risk his sanity on an
attempt to see things in the present time, and so his stories were
redolent of the ante-bellum sentimentality common to the time. Even
so, they were well crafted, and good enough to make a dollar now and
again. But now, in 1898, as he sat writing in his secret journal, on
pages he ruled himself, he was broke and dependent.

He couldn't afford to go down to Lazarus Brothers Department Store and buy a ruled book. And, after thirty-three years as a writer, it was still a goose-quill pen he wrote with, not the fountain pen he wanted. But Little Sam, watching from the doorway as the old man wrote in the book, didn't know these things, didn't know that his grandfather was begging, in his elegant handwriting, for Jesus to give him some money nor that Jesus said no.

When the old man was done with lamenting his condition, he would write about the way the weather was, what flowers he had seen in his solitary walks along the bank of the Catawba River, memories of old girl friends, plans for new stories, hopes for his grandchildren. He would write about politics, too, and not as something ruled off in heavy lines from the way the flowers grew or what the neighbors were up to or who had been sent to the madhouse. Because politics in Burke County, North Carolina, then and now, was personal, had faces and names and even smells, and sounds, too, which were familiar sounds and not piped down from New York City or anywhere else but manufactured in Burke County as surely as the few sticks of furniture they made there were. Politics was home-grown, personal, as were the words and oaths that led up to the pistol shot that came in the night.

It happened a few hundred yards down Lenoir Street, where a Mr. Small, full of liquor, declared he was going to vote the straight Republican ticket, and where a Mr. Suddereth, equally full of liquor, said, "You can't do that; you shouldn't say that." But Small responded, "I will say anything I damn please, and do it, too, because it is a free country." Upon which Suddereth blew out Small's brains.

And the old man, writing in his secret journal, saw it this way: that the Republican Party was made up of carpetbaggers, scalawags, and Negroes; that these people were destructive of order and rapacious toward white womanhood, that the carpetbaggers and scalawags courted the Negro vote for the sake of sordid gain. So that while it might be deplorable that Mr. Suddereth blew out the brains of Mr. Small, it was understandable, it certainly wasn't insane; not like the case of the sheriff who wandered off one Saturday night into the mountains, where he was found gibbering in nonsense syllables to himself.

To John Witherspoon Ervin, as to most white men in Morganton, the notion that the sheriff carried madness in him was no more remarkable than the fact that Suddereth carried a gun. Most grown men in Morganton toted guns in those days. After all, Morganton wasn't part of the wisteria and magnolia South the old man wrote about in his novels, and never had been. It was more like the frontier, and the chief difference between it and the land of the wild-west dime stories was that in Morganton the guns and the madnesses were concealed as long as possible.

You did the best you could and tried to keep going. One morning the old man set out on foot to walk the mile to the town square, and saw, coming down the sidewalk, first one black ant, then three, then hundreds, thousands, millions of them surging blackly in a three-foot-wide column, coming toward him from the direction of town. He stamped his foot and saw them writhing there in the hundreds in death-agony, and thought, this isn't real, and stopped some passerby to ask if they saw the ants. To which they replied, no.

So the old man kept on about his business, walking down to the town square through the massive column of ants — and returning home to see the bare white walls of the Ervin house covered with gorgeous, brightly colored floral prints, and the ceiling so covered, and everything covered that way, and thought, well, I can't do anything about it. And so went on with the garden-tending and the lesson-teaching, and day by day meticulously recording everything in his journal including the ants and flowers. Madness was part of life, as were flowers, as was politics. And he wrote of politics urgently, as a warrior.

Because the War Between the States wasn't over yet. The rise of the agrarian populists in the early nineties had led to the ascendancy of a successful coalition of Republicans, populists, and Negroes, and since then the state had been ruled, for the most part, by them. And the old man was outraged by this; wrote about it in his journal.

Year after year the northern papers, knowing nothing of the negro and of the conditions that surround us in the South will declaim against our treatment of the negro and keep alive and increase the prejudices of the northern people against those of the South. It was the most bitter and cruel act that a civilized government ever perpetuated against one section of its people when it gave the ballot to the negro knowing that in many parts of our country it meant the complete subjection of men of the Anglo-Saxon blood, to a race that sinks back ever into barbarism when left to itself, and knows nothing of the rights and duties of citizenship. It was a cruel and malicious act to impose such conditions on the people of the South. We can never be a *thoroughly* united people until this great evil is removed, and we reestablish the wise, sound doctrine of our fathers: that in every section of our country White Supremacy must prevail.

This theme dominated the Red Shirt campaign of 1898, when Little Sam was two, and the Democratic Party, the white man's party, decided once and for all to rid North Carolina politics of the Negro. Most of that fall the father was gone, stump-speaking along the railroad lines in favor of the Democratic Party and the white man.

He did it for the principle of the thing, because, there weren't many Negroes in Burke County. They had never been brought there in great numbers because land parcels were small and people couldn't afford them. This was mountainous, western North Carolina. It wasn't like the flat, sandy, tobacco- and cotton-growing eastern part of the state, where Negroes abounded, where the wealthy landowners, before the war, had been able to afford them.

Thus it was difficult for the voters in this part of the state to imagine how thoroughly they dominated the political life of the east. So Sam's father was traveling the railroad lines, showing photographs of the black candidates from the east, by way of proof, passing the pictures around in torchlit crowds, then mounting the stump to speak with fervid precision in favor of white supremacy.

Sam's father, riding the train grimly through the reds and yellows of autumn North Carolina, believed that by taking action, he was working for his children in a practical way. All that otiose journal-writing stuff did no good, and left you at the mercy of events. He still regretted not having been sent away to college, and none of his own children was going to miss that experience if he could help it, and none of them was going to be debilitated by dreamery. And for them to have any future at all, the white man would have to rule North Carolina once more.

North Carolina, was its own republic, as remote from the rest of the United States as South Africa. It was a green and private world, and not many people lived in it. Wilmington, the largest town, 400 miles away on the coast, had only twenty thousand inhabitants. Raleigh, the state capital, had about twelve thousand; Charlotte, a few hundred less; and Winston-Salem and Asheville maybe ten or eleven thousand each. In this world through which he was traveling, people knew one another, personally, and fought one another, personally, in the Red Shirt campaign of 1898. It was so bloody that North Carolina's Republican Senator Pritchard wrote to President McKinley, asking him to send in troops to keep peace on election day. He said that threats had been made by Democrats which put the Negroes in a state of alarm.

Which was the truth, although McKinley was quick to discount it, and sent no troops. Negroes had been threatened, all right, and at best, the Negro who showed up to vote would not be regarded as a good Negro anymore, and hence would not be so likely to land a job. Or, if he had one, would be more likely to lose it, and plummet down instantly from the world of the good Negroes — such as Betty and her little daughter Polly, who helped her about the Ervin house, or Miles Tanner, who worked in the yard and cut the wood — into the world of the low-down Negroes — such as those who lived squalidly along the creek.

The grandfather cared enough about the election to walk down to the polling place and stand on his feet as chairman of the board of judges for sixteen hours, and then walk the mile back home, having turned away scores of unregistered Negroes during the day. In the end, the Democrats won, carrying the state by twenty-five thousand votes. They acted quickly, too, passing an amendment to the state constitution requiring that Negroes pass a literacy test before they were allowed to vote. This put the Negroes out of business. These Democrats, these white men, were to rule North Carolina for another seventy-four years.

That election of '98 had other consequences for the Ervins. Emboldened by his success on the stump, Sam Sr. ran for the Democratic nomination for Superior Court judge a couple years later. And thereby learned something about himself, or perhaps confirmed something he already knew: that he was not universally loved. He was defeated, and never ran for public office again. Although he still gave a lot of speeches.

That was the way he talked to people, by speeches. That was the way it was, even out on the narrow front porch of Fern Hill, with his family fanned out in a long row to either side of him. He would speak with great precision and at great length, brooking no interruption except for the occasional polite question, basking righteously in the murmur of laughter that formed the scrollwork around the stories he told over and over.

When Little Sam got to be four, he was admitted to the front parlor in the mornings, where his grandfather, who was nearly blind now, began to teach him his ABC's, thumping him smartly on the head with a flipped finger when the lesson failed to take. So that in later years all he could remember of his grandfather were the words punctuating the flips of the finger to the skull: "Mighty thick. Mighty thick."

MURDERER

Morganton was a disappointment; in fact, not even there. There was just the concrete trough, called U.S. 40, and a turn-off ramp that said Morganton, and, through the dense and rainspattered January-gray fog, the pink neon acclamation of a Holiday Inn. I checked in there, and set out on fogshrouded State Route 18 toward where I thought the town was. I drove for a couple miles through the fog, seeing nothing but a filling station here, a Colonel's Pantry there, until I came over the top of tall hill and saw, looming through the dense gray fog, massive redbrick buildings, many of them, hulking on a slope near a tall smokestack: the State Hospital for the Insane. Morganton.

Sam's address was in the phone book, but in half an hour of driving around I couldn't find the place. What I did find was a shabby little town, of no particular antiquity, the town square, with its old gray court house only a tone lighter than the cold wet fog, and finally, the First Presbyterian Church.

This was the new one, the old church having been torn down in 1960 to make way for a building and loan association. This was of red brick, with white columns, and lots of grass and boxwood hedges around it. It had acquired, in a decade and a half, that look of instant venerableness Southern churches are so good at getting.

Tucked away from the big street was a small graveyard, which had been dug up and brought from the old church. And under the dripping black branch of a small tree that had been planted there was, among the other gravestones, a large rectangular marker boldly chiseled JOHN WITHERSPOON ERVIN. There were a few empty Miller beer cans on the grass. Apparently the kids came here to drink.

When I got back to the motel room I phoned the Senator, who suggested I come over the next day. And so, early the next afternoon, which was a bright afternoon, with the blue mountains standing out crisply now above the town, I went to his dark brick house, and stood there with the tape recorder slung over my shoulder, waiting for Sam Ervin to answer the door.

Which he did. He was taller than I expected, about six foot one, and was wearing a handsome dark blue suit and a fresh white shirt. His complexion was ruddy, healthy; something that couldn't be brought over on TV, not even color TV. The eyes were deep blue, like the suit, and made a startling contrast to his ruddy skin. The eyes didn't look at me, but over my shoulder. His hand was gnarled and large and he drew me into the hallway, murmuring amenities.

I walked with him to the library, which was just off the front hallway. He moved like a man who has been in fist fights, and that, too, was something that did not come through on television and, in fact, was a bit surprising because Washington politicians tend toward jogging and badminton. But Ervin moved husky at the neck and broodingly self-confident in body.

I took his own armchair, by the phone, and Sam sat in the small hardbacked chair opposite me. I asked him if he minded the tape recorder, and he said no, and so I began with a question about a secret political organization he'd belonged to during his student years. Then the phone rang.

I went back out into the hallway and waited. It was very quiet out there, floor-to-ceiling books and a deep blue carpet, very quiet in all the house. I heard him on the phone, speaking precisely and in great detail, to someone at the Nixon White House. He was telling the fellow about what tapes he wanted, and giving the dates of each of them, and the dates, as well, of his previous requests for those tapes. When I went back into the library it was evident he had no notes with him. So the whole long series of facts he'd just recited had been given from memory. Now, without any sign of effort, nor the slightest pause to recollect, he took up in mid-sentence what he had been saying about the secret political society, together with dates, facts, and the names of boys who had run for minor political offices at the University of North Carolina sixty years ago.

The questions had been designed for quickness, so that the Senator would not tell me any of his funny stories. I liked the funny stories, all right, but this was business. He answered all these questions without strain, without losing his poise, giving me lucid and detailed accounts of his boyhood, the University of North Carolina, World War I, the North Carolina State Legislature of 1923, his family life, his friends, decisions of the North Carolina Supreme Court, and his relationships with Thomas Wolfe and Robert Welch.

So I was confirming a suspicion or two. Like many Americans, I more than half-believed that, because most intelligent persons are powerless, most powerful persons are unintelligent. But that doesn't follow, does it?

When Sam saw the mood of the interview shifting in a direction he didn't like, he suggested that we move over to the sofa, where we sat closer, away from the phone, and where he began to advance the pseudopodia of his stories. The first one was about a colored man who was brought before a white judge, circa 1877, and charged with chicken-stealing. The judge asked, "Cuffey, where did you learn to steal chickens like that?" To which the colored man replied, "Cap'n Boss, it was at Fredericksburg during the war when you told me to get some chickens and make a stew for you and your friends. You knew I couldn't get any chickens except by stealing them."

Then Sam began laughing, baring his big, white teeth, crinkling his eyes, laughing silently and deeply from the gut, and went over that threshold into the deeper mirth, his eyes holding mine, and I went with him, not much amused by the story, but interested in watching him laugh and, like him I suppose, enjoying a private joke having nothing to do with the real one. Until suddenly I found I was still laughing and saying weakly, "Oh my," for all the world like a good boy, whereas the Senator's eyes had gone bleak and hard and the laugh had been bitten off with such utter suddenness that one hadn't seen it go. So that's how he handles his aides, I thought.

My last question had to do with something he'd told me over the phone about Boswell and Johnson, something to do with murder.

He looked puzzled and I said, "I'm not going to murder you."

"No," he said. "I was thinking about what I told my other biographer when he was pestering me with questions." Then his laughter, very loud, came again and he said, "Murder me? I was thinking the other way around." Then he threw back his head and really laughed, big belly-shaking guffaws, and finally down into that silent breathless laughter that is the deepest of all. Catching him in the middle of that, I said, "I don't get it."

"Just joking," he said.

When it was time to leave we strolled out on the front porch. I was seeing him close up now, a foot or two away. He was a strikingly handsome man, and none of his photographs disclosed this. For one thing, they showed him as having wattles on the side of his jaws, and he didn't.

"I was born right there," he said, indicating the old, white family house, still

surrounded by its oak trees, fifty yards away. "So you can see, I haven't gotten very far in life."

Then he jingled the keys to his New Yorker sedan and offered me a lift back to the Holiday Inn.

I said no thanks, and he reminded me that it was a long way from his house to the Holiday Inn.

Chapter 2

By the time he was four and a half he was beginning to get acquainted with his father. Often, Sam Sr. would be home in the evenings, with his little gold-wire Ben Franklin glasses glinting in the kerosene light as he sat across the parlor table from Sam's mother, reading.

The grandfather was dead, and the father wasn't content, as the old man had been, merely to sit around after dinner and placidly watch the stars wheel by, but would read out loud to the assembled children — stories out of the Bible, or Sir Walter Scott, or Uncle Remus — highly colored dramatic readings, punctuated by gestures as schooled, stiff, and emphatic as those that accompanied his courtroom orations. He would become worked up when he read the Old Testament story about Joseph and the coat of many colors. He would be indignant, almost hurt, at the way the youngest child had been treated. Or he would sit out on the long, narrow front porch, with his family spread out alongside him, and his cuspidor beside him, chewing, talking, spitting. The little man's eyes would glisten fiercely in the darkness and all this was set in the long silences in which the only sounds to be heard were bullfrogs croaking down along the creek.

He would talk about his own boyhood: working in cotton fields all day, bringing home all his money and giving it to his mother, then plodding out leaden-legged, with his rifle over his shoulder, to shoot partridges, possums, squirrels, and doves. Going out on Sundays, too, fishing and picking strawberries, and bringing the proceeds home to give to his mother to feed the family. He'd punctuate these reminiscences by declaring fiercely, "I loved my mother." Then repeat it more softly. "I loved my mother," he would say.

In spite of the money he had in the bank, and the cotton mill stock, and the Charlotte Hotel stock, and the retainer from the Southern Railway, whose attorney he was in that part of the state, Sam Sr. had hard, bitter knowledge of the precariousness of all things. By daily, hourly acts of the will, he forced himself to carry out meticulously what his newspaper advertisements promised: "Sam J. Ervin, atty at law, special attention given to all business." And his contempt for the dangerous dreaminess he'd seen in his own father had a lot to do with the policies he had in raising his children. For Sam Sr., it had been a difficult and clawing climb from the South Carolina cotton fields to his book-lined law offices on court-house square.

He had ridden into Morganton, aged nineteen, on a wagon he drove himself, bringing with him his father and mother, and a few sticks of furniture. Immediately, they'd had to sell the horse and wagon to get something to eat. He'd gotten the job as postmaster, at $100 a year, and they'd lived on that. He'd done the chores of four or five men, working twelve-hour days of hard physical labor, and reading law at night. Then he found he was entitled to $250 a year to hire clerks with; and so had paid himself that, and went on studying law at night, studying harder than any ordinary man would have had to, because he was incapable by temperament of reading law under anybody. He was not going to do anything under anybody if he could help it, because his experiences in the cotton fields had burned into him a detestation of any kind of subordination. Thus, now, although his muscles were sore from throwing the mail sacks around, and his nerves weary from money worry and long unguided expeditions through the midnight pages of Blackstone and Coke, and though he had no help from his dreamy father and no guarantee about anything, he had made himself a free man and determined to remain that way. So when illness came to the family, and more expenses, he'd added to his other tasks the chore of lugging the mail sacks the half-mile to the train station, and for that had received another $200 a year. After half a decade of that, he was admitted to the bar.

Early in his practice, having no clients and nothing to do, Sam Sr. had read and annotated every single decision ever handed down by the North Carolina Supreme Court. As time went on, he did the same thing for the rulings of the Supreme Court of the United States. By effort, he made himself into a learned lawyer, and by effort and character both, into an accurate one. He was highly respected by lawyers and judges throughout North Carolina, and at the end of his career, he would have argued more cases before the Supreme Court of North Carolina than any other lawyer of his generation who engaged strictly in the private practice of law. Study gentled him, and deep experience of life made him compassionate, and sometimes he would look back with awe on the wildness that had been in him during his youth.

"I have always been ashamed of one thing I did," Sam Sr. said one evening out into the stillness of the front porch. "When we lived in Paxville there was a beautiful white heron about six feet tall. The heron was eating frogs. I aimed the rifle and shot the ball right through him. He flew to a tree then got sick and fell down. He got ready for a fight. I broke a limb and beat him over the head. What possessed me to shoot a beautiful bird like that, I have never been able to understand."

Everyone knew Sam Sr. from seeing him walk down the Morganton streets, always in the same Prince Albert coat, with the Prince Albert beard, too, and the same black homburg hat set precisely on his head. They saw him going to the court house, thence to the post office, and back to his own office. Where he would work on his cases, then go back to the court house again, back to the post office, back home, always at the same time, always following exactly the same route, and nodding briskly to those he passed. Except, of course, on the days when there was court he would adjust his schedule to what the court was doing. He was a man of great uniformity of behavior and with no exceptions other than on those few summer days when the mercury stood over 90 degrees and he would come out of his office walking stiffly, carrying his rocking chair at arm's length in front of him, and sit there stiffly on Mrs. Galloway's lawn, under the apple tree, writing out his briefs on long yellow ruled pads. He never took off his coat.

He was a good, hardworking lawyer, and many of the town's citizens, and almost all of its Negroes, brought their cases to him.

Little Sam, aged six, had a sense of order, too. He had a box full of wooden compartments and he would keep bird eggs and brightly colored stones and things like that in there, and show them to his mother. He was already, in a way, a smoother article than his father: a good little boy, gentle, humorous, and kind, who looked at you levelly; who always had time for you, to talk, to do nothing together; whose speech, already, was somewhat stumbling and hesitant; who never was in a hurry about anything; who laughed a lot.

That summer, a few times, he went downtown with his father to the law office. He could see the mountains better from down there than he could at home, because the ash trees his maternal grandfather had planted around the court house were young enough so that there were spaces to see through. And those mountains, too, told what Morganton was: the frontier. Table Rock, a nearly square outcropping, dominated those mountains and stood out harshly over the town. It was not the way the Blue Ridge Mountains are supposed to be, not gentle and sloping, and not even blue, but a gashed yellow cube.

Morganton was the frontier, all right, and it wasn't only the moonshiners who carried pistols. Sam's father carried one, too, and was the sort of man who would use it. Once, when Sam was a boy, and a bunch of Morganton toughs were chasing a Negro down the street and happened by ill fortune to run athwart the man in the Prince. Albert coat, they did not stick around to ask if he was serious when he drew his gun and told them to disperse. Because everybody knew what was in Ervin, and that thing which had clubbed the heron remorselessly down into death was never entirely absent, but would peer out at you.

Morganton justice, in those days, smacked of the frontier, too, criminal matters were resolved swiftly, and some of the town's residents remembered when whippings were more common than jailings, and brandings ("T" for thief, "B" for bigamy) not unknown. Morganton law was suited to the sensibilities of the men who lived under it. Who were tough.

All this seeped down to Sam, as it did to most children in the South, in the form of good manners. For instance, a Southerner then, and even now, was not so quick to call another man a damn fool or a son of a bitch as a northerner might be, because he knew that saying something like that obliged the other fellow to hospitalize him. So that the Southern soft-spokenness Little Sam was developing devolved from a world of men whose self-respect did not allow them to endure light treatment. Thus Sam found out, very early, that life was more pleasant when lived as gentlemen live it, which meant allowing the other fellow his essential privacy and self-respect.

Sometimes, when Sam was downtown with his father, he would sit out on the park bench under the ash trees, beneath the green-bronzed statue of the Confederate rifleman, and watch the life of Morganton go on around him, sensing already that he could have a part of that life, if he wanted to, and no small part, either.

Because, by now, his father knew that Ed wasn't going to make it; that however much care he would continue to lavish on the older boy — sending him to a Virginia boarding school, and to Arizona, and paying for the treatments, which tried without success to remove him from his addiction to opium — Ed was not going to make it. So heavy expectations were coming down on Sam.

Every Sunday morning, his father took him and the other children to the First Presbyterian Church, with the older girls in their long flowing dresses and Gibson-girl hair, and Sam and the boys in starched white linen, which Betty had done up back in the steamy damnation of the kitchen. Lap babies, knee babies, yard babies — all of them went to church.

As an elder, Sam's father was a ruler of that church, and, as such, was the boss of the ministers. He was one of those who laid down the terms of their contracts, determined how much money they were to be paid, and, when it became necessary, fired them.

Thus, the First Presbyterian Church of Morganton was like the other Southern Presbyterian churches, in that the minister was an employee, and every man stored up as much of the Bible as he thought he needed, and became his own priest. So that in the summer before he started grammar school, Sam was storing in Scripture from the Bible Memory Cards, and reciting them to any white adult who would listen. Sometimes he would cross the street, to his mother's mother's place, to do that.

As he got older and was allowed to cross Lenoir Street by himself, he began to see more of his grandmother. More than anybody else did. He knew already that his father's visits to the old lady were limited, strictly, to one white-cravatted formal call each year. His father called her "Mrs. Powe" and she called him "Mr. Ervin." He was that even to his wife: "Mr. Ervin."

Thus life went on in Morganton. Many people were poor, none was rich, and the town was not different from a hundred like it in North Carolina. Except for a couple of tobacco tycoons who lived over in the Piedmont, and a few cotton moguls from the old aristocracy over on the coastal plain, nobody in North Carolina had much money. The towns were essentially places where farmers came to trade and to get their lawyering and doctoring done. And there was no special sign that any of this would ever change.

But over in the Piedmont, Buck Duke, a billionaire who was bored with tobacco now that a couple of anti-trust suits had gone against him, was looking all along the river to Morganton and all the way down to where the Catawba became, in South Carolina, the Wateree — with an eye to developing electrical power from the mountains to the ocean. And over on the edge of the ocean, a couple of fellows were working on a machine that could fly. But all Sam knew about power now was that it slid through the town in the evenings, screamed its wild halloo at the madhouse, and raged on north toward Washington.

THE CHARACTER OF AMERICANS

I lay on the bed in the pastel anonymity of the Morganton Holiday Inn and began to read a book Sam had given me. It was called Senator Sam Ervin's Best Stories, *by Thad Stem, and I was thinking, this will put me to sleep all right. It was the transcript of a conversation Stem had with Sam one afternoon when he'd come strolling by the house on Lenoir Street to find Sam sitting out by his breeze-ruffled azalea bushes, and with his mind no more on legislative ponderosities than the breeze's was.*

This conversation, which took most of the afternoon, meandered over the old stories from the North Carolina courts of generations gone by, skirted the subject of the Civil War, and lightly rushed by moonshining, hill dialects, and the trial of Frankie Silver for the slaying of her husband Charles — which had taken place in the Morganton Court House and given rise to the ballad "Frankie and Johnny." Finally, as the sun got lower, the breeze cooler, their conversation had come up on the subject of death.

It was merely the transcribed tape of a casual conversation, but it was like no conversation I'd ever heard, and in the course of it Sam quoted Mark Twain, Charles Dickens, Rudyard Kipling, Samuel Johnson, Shakespeare, Josh Billings, Petroleum V. Nasby, George Washington Harris, the Bible, Daniel Webster, Irvin S. Cobb, Oliver Wendell Holmes, Francis Bacon, Alexander Pope, Frederick Jackson Turner, Thomas Wolfe, Benjamin Disraeli, Edward Everett Hale, P. G. Wodehouse, Samuel Butler, John Milton, Winston Churchill, Oliver Goldsmith, George Bernard Shaw, Lord Byron, William Makepeace Thackeray, Ralph Waldo Emerson, Eugene Field, James Whitcomb Riley, Davy Crockett, Washington Irving, Samuel Pepys, Thomas More, Henry Ward Beecher, Finley Peter Dunne, Seneca, and Robert Browning, whose poem "Prospice" he recited in its entirety, as expressing his own sentiments.

> Fear death? — to feel the fog in my throat,
>   The mist in my face,
> When the snows begin, and the blasts denote
>   I am nearing the place,
> The power of the night, the press of the storm,
>   The post of the foe;
> Where he stands, the Arch Fear in a visible form,
>   Yet the strong man must go:
> For the journey is done and the summit attained,
>   And the barriers fall,
> Though a battle's to fight ere the guerdon be gained,
>   The reward of it all.
> I was ever a fighter, so — one fight more,
>   The best and last!
> I would hate that death bandaged my eyes, and forebore,
>   And bade me creep past.
> No! Let me taste the whole of it, fare like my peers
>   The heroes of old,
> Bear the brunt, in a minute pay glad life's arrears
>   Of pain, darkness and cold.
> For sudden the worst turns the best to the brave,
>   The black minute's at end,
> And the elements' rage, the fiend-voices that rave,
>   Shall dwindle, shall blend,

Shall change, shall become first a peace out of pain,
Then a light, then thy breast.
O thou soul of my soul! I shall clasp thee again,
And with God be the rest!

The next afternoon at Sam's place I met Margaret, his wife, whom he called out of the kitchen. She came out into the entrance hall to shake my hand; a short, friendly lady of seventy-six whose eyes, behind the thick lenses of the glasses she wore, were not recognizable as the eyes of her younger years, which I had seen in photographs. But the younger voice was still there, and after we'd spent a few moments passing hall amenities back and forth that younger face, too, emerged. I could see her now as young and I wondered if Sam could.

So Sam and I went into the study together, and the afternoon began, much as the previous day had ended, with the study very quiet, almost still, except when the phone rang. He took calls from ABC, NBC, and the Associated Press. And there was another call, from his Administrative Assistant, Patricia Shore, with whom he conducted a great deal of business in a short time.

These interruptions annoyed me, because I was trying to frame a complicated question having to do with the possibility that the character of Americans had changed radically in the nineteen decades since the Constitution was written. The rationale went something like this: In 1787, four out of five Americans who worked were self-employed. And, because of that, the America of the Constitution was a masculine nation, where what counted was toughness, inventiveness, get-up-and-go. Now, however, nineteen out of twenty Americans who worked were employees, who spent their days, whether at $5000 or $50,000 a year, doing what they were told. Therefore America, some thought, had become a feminine nation, feminine in the worst sense, and deeply imbued with the employee's virtues; affability, a propensity for time-serving guile, a whore's ability to feign good will, a churl's determination to repress hostility. So maybe Nixon was what we wanted. Maybe the Constitution was of no use to us any more because we didn't want to be free. Instead, we wanted to be good employees, and thus we had the government we deserved. I wanted to ask him what he thought about that.

It was a complicated question, hard to frame, and every time I got it about half-said the phone would ring. So I tried to compress the thing.

"You may win this battle with Nixon," I said. "But a lot of people believe the type he represents will win the war. That our country will continue to be run by men like him. And that men like you will disappear."

There came a loud knocking at the front door, and he got up to answer it. By the time he made it to his study door, however, Margaret was already standing out in the hallway talking to whoever it was, and Sam was peering out hawklike through the crack in the door. He seemed to be ready to leap into action to help her. I was later to learn that many of the callers at that house were strangers.

This fellow had motored in from Ohio to get Sam to help him with a problem concerning the Veterans' Administration. Now Sam stepped out of the study into the entranceway and went to meet the man, coming to stand between Margaret and the caller, who could have been deranged and who, for all Sam knew, was.

Sam listened to all the minutiae of the case, asking questions, as Margaret came into the den with me, where she used the phone to make a date for playing bridge, a game she'd been at for sixty years. She had none of that plasticized greasy chic sometimes found in Washington political wives, but was home folks for good or for bad, and spoke plainly. I liked her, and wondered whether she was bored by sixty years of bridge.

When Sam came back, I asked him once more if he thought the character of Americans had changed since the days of the Constitution. He answered in a manner that was dispassionate and devoid of any effort to charm.

"There have been quite drastic changes in the lives of people," he said. "For example, in the days when the Constitution was written, you had what was essentially a rural population. You had every man who was more or less master of his trade and captain of his soul. He carried on his own vocation. You've had the urbanization of people; you've had individual crafts succeeded by giant manufacturing organizations. And, I think, very unfortunately, people have been crowded into urban centers. And to them — unlike the people in Jefferson's day, where they saw vegetables and things growing in the ground — to them, food comes off the grocery shelves and they have to have money to get food.

"And I think when people are urbanized to that extent that they have a tendency to lose confidence in the future. They are subject to being deceived by a lot of demagogues who promise a whole lot of something for nothing. I do think the character of the American people has changed."

Not only that, he continued, but also their knowledge of government had deteriorated. He said that people in the past would make an occasion out of attending the quarterly Court Days in whatever county they lived in, and that there, in the orations of the lawyers and courtyard discourses of political figures, they had received a firsthand education in government, firsthand proof that the American government was indeed made of flesh-and-blood men. But now there was very little contact between the governed and their governors.

These were precisely the ideas that had led many Americans to political despair, and I was surprised to hear them coming from a man so active in politics. He came up to the point of saying, "The Constitution is just so many words on a piece of paper and it cannot enforce itself," at which point I shut off the tape recorder, a movement his quick eyes caught. I asked him whether the destructive servility of the American citizen wasn't the central cancer of our century, and whether Watergate wasn't the distilled malignancy of that.

He became very quiet, waves of pure energy coming off him like a gale off an iceberg, face very mobile, eyes moving quickly from me to the tape recorder.

"Are you sure that thing's turned off?"

"Yes."

"All right," he said. And began speaking of Nixon in a graphic, colorful way that any man could understand. Given the circumstances, his daring astounded me. I could have been, for all he knew, working for Nixon.

I had come across hints of this before, a trustingness on Sam's part that tended to draw deep loyalties toward him from other people.

"You know, I used to be a very intense person," he said when we were done. "I at one time had an ulcer. It was one of the most terrible things that happened to me."

He then mentioned one of his brothers, a United States Congressman whose suicide, I had reason to believe, had leered in his nightmares now for many years.

"I think his temperament and mine were different," he said. "Anyway, I started reading what caused ulcers. Among other things, I read Dale Carnegie's book How to Stop Worrying and Start Living. Which is a very good book on psychology for anybody that has any ailments."

I asked him if he knew anything about Carnegie's own life, and when he said no, I thought to myself, it is just as well.

Chapter 3

WHEN SAM ENTERED grammar school in the fall of 1903, there wasn't any special shock of transition, of having crossed over into another world. The school was part of the community, run by the community, and what went on there was what the people who ran things wanted to go on. So it was like the rest of his life. The Morganton Graded School was brand-new, and the chairman of the School Board was his father.

He knew all his classmates, knew just about everybody in town. He knew where most of the dogs and cats belonged, and some of their history and ancestry. Schooling for him, like politics for his father, was personal, and, as a matter of fact, was a sort of politics. Sam got along, was well liked, was included in on everything, was one of the includers. Most importantly, perhaps, he wasn't bullied. He was of a sunny disposition, which was proof against punches and assorted humiliations, and thus, for him, life droned on richly in the quiet town, and he would sit at his desk in school, bent over his blue-backed books, or waiting to take his turn in the spelling bee, and not paying too much attention. Some spring mornings, he could hear his father's voice marching across the green town square in measured rhetorical periods, and knew that the court-house window was open, just as the schoolroom window was. It all fit together.

He was glad to be in school, because there wasn't as much to be gained at home as there had been before Hugh Tate, and Joe, and Eunice, and John had been born. Now his mother, whom he adored, and whom his father had taught him he had damn well better adore, had eight other children to think about, four of them younger than he, and there wasn't much time to show her his box with the bird eggs or for laughing together on the front porch.

He was ranging a bit farther now, and after he'd been in school two or three years, he was allowed, finally, to go down to the creek by himself, where he panned for gold. This had a patina of practicality about it, like almost everything he did now. After all, only the year before, a peg-leg prospector named Moses had spent an entire summer prospecting down there, and paid Sam's father $10 for the privilege. There was gold in North Carolina.

And his father would sit on the front porch in the evenings, regnant and content. His theoretical esteem for his fellow citizens did not propel him toward fraternization. He made no social calls, none. Either it was the Lord's business, or plain business, or it was nothing. The rest of the time, in the summers, he sat out on the front porch in his rocking chair. "Always tell the truth," the father would tell Sam. "Never tell a lie. Never. Even if it hurts you, never tell a lie." At other times he would mutter, "You have to be a good animal before you can be a good man."

There was a curiosity in Morganton now, an "automobile." And Sam, who was old enough to swim in the Catawba, lolling in its slow brown waters, more than once heard the thing rattling across the plank bridge. It was a Harvester, and its wheels were about three feet high. It would struggle mightily across the bridge, and when it got across it would turn around and back up the hill on the other side; an absurd contraption, and Sam would laze there in the warm lapping waters, listening to the thing. It felt good being away from the big white house, a good animal on his own. Sometimes he would go down below the bridge to the deep place, Granny Hole, and spend the afternoon with the other boys diving naked off the rocks or sprawled out on the banks browning. Or else, swim still farther down the river, to where the watermelons grew fatly in the fields along the bank, and steal one of them, hug the thing to his chest, and ride it down the river, coming up finally on a flat, sandy place, where he and the other boys would bust the thing open and devour it, before civilizing themselves with clothes and beginning the long trek back to where his father sat on the porch, as inscrutable as ever, a potentiality not yet tested.

Sometimes the older man seemed eccentric, even ridiculous. The Prince Albert get-up had never been in fashion, except among a few professional risers of the 1880's and '90's, and in any case, was out of style now. But his father would send his mother down to Lazarus Brothers Department Store to say, "Mr. Ervin wants another suit." Which, in a few weeks, would appear, same size as always, same style — and the little man kept about his punctual rounds with the brisk efficiency that extended into all his doings. When one of Sam's sisters stayed out late, the father would march down off the porch into the darkness carrying the lit kerosene lantern, calling out methodically for her to come home, and reappear, fifteen minutes or half an hour later, face still impassive, girl in tow.

They were good-looking girls, these three eldest Ervin daughters, and the father's efforts with the lantern weren't going to keep them from going about their natural business, but the father was determined. He would even make them stay at home and play setback with him. He seemed to want to keep them there with him forever.

Other things, as seemingly harmless, were going on in North Carolina that year. Thomas Dixon was writing a novel called *The Clansman,* the state legislature voted in Prohibition, and Sam's six-year-old brother, Joe, slipped and fell out of an apple tree in the Ervin back yard. Sam was looking right at the boy when it happened, and it didn't seem to amount to much.

But the boy was stricken with severe pain, became unable to walk, and had to be operated on for osteomyelitis. He could get around only by using crutches, and was in pain.

Before the fall, Joe had been a strong competitor for familial attention; was bright, winsome, and more outgoing than Sam. After the fall, Joe began to get bigger doses of attention than the other children did, especially from the mother, who spent long hours reading Uncle Remus stories to him, and teaching him how to walk on crutches, or sitting by him holding his hand when the pain was severe. There would be no opium for Joe, the parents decided; he would bear the pain so he could have the world.

In the meantime, Sam's distance from his father was beginning to express itself in a form of insouciance which bordered on contempt.

He wants me to work in the garden? No. I'm studying. He wants me to milk the cow? You do it. I am reading the Sir Walter Scott. He would send word down to his father from the high-ceilinged bedroom where he did the reading, and would hear no more of it, although requests for his services continued to come in. As for Joe, he had another operation, then another. The more crippled he became, the more attention he received from his parents.

In later years, Sam would not remember what it was, exactly, that brought on the confrontation. All he would remember was that his father ordered him to carry out some chore, and he refused. Sam had never been whipped. But now his father got a switch and said he would teach him to be "obedient." And that the whipping would hurt him more than it would hurt Sam.

But the thing Sam listened to, then, was the part about being "obedient." He did not want to be obedient, nor did he consider obedience a virtue — at least not for himself. His father beat him across the butt with the switch and asked him if he would be obedient now, and Sam said no. Then he beat him some more, and asked him if he would be obedient, and Sam said no. As the father was beginning to beat him again, the mother intervened.

"He has been punished enough," she said, and led Sam away. The boy was sobbing. She took him up to her room and he cried there and when he stopped he came back down. What had been at issue was whether he was going to be an obedient person, and it was at this point in his life that the contumacy, which had hitherto been experimental, became rooted in his character for good. Much later, he would decide the whipping had been merited, but it did not matter whether it was merited or not. The point was, that the confrontation with his father had come at last, and Sam had emerged from it unbroken, and this was fraught with consequences for the rest of his life. For instance, when manhood came, he would go to great lengths never to be an employee, and would expect his own employees to be obedient. Thus he became his father's son. All he knew was, his father had whipped him and his mother had saved him, and he came to the conclusion she was a saint. And he was determined never to allow himself to be violated by anyone, under any circumstances.

His mother did not say anything to him about the beating, not directly, although somewhat later she was to tell him he must not judge people, that he must take them the way they were and not try to reform them. And Sam heeded this advice. He became more tentative, more awkward of speech, and this actually worked to his advantage. People liked him for it; here was a young man who wasn't so arrogantly sure of himself as the father was. And his indulgent, Chaucerian geniality went well with his hesitant speech, making him something close to beloved by the citizens of Morganton. So it was beginning even then. He was aloof and genial at the same time and was known around town as a boy who was extremely good to his mother.

THE MASTER OF THE WORLD

I stood in the parking lot of Morganton's Holiday Inn, gazing through the binoculars toward Table Rock Mountain, which glowed a chalky orange in the morning sunlight. Jules Verne had called it "the Great Eyrie." That was in his last novel, The Master of the World, *which was set in Morganton. The villain of that book was Robus, a darkly brooding, isolated genius who resembled Captain Nemo of Verne's* Twenty Thousand Leagues Under the Sea.

Those steep cliffs, seen through the binoculars, were beginning to take on a hard lemon shine, and I didn't see any place where they could be climbed.

In Verne's book, written when he was seventy-nine, the Great Eyrie was the homing-place of the Terror, *which was Robus' ship, automobile, submarine, and aeroplane all crafted into one; a machine whose power emboldened the man to call himself the Master of the World.*

The sheriff of Morganton, who was alarmed by the fires glowing up out of the mountain at night, and annoyed by the fleeing mountaineer refugees, had set out with his dog to scale the Great Eyrie and capture Robus, but he hadn't been able to locate a place where those cliffs could be climbed, either.

Now the morning breakfasters were coming into the Holiday Inn. There was no telling what the Master of the World might have done if it hadn't been for the pride that led to his destruction. He had fancied that he could defy anything, had flown the Terror *straight up into an electrical storm, and died.*

That day I asked Sam if his own aides, in their eagerness to please, ever reminded him of Nixon's. And he said no.

Let him who would be Master of the World beware of electricity.

Chapter 4

For little Sam, politics was watching people he knew, and on Tuesday of Court Week he'd walk downtown early and hang around the Old Court House waiting there under the ash trees to see what would happen.

Court Week, when the Superior Court came to town, was Morganton's biggest event, bigger even than the Summer Revivals or the political dinners-on-the-ground. The boarding houses would fill up as lawyers, plaintiffs and defendants, and just plain citizens blew into town to see the trials and hear the political speeches. They would gawk at the medicine show, which traveled where the court did, at the hawkers and vendors, the balloon sellers, the fried chicken stands, the red white and blue bunting; and there would be the pretty girls Sam hadn't seen before. The town called him Little Sam now, and would continue to do so long after he grew to stand head and shoulders over his father.

By now, there was more than just charm to him, and he cared enough about himself to get into some fist fights. But he hadn't forgotten the confrontation with his father. One day his mother found him up in his room making paper soldiers.

"What's the matter?" she asked.

"Nothing."

"You look unhappy, son, like something's the matter."

"It's just that all the wars are over. That there won't be any wars to fight any more."

"Perhaps that's a good thing," she said. "Did you ever think of that? Because they kill people in wars."

"I know."

"Surely, Samuel, you wouldn't want to kill anyone?"

"No mam," he said.

Meanwhile his father went about his rounds, still wearing the Prince Albert coat, nodding stiffly to those he passed on the street. There were a few more automobiles in town now, and occasionally, one of them would stop and offer him a lift. Which he refused. No "lift" was necessary for one who was attending to his business, the old man believed. Besides, you spent more time getting in and out of the thing than it would take you to get there on foot.

He was making a lot of money. He was attorney for the Southern Railway in that district of North Carolina, and had half a dozen other corporate clients, and held a goodly amount of cotton mill stocks and other securities. He wasn't spending much, either, because his dream from the beginning was to put all of his children through college, all who were able to make it.

In 1909, the year the last daughter was born (Jean), Sam's parents sent the third oldest daughter off to a women's college in Greensboro. This was Margaret, a pretty blond girl of eighteen, tall and graceful like her mother. Within a week, there came an official letter from the college, and late into the night Sam heard his mother and father talking down in the darkened parlor. He heard his father saying, finally, "We can't send her away. There is just no use and we can't send her away. It would be shameful to do that."

And the mother: "That's right, Sam. We can't do that."

The young girl, Margaret, came back the next week on the Southern Railway, and walked upstairs, valise in hand, with all the chagrined silence of one who is about to undergo a whipping. And underwent it, death's whipping, closing the door behind her for the last time and undergoing it there in the room, for months, with Sam's tall and gentle-seeming mother now taking up her meals on trays, and bringing the dishes down to scour them herself in boiling water with lye and potash. Then returning to the room to sit with the stricken girl in the long hours between meals, or in the longer hours of the evening, feeding her when she became weak, praying with her, giving her whatever useless medicines the Morganton Pharmacy sold. They had all known since the letter from the college that one lung was gone, eaten away by pulmonary tuberculosis, that the other one was going, too. So now there were two Ervin children having difficulty in getting breath, and one in great pain from the crippling bone disease. Real things happened to people and Sam didn't grow up planning to be old. Getting old would come as a slow and genial surprise.

Then Margaret died. Sam's mother was with her when she dropped away down into death, and the wagon came and took the body to the mortuary. The mother brought all the things down from the girl's room — bedding, clothes, everything that would burn — heaped them in a pile out in the back yard, poured coal oil on the stuff, applied the match, and walked back to the house while it was burning. And never spoke of her again.

This was the year the movie-house opened in Morganton, and, a decent time after his sister's funeral, Sam went down there and saw his first movie, starring Ben Turpin; it was very funny. The movies cost ten cents and it was a great relief to go to them. Custard pies in the face and cowboy train robbers and mustache-twirling villains and heroines who always got away. You did not go down there to see things about the heroines who did not get away, because reality would give you plenty of that. At the movies, too, there were Morganton's young girls, as lovely and promising as movies themselves.

He was beginning to get the sense that one day he would grow up and be a man. He was in the ninth grade now, and was required, as every other student was, to answer the morning roll call with a verse from Scripture. One morning the verse he chose was "I have more understanding than all of my teachers." He had to stay after school for that one. It was a verse he more than half-believed.

About this time the father took Sam and Hugh Tate up to Washington, D.C. They went up on the Southern Railway — which was free, since the father had a pass — coming into Union Station, riding in a taxicab down to the Willard Hotel, and from there venturing out on foot to the White House, the Capitol, and the Supreme Court; then down the Potomac by boat to Mount Vernon. Through all of this, their father was no different from the man he had been at home, the same Prince Albert coat, same impeccable grooming, sitting stiffly by the window chewing tobacco as the train moved through the countryside, lecturing the boys on American history and the Constitution. There were no pats on the shoulder, no hugs, no rough-house, no laughter, no reminiscences of his own boyhood beyond the usual recollections of how hard he'd worked; and, in truth, no explanation of why he was doing this thing in the first place. He had done it with all the children, beginning with Laura, and was to keep it up with all of them, ending with Jean.

Sam was in his teens, and had been tossing a baseball since he was four or five, and playing in pickup games since he was seven or eight. He was good at baseball because he hadn't had to work and because, in the South, the weather was such and the disposition of the players was such that you came out there after breakfast when the grass was still wet and you played all the morning and skipped lunch if there was any way of getting out of it, and played all through the languid hot afternoon and kept on playing until supper. Then you had to go home for a few minutes. But in the summer there were two or three more hours of light even after supper and Sam came out and kept on until dusk, when he could not see the pitches coming in and had to shy away if he happened to be in the field when the bat cracked because he didn't know whether the thing was coming at him or not. Sometimes the ball would be lost in the dark and firefly-behung honeysuckle bordering the field. When they found it in the morning it would be waterlogged and had the heft of iron. Playing all day, every day, for two or three summers, Sam got ready for the serious games. He caught for the Sandy Flat team, first as substitute catcher and occasional right fielder, then, as he got older and filled out, as first-string catcher.

There were two types of boy who played that position. The first was the squat, muscular, ugly scrap-iron sort of fellow who was born a catcher, and who could have been nothing but a catcher, who, on the football team, was a center, and who was the last fellow to get a date, and who made C's in school when he worked hard; the sort of fellow who scratched his balls a lot and spat more than he needed to. Most catchers were like that. The second, rarer sort of catcher was like Sam — lanky, aloof, looking as if he doesn't belong on the baseball diamond, or who seemed like some sort of pitcher until you saw him put the equipment on. This was the sort of fellow who wanted to play so much that he was willing to take the toughest job.

Sam paid for his place on the team, paid in foul tips that smashed into his face guard and knocked him silly, in flung bats cracking across his shins, most frequently in jammed fingers, and occasionally the worst of the things, the foul tip that went cannoning into his groin and left him writhing on the ground. The rest of the players would lounge around matter-of-factly waiting for him to get up because that, after all, was the prime expectation one had of a catcher, that he would get up, that he would shake the numbness out of his leg or hand or whatever it was, and keep on. Which Sam did. He became team statistician, too, filling ledger after ledger with the box scores of the games, plus the batting averages, fielding averages, all computed by himself, all entered neatly and voluminously in the ledgers. He was a little surprised not to be holding a job. Most boys in town did, even those whose fathers were better off than his own.

Now he began to have his first dates. Girls from church, girls from school, girls he'd known all his life. A date cost thirty cents, which paid for the movie admission and the Coca-Cola afterwards in the dim marble fan-cooled fastness of the Morganton Pharmacy. Then there was the walk home under the ash trees, maybe holding the girl's hand if he was serious, or, if he was very serious, kissing her good night. But all of Morganton's girls represented — Morganton. And Sam was half in love with easeful elsewhere.

By the time he was in his senior year of high school he knew he had to do something. He had to decide how he was going to be grown up. And he was a troubled lad because after high school was over, which was to say, after youth was over, there seemed to be nothing, a stone wall. And nobody seemed to know about that but himself. Already members of his high school class, boys and girls his own age, were engaged to be married. Everybody seemed to know what he was going to do with the rest of his life. In almost every case, this meant — Morganton. If not the hardware store now, then the doctor's or lawyer's office later. But Morganton.

His teen-aged years had been good so far, with the baseball and the dates and swimming in the Catawba. It was magic to be in perfect shape so that your legs felt strong when you walked, almost as if you had no legs at all; and when you ran your lungs only felt good, and you could feel them getting stronger; and when you swam now it was effortlessly and for long distances and you didn't need permission. It was magic to have two or three hundred people watch you step up to the plate on a weekday afternoon when all the stores in Morganton closed so that the town could come out to see the baseball game, magic to walk down the street and have some oldster step up and congratulate you on your performance behind the plate. And to walk with that nice girl under the trees, to know she liked you, and maybe even more, to know that you could fall in love with her if you wanted to, and be thereby empowered to fight for her; that was magic.

Morganton was all right until you were sixteen, but after that it strove for nothing, fought for nothing, risked nothing, and he would get out of it, and keep the spirit of whatever it was that was gorgeous about being sixteen; that thing the older people had forgotten and the others his age spat on as casually as his father squirting a plug at the azaleas.

He would go to Annapolis, to the Naval Academy. It wasn't as if his father had said anything to him about the law. It wasn't as if his father had taken him down to the office and said, "I have done this and I want you to do this." So he would go to Annapolis, cautiously, if he could get there.

The obstacle was the math. Sam had never liked the subject, never been good at it. He had enough for the batting averages and that was all. But now he had to have enough to pass the entrance examination for Annapolis, time was short, and there was no way in Morganton to learn as much as he needed, as quickly as he needed to. So he decided he'd go away, to a preparatory school in Annapolis. To accomplish this, he'd have to get the money from his father, and when he asked for that, it would give his father the opportunity to tell him, finally, after all these years, what he expected of him by way of a life's vocation.

Sam primed himself for the scene with his father, thought about it furiously and without stop, day after day, absorbing himself in it to the point where he would pass by his friends, or one of his girls, or one of his sisters and brothers, and walk on down the street not having seen them. So that the people of Morganton were beginning to say, That's Old Sam's son, all right, at the time when he himself was least sure of that. For days this went on, the planning, the building up to the confrontation with his father. And it may very well have been that the wily old man saw this, too, because when Sam looked up out of his planning stupor the old man was gone, vanished. To the mountain courts when there was no ostensible reason to go there, leaving Sam with a fully prepared and memorized script and the theater nailed shut. The old man stayed away, and was mute. No letters. And the time was coming when he had to leave for the Annapolis prep school. So finally Sam went to his mother, told her what he wanted, and asked her to write the old man in his behalf.

The response — and it came quickly — was unexpected. No personal letter, no warnings, no advice, no call to come up to the mountain courts to talk things over; just a parenthetical aside, in an otherwise long letter to his wife, saying it is all right about the prep school and the Naval Academy and to draw the money out of the bank. There was more on the weather than there was on the prep school. And now it was January 1913, and there was nothing to do but go. It wasn't until Sam was on the train, alone, headed north, that he had time to think about it. Then he remembered the boy with the crutches waving good-bye to him and thought, so that is it. Joe is the one he has the expectations for.

Sam disliked the prep school. He felt bad, and wrote frequently to his mother. Nobody here knew anybody else's family; nobody had known anybody else for very long or expected to know them for very much longer. It was a cold place and there was a lot of math. There was a great deal of Bob Cratchet and nothing at all of John Paul Jones.

It was cold, too. The ground was like iron. The wind cutting in from the gray Severn was cold. Outdoors everything was gray. Occasionally, for a touch of color, there would be some drab brown grass and all this was crosshatched with monotonous voices, accented like machines, talking about math. If he did well in his courses, then his score was up on the bulletin board for a couple of days before the rainy wind from the gray Severn blew it away. If he stuck it out through four years of the Naval Academy he would get to sail down to the cold, ugly sea on a floating office ship, with all wars fought and all striving forever done, and nothing left to do but sit at a gray iron desk fooling with math.

He was thinking about these things when he went down to Washington that March to attend the inauguration of the new President of the United States, Dr. Woodrow Wilson. Standing on Pennsylvania Avenue, on strong young legs, watching for hour after hour as the floats and riders went by, sensing a murmur of spring in the leaves coming out on the avenue then, seeing in the jollity of red Southern faces something that had more gusto than the binomial theorem. He thought, this is more like it.

There were a lot of good Southern faces in the parade passing by, because Wilson's inaugural was the outward manifestation of a profound change in the political fortunes of the South.

Southern faces. Wilson's, for one. He was the son of a Southern Presbyterian manse, schooled at Davidson College in North Carolina and at the University of Virginia, who had practiced law in Atlanta; who had been born Southern and lived Southern while his essential self was being formed, and who therefore was untouched, could never be touched again by hiatuses spent as President of Princeton University or Governor of New Jersey or any such secondary thing. Five of Wilson's ten cabinet members were Southerners, too. In addition to that, the Southern members of Congress were just coming into the power of seniority and assuming the important chairmanships. To Sam's way of looking at things, then, this inaugural parade marked the end, at last, of the War Between the States. The South had won, and was in control of the national government. Washington was a Southern city again, gracious in its manners, lovely in its young women.

On the other hand, there was the Annapolis prep school, squatting toad-like up there on the Severn. There was about a week or ten days more of that, and then the entrance examination, and if he did well on that he would be rewarded by forty years in a floating office building. He went back and took the exam.

He had learned all the math they had to teach him, but sitting here at the examination he had the feeling that he didn't know any of it. And flunked. And was beholden to his father for the prep school because it had been Sam's own idea and had cost money. Cost shame, too, coming home beaten, with everyone in town knowing what he had gone away for and why he was coming back. So he went back to the Morganton high school, to finish the month or so left, and graduated. His father didn't reproach him. But Sam felt it. And still there were no suggestions like, maybe you want to go to the University, maybe you would like to study law.

The day high school ended, Sam walked the quarter-mile to neighbor John L. Anderson's place, asked for a job working on the roads, and got it. The next morning, which was a hot day, hot already when he started out, he walked the mile out the Lenoir road to where they were working on the highway near the Catawba Bridge, and was introduced to the mule that pulled the scraper. His job was to get the mule moving and walk along behind it while it scraped up the dirt, smoothing out the ruts and gullies that had developed in the road over the winter. He worked there all morning, five hours in the sun walking behind the mule, then went to sit in the shade of the bridge looking down at the Catawba, where the free boys swam or floated idly on their backs looking up to where Sam sat stolidly with the other workmen, chewing on the sandwich his mother had sent out with him. He was tired of the road construction job already, and wished he could be floating down there in the river again, looking up.

It was hot and he was tired and he plodded on behind the mule for five hours more. It was an eleven-hour day when you counted the hour for lunch. Then walked the mile home and that was one day's work done and one dollar earned. He got up the next morning and did it again. He kept on doing it until he had worked the edge off of the beholdenness enough so that he could apply to the University of North Carolina.

By the time he was ready to go away to Chapel Hill he was a tanned, hard, serious-looking young fellow with a bowl haircut and a stiff collar, and knew that the penalty of having to work life-long at a job one detested was not to be borne. So the stakes at the University would be mortal.

HERMAN BAITY

Herman Baity was a handsome, vigorous old fellow with a black brush moustache and hair mostly still black. He was wearing a rugged, expensive British tweed suit and spoke precisely in a deep, growling voice. We were sitting in his elegant living room in Chapel Hill, where I had come to interview him on the strength of Sam's having told me that Baity was one of his best friends. Now

Baity answered my questions, recalling those days when he and Sam had been students at the University. He kept apologizing that he didn't remember more.

"You see I don't have a graphic memory," he said. "I remember the sense of things but I don't recall images very well because I don't think in them."

Baity had come up to the University of North Carolina in 1913, from rural Iredell County, with sixty dollars in his pocket to get him through the year, and had made it, and the next three years too, working in the laundry and anywhere else he could get a job, and was no doubt all knees and elbows, a rough rube. He'd graduated in the liberal arts with Sam, then returned to the University and gone through in engineering. After serving in World War I he had worked, saved money, gone to Harvard and earned a doctorate in environmental health. Later he'd worked in public health in North Carolina for a few years, traveled for various foundations, and lived in South America. He became a high official in the World Health Organization, and lived in Zurich, Switzerland, for sixteen years. Now he had a home in the south of France, where he and his wife — a well-known anthropologist — spent six months each year. He had also managed to become a full professor at the University, now professor emeritus, and he taught when he felt like it. He was elegant, urbane, and manly, and was able to wear a British suit without pretending to be British. He was a handsome old man who might have been a movie star once but whose masculine vigor of intellect was beyond that of any actor's, as was his hard and genial self-knowledge. This University, which was the best in the country when he was attending it, had made him what he was, and he loved the University.

He'd prepared for the interview, and had a list of things he wanted to tell me in case I forgot to ask. But I was still searching for something he'd not planned on, when I noticed a smile cross his face, and I asked him what was funny.

"It's nothing," he said, and started in on something else, the old-time debating societies or something like that, when the smile broke in again and he began laughing to himself.

"Well, you see, we had our fiftieth reunion a little while back," he said. "Nineteen sixty-seven. We had a dinner and Sam was presiding. Everybody would get up and make speeches, you see. About what he'd been doing since the last time, things like that.

"Well, this fellow stood up to be recognized, and Sam gave him the floor, and the fellow — and he looked around over the crowd — you know, there aren't as many of us now as there once were — and he said, You know, time changes everything.

" 'Time changes everything,' he said. 'Why, the passage of years has done such things to faces — that there are men here today, friends of mine in years gone by, of whom I had to ask their very names. Even I myself have changed,' he said. 'Yes, Time has come, all right, and wrought its changes. On all save one.

" 'On all save one,' he said. 'For there is one among us whom time has not changed, one who miraculously has escaped the ravaging forces of the years, coming down through the decades practically unchanged. And who is that man? Who is he?

" 'Mr. President,' he said. 'That man to whom I refer is none other than yourself.' "

Here Baity's laughter began to come again, so that I had difficulty understanding him.

" 'Yourself, Mr. President,' he said. 'Because . . . ' " Here the laughter became severe. " 'Because . . . because . . .' " ha ha ha ha ha " 'Because you looked like an old man when you were a freshman, and you look like an old man now!' " Then Baity was lost in his laughter and it was a good long while before he came back. He was a lusty, solid old man and the University had made him.

Chapter 5

WHEN THE TRAIN STOPPED at the University Station, Sam looked for the school, but it wasn't there. And so he waited for Captain Smith's train, which he got on and rode to Carrboro, eight or ten miles away, then got off with the other students there and walked the mile to Chapel Hill, which was a village of maybe 500 people set across the dirt road from the University of North Carolina.

Sam didn't see the University at first because the leaves were still out and the buildings were set back among the trees. He crossed over the dirt road and went down a brick walkway under the trees to where the buildings, old ones of soft and weathered redbrick, stood in austere simplicity in a sort of quadrangle. There weren't many buildings. Nor many students, less than a thousand, and the tradition was that you got to know everyone on campus by his first name.

By Christmas he would know them all, his fellow students, and was to find them, from the beginning, very much like himself, in that they spoke with the same human accent and came from the same state. North Carolina, for almost everybody, was the ultimate reality, the United States of America existing only mistily, as sort of a Platonic ideal; but the state was rich, raw, real, and green, a human state that had nurtured them and toward whose leadership most of them were tending. They had come from the same sort of stock, too, which was to say, mostly English, Scotch-Irish, and German with a bit of Huguenot thrown in. Their people had been in the country a long time and didn't have to be sent to Americanization school to learn its ways. So that the North Carolina they all came from, in which only one man out of a hundred had a foreign-born parent, was a profoundly different place from, say, Connecticut, where most of the citizens (58 percent) had a parent who was foreign-born.

They came from the same stock, the students and professors. This seemed to Sam a good arrangement because, since you all came from the same thing, presumably you needed to know the same things. They all read Kipling, poems like this:

> The Stranger within my gate,
>   He may be true or kind,
> But he does not talk my talk —
>   I cannot feel his mind.
> I see the face and the eyes and the mouth.
>   But not the soul behind.
> The men of my own stock,
>   They may do ill or well,
> But they tell thee lies I am wonted to,
>   They are used to the lies I tell;
> And we don't need interpreters
>   When we go to buy and sell.

These boys shared with Kipling a sense of siege; a belief that Anglo-Saxon civilization was under an attack, which manifested itself not only in the war that might break out at any minute in Europe, but also in the unrest caused by the hordes of Eastern European immigrants who were arriving at Ellis Island each day, bringing with them, as it seemed to some, servility, dirtiness, and an ignorance of American ways; bringing with them, in some cases, peregrine ideals aiming at the destruction of Anglo-Saxon civilization. So that the Kipling poetry, which Sam began to know then, and to love, was as much an expression of what went on at the state's marsupium as were the old buildings themselves, or the memorial tablets to Confederate veterans, or the reproduction of Guido Reni's *St. Michael Slaying the Dragon,* which hung behind the rostrum of Gerrard Hall chapel and which the student body saw when it gathered together that first day, when Sam and the rest of the freshmen got introduced to the Carolina spirit.

The Carolina spirit, then, wasn't just to go out and beat somebody in a football game. It was preparation for a more mortal battle that would take all of life and not just a couple of hours. These four years there would be this time and this place, in which to study and have fun and learn to live with those your own kind. The faculty, which was brilliant, and the University president, who was a charismatic genius, all believed in the same thing: Christian civilization and the ideal of the Christian Gentleman, and it was this, above all, that the school taught.

It wasn't just something the faculty and administration wanted and that the students could take or leave. No, it was what the students wanted, too; it was the culmination and capstone of coming from the same stock, because good blood meant nothing if it was not ennobled by high ideals and gentled by good manners. So the picture of St. Michael slaying the dragon was not there by accident, and Sam was to sit looking up at it five mornings a week for the next four school years. Chapel was compulsory; it was when you learned what the whole thing was about, what the purpose was.

Because you couldn't tell anything by reading the catalogue. For instance, the catalogue said that you couldn't leave the Hill without your parents' permission, which wasn't true, and that you would be expelled if you were caught drinking intoxicating liquor, which may or may not have been true but was very seldom tested in spite of the cases of stuff coming into Chapel Hill Station each week. You could drink if you were halfway circumspect about it, and you could leave the Hill if you could think of anyplace else to go.

Some of the things in the catalogue couldn't be depended upon, while other things could. For instance, the catalogue said, "the University endeavors to make young men manly and self-reliant, and to develop character by educating the conscience," and that was true. But this was a thing so mysterious and immense that it could not be taught by any written words; was a mystique that even the chapel exercises could only allude to, and it pervaded everything.

The most conspicuous Christian gentleman of all was Edward Kidder Graham, acting president of the University when Sam arrived, who was to be named full president that year. Sam saw him the first day up on the podium in Gerrard Hall. When he stood up you forgot about St. Michael and looked at him. You watched him whether he was saying anything or not because he seemed to come from a more intense order of being; he was closer to being your true self than you were.

He was tall, ascetic, almost gaunt, a man who could be called beautiful, with some sort of spiritual power coming out of him so strongly that it could project itself through faded photos sixty years later with unmistakable authority. A scholar and, in spite of that, a genius who looked a little bit like Emerson, without the gawkiness, and a lot like Woodrow Wilson, without that vacant stare Wilson got when he was in a public place trying to appeal to a lot of people. No, Edward Kidder Graham was a man who never deserted himself to appeal to the mob, was truthful in being. His elegance of dress, athletic grace of movement, and simple, lofty eloquence of speech — all these were secondary to the central thing he was, a Christian gentleman.

What Graham talked about in the chapel exercises was "democracy," "leadership," "education for the good life," "service," and "ideals." And to Sam it began to make sense. "Democracy" meant that you honored your fellow citizens of whatever rank in life, and trusted, ultimately, the wisdom they expressed when they voted. "Education for the good life" meant that the University was there to strengthen your moral character, enhance your aesthetic sensiblities, and make you wise, so that you would live in a high state of perceptual awareness and rightly decide the things that would be brought to you to decide. "Service" meant you were destined to lead; "ideals" meant that you honored God and refused to lie to yourself or anybody else. And "leadership" was what you were headed for. Because the state was run by Christian gentlemen, and so was the nation. Thus, underlying everything, including the Constitution of the United States, was the notion that Christian gentlemen ran things. When the laws didn't fit together exactly right, Christian gentlemen made them right, because they were wise, benign, and strong.

This year Sam studied long hours in the golden pool the electric light made on his desk, went down for dinner, and came back to study some more. There was no way to let things slide for a couple of weeks and then catch up by cramming. Classes were small, with never more than twenty students and sometimes as few as four or five, and the professors knew from day to day what you were doing. Sam was close to being the perfect Carolina student; everything he was now added up to that, but he didn't know it. And this made him even more perfect, because he had the humility, too, which wasn't required, say, at the University of South Carolina, and certainly not at the University of Virginia, but was mandatory down here. If you were conceited at the University of North Carolina you had to have a good excuse, like being twelve years old — as was one of Sam's schoolmates, Robert Welch, the candy-man, a shrill, brilliant little fellow who still wore short britches, and who had a national future ahead of him as founder of the John Birch Society.

The University of North Carolina had the most distinguished faculty in the South, and this was before the days when the only way to be distinguished was to avoid the undergraduate students. As often as not, classes were held in the professor's house. Sam was close friends with Frank Porter Graham, later president of the University and a United States Senator. For freshman English he had Edwin Greenlaw, who was shortly to become the Dean of the Johns Hopkins Graduate School. For American literature he had Norman Foerster, the distinguished founder of interdisciplinary curricula in American Civilization.

These professors not only knew Sam by name, they knew him well and intimately, and this was what he got for the sixty dollars a year tuition and the $15.00 a month for board. His faculty advisor was Archibald Henderson, a mathematics professor who wrote and published extensively on historical subjects and who, on the side, was the official biographer of George Bernard Shaw.

Many of the professors had independent means; all of them were men of quiet pride, intellect, and self-sufficiency. During the first few months Sam dealt with them carefully, the way he'd learned to deal with his father, by doing everything that was expected of him, before it was expected, studying long hours in the evening, and then, maybe, when he was feeling far enough ahead of the game, stopping by Nick's Restaurant on his way home and paying fifteen cents for half a dozen fried oysters. When he was really feeling free he would shell out the dime to go to the Pic, the town's one movie house, to watch the Charlie Chaplin films and eat roasted peanuts and listen, in the intermissions, to Mabel, the piano player, pounding out "Ballin' the Jack," "The Curse of an Aching Heart," or "There's a Long, Long Trail" — all new songs that year.

He was seventeen, and saw the world pretty much the same way

Edward Kidder Graham saw it, as peopled by self-contained and self-sufficient men, each of whom was ultimately and completely responsible for himself. He was able to believe most of the corollaries, too, such as the one that held that whoever organized a business or built a factory — thereby offering employment to some of the other self-contained men — was thereby a social benefactor, a patriot, and a noble soul.

Of course, that he believed all this at seventeen was no sure signal that he was going to go on believing it. Maybe he would and maybe he wouldn't. But if there were those who were bored by the Edward Kidder Graham business and saw it as sham, Sam wasn't very much aware of them because, clever minority that they were, they kept their mouths shut.

One of that minority would be Thomas Wolfe — who wasn't at the University yet, but was to come along in Sam's senior year — and who was to see Edward Kidder Graham through the lens of a different sensibility:

> His pale, pure face, somewhat gaunt and emaciated, a subtle air he conveyed always of bearing some deep, secret sorrow, and of suffering in some subtle, complicated way for humanity, began to afflict Monk with a sensation that was akin to, and in fact was scarcely distinguishable from, the less acute stages of nausea.

But Sam liked Edward Kidder Graham fine, liked his professors, too, including Horace Williams, the philosophy teacher whom Wolfe was to call the Hegel of the cotton patch. They never did get to the textbook in Williams' course. The fellow just stood up there, thinking out loud, and, when he felt like it, engaged the students in dialogue. When the semester was over the final examination required them to trace the movement of thought in the course. The important thing, Sam began to learn, was to look the professor in the eye and to go on talking to him, and let him educate you that way. You were educated by people; you could slack off on the books without the world caving in.

One evening, when he could have been studying but was sitting around, instead, with a bunch of new friends, someone suggested that they take a stroll to Durham and Raleigh. So Sam hiked thirty-eight miles that night, and rode back to the University Station on the next train. Other things besides books were part of his education, the thing his father was paying for. There were dinners at the professors' houses, chamber music in the evenings, and dramatic productions from time to time. And there was Christianity, or what passed for it. The YMCA met three nights a week and, as often as not, Sam went to that. And there was a Bible class, which met every Sunday in the dormitory room of Bill Umstead, a sophomore. Sam went to that, too. He was a Christian and it seemed a natural thing. On Sundays, after the classes in Umstead's room, there were long rambling walks across the raw fields and through the endless groves of pine.

He was finding he could do a great many things at once, that he had a superabundance of raw energy. He was smart enough to keep his mouth shut about it, too: he knew without being told that at Carolina the greatest hindrance to being bright was the desire to be thought so. Even before the flowering dogwoods, redbuds, and quince apple blossoms came out that spring, turning Chapel Hill into something like heaven, Sam was handling many things well: the Sunday school, the cultural events, the night-long bull sessions, the debating society, the ordinary course of study (except for physics, perhaps, which he detested), and a special paper he was writing for Dr. James Gregoire deRoulhac Hamilton, Professor of North Carolina History, for which he won the Colonial Dames First Prize.

Even now, in repose, his face had the seriousness of an older man's. But it was seldom in repose anymore. He was talking to people more, and when he did he laughed a lot. By the end of his freshman year he was beginning to feel very good, was gathering strength, building up to something. It was a plain, small university, a good place to be with those of one's own stock.

TOM WOLFE?!

I sat in a booth at Chapel Hill's Pines Restaurant, looking out the window and listening to the conversations of the other customers. The men in the booth behind me were discussing forestry, and those in front of me were talking about a computer projection that was supposed to tell what North Carolina would need in 1995. The view out the window wasn't so hot, just the omnipresent four-lane highway, grass strip in the middle, and beyond that a sign at the entranceway to a housing development for the well-to-do, the Oaks. I did not see any oaks over there, only wet pine trees. Everything was gray from the February drizzle and the wetness seemed somehow to have invaded this restaurant. At a table over in the corner they were talking about Schopenhauer.

My waitress was a pretty girl, brunette, blue-eyed, a fair complexioned, cream and roses, of the type a Yankee might call zoftig. *I watched her as she waited on the Schopenhauer table. She seemed to know what they were talking about and entered into the conversation. When she brought my order, I asked her if she went to the University. She said yes. She was in her third year of graduate school and was taking a seminar from a famous literature professor there. She had been going to the University for seven years, and was now sufficiently advanced to be allowed in one of his courses.*

"How do you like it?"

"It's all right," she said. "Only we don't get to see him much."

"That's too bad."

"He assigned me a paper on The Bostonians, *and I want to do one on* The Spoils of Poynton. *But I haven't been able to find him yet to make the switch."*

"I expect you'll be a Ph.D. pretty soon."

She shook her head. "No," she said. "I'm going home next month."

"How come?"

"It's the market. No jobs. There's no point in it."

"Well, maybe you have had the education for the good life," I said.

"It's more like the education for stenography, if you ask me."

"That, too."

"It's a pain in the ass," she said.

I had an appointment that night with another of Sam's old friends, Dr. Albert Coates. His place reminded me of Herman Baity's. It was a large, beautiful house on an old street, surrounded by big trees, where there was no way of seeing the four-lane highway or the new shopping centers or the Danish X-rated movie playing on Rosemary Street where the professors' houses once stood. No, Coates' and Baity's houses were situated in places where it could just as well have been 1913 still.

Coates was the same age as Sam, seventy-seven, and there was something of the relaxed undergraduate about him, not only in the cardigan sweater he wore, but in the mobile face, in the way he strolled instead of walked. He was watching the last part of Neil McNeil's show on public television and had invited me over there to see it with him. The show was about President Nixon and whether he'd be impeached. Coates was very exercised about Watergate, and saw in it the ultimate confrontation between the old America, which he loved, and the new America, in which he was not very comfortable.

His wife came in with coffee and sat watchfully on the sofa opposite us. She was an attractive, silver-haired woman perhaps ten years his junior and she sat on the sofa crocheting and listening closely to our conversation. She had some memories of Sam in the 1920's, and when there was a lull in the conversation she told them to me. Meanwhile, Coates left the room, and came back with two books: one hardback, The Speeches of Edward Kidder Graham, *and the other paperback, his own* What the University of North Carolina Meant to Me. *It was a book that spoke fondly of the University in the days when there had been 900 students, not 20,000, when everybody had known everybody else's first name.*

"They have professors now every bit as good as those we had," Coates said, "but the student doesn't get to see them till he's in graduate school. More than likely he's taught by an assistant of some sort. No personal contact. What's more, there's no one to lead. The president is an administrator, a fund-raiser, a dealer with legislatures. And is very good at that, I expect. But he doesn't lead. Lastly, there's no attention given to the fundamentals of our government. You can get out of here with a Ph.D. in political science and know nothing of the Constitution of the United States."

"I wonder who in the Senate will take Sam's place when he retires?" I asked.

"That's just it," Coates said. "Nobody."

We got to talking about Edward Kidder Graham.

"Every student at this university loved him," Coates maintained.

"Except one," I said.

"Tom Wolfe?!" Coates snorted.

"Yes."

Coates grew animated, red-faced. "Let me tell you," he said. "The last time Tom came down here, we sat down to breakfast, right over at that table, about ten in the morning — and, you know, we had a little refreshment — and the breakfast lasted until four in the afternoon. Tom had just published that damned thing. He was sitting in that chair right over there. And I said, 'Tom, you ought to be sued for libel on that.' I told him he was just trying to get at that literary bunch who made Graham into an object of worship — and who did the same thing to Tom, too, once he'd died. And he admitted it. Admitted it . . . jackass . . ."

"You knew Tom Wolfe," I said.

"He was my roommate at Harvard," Coates replied.

Back at the University Motel, the pastel colors of the walls were the same colors that came out of the television set. I lay down on the bed and began to read the speeches of Edward Kidder Graham. They were good speeches, lucid and eloquent, and I was inspired by them. I, too, had been raised to be a Christian gentleman and I did not think it such a bad ideal if one had the money for the "gentleman" part of it.

Meanwhile the news kept coming out of the color television set. There was sporadic shooting along the interstate highways and one trucker near Greensboro had gotten his in the stomach. Also, it was Women's Week at the University of North Carolina. Gloria Steinem was in town, and so was Jane Fonda. Mrs. Norman Mailer was appearing with the Carolina Players. Chapel Hill's black Mayor was explaining the gas-rationing program. As I drifted off to sleep, I remembered that Richard Nixon, an outsider, had spent three years here in North Carolina, going to school with the Christian gentlemen, and I wondered how he'd liked it.

Chapter 6

IN MORGANTON, that summer of 1914, Sam and Jim Kirksey got jobs in the tannery. Kirksey was his closest friend; he had gone through high school with Sam and was to go through the University with him, too. For five days a week they worked side by side way up under the eaves, in the intense heat, choked with the thick dust, packing tanbark down into the sheds. Every day at quitting time they were obliged to pass through a line formed by the older workers, who shook their hands and told them good-bye, on the theory that they wouldn't have the gumption to come back the next day.

Sam didn't have to work; no one had asked him to, and besides, there was a tennis court now on the Ervin property, which attracted half the young people in town, including the pretty girls who were among the summer visitors. But every weekday morning, before the tennis players were out of bed, Sam would leave the house, walk the mile and a half to the tannery, and climb up there into the rafters, into the heat and damnation of dust, to toil the ten-hour day that would earn him a dollar. On Saturdays he and Kirksey went down to the train station and unloaded cattle hides that came in from Argentina. These were very heavy but the air on the train platform was better than it was under the eaves of the tanbark sheds, and they could quit for the day when they had unloaded their quota. So they worked hard and got home by noon. Well, it kept him in a right relationship with his father, and he wasn't passionately involved with any girl yet. Didn't have to be at the tennis court. He knew that once he commenced getting serious with a girl the next step was to declare what he was going to Do, but he wasn't ready for anything like that. Although it was beginning to look like he might follow his father into the law. Indeed, there didn't seem to be much else, although a couple of his professors had suggested to him that he might go into university teaching.

He went back to the University that fall tougher and with a harder edge of self-respect; this was the bedrock under the smiles, stories, quips, cranks, and miscellaneous genialities. The sense of siege was more urgent. The Great War was on in earnest now, and instead of joining a social fraternity, which he might have done, Sam decided to devote the time to the meetings of the International Polity Club, an organization meeting regularly to study and discuss the war. What America ought to do hadn't yet been settled. Among the small farmers, and the sons of small farmers at the University, there was strong isolationist sentiment; they didn't want to be robbed by the munitions-makers, nor did they want to die for somebody else's gain. These boys had, as their chief spokesman on the national scene, the powerful North Carolina Congressman, Claude Kitchen, who, within the year, was to become Democratic Leader of the House.

And Sam watched all this, not as an intellectual watches such things, but the way a young sub on the sidelines watches a football game. Politics was full-time sport. The hundred boys in his class would, in time, be running the state, and they all knew it. Wolfe was to write:

> The campus had its candidates, its managers, its bosses, its machines, as had the State. A youngster developed in College the political craft he was later to exert in Party affairs. The son of a politician was schooled by his crafty sire before the down was off his cheeks: at sixteen, his life had been plotted ahead to the governorship, or to the proud dignities of a Congressman. The boy came deliberately to the University to bait and set his first traps: deliberately he made those friendships that were most likely to benefit him later. By his junior year, if he was successful, he had a political manager, who engineered his campus ambitions; he moved with circumspection, and spoke with a trace of pomp nicely weighted with cordiality. "Ah, there, Gentlemen." "Gentlemen, how are you?" "A nice day, Gentlemen."

Sam kept in the background at first, as a member of a small, clandestine group whose activities were directed, not toward electing its own members to the campus offices, but at naming those who would be elected. He liked running things while seeming to be uninvolved. He gave up the idea of university teaching. His class-mates began to poke fun at the professors. One morning Professor Bacot found a cow in his seminar, and remarked casually that the intellectual level of the class seemed to have been raised somewhat.

Sam decided that he could not be a professor, because he wanted to be more active and more independent than that. And there weren't many other things open. He wasn't going to be an apron-wearing store fool, and couldn't be a minister because a minister was merely an employee. In short, his prime directive — to be free, never to be violated — was driving him toward law. He had been reading it in his spare time now for a couple of years; Blackstone's "Commentaries on the Laws of England."

And he loved the University of North Carolina. This was the world that Thomas Wolfe wrote about in *Look Homeward, Angel:*

> In this pastoral setting a young man was enabled to loaf comfortably and delightfully through four luxurious and indolent years. There was, God knows, seclusion enough for monastic scholarship, but the rare romantic quality of the atmosphere, the prodigal opulence of Springtime, thick with flowers and drenched with a fragrant warmth of green shimmering light, quenched pretty thoroughly any incipient rash of bookishness. Instead, they loafed and invited their souls or, with great energy and enthusiasm, promoted the affairs of glee clubs, athletic teams, class poli-tics, fraternities, debating societies, and dramatic clubs. And they talked — always they talked, under the trees, against the ivied walls, as-sembled in their rooms, they talked — in limp sprawls — incessant, charming, empty Southern talk; they talked with a large easy fluency about God, the Devil, and philosophy, the girls, politics, athletics, frater-nities and the girls — My God! How they talked!

But that was Wolfe. Sam kept up the scholarship; and his history papers became larger, more ambitious, and continued to win prizes. He was, perhaps, "influenced" by Professor Hamilton (for whom he did the papers) in the sense that Hamilton's thought provided the larger justification for what Sam had come to the University thinking, anyway. Hamilton believed in the ascendancy of the true blood, believed that with the 1898 election North Carolina had "come into the hands of the class best fitted to administer government, and the supremacy of the white race and of the Anglo-Saxon institutions was secure."

Hamilton predicted that one day the white supremacy would be tested. And in the spring of Sam's sophomore year, as if to signal the future confrontations, Booker T. Washington died, and the NAACP took over the leadership of the black cause. And *The Birth of a Nation* began a record run of forty-seven weeks at the Liberty Theatre in New York City. That was the movie they'd made out of Thomas Dixon's *The Clansman,* and it served to increase the membership of the new Klan.

But Sam was already above all that. He was no candidate for Klan membership, knew that the organization was made up mostly of the Anglo-Saxon varletry. He knew — as his classmates did — that their own part in the coming struggle would take place on a higher ground. He did not intend to waste his time night-riding.

The next year, his junior year, the mood on the campus began to tighten up. No longer were voices raised for the German cause. And it had been collectively decided, in the deliberations of the International Polity Club and in the bull sessions endlessly taking place on the isolated little campus, that war would be fought in defense of civilization itself — that is, in defense of that part of the world run by Christian gentlemen. This would be the final war, and Sam's own generation would fight it.

So he would have his chance at glory without having to put in forty years to get it. He went about his business, as assistant editor of the University magazine, class historian, and commencement marshal, and was active in half a dozen clubs. And kept up the historical research for Professor Hamilton. This year he wrote a paper entitled "The Provincial Agents of North Carolina," and in so doing learned more about his mother's side of the family. They had come from Cheraw, South Carolina, just as his father's family had, and his mother and father were, in fact, second cousins.

He took delight in writing his mother about his research, especially when anything in the books and records told a tale, however fragmentary, that smacked of the dignity of her family. Such as when he discovered in old records that some of his maternal ancestors had belonged to "a prominent and well-to-do family who built their home on a bluff overlooking the Yadkin River near Salisbury." He wrote her about that. The records also showed that some of his ancestors had been pillars of assorted Presbyterian churches, or Revolutionary War soldiers, or businessmen of good repute. Working long into the night searching for his ancestors gave him deep delight, because in so doing he was establishing firm connections with many men. No aberration from greatness on the part of any one family member could alienate him from all that. He was of the good blood, the records seemed to show, and good blood was what counted.

Although Sam was only dimly aware of it then, he was part of a movement that had been going on for thirty years or more. The Americans who'd been here longest, those of Northern European descent, felt themselves menaced by the millions of new arrivals from Italy, Eastern Europe, the Balkans, Russia. Feeling their culture and their dominance threatened, they formed their private schools, their country clubs, their Colonial Dames and Sons of the Revolution, and their cults of genealogy, which upheld the view that the Anglo-Saxon race was the great race, and that the Christian gentleman, by his intrinsic excellence, should continue to rule the world. Sam went on writing the papers for Professor Hamilton, and was elected Secretary of the North Carolina Historical Society. In the commencement that took place that spring, he again took first place in North Carolina History, and went home carrying the ribbon.

By the summer of 1916, German U-boats were already sinking American ships in the Atlantic, and it seemed certain that America would enter the war within the year. That was the summer the Catawba flooded, the biggest flood in anybody's memory. Nobody could get out of Morganton. And then there were the Brown Mountain lights.

Many of the citizens of Morganton believed that these mysterious lights had been there since the mountains were formed, or even before. And there were authenticated records of these lights' appearing as far back as Revolutionary War times. There wasn't anybody in the town who at one time or another hadn't taken a picnic basket and some friends up to one of the adjoining mountains to watch them. They would most frequently pop up after a rain, discrete, shimmering at first as they were rising, spherical, then becoming ovoid as they ascended slowly into the atmosphere, finally vanishing. No man knew what caused them. Not even Jules Verne knew.

The federal government, which even then hated mystery, was trying to explain them, and had even spent the taxpayers' money sending some fellow down from the Department of the Interior; who had come up with a report saying that they were the reflection of the headlights of train engines. Now, this summer of 1916, the Brown Mountain lights came again. But the flood had washed out train tracks for thirty miles around, and no trains were running, and the lights continued to rise above Brown Mountain, more brilliantly than ever before. So it was not absolutely necessary to move into the modern age just yet. There could still be mystery. And Sam was thinking about war and mystery; was in that frame of mind when he met Margaret Bruce Bell, a summer visitor who was visiting her uncle when she was stranded by the floods.

He first saw her seated up high in her uncle's automobile, which she drove around Morganton that summer. The windshield was down, and she was laughing as she sped by on her way to some frolic. She wore a white dress, ankle-length, and a broad-brimmed hat, also white. And Sam thought he saw something about her that could not be reported or explained, something he alone could see. Besides, she was damned good-looking, and anybody could see that. The next day, he met her at the home of Judge Avery.

Now, Margaret Bruce Bell, at seventeen, was already an experienced campaigner. She had been raised to handle young men, and for the past four or five years had been handling them skillfully. There was another young fellow or two down in Concord, North Carolina, where she came from; and maybe half a dozen from other places, who had been drawn to her at Converse College in Spartanburg, South Carolina, where she'd just completed her freshman year. There were lots of young fellows, many of them serious, and each of whom seemed to think this girl had something special only his eyes could see.

Sam asked her out to a dance, and she went. He asked her out to the motion picture show, and she went. To a hayride, and she went. Then he kept on asking her out, only sometimes she did not go with him now; sometimes, she had other dates — and with fellows he knew! Which was intolerable. He even began to look forward to the

time when she would leave Morganton, because when she did, although there would still be other young men, at least he would not
have to know about them.

He could not understand her. She would go out with that other
fellow, and Sam would walk maybe ten or fifteen miles through the
night, thinking about that. The next day he would find her in his own
kitchen, or upstairs in his sister's bedroom, talking to the women in
his family with an intimacy that seemed to dissolve when he approached. The talkers would fall suddenly silent or else leap out at
him with banter he knew had nothing to do with whatever it was
they'd been discussing.

That Sam and Margaret liked each other showed in the photographs which were taken of them that summer. There is Sam in his
shining bowl haircut, trying to hang on to the underside of some car's
running board while Margaret sits in a white dress on the rear fender
looking down and laughing at him, obviously delighted with him.

She liked him, and he sensed that. But she kept him away. No
engagement. No going steady. She would think about that one, the
going steady, and maybe later on they would see what they would see.
She was shy, winsome; she clowned around, giggled; and she was
subjugating him.

This was a necessary thing (because this was the South), and she
knew it even if he did not, and went on breaking him into the thing,
taming him. There was a certain sort of control she had to achieve.
She knew absolutely that without it there could be no marriage, or, at
least, no marriage any more permanent than the hired minister's
empty words fading away in the rafters of the First Presbyterian
Church — of Concord. Which was where they would have the wedding, if they ever had it: in Concord, her home town, and on her own
terms. Because she was a fit match for him, was as determined, and as
gifted in what she did — handling young men — as he was in what he
did.

Not only was she a Presbyterian, as he was, no small boon, but what
was more, what stirred his imagination — she was, authentically, of
the good blood, a direct descendent of Sara Hutchinson Leslie, an
aunt of Andrew Jackson's. She was beautiful, witty, spirited, and he
could marry her if he could only teach his leaden catcher's feet to
dance the tunes she called.

But he was glad, in a way, to be returning to Chapel Hill for his senior year, to continue the campaign from there. Once back at the University, he knew, he would not feel himself to be so clumsy. Back there, he knew, he would be in control, not only of himself, but of others as well. And this would have to continue, his growing feeling of control, of incipient mastery. Because even true love itself would smash up on the rock of his self-respect if it came to that.

She sensed this in him, knew better than to push him too far, always salvaged him, finally, from buffoonery. This summer, therefore, when he made a point of asking her to the Commencement Ball, which would take place at his graduation, nine months hence, she made a point of accepting. After all, it wasn't so unusual for a popular girl to be asked that far in advance. So they made the date, probably not knowing how close war was, not knowing there would be no Commencement Ball at the University of North Carolina in 1917, or any commencement, either.

When Sam went back to the campus that fall, he found that not all his classmates had spent the summer of 1916 chasing girls. Many of them had been at nearby Plattsburg, drilling with rifles, and what they were talking about in the bull sessions was not girls nor God nor Edward Kidder Graham, but whether there ought to be any University at all, whether it wasn't weak and foolish to go on studying in the face of the threat to civilization. They were even drilling on the campus itself, and victory gardens had been planted in back of Peabody Hall, and men who had seen action overseas were showing up to speak in the chapel exercises on life in the trenches. The summer had been full of reverse for the Allies, and it was not certain that democracy would triumph.

Things did not seem solid anymore. Sam was named class historian, assistant editor of the University magazine, most popular in his class, Best Egg, and yet things were not solid, the drilling went on, and the trench-lecturers continued to fill the chapel with indoctrination as Sam and his classmates sat there flanked by the cool marble tablets listing in old script the names of Carolina students among the Confederate dead. Nothing was solid. He didn't even have the girl. He knew she was seeing the others when she wasn't seeing him.

Nor could he take any comfort in the younger men who were coming up behind him at the University, because there was no solidity there, either. One of them was his brother, Joe, who arrived on campus that fall, limping on a walking stick, grinning, politicking from moment one. Then there was that friend of Joe's, the tall, skinny, scowling redheaded one, Tom Wolfe, who loped sullenly around the campus exuding a truculent contempt for its traditions, its sacred spots such as the Old Well and the Davie Poplar, and even for Edward Kidder Graham himself. Although, for all that, it was Sam and the young men like him who ran the University, set its tone. They were the Christian gentlemen now.

On Thanksgiving they filled the train that was headed up for the annual game with the University of Virginia, went out to the stands, and were led in cheers by Si Parker as the Tar Heels beat the Cavaliers for the first time in eleven years. Then suddenly it was Christmas and there wasn't much time anymore.

They had to finish up. There were all the usual campus activities, there was the largest and most ambitious historical paper Sam had ever attempted (the equivalent of a master's thesis), and, in addition, he was taking the first year of law school at the same time he was finishing his last year in the University. He got down to Concord when he could, during the holidays.

As a law student, he was beginning to get some firsthand notion of how prodigious a lawyer his father was, and he would write the old man when he came across one of his North Carolina Supreme Court cases, write him flatteringly. Yes, if anybody was going to meet the old man's powerful expectations, it was going to be Sam now. Because there was no longer any question about Ed. Time and ill health had settled all that, and Ed now dwelt about the fringes, wheezing for breath, and the father would sit out on the front porch, muttering "I have no son."

Just writing the research paper — "A Colonial History of Rowan County, North Carolina" — could have absorbed the full energies of a normally active young man, but Sam did that almost on the side, while courting Margaret and going to the meetings of the International Polity Club and the debating societies and editing the magazine and attending all his regular classes and the law school classes as well. He did not quit, did not fall down on anything, did not yield to self-pity about the possibility of his being killed in the war, did not act uncomfortably as did Robert Welch, who, still wearing short britches, ran away to Roanoke, Virginia, on the theory that the University of North Carolina was no place to be a man.

But Sam believed that the place to be a man was at the place you were supposed to be. That was the only chance you had, and if it meant that someone else got the attention of your mother and the companionship of your father and the high prizes, if another man kissed your girl, and if, finally, you got killed because you were where you were supposed to be, all right. Because if you sniveled or ran you lost everything.

Early in April, in the spring of his senior year, the United States declared war on Germany, and Sam went down to the gymnasium, together with all the other men in his class, and volunteered for induction into the army. This, in spite of his father's having suggested to him that he wait until he was drafted. He was sworn into the army, went back to Morganton for a few days, and then rode the train down to Oglethorpe, Georgia, to begin officer's training. Before he left the University, he was elected Permanent President of the Class of 1917. But there would be no Commencement Ball and no commencement for that class, and this came down on Sam very hard because it was at the commencement, he'd always assumed, that he would speak to Margaret.

Three months later he rode back into Morganton with his lieutenant's bars shining on his shoulder, and his father took him aside into the parlor and showed him the war bond. It was for five thousand dollars and his father had bought it the day he went in. Presumably, it was a gesture of approval, to be cashed in later.

That afternoon, Sam marched in the parade. It started at the Court House Square, and was led by the Morganton band. Waits Harbison, dressed as Uncle Sam, rode a decorated mule; Bobbie Cobb, dressed as Miss Liberty, followed in the fire engine, which had been draped with red, white, and blue streamers, and was followed by the draftees, who wore arm bands that said "Burke's Boys." Then there came the Exemption Board and the Home Guards and the Red Cross, followed by the Confederate veterans. There were still plenty of the Confederate veterans. Then there came the Boy Scouts and several hundred school children. Little Jack Barefoot wore a sailor's suit and represented the navy. Then, after the marching and the band music, the speeches and the fireworks, the Red Cross ladies served up dinner to the new soldiers and the Confederate veterans, who sat side by side at the tables.

The next day Sam was on the train for New York, headed for the embarkation point, and two weeks later was out on the Atlantic, aboard a troopship. He spent his twenty-first birthday — September 27, 1917 — at sea. And although he could not find the place on any map, he knew where he was. He was inside himself, unviolated and in control, doing the things that were expected of him.

DAUGHTERS

I was down in Morganton again, and one evening, after dusk, I set out to look for Laura Ervin Smith's place. It was that time of evening when, as a boy in the South, I used to set out to pick up my dates. It took a long time to find the place, because it wasn't in town, but somewhere out at the edge, and the street signs were poor. There was a road running along a bluff above the Catawba River, and she lived on that. At the end of the road, which was Morganton's Lovers' Lane, intense spotlights glared in my face and there were high white walls and I thought it was a prison. But I drove into a courtyard, where the lights weren't so bad, and saw it was a house after all, a large white place made out of something like stucco, but that seemed smoother and more steel-like than stucco. Spanish architecture, red tile roof, big; the sort of place they would sell you for a quarter of a million dollars in Washington, D.C. I didn't know what it would cost down here.

She met me at the front door and led me back, across the polished bricked floor, to a room that might have been called a den, but that was somehow more impersonal than that, like a waiting room in an expensive restaurant. There were large hand-hewn darkstained rafters in the ceiling and copper implements hung from them and there was a big copper kettle, two and a half feet high, sitting on the brick hearth. Either it was of great antiquity or had been battered to make it look that way, and I thought to myself, as she showed me to a place on the sofa, I knew your great-grandmammy, girl, who cooked with one of those.

She was wearing gray slacks and a red jacket, and was as good-looking as I remembered from times gone by. Beautiful.

"We're going to be alone tonight," she said. She was standing near the fireplace. Beyond that was a wine cellar with dark wooden racks and the red

snouts of a hundred wine bottles. She poured us some dark red port, and came to sit on the sofa by me.

"Where's your wife?" she asked.

"Back in Virginia."

"Too bad."

"Yes."

"Bill is gone most of the time," she said. That was her husband, William Smith, who was sales manager of the Henredon Furniture Company.

The room was opulently decorated. Here was where they entertained the buyers who came down from Chicago and New York and places like that. It looked like the set of a Rock Hudson movie. She did not seem at home here.

"I don't know what I can tell you about Daddy," she said. "He was a good father, I suppose, but he was very busy, and mother raised us. All I can remember is playing across his shoes while he sat in a chair reading a book."

I told her of the many pictures I'd seen of her: the ones where she was a Cherry Blossom Princess, the ones when she came out, in Raleigh, as a debutante. (I couldn't keep my eyes off the copper kettle.) And the photos of the first wedding: the one with the marine lieutenant who had squired her about to the Cherry Blossom festivities, the one with crew cuts, starched uniforms, Eisenhower smiles, crossed swords and four hundred guests.

"What do you think of all that?" I asked.

"It was ridiculous."

"Why did you do it?"

"Let me see . . . Because Mother wanted it, I suppose."

"What about Daddy?"

"He wanted what Mother wanted."

"So I gather."

"Listen," she said, "you can't pin that on Daddy. I was an adult. It was nobody's fault but mine, if I wanted to play the Little White Bride. Remember, that Little White Bride scene has worked very well for Mother. She's had a good life out of that scene."

Sam's other daughter, Leslie, lived in that part of the country where it is more important to be decisive than to be right, and to see her it was necessary to drive up the New Jersey Turnpike to where the thing is twelve lanes wide and to exit on one of the numbered ramps. Because of the traffic, one was obliged to turn off decisively whether it was the right ramp or not. It was okay to take the wrong ramp, but indecisiveness would be punished by death. After a few hours of searching among the New Jersey towns, I found her place, a good-sized house set back under the trees in a comfortable community.

Like her sister down in North Carolina, Leslie met me wearing trousers — an aquamarine business suit. She, too, was alone. Her husband, Jerry Hansler, was at work in New York City, where he was head of the Environmental Protection Agency for the Northeastern United States.

Leslie, too, was a good-looking woman. But she came on more like a tomboy, all earnestness, slang, and level gaze, a bit of Carol Burnett, a bit of the mechanic down at the garage who is also your pal. She told me she remembered very little about Sam.

"He was always reading a book," she said, "so I was raised by Mother."

"You don't come on very much like Mom."

She grinned like a shortstop.

"That housewife bit might be all right for Mother's generation," she said, "but I believe in other things."

"Such as?"

"Options."

We talked for an hour and a half but she did not tell me very much about Sam, except that he was always reading a book and that he would sing in the car when they took long drives. She wanted to tell me stuff I already knew about Sam's years in the Senate and the legislation he'd had passed. For years before her marriage, she had worked on one of his subcommittees, and her life had been drawn into his.

She'd just passed her bar examination and I congratulated her on that.

"Yes," she said, "I'm looking for a job. I have to decide pretty soon."

"Did Sam give you any advice on that?"

"Not specific advice," she said. "He gave me a copy of Dale Carnegie. I have it in the back room somewhere."

"Do you ever consult it?"

"Would you?"

"No."

"Well, neither do I. What's Dale Carnegie got to tell me about handling my options?"

Chapter 7

Sᴀᴍ's sʜɪᴘ, the *Kroonland*, hove into Liverpool harbor, all dull slate gray with the yellow band around its middle getting yellower as she loomed in. Only as it came in very close could the people on the shore see that the yellow band wasn't painted on but was comprised of hundreds of soliders. Sam was one of these. This war wasn't going to be like a Sir Walter Scott novel. There would eventually be four million men in the American Army, two million of whom would end up in France; the first division to get there was the Big Red One, Sam's division. It was an exercise in impersonal vastness with the four tons of cargo provided for each man unloaded from the ships by the battalions of sweating Negro stevedores.

And yet, in spite of that vastness, the moral tone of the operation was somehow kept up, and one of the first things Sam saw, shortly after he landed at Le Havre, was a circus banner stretched across the street reading: "This way to the YMCA. Get your money changed, and write home." The Red Triangle Man was everywhere, along with the ubiquitous YMCA hut, which was a combination theater, reading room, coffee stall, baseball locker, post office, and library, but which was most of all a chapel in which one was taught how God loathed the Hun, and exhorted to write home to Mom. But the YMCA was no use at all in preparing him to lead a combat infantry platoon made up mostly of hard-bitten career army men, fresh from whatever moral uplift there was along the Mexican border, some of whom could neither read nor write, and few of whom had any use for the YMCA, that haven of all mama's boys. This was Company I of the 28th Infantry Regiment, 2nd Brigade, 1st Division.

The 1st Division — the first of forty-two American divisions to be sent to France — assembled in and around six villages in the Gondrecourt training area and set about to make the place clean. That was the American way, then. So Sam supervised his platoon, or tried to supervise it, as dung piles were scooped up on wagons and hauled away, water bags set up on tripods, windows knocked out for fresh air, and bathing areas marked off along the streams.

There were bugs, everywhere, which the cuteness-loving Americans called cooties, and no amount of cleaning and spraying seemed to get rid of them. They were all over Sam's body under his shirt, and as he stood there telling the men what to do he would feel them crawling up his neck; he'd reach up and pull off a handful of them. All this cut into his dignity. In North Carolina there was a line between gentlemen and other men that could be eradicated only by murder, but here, in France, in front of these soldiers, Sam felt that line disappearing. It was nothing overt, nothing to send a man to the stockade for. It was just the absence of that deference with which he was used to being addressed. And what with the cooties, and with no place to sleep that was truly comfortable, Sam was finding that there were realities the chapel lectures had not described, and was beginning to wonder whether hard work would get him out of this one.

But he did work hard, as they went into training now under the supervision of the British bayonet instructors and the French Alpine soldiers, the "Blue Devils," who taught them squad tactics and the use of the Mills bombs, Livens Projectors, and Stokes mortars, but who provided Sam with nothing of what he needed most, which was some way to handle his men. No matter what he did, he never got it right. It was as if the men could do everything without having him around, as if he were unnecessary. Every day was the same. They'd be up at five, have roll call at five-thirty, followed by calisthenics in the warm autumn sun. Then, after a breakfast of cold griddle cakes and corned beef hash, and after sick call, they'd begin work at seven. Mornings were given over to bombing, machine-gun and automatic-rifle fire practice, followed by a quick cold meal on the training grounds. Afternoons, until four, were devoted to rifle and bayonet practice. Then the men got the rest of the day off, while Sam and the other lieutenants went to classes to try to learn a little in advance whatever it was they were supposed to teach the men the next day.

At nine o'clock he would be in his sleeping bag for the night, trying to imagine what it was that had been done that day that could not have been done without him. Then it got cold, and during the training period, he had to get up early in the morning and light a candle to thaw out the wet shoes that had frozen and stuck to his feet. The time was drawing near when his unit would be sent forward for its indoctrination tour in the trenches. He was issued his gas mask and, with his men, made to walk through a gas-filled chamber. One whiff would be fatal, they were told. He learned to put on the gas mask within five seconds after the green alarm rocket burst in the sky. But he was no closer to his subordinates than he'd been before, was still a YMCA boy who was struggling within himself to find a way of dealing with men.

Given the time, he might have worked it out, but one day he was called from his tent and assigned to the headquarters of General Pershing at Chaumont. There, everything was clean, and almost everyone in sight was an officer and a gentleman.

Sam's task was to prepare tables of equipment. At Pershing's headquarters, even the cooties could be managed; he felt more at home. It was like the University. There was no need to worry about the vulgarities of the men. And in Pershing and his staff of officers was the final proof that, in spite of all poison gas, blackness, and shellfire, the war was being managed by Christian gentlemen for the sake of civilization, for the sake of those places where there were books and baths, places where light shone. He wrote to his sister in Richmond and asked her to pick out a Christmas present for Margaret Bell.

Suddenly, early in February, he was returned to his troops. They were getting ready to go into the line now, not supported by the French or anyone else, and on January 15 the 1st Division occupied the Ansauville sector, before Toul and confronting Montsec on the St.-Mihiel salient. On January 30 the area passed under American command, the first American sector. And now those things Sam had not been able to learn about handling the men began to move toward a showdown.

They were down in a deep hollow on a front that was denuded of vegetation, that was mud, little more than a succession of shell holes connected by shallow, water-filled ditches. The days were short, wet, lit dully by murky gray light. The nights were cold and the water froze. He squatted there in the ditch with his men on either side of him, looking out through the barbed wire into the night toward where the Germans were. Then, there was a faint pop, as of a hand-clap, and, whooshing high above his head, spark-arching up into the black sky, the green rocket rose. He fumbled with the gas mask, clamped it on his face and now he was inside the goggles and the sound of his own breath was loud. He was staring out into the ghastly and menacing void, having learned, or having believed, that he had a place in the world and the place was here. Later he learned the green rocket had been fired from the German side.

He was not ruthless, yet, and assumed all men hated being ordered around as much as he himself hated it; he was an apologetic kid, and, rather than give orders for difficult assignments, took the watches himself, took the patrols himself, perhaps thinking he would master the men that way, the same way he had mastered his fellow students at the University of North Carolina, by setting an example and drawing them to himself. Thus his will power, which had burned up everything in its way until now, was turned on to fullest intensity. He didn't even watch to see how his men were taking it because, politician that he was, he knew that if they caught you looking uncertainly over your shoulder they would never follow you.

In the ditches and trenches where he forced himself to go on, hour after hour, day after day, the water froze and his feet froze, too, cracked open and bled, and still he went on. On top of it he caught the flu — the same kind that killed Edward Kidder Graham that year — and developed a pulmonary infection. Still he carried on his duties, counting on his will power to burn away the infection and the resistance of his men.

They were in front of the French village of Seicheprey, in the most depressed and waterlogged part of the first line. Their dugout was filled with water and there was no place to sleep. The closest dry dugout was an eighth of a mile to their left, where another I Company platoon was stationed.

By arrangement with the lieutenant in command of the other platoon Sam permitted some of his men to leave their own sector and go over to the dry dugout to sleep. As one of them was returning, the sentry challenged him and demanded the password, and in his panic, the soldier lapsed into his native tongue, which was not English, and was shot dead. Sam, hearing this, panicked and sent up a rocket that called down artillery fire in front of them. After it lifted, he realized there had been no German attack, and that he himself had been partly responsible for the death of the soldier.

Worse, he quit his platoon, leaving it without pemission, went to the next sector, and fell asleep exhausted in the dry dugout there. The next day, he was relieved of his command and told that he was subject to prosecution for abandoning his post in the face of the enemy.

He was allowed to write a letter in his own behalf, explaining what had taken place, and pointing out that he had left a non-com in charge, and after numerous communications and meetings it was decided that his actions had been the result of inexperience, illness, and overexertion. He was discharged — honorably — for inefficiency, and allowed to reenlist as a private in his old platoon. Deep in humiliation, there in the ranks beside the men he'd tried unsuccessfully to command, he was to have a chance to redeem himself by the military standards of that time. And he did redeem himself.

In spite of that, he kept the full facts secret for fifty-seven years. In his political campaigns, his official literature, and his authorized biography, he promulgated misleadingly incomplete versions of what took place.

In our age, perhaps, it is difficult to understand what he was ashamed of — especially since he subsequently won the Silver Star and the Distinguished Service Cross for gallantry in action. But that was another age.

On Easter morning, with Sam now a private in the ranks, orders came to prepare to move. Before the evening of the next day the 1st Division was marching through the night toward what was called then the Big Show. By April 14 he was marching through the fields of Picardy, where it was springtime, and where the people in the villages they went through were poised for instant flight. Because the Hun had broken through the Allied lines, and was at Montdidier, looking hungrily over their heads at Paris.

It was toward Montdidier that the 1st was moving by forced marches. The men went on from late morning until late afternoon, covering sixteen miles a day. They would halt for supper and be assigned their billets. Then one night, just as Sam was going down into the deep sleep those sixteen miles demanded of him, First Call blew, and, a few minutes later, Fall In. From midnight — in a night so black it was barely possible to see the man in front of him — he marched until dawn. And, after pausing briefly, marched on until four in the afternoon, twenty-seven miles more. Forty-three miles without sleep, under full field equipment, seventy-five pounds of it. Fifty minutes' hike, ten minutes' rest, and that ten sometimes reduced to three.

A few days later, they took over a sector several miles to the west of Montdidier, near the top of the salient the German mailed fist had thrust toward Paris. Trenches were mere broken scratches in the earth, hardly waist-deep. Dugouts were no deeper, roofed only by a thin sheeting of iron and a layer of sod. They were under fire, now; there was no protection against a direct hit, and direct hits were plenty in a constant shellfire that sometimes reached the density of a barrage.

Broyes, Villers-Tournelle, Coulemelle, which once had been villages, now were mere shapeless heaps churned and rechurned by exploding shells, their air befouled by the garlic odor of mustard gas. Like everyone else, Sam lived underground, burrowing deeper when he could. And he wasn't prepared for it. Again and again it came, the sudden, rising shriek through the air, a crash. Then silence, followed by the calls for the stretcher men, and, after dark, burial parties. Every day, every night, men he knew died in bombardment. In Coulemelle one night twenty thousand gas shells fell. On another night Villers-Tournelle, which was no more than a quarter-mile long, received ninety thousand shells in two hours, and when the firing paused, they took out eight hundred casualties. Then, just before Mother's Day, Sam and his unit were ordered to the rear, where they were to train for a "special exercise."

But first there was something else. Pershing had ordered the enlisted men to write their mothers. After that there would be the special training and they'd be sent back to the front. Sam did not expect to live long, and as he held the unfamiliar pencil and stared down at the whiteness of lined paper, he tried to frame the sort of letter that a mother of that time might treasure after her son was dead.

Dearest Mamma:

Today is "Mother's Day," and according to orders from General Pershing it is to be most fittingly observed by each member of the Amixforce writing a letter to his mother. No order heretofore given has, in my humble opinion, contained so vast a store of true wisdom.

Humanity is not constructed in such a manner that it can realize, even to the slightest degree, the tremendous magnitude of the debt it owes to motherhood.

I feel, however, that the events of the past twelve-months have given me a far deeper insight into the true significance of things than I ever possessed before. And my hope and prayer is that I may be spared to come back in honor and safety in order that I may repay a small part of the great debt I owe to you. No one can be under a greater obligation than I, for my mother is the most beautiful and self-sacrificing mother in the world.

But unbeknownst to Sam, the one taking the most interest in him back home was his father. The old man would go down to the train station every day to get the *New York Times,* bring it home and spread it out on the kitchen table, together with the big colored *National Geographic* map with the pins in it that he moved as the battles moved. Or he would go out on the front porch to sit close beside the blue-star flag that hung out there demonstrating that the old man had a live boy in the service. Or he would stand in the living room, looking at the big photograph of Sam in his soldier's uniform, which had taken its place on those walls together with the Victorian prints of Romeo and Juliet and the three witches from *Macbeth.* Going regularly to the First Presbyterian Church, on Sundays and Wednesdays both, he would pray for the boy.

Back in France, the training was taking place with the aid of about a dozen French tanks, and consisted of storming and restorming a high hill, on the top of which there was an imaginary village. They did this until they got to be very good at working with the smoke screens and at running up hills.

The German salient came to a knuckle at the village of Cantigny, and that was where they were needed. The village had been twice taken by the French, and twice lost by them. Pershing himself, they were told, was going to be on hand for this one, as were the general staffs of all the Allied nations. Cantigny was to be the first place where American troops would be committed to battle, and there it would be determined whether they could fight.

On the night of May 27, Sam marched forward with his unit to the trenches opposite Cantigny. There was heavy shelling from the Germans. At midnight, the food came up, slumgullion, and Sam had time to bolt some down before being ordered to join a carrying party to move up barbed wire and posts. In the hours after midnight, he went out again and again into no man's land, while behind him the 28th was resting at the American aid station set up behind a cliff.

Everything seemed to shine, men's faces, everything from phosphorescent chalk, which had been dug out of the cliff and which now was spread out so that the ground shone. At 3:00 A.M. the American artillery began a slow, destructive shelling of enemy trenches and communications. Sam and his party went on working, lugging the posts and wire forward, then going back past the place where their comrades, some alive, some dead, lay shining in the night, to get more of the stuff and go forward into that mud-blackness of no man's land. At four-thirty the final artillery preparation began, an ear-splitting, earth-shaking noise-fury beginning with the first whisper of light and lasting the hour on into true dawn, when the American troops went over the top.

And Sam, who was to move out later, stood back at the observation post watching the attack. First, the rolling barrage, a wall of whitish smoke punctured by sharp flashing and spoutings of the Picardy chalk soil. Fifty yards behind, the tanks and first wave of infantry, bayonets glinting in the sun, which was rising now. Two hundred yards farther, the second wave, and five hundred yards beyond that, the third wave, walking forward steadily through the enemy counter-barrage, doing exactly that thing they had been taught to do in maneuvers, while behind all this, on a high rise of ground, stood jack-booted Pershing himself, flanked by the beribboned staffs of Europe. Sam's carrying party moved forward with the third wave, bringing up wire and ammunition to a post near the cemetery on the left of the town, a mile inside what recently had been the enemy front line.

The Germans had converted that cemetery into a strongpoint, emptying the mausolems of their former occupants, and using the vaults as dugouts for machine gunners and riflemen. By the time Sam came up, the place was again occupied mostly by the dead, and a semicircle of other dead lay before it. Shells were falling on the cemetery, and he jumped down into a hole with half a dozen engineers who were there to supervise the stringing of the barbed wire. A

few feet away an American soldier was hit, and Sam came up out of
the hole again and scuttled toward him, as a shell landed behind him,
killing all the engineers. There wasn't anything he could do for the
wounded man, either, and now Sam headed toward the rear again for
supplies, wading through a field of high green grass with German
automatic-rifle fire whipping through the grass as he moved.

There was a man down there in the grass, a live man in a gray green
uniform, moaning. Sam knelt down to talk to him in University of
North Carolina German but it was no use. The man was in pain and
his arm was broken. There was some pasteboard lying nearby and
Sam knelt, trying to tie up the arm in the pasteboard, with the bullets
whipping past him. That line between the living and the dead was
disappearing. Men died and were still there. Men who were alive
seemed unreal. As Sam knelt there trying to fix the arm, something
smacked his foot; he looked down, and saw that a bullet had gone
through it. He went on fixing the arm, finished, stood up, went
hobbling back, walking on the heel of the shot foot, through his own
lines, bleeding profusely with the shoe full of blood now, the blood
oozing out over the sides as he walked, the sound of the gunfire
behind him growing fainter as he walked back toward the aid station.
At seven-thirty, a white rocket rose high above Cantigny, dim against
the smoky sky, a signal of victory that Sam didn't see. The Americans had held the village in the face of five German counterattacks.

He spent a month in the hospital being treated with various medicines and thinking things over, trying to absorb what had happened
to him. One day an officer came in and told him he'd won the Silver
Star. The citation from Major General Robert Bullard went like this:
"Private Samuel J. Ervin, Company I, 28th Infantry, with exceptional
courage and perseverance, led a carrying party through heavy fire;
he made several trips from the rear to the front until wounded." So
he could go home in good grace now. He had won a French decoration, too, the Fourragère, and had been among those chosen to march
in the Bastille Day parade in Paris. By the time July 14 came, his
foot had healed and he marched in the first squad of Americans, the
squad that led the parade. If rumor had it right his unit would be
sent down to the south of France for rest and recreation.

The next day, he was loaded onto one of the little French boxcars,
one of the "40 & 8"s (forty men and eight horses). The door was

bolted, and he felt the train moving on through the night, and fell asleep in there on the straw. Before dawn broke in through the car's wood slats, he woke to hear boots marching by. The train was at rest. Sam and the other troops had arrived somewhere and the boots kept marching and they broke open the door of the boxcar to see French soldiers moving up in full battle dress and knew that this was no spa. Sam didn't know the name of the place, or in what direction from Paris it was. It was the officers who knew the names and coordinates. He jumped down off the 40 & 8 and lined up for marching. It was strange. He had resigned his commission and come back as a private, partly to prove something to the men who'd been under his command. But now many of those men had gone back to the hospitals or down into the French soil, and the ones who were left didn't seem to care one way or the other. He himself didn't care. Not anymore. That had been boy's stuff and the thing that had happened at Cantigny and was about to happen now obliterated all such considerations as surely as the line between the living and the dead was being obliterated.

As day broke, they bivouacked in a forest, hiding from the German Fokkers. Then the order came to move. On every road, from every direction, came an endless stream of camions, along with whole battalions of 75's, and huge pieces of heavy artillery drawn by tractors or by teams of twenty horses straining together at their giant leather yokes. Cavalry trotted across the open fields and troops in every sort of uniform camped along the roads; and noise, always the noise, as they marched on, a nervous cacophony of wheel-clatter and hoofbeat, of orders shouted in a dozen tongues, with gesticulating, cursing MP's everywhere fighting to prevent traffic jams at the crossroads, and · always the Fokkers snarling by or screaming down, all the so-called civilized world and its engines moving in one direction and the darkening afternoon sky hazy with the dust of it.

As night fell, rain came on, heavy rain from the instant of its beginning, and becoming heavier. They plodded on into the blackness in mud that was up to their ankles fifteen minutes after the rain began, making slow progress or sometimes no progress at all, with Sam clutching now the shoulder strap of the man in front of him and at the same time feeling a tug at his own shoulder as the man behind him clung on. They would slide down into holes or slip precipitously

down through the blackness into ditches, four or five of them together, still hanging grimly on to the shoulder straps and tangled
together, heaped and clotted in the blackness, and, even as they were
falling, struggling to rise. They were moving into the Second Battle
of the Marne, though Sam didn't know this, knew only the shoulder
strap clutched in his hand and the wet howling night. They arrived at
the jumping-off place half an hour before the attack was to begin.
Suddenly, the rain stopped, and there, high above them on the hill,
shining luminously in the dawn, was the town of Soissons. In front of
them was a wide, rolling plateau cut by deep, raw ravines.

That town was a heavily fortified strongpoint squatting guard over
the highway and the railroad. It had to be taken if the Allied coun-
terstroke was to succeed. Now, with Venable, the new lieutenant, in
the lead, they moved up quickly into position at the base of the
plateau. The German artillery opened up, American guns began to
reply, and Sam and the men rose up out of the shallow trenches,
moving out of the mist-shrouded valley into the sunshine of the
enemy's fire.

One of the lieutenants, Morrison, went down. A shell, exploding
behind him, ignited the signal rockets in his knapsack and he died
whirling in the mud like a hog being butchered with fireworks. Sam
looked up and saw Venable gesturing at him to take charge of Morrison's platoon, and so he ran on forward, leading his men down into
knee-deep swamp water and out onto the hard ground again and up
the steep rise.

WHAT IT TAKES TO WIN

*I went to Concord, North Carolina, to see Si Parker, who'd been cheerleader
at the Virginia-Carolina game in 1916. He was eighty-two now, five years
older than Sam, who referred to him as one of his best friends. Parker had
been older than the others in the 1917 class because of poverty. He'd been
forced to drop out and work, and there'd been a five-year hiatus between his
sophomore and junior years. After the war he'd had a long, successful career
as vice president of an international pharmaceutical manufacturing corporation and, judging from his house, was in comfortable circumstances.*

It was a large, white-frame place set back among old trees at the top of a wooded hill outside Concord. Spotlights shone in the fog and lit up the house with soft white light. A pair of white and black English setters came around the house and barked in a friendly way. It was quiet up on that hill, no super-highway sounds.

Si Parker opened the door for me. He was a handsome, deep-chested man in a clean starched white shirt and bow tie. His skin color was good and his face was creased by a big white smile. As he led me to the stairs and then up to his den on the second floor, his walk was muscular and athletic. When we got to the den the heavy leather easy chair wasn't where he wanted it, so he grabbed hold of the thing and wrestled it across the floor to another spot.

There was a glass-covered case on the wall with some medals in it, the Purple Heart, the French Fourragère, and the Distinguished Service Cross, which he'd won several times. And the Silver Star, which he'd won twice. At the top, by itself, was a light blue medal with little white stars on it.

"Which one is that?" I asked him.

"The Congressional Medal of Honor," he said.

This, then, was not the sort of cheerleader you patted on the beanie, but another kind of cheerleader. He was manly, lucid, genial. We began discussing the old days at the University of North Carolina, and he told me about the 1916 football game, campus politics, Sigma Chi (of which he'd been a member), and the meetings of the International Polity Club.

But I was not here to talk about the University of North Carolina, and it wasn't long before the conversation got around to the war. Parker and Sam had enlisted together, trained together at Oglethorpe, gone over on the Kroon-land *together, fought together at Cantigny and Soissons; Sam in Company I, and Parker as a lieutenant in K Company; neighbors.*

I asked him to tell me about Soissons, and he began to talk seriously and intently, a story having to do with Sam. He said:

"We went up a hill and down a hill. All kinds of ways. I was on the extreme left of the American sector and the French were on my left. They were French Colonials. In going forward that day, the French pulled off at an angle so that my left flank was exposed.

We went down through a hollow and started up a hill, and in between our left flank and the right flank of the French army, there was a big gap in there. We were fighting and they were held up by heavy machine-gun fire from in front of us. And to my left oblique there was a rock quarry right at the top of the hill. There were machine guns in the rock quarry . . .

So I took a bunch of men and went down to the valley to work my way around to *attack the machine guns and put them out of commission so we could take our front-line position. Well, I got down into this low ground and I met a bunch of French Colonials down in there, they were strays, they had fallen out of the French army and there was a bunch of them down in there and I didn't know much French language but one of my men could speak French and acted as interpreter.*

And I told them that the machine guns in the quarry up there were going to be taken by us, and to come on now and help us. We were not under fire down there because of the hill.

We lined them up down there and I told them we were going to crawl right up under that terrace. And for them not to make any noise. Nobody was to speak a word or anything and we were going to get up behind that terrace and then we were going to storm that rock quarry. I told them not to fire a shot, make a sound. Not to fire until I jumped up and fired my pistol and then for them to come out screaming and hollering. We were working our way up to this rock quarry to attack it from this side and surprise them.

While we were working up I saw a machine-gun crew come out from behind that rock quarry up there, come up and establish a position off to my right flank. And it was too far for me to attack this machine-gun crew.

Well, that upset me, but it was too late. The only thing for me to do was go ahead and take that rock quarry. I thought I would get the fire on my right flank from this machine-gun outfit that had just been set up out there. But we weren't going to stop. We were going to go ahead just the same.

I jumped . . . We got deployed and I jumped up on the bank and shot my pistol and said, "Let's go," and yelled. And those fellows came out there, those Moroccans and my army, all yelling and shooting, shooting at everything that came up . . .

And that bunch of men, the Germans that established that machine gun on my right flank . . . there were three of them. They didn't fire a shot at us. And I saw some of our men run out from over there and put that machine gun out of action. So we captured that nest of machine guns up there in the rock quarry and the record says that we took six machine guns and at least forty prisoners up there.

Well, when we got that position, we had to fortify ourselves against a counterattack. Because a counterattack, chances were, would come again. And I remembered these men who'd come out from over there and put the machine gun out of commission. So I sent a man back and told him to tell those men to come over and join us.

In a little bit I looked back and saw a man coming. He had been hit in the hip and he came on up and the other two men had been killed. He had killed the gunmen; put it out of commission. And that man was Sam Ervin.

He was using a gun for a crutch. I saw him and said, "Sam, you are crippled, you ought to go back." He said, "Let me stay and help you fortify the position." He couldn't move so I told him to give orders up here and I would fortify from here on down. So he fortified that bunker and I went on down.

And got ready for the counterattack. Then I ran back to Sam to see how he was getting on, and I said, "Sam, you've got to get out of here." I saw Sam crawling off to go back. I recommended Sam for the Distinguished Service Cross. He saved my group of men that were attacking that place. If he hadn't been there and knocked out those men they could have swung that gun on us and we wouldn't have had any chance, you see.

Later, much later in 1932, Sam would be awarded the Distinguished Service Cross for this.

"Was that the last time you saw Sam during the war?" I asked him.

"Yes. Sam was badly wounded there, and the next time I saw him was after the war was all over. I had been in the Army of Occupation and attended school in England and I came to New York and came right down on the train. Sam didn't know I was coming; we hadn't seen each other. We ran into each other in the lobby of the hotel down here. He had come to see his girl and I had come to see my girl."

"I have another question," I said. I kept looking at the little blue and white medal and felt as if I were talking to it. "Why did he do it?"

"What is that?" Parker asked.

"Charge headlong right straight at a machine-gun nest. When he wasn't ordered to do it."

"They were the enemy," Parker said. "They were shooting at us."

"I'd think that a young man that age, with his prospects, would want to enhance his life rather than charging straight on three men in a pit who are shooting at him with a machine gun."

"It must not of seemed that way to Sam."

Now Parker made fists of his hands and crossed them in front of him, at the wrists.

"You know, I'm like this about that Watergate thing," he said. "I have always been a Nixon man, have always supported him. But I was a Sam man way before that. This thing has really got me."

He helped me on with my coat. "You know, it's funny," he said. "I never will forget one thing, going over to that quarry up there. I don't know where they came from. Two horses came flying across that field in front of us, but these soldiers shot down those two horses. I'd said, 'Shoot everything that comes.' They did, and killed those two horses. But that is what it takes to win, you know."

Chapter 8

THERE WAS too much pain in his hip to walk or even to stand and he crawled on down the hill as Parker had told him to. He did not crawl far; fell asleep in a shallow trench, not knowing whether he was dying or going to sleep and so tired he did not care. Fell asleep next to a several-days-ripe German corpse, and didn't care about that, either.

That was the end of the war for him. He was wakened by a Frenchman and taken to the cellar of the man's house, where other wounded Americans were, where there was much wine. Sam drank plenty of wine, slept, and drank some more. After a while the corpsmen came and carried him back to the divisional evacuation station in the ruined village of Cœuvres. There were hundreds of wounded men there.

They filled the station, lying ranked and tagged along streetcorners, crowding courtyards, chattering frantically in the delirium of pain, not making sense and only glad to be talking because they knew as long as they could do that they were alive — although many of them had stopped talking and were not. Sam lay there in white silent agony, breathing the fetid odor of rotting flesh, stale blood, burned hair, not knowing or caring that up on the heights from which he had been taken it was worse. Up there the roadsides were littered with dead horses, dead men. The trampled wheat fields were dotted with rifles thrust bayonet down into the earth, guides to oncoming legions of burial parties. A white rag flew from every rifle where an American lay. Fields and hillsides of white rags. There had been many machine-gun nests, every one of which was taken by direct frontal attack, by these ballooning corpses.

Sam was evacuated by ambulance to Beauvais, examined by fluoroscope, laid out on the operating table, and knocked out. When he woke up he was told that they'd taken a shell fragment from the hip. Afterward, there were months in various hospitals, watching from what seemed a great distance as the doctors fought to control the infection. He was moved from place to place and the mail did not follow him and he was cut off from home, although he himself kept writing, kept sending letters into the abyss.

The months went by, he was walking again, but he had no contact with anyone. On April 12, 1919, he was put on a ship for home, and a couple of weeks later was mustered out of the service at Fort Lee, Virginia.

He stopped off in Richmond, at his sister Laura's place. She was living in the mental institution run by her husband. From there he took the train up the rolling Piedmont, which simmered in its spring's haze, with the mist drifting up from places where the river ran and moving out over everything, obliterating distinctions.

Back in Morganton, life flowed on as sluggishly, as unremarkably, as ever, although now there was in it the detritus of ruin, a sense of things not quite right.

Something was wrong, awry; it showed up even among the Negroes, whom no one had noticed especially for the past couple of decades or had needed to notice. Even the way they talked to you was somehow changing; everyone sensed it, and that oncoming summer it was to explode throughout the nation with twenty-five major race riots and hundreds of minor ones.

Soon after he arrived home, his father took him aside.

"Why didn't you answer my letters?"

"I didn't get any, sir," he said.

"I wrote you two or three times a week, right along."

"I am very much obliged."

"Didn't you get any of them?"

"No sir."

"Your mother wrote you, too."

"Well I am very much obliged," Sam said.

"What are you going to do?" his father asked him.

"I expect I will go down to Converse College and see Miss Bell," Sam said.

His father took out his little gold knife, cut himself off a plug of tobacco, tucked the chaw in his cheek.

"If it is going to be the law I'd be proud to have you practice with me," the old man said. And began slowly to chew, looking out down the hill toward where the tall pines grew along the branch.

Sam was tall, tanned, hawk-nosed and hawk-eyed, six feet one, erect, young of skin and lithe of stride; seemed more certain of himself than he had ever been before.

"You know," the old man said, "it is a dangerous thing for a young man to practice with his father. Especially if the father's any good. Because then the father, see, might not believe the young man is grown, might not give him his chance."

Sam stood there, looking down to the pine trees.

"But if you decide to practice with me I will give you a chance to make a lawyer out of yourself if I lose every client I've got."

This was on the first day, after Sam had been driven home from the train station by his cousin, Frank Tate, and had stridden down the sandy walk in his leather-legginged army uniform with the broad-brimmed hat. The younger children, John and Eunice and Jean, had the hat now, and the chocolate bar that had been in it, and Sam was standing out in the back yard with his father, just the two of them. Standing out there bareheaded, crew-cut, his young hair shining handsomely in the sun.

"Was it hard on you over there?" his father asked.

"Yes sir," Sam said.

Sam rode the train down to Converse College. Margaret was as he remembered her, except a bit more mature about the eyes, more decisive of speech. He didn't want her yet, not right now, because it was too complicated, proposing, speaking to her father, deciding what he was going to do. Besides, he didn't know where his rivals stood now, or even how many of them there were — let alone who they were. Years, he knew, could be consumed with negotiations, coquetries, assorted treacheries and worries. It was better to concentrate on simple gratifications like cigarettes. He was smoking two packs a day. So the yearning he felt at Converse College, on the greensward, with the girls all in their spring dresses, was for a Camel, and he was glad when he was able to duck out and have one. His conversations with the girl were vague; he kept them vague; and by and by he noticed he was back in Morganton, alone.

Or it felt as if he were alone, although they were all here, still, in the big white house, his parents and his seven brothers and sisters. Hugh Tate shared a room with him. Now Sam would talk about anything, except the war. And in the bad hours, there was no one to talk to at all.

Those were the hours from midnight until dawn, when everyone else in the house was asleep, and Sam was most awake, with nothing to do but listen for the wild noise knifing down out of the mountains, the train's scream at the madhouse, which had kept on across the years with the old, pneumatic regularity of things that never changed. He'd lie there in the darkness with nothing to wait for except the train and the occasional trapezoid of light sliding across the ceiling.

He could not keep the war out of his mind. He'd light a Camel, and sit there in bed, knees clutched up to his belly, staring at the moonlight on the wall. Or get up, pull on khaki trousers, and tiptoe down the stairs and out into the back yard, to stand alone where he had stood with his father.

One day he announced he was going back to Chapel Hill that summer, to the law school. It was a six-week refresher course for those who were going to take the state bar exam. Sam, who'd had only one year of law, had no business being here.

But he loved the books, the thick, rich, calf-skin volumes, stamped in red and gold; loved the odor and heft of them, the way you could open them and by an effort of the mind be lost in what they said. When the cram course was over he drove with friends up to Raleigh, where the state Supreme Court was giving the bar exam, and checked into the Yarborough Hotel there. He sat up all that night throwing questions and answers back and forth across the room with his friends — Emery Denny, Harley Gaston, Bill Chandler. When they went into the bar examination, they found it was easier than they'd expected, and when they emerged from the building and stood out front together, someone guessed that the Supreme Court had decided to lighten up because of the war. A few days later, back in Morganton, Sam got the letter certifying him as a member of the North Carolina bar.

Except he wasn't ready to practice, not ready to go grubbing around the court house collecting any hardware merchant's back debts, or to sit nailed to his desk in that hot little building where his father had his office, listening to the sweaty marital complaints of some hillbilly's wife. And there was no excuse at all for going back to the University of North Carolina Law School now, because it would only prepare him for the bar examination he'd already passed.

Sitting in the family living room, alone, in the cool darkness there, was his older sister Catharine, the best-looking of the Ervins, maybe the smartest, and, up until recently, the most athletic. She was reading a book and she looked up when he came in. She always read a lot and liked to go to the big places — Charlotte, Richmond, even New York — to see the plays, museums, and art galleries.

"You don't look too happy for a young man who's just passed the bar," she said.

"I'm not."

"That's understandable. It's because you're not ready to settle down."

"I expect not," he said.

"There's no reason why you should be."

"But there doesn't seem to be much else," he offered.

"You might go to Harvard Law School."

"What for?"

"Because it's the best law school in the country. Because it will help you to grow. Because it will be worthwhile for its own sake even if you never make any money out of what you learn there."

He took her advice, applied to Harvard, was accepted, and went, climbing up on the train there in the Morganton station, with his bags packed, before he was even solidly back from the war. He would go up and see how he liked it, take a few of the third-year courses. As for graduating from Harvard, he wasn't sure that he wanted to, or could. His status was unclear because of the year's courses he'd had at the University of North Carolina Law School. Harvard didn't seem inclined to accept those credits.

Anyway, it wasn't just credits he was after, but other things, the external discipline of the books and the testing of his abilities against young men who were as gifted as he. Because he wasn't sure how much of his "success" at the University of North Carolina had been just charm. A lot of it, probably, and he'd just been through a war where charm had not gone very far. He took a room a long way from the law school, on Bigelow Street in Cambridge. He'd already put the girl, Margaret, into the shadows of his mind. He would write to her regularly, as he tied his shoes regularly, but with no more sense of commitment than that. The indoctrination lecture, given by Professor Bull Warren, suited his mood:

> Young gentlemen, if your *moral* character has not been nourished by your parents, the kindergarten, public school and college, there is little the Harvard Law School can do for it this late in the day. What this law school is concerned with is your *mental* character, training a mind that refuses to do a sloppy piece of work.

Well, he had done many sloppy pieces of work at the University of North Carolina. Latin, German, and physics (which he'd barely passed) had been like that. But here, he knew, it would be different, and he carried his armload of books back to the room and began studying. No one here was going to give him points for having been shot at in the war. He'd be questioned daily on the facts of cases, what each side had said, how the court had ruled, and why, and whether it was a valid ruling. This would go on, day after day, with no remission except for the once or twice a week when he went with his good old North Carolina buddy, R. Floyd Crouse, to play handball. On Saturday nights he would get dressed up and go to the theater with his fellow North Carolinians: Crouse, Albert Coates, Billy Polk, A. Thurman Castelloe, and that tall, skinny, redheaded fellow, Wolfe, who had been a classmate of Joe's down at Carolina and who was now up here in the graduate school studying playwriting or some such damn fool thing. Then back to his room and the books again. His home was the cone of light his study-desk lamp made. He knew, as he worked on into the night, that his classmates were working, too. There were men in the law school who studied twelve hours a day.

The great teachers were here — Williston, Chafee, Pound, Scott, Beale, and Frankfurter — and you never asked a man what he was taking, but whom he was taking. The method all these men used was the case method, which had been introduced at Harvard, and which was radically different from what Sam had known. Which was the old way, the textbook way, where bedrock general principles were enunciated by Coke or Blackstone or whomever. But now Sam learned by reading, and memorizing, and discussing actual cases, hundreds upon hundreds of them. At first it was confusing. Sometimes, amid the babble of so many cases, Sam would feel it slipping away from him, the sense of foundations, of principle.

Which brought him back to the Constitution. Throughout all his courses — contracts, evidence, equity, public utilities, procedure, conflicts — he began to see interconnections, and from that there began to emerge a world view of the law that was almost Biblical in nature, and that put together, in a solid way, all those old things which he could still believe in, which had survived the ruin of war.

It went something like this: First, there was good blood and bad blood; he had always been sure of that. The best of the good blood was Anglo-Saxon, the best and maybe only civilization was Anglo-Saxon, and the finest flowering of the Anglo-Saxon genius was the law, the common law buttressed by the Magna Carta and the 1688 Bill of Rights. Those documents were like the Old Testament of law, wherein the right things were taught, albeit, at times, dimly. But the way Sam saw it now, the full flowering of law, and hence of Anglo-Saxon civilization, was the Constitution of the United States, which he like many other Southerners, was to call the greatest "human" document ever written — human, so as to separate it, in a decent way, from the Bible. Although any man could stop believing in the Bible any moment he had a notion to. Whereas with the Constitution it didn't matter whether you believed in it or not, because it pervaded all American law, and men had to live by it. It was something solid, far more permanent than a man. It was a religion of which he could be priest.

He loved the law. It was giving him a life, making him free. For Harvard, unlike the University of North Carolina, did not put fragrant and debilitating tendrils about her sons, and campus activities didn't matter. What meant something was being good at your studies.

He was experiencing that special thing that comes to all men who have studied long and hard: his repeated acts of disinterested self-discipline were charging him with an access to power. In this, then (if in little else), he resembled his contemporary, Ernest Hemingway, in that solitary, actinic discipline was nurturing him into a profound aloofness from his fellow men.

Everything else during these years from 1919 through 1922 was a phantasm, no more substantial than the mists in the pines of North

Carolina. His home was the pool of light on his study table, the long yellow note pads, the sharpened pencils, the cigarette smoke curling up under the lamp, the steaming cup of coffee. Three whole years were spent this way, floating dirigible-like in Massachusetts, tethered to Morganton by cables of steel.

TOAD GOING DOWN

This time we were in Sam's office, a spacious, high-ceilinged room, all marble and mahogany, with a view out across the Capitol grounds to Union Station. The trees were beginning to turn green. We were spending a lot of time together this spring, although he had plenty of Senate business. This day, there were several key votes coming up. These were announced by a system of buzzers and lights connected to the electric clock up above the mahogany door frame. Now the buzzers began to make noises and I asked him if it was time for a floor vote.

He listened to the clock for a little while, then said, "Naw, let's go on." So we did. He was looking healthy that day, his skin color was ruddy, and he was laughing a lot as he told stories about his youth: swimming, baseball, dances, and the men he'd worked with in his summer jobs. He would pause frequently to spell out carefully the name of each person he was talking about. He was fond of his old friends, and I think he wanted to save them from oblivion by having their names in this biography.

I told him I'd read every book on Morganton history I'd been able to find, and still didn't know enough.

"I wrote one," he said.

"I didn't know that."

"Oh, yeh."

"Where can I get hold of a copy?"

"I got one here," he said. He stood up, stepped briskly over to a bookcase, and returned with a heavy document, four or five inches thick. This book, which I was to read later, covered more than 200 years of Morganton history, and was full of names, statistics, private stories, and accounts of public events. He had done it in his spare time, the research and writing both. Later I learned that the volume he was lending me now was the only copy in existence.

It was like him to trust people like this, and the open way he had about him extended to some of the members of his staff. For instance — to digress for a moment — there was the first time I came to the office, before I'd ever met him. I was looking at some newspaper clippings, and Patricia Shore, his gorgeous Administrative Assistant, had said to me, "You need some place to work, to spread those out." And had led me into the Senator's office, this office, where she'd told me to go ahead and work at Sam's desk. Covering two thirds of that desk was personal, private correspondence. And this was in the most intense part of the battle between Sam and Nixon. But they trusted me not to read it. Most of the staff were like that; they were trusting, like Sam.

Now the clock over the door began making some insistent noises, and he squinted up at it, screwing up his face behind one eye like an old sea captain staring into squally weather. He got up from his desk, still talking, and I accompanied him out the door and down the hall. He walked very fast, his step long and certain, his body erect, and he snorted away at a Vicks inhaler as we went. Maybe he gets his power from that, I thought.

When we got to the elevator there were already a couple of high school students inside wearing red, white, and blue blazers, which proclaimed on the lettering over the pockets that they were members of Hugh O'Brian's Legion for American Decency. One of them, a short, crew-cut young man of about sixteen, who was wearing horn-rimmed glasses, stood there with his hands clasped in front of him, staring up at Sam. Then we got in and he was standing right next to Sam, staring up at him from about half a foot away. He looked, for all the world, like Toad in American Graffiti.

The elevator wasn't moving because the operator was waiting for Senator Frank Church, who was running down the hall to catch it. He still had a long way to go and now Toad began to speak.

"Well, well, well, Senator Ervin . . ."

Sam blushed, sort of looked at him sideways out of the corner of his eye, beamed, and said, "How do you do sir?"

But Toad was in a celebrity-trance. ". . . well, well, well, Senator Ervin," he said.

Sam harumphed and tried to keep on grinning and looked around as if seeking a way out of the elevator.

". . . . well, well, well, Senator Ervin," Toad went on. Sam tried the how-do-you-do-sir routine once more but it was no use and Toad stood there, looking up as if he were watching a kite, and went on with the litany. Sam was now looking longingly out into the hall where Church was running as if he were under water.

Chapter 9

WHEN HE CAME BACK to Morganton, in the summer of 1922, to set up law practice with his father, he'd already been named the Democratic candidate for the state legislature from Burke County. Harry Riddle, a friend of his father's, had managed that without his knowledge or consent, and Sam had received a telegram from the Democratic county chairman on his last day at Harvard. This was a sort of graduation present, one that was appropriate to Sam's station in life and was designed to help him get set up in the practice of law. So he went back to Morganton determined to run in the fall election against whomever the Republicans might field. The state legislature, which took only six or eight weeks to transact two years' business, would help him make money. Margaret Bell was a woman now, even better-looking than she'd been before, and still not married. She was teaching English in the high school down in Concord.

In those days his father kept a little one-story office building just across the street from the Burke County Court House. It was a small office, two rooms with a fireplace between them, floor-to-ceiling windows. There was a large, ancient wooden secretary with pigeon-holes, and in the front room was the old man's massive roll-top desk and the rocking chair. While Sam was away, his father had built on a new room for Sam's office, one that was as long as the two little rooms combined. And now Sam set about arranging it, putting in a new flat-top desk, an oilburning Heatrola, and an Ediphone. Worst of all, from the old man's point of view, was the telephone Sam had hooked up the first day, which the old man distrusted and wouldn't use in the beginning, and never did use it without the greatest suspicion, holding the receiver about a foot away from his ear, as if a snake might come out of the thing.

After installing the modern equipment, Sam moved in his own law books, which he kept in the bookcases that most lawyers had in those days, with the glass windows he could lift and push back when he wanted to get a book. For the first few weeks, business was slow. Much of his father's practice was with corporate clients, such as the Southern Railway, clients who wanted the old man, not the son, and Sam went on reading just as if he were still at Harvard. His first case was an attempt to remove a lien that had been placed against some fodder stacks in a client's corn field. He lost it, and since the client was too poor to pay the court costs Sam ended up paying them himself. And went on reading.

When he wanted to know what was going on in Morganton, he had only to look up from the book, because he was right on the town square. There were a lot more automobiles now, all black. It was a rare month when Sam got to ride in one. He wasn't sure whether he needed an automobile, either, since he walked the mile to and from work. Anyway, it was a moot point, because he couldn't afford one, and his father, who could, would no more have invested in one of those things than he would have bought a rhinoceros. Still, there were a lot of them around, and a man could get a Ford touring car with clincher tires for $427.00, or one with a starter for $500.38, or, if he was rich, might buy a sedan for $745.00. In the shops along the square a man could get his wife an all-wool serge outfit for ten dollars, and, if he wished, buy himself a fine red union suit for seventy-five cents, which he would need in the winter, when Morganton went back into the past, becoming a chilly oasis in a desert of deep mud. A man who owned a car would jack it up, remove the tires, and stow the thing away in the barn until spring. The winters were cold, and there weren't half a dozen homes in town with central heating. There was not much more to do, either, than in the old days, although there were a couple of men in town (A. C. Chafee and F. Jerome Wortman) who were said to own a thing called a radio. That was one of the things you could hear the people in the square talking about, that gadget through which, it was rumored, you might listen to a man talking down at you from Pittsburgh. This was the year Samuel Huffman died in December, having heard a radio just once in his life.

But Sam had heard radios plenty of times, and been to concerts and plays, and it was not for nothing that he wanted his office stocked with the most modern things. He was enough of a true sophisticate behind those sleepy hawk's eyes to know that the gadgets were okay but that the Harvard stuff would be resented if it were displayed. And he knew that to make it on his own he would have to do more than just read the books or stand for the legislature when they told him to. He'd have to mix in with the town, join things.

Then there was the girl. That had to be settled, now, one way or the other. So one Saturday Sam got on the train and rode the 90 miles to Concord and stepped down on the platform carrying the Kipling poems under one arm and the five-pound Whitman Sampler candy box under the other, determined to speak to her this time. This was five years after the first time he'd been determined to do it. When he got her alone he asked her if she'd marry him. He knew what he'd say no matter what she said. If she said yes, it would be easy; he even had a poem marked for that. And if she said no, he had a bowing-out speech that was so strong and gracious she'd be bound to look down contemptuously forever on whoever it was she finally married. He had a poem marked for that, too.

But she wasn't going to say yes, or no either. She wouldn't become engaged, wouldn't Wear His Ring, wouldn't even agree to Go Steady. What he could have was, a Private Arrangement. She agreed that, if things kept on as they had been, she expected they'd be Married one day, hence she'd not Get Serious about anybody without Letting Him Know. All he could do was Wait. She wouldn't stop Seeing Others; he'd have to Trust Her, because if he didn't Trust Her, why in Heaven's Name would he want to Marry Her and have her be The Mother of His Children. So he climbed back on the train, not knowing whether to be elated or not, and went back to Morganton to start joining things.

There were more things to join now than ever. When he'd been born there'd been the First Presbyterian Church and the Democratic Party and not much else, but now every town and hamlet was beginning to have its Chamber of Commerce, its Rotarians, Kiwanians,

Lions, and what have you. They vied with every other town and hamlet in promoting new industries and commercial enterprises, which would feed off the electric power now being produced by Buck Duke out of the Catawba and already changing the order of things. North Carolina was shifting over from an agricultural to an industrial state, and political power, accordingly, was shifting from the plantations of the coastal plain to the electricity-rich Catawba basin of the industrializing Piedmont.

This year Sam joined the Chamber of Commerce, Masons, American Legion, Kiwanis, and, not least, the Junior Order of American Mechanics, a nativist group that shared the Klan's prime vision — of Christian civilization threatened by non-Anglo-Saxon stock — though it used more sophisticated ways than the Klan did in achieving its objectives. This organization had taken the lead in securing the passage of the previous years' restrictive immigration laws, and two years hence would help see to it that those laws were made permanent.

Sam joined all these clubs, entering into close relations with men of his own town, men of his own stock. There was no lingering, no lurking back. The time for all that was past. He was not going to make a career out of law school, nor loiter sullenly among the gangrels of Paris, nor set up some lawyer's warren high above New York's cold canyons. No, he was going to be a citizen of Morganton. He cast his lot with this community, this time and place, and entered deeply into the spirit of it — the boosterism, the religion of progress, the glad-handing and group-singing, this new optimism whose tone was set, often as not, by the Protestant clergymen who stomped up and down the aisle at the weekly luncheons, leading the singing.

This was the year of "Carolina in the Morning," "My Buddy," and "Three O'Clock in the Morning," songs that were to this new religion what "The Old Rugged Cross" had been to the religion of his father, songs that had in them the very marrow of the thing he was entering into: a bouncy, bright-eyed, faith in progress; a homophilic sentimentality that transferred easily from one's buddies in the 1st Division to one's buddies in the trenches of business, together with a liberation from the grim and nine-o'clock-going-to-bed ethic of the older generation. Yes, you could stay up until three o'clock in the morning now, swilling the booze the increasingly affluent moonshiners sold you, so long as you did it with other good buddies, and so long as Carolina in the morning found you at your business with your traps set as firmly as the smile on your face. Yes, and when you sang these songs at the Kiwanis meetings you knew that the minister bouncing up and down there between the aisles was of your breed, too, was a booster, was the sort of fellow who talked in terms of his "plant," and published the Sunday school attendance figures in the Morganton *News-Herald,* and used periodic revival services shrewdly, and was always on the hawk for a better deal in the buckets of industrial wax that kept his linoleumed halls shining brightly.

Business, politics, patriotism, and religion were yoked together, were one thing, and it came as no surprise to Sam when he was asked to take over the Men's Bible Class at the First Presbyterian Church. It made no difference that he hadn't gone to church in Boston. In a sense, there hadn't been any church in Boston, because the church was people you knew all your life.

Of course, you could sneak away from all this, if you wanted to. Even in Morgantown, you could waste time feeling sorry for yourself, or reading the works of Sinclair Lewis, or maybe both. You could read all of Mr. Lewis' books in a month, and when the time was up you still had your life in front of you. It seemed self-indulgent to waste time whining and criticizing the men you'd thrown your lot in with. Mr. Lewis was all right in Boston where the intellectuals floated around with their heels about two feet above the ground, but this was the true world down here, meaty and wonderful, and Sam was going to live in it. And he didn't read Sinclair Lewis, not one word.

In the fall he ran for the state legislature and won. And in January got on the train for Raleigh, having spent the day before touring the madhouse, to see what it needed. Now he was a legislator, at four dollars a day plus traveling expenses.

The train to the legislature was the same train he'd taken to the University, but the things he saw out its window were different. Whereas the mill villages had once been mere clumps of gray shacks, not a lot different from assorted Negro towns, they now had electric lights, sewers, sidewalks, and plumbing. There were more of them, too. Sharecroppers, yeomen farmers, and mountaineers alike were being drawn into them and were being gelded and tamed. The cities were different, too, and when Sam passed through Winston-Salem, Greensboro, and Durham, the sky was punctuated with the exclamation marks of the empty skyscrapers the boosters had thrown up in defiance of all the North's black factories. The South could do as well as the damn North. There was thick industrial smoke in the air, and it was good.

In the legislature Sam was going to, bankers, the larger manufacturers, and utility magnates wielded an increasingly greater share of power, living comfortably in symbiosis with the Klan, which now controlled a third of the North Carolina counties. The Klan, like Coca-Cola, was being sold out of Atlanta, but that made it no less refreshing to many North Carolina men. Most of them were still free, still had not been drawn into the mill villages or any other form of helotry. As W. J. Cash wrote in *The Mind of the South:*

> In every rank they lolled much on their verandas or under their oak, sat much on fences dreaming. In every rank, still, they exhibited a striking tendency to build up legends about themselves and translate these legends into the explosive action; to perform with a high, histrionic flourish and to strive for celebrity as the dashing blade. In every rank they were much concerned with seeing the ponies run, with hearing the band, with making love, with dancing, with extravagant play.

These were the majority of male North Carolinians, and it would be men of Sam's class who, in serving the cause of Progress, would shoehorn them into modernity and servility, while at the same time seeming, themselves, to belong wholly to the older traditions of the gentlemanly businessman or the great small-town lawyer.

In the mill villages, among the new men, the price of the sewers, sidewalks, and cinder-block sameness came high. Mill hands were now being obliged to work by the stretch-out system, a program by which a spinner or weaver was obliged to tend more machines for more hours or else be laid off. The sixty-three-hour work week was a luxury still being enjoyed only by their wives and children. But none of this was Sam's business, to his way of looking at it, nor the legislature's either, and when he got to Raleigh he concerned himself with the game season in Burke County, the drainage of Muddy Creek, and whether to charge three dollars and fifty cents or five dollars for a license to a filling station operator. They debated that issue for days. There was the shine of newness about the question, whereas the matter of the mill villages was an old, dark, settled thing. If a man did not like it in the mill village he could work harder to better himself.

And if he didn't, he could take the consequences. Because, after all, everybody was obliged to look after himself — although there were some who couldn't. Sam recognized this, too, a little, and went to the trouble of sponsoring legislation for a bond issue to improve the Negro school in Morganton.

The legislature was like a vacation for him. He had no political ambitions, no thought of rising or even coming back, and there wasn't the strife he always felt when he was trying to get ahead. Not that a political career was, in itself, to be despised. It was just that there was no money in it, and that conditions in North Carolina politics, at this time, precluded his even thinking about it. To have a career in politics (as opposed to this vacation) would mean going against his prime inner directive: that of never being beholden to anyone, ever.

Because the state was run by the political machine of Mr. Furnifold Simmons, who was now up in Washington, D.C., being Senator, it was a closed hierarchy in which a man had to make himself into something like an employee. The men who were to have the high offices were carefully hand-picked by Simmons years in advance, sometimes even before they had reached their majority. Usually they were from families who were already well connected; they were conservative and required to remain so. They would serve the party, which is to say, Simmons, for years, speaking when and where they were told to, saying what they were told to say, working whatever hours were required in local organizing activities. They came up through the successive grades only as men ahead made way for them and Simmons said okay. In any given election year, only two or three of them would be eligible, and sometimes only one. This was how the state was run, and Sam wanted no part of it. While he had no trouble with the conservatism, and actually liked to speak in public, he was damned if he would have another man telling him what to do. No, that was what all the work had been for, at the University of North Carolina and at Harvard, too. That was why he'd charged the machine-gun nest, so as to have a place to come back to, where no man would dare condescend to him or tell him what to do. Thus, as long as the Simmons machine remained in control, there could be no question of a political career. Although Sam enjoyed politics as a spectacle, as a leg up in the law, as a phenomenon that, in North Carolina, was as yet unseparated from life. In a sense, every North

Carolina lawyer then was a politician whether he wanted to be one or not. All public occasions were political occasions; it was all bound together.

When he came back from the legislature he began to travel up to the mountain courts that the maple sugar candy had come down from, riding way up in the Blue Ridge to the county-seat towns, often as not alone. He practiced in Avery, Mitchell, Caldwell, Catawba, McDowell, Cleveland, and Watauga counties. His father was sixty-six now, with plenty of money and plenty of things to do back in Morganton, leaving Sam to follow the Superior Court around.

He was always present on that best day of all, Court Day, when the farmers brought in horses, mules, cattle, hogs and poultry, and anything else they could think of to sell. Watermelon wagons would be parked along the curbs, high-piled with the green, fat things, and you could get a generous red slice for five cents and stand there spitting the slick black seeds out of your mouth, talking to your friends, and watching the people pass by: politicians, peddlers, patent-medicine quacks and their minstrel shows, women's bazaars, assorted court petitioners, plaintiffs and defendants, sheriffs, salesmen, and noisy evangelizing preachers.

He was beginning to make a name for himself, too, what with the ability he'd had to get along with people in the first place, the Harvard training, and, on top of that, hard work. He always had a book in his hand, always was prepared. He worked a lot at night, alone, his eyes gazing down into that faithful pool of light that seemed to travel with him everywhere, with the books in front of him, the notes, the long yellow pads, and the rows of delicate, pointed pencils.

But he didn't offend people with his knowledge, and was always ready to deflate things with a quaint story when he found himself coming on too smooth. He didn't overpower people in cross-examination or in his summation speeches to the jury, but was tentative, courtly, humorous. People liked the way he spoke, hesitantly, almost stuttering.

He didn't have to worry about Margaret anymore, either. She had finally said she was going to marry him. He would go down to Concord for the wedding, his final surrender. Because he was ready for that, too. She had educated him without his knowing it, and it had taken her only eight years.

He was twenty-seven and still living at home. He would sit in the

parlor, watching his mother, father, and older brother, Ed, fiddling
with this contraption Ed had brought home, a radio. They would
take turns with the one headset, passing it back and forth among
them and listening to the fellow talk from Pittsburgh. Every now and
then they would look up, asking Sam if he didn't want to come over,
proffering the headset to him. And Sam would go over, take the
thing and clamp it to his ears and, not listening or caring what KDKA
had to tell him, just feel himself close to his parents and his older
brother in a way he would never be close again. He was glad the
house would keep on going, glad Ed had a place to stay. There were a
lot of people in the world who never could make it beyond their living
rooms, who were lost beyond there.

His father got up from the radio, beckoned to him, walked with
him outside. With Sam, six foot one and filled out, walking alongside
the little fellow, who was no more than a hundred and thirty-five
pounds. They were on the south side of the house and it was dark,
quiet except for the crickets and the frog down at the creek. They
were looking out toward the weed-grown baseball diamond shining
there in the moonlight beyond the trees.

His father cleared his throat.

"I am going to deed that over to you," he said.

"What?"

"That lot."

Sam had to stand there for a minute thinking what it meant. Because he did not think of it as a "lot," only as a baseball diamond; had
never even thought of it as belonging to the old man, especially.
Rather, it belonged to everyone who'd ever played baseball there; was
almost a public park.

"You can build you your house there," his father said. "And if you
need some money I'll lend you the money." He didn't say, "You're a
good son; I'm proud of you." But the tone of the thing — it was as if
he'd said that.

Sam and Margaret were married over in Concord, at a big, brick
Presbyterian church with a tall steeple. It was June 18, 1924. There
were three hundred people at the wedding, just about everybody Sam
was close to, except his father, who never went to weddings (or
funerals), and his kid sister Jean, fifteen, who stayed home to cook for
the old man the only thing she knew how to cook, rice, three meals a
day until the mother came back. Everyone was there; it was a big

wedding, a big reception, with many hands to be shaken. Then Sam and Margaret got on the train with a pass the Southern Railway had given him, and set out for Yellowstone Park. The train slid through Morganton on the way, with the whistle shrieking, as always, only now Sam was inside the power, where the shriek was not so loud. When she asked him where he thought they'd be on their golden anniversary he said he didn't know.

TEA FOR TWO

The signs in the lobby of the L'Enfant Plaza Hotel said, "50th anniversary celebration for Sen. and Mrs. Sam J. Ervin, Jr." We saw the reception line was ahead of us. Sam was there, red-faced and beaming, and at a level below, down nearer the figured carpet, was Margaret. There were easels everywhere, carrying blown-up photographs of Sam and Margaret, some of them fifty years old, some older. When we got to Margaret, she took my wife's hand, and mine, in both of hers, and moved us down to Sam while beaming in our faces, for all the world like a woman passing the fried chicken.

There were a couple of hundred people in the ballroom, and some tables, and up at one end an orchestra was playing. The woman singer, who was about fifty-five and plushly upholstered, was rendering "Tea for Two," which had come out the year Sam and Margaret were married.

It was June 18, 1974. Sam and Margaret had been to six golden anniversary parties in the past seven days and this was to be the last one. I watched them standing together in the reception line. Margaret was passing him the people and he was beaming at them. When they got to him he did not pass them on but smiled down at them and spoke quickly. He was a healthy, mirthful old man, seventy-seven years old and still six feet one. He had been working since eight o'clock that morning, much of the time on his feet; had given a speech on the Senate floor, participated in debate, met with the Watergate Committee, met with the Constitutional Rights Subcommittee, conferred with his staff, written letters, answered the phone, and moved about on his feet a great deal. Now this party was going to last three more hours and he would be on his feet for it, too. Nor would he neglect the bourbon.

Scoop Jackson came in the door, surrounded by his retinue. There was a cluster of excitement as the people sniffed the power of a possible President.

Jackson was a red-faced, merry little fellow about five feet seven, who drank bourbon and lay back there behind hooded eyes watching the sniffers.

I saw Sam's son, Sam III, whom I'd interviewed down in North Carolina the day before. He was red-headed, ruddy-complexioned, blue-eyed, close to beautiful. We'd had a good interview and he'd told me everything I wanted to know, looking me in the eyes as he spoke. I watched him now, shaking the hands of well-wishers who came up. Some months before, when his father had announced his retirement, there'd been some pressure on him to announce for the Senate seat. But he'd declined. He was a Superior Court judge in North Carolina, forty-eight years old.

Ed Muskie came over and shook hands. He was taller and broader than he seemed on television, and his eyes were self-possessed, piercing, intelligent. He looked like a President of the United States, whereas Scoop Jackson looked like a little fellow having a drink. There was much noise, the orchestra was loud, it was impossible to hear Muskie or anybody else. Then Hubert Humphrey came up and stood near us, drink in hand. His trousers were run-down at the cuffs. Folds of skin came down in parentheses over his eyes, and he sipped deeply on his drink. When he looked up, I saw the eyes under the parentheses. They looked scared and sad.

There were many dancers out on the floor and they smiled and laughed a lot at one another, while over at the other side of the room, back among the tables, white flashes from the cameras went up along the walls. Sam and Margaret were cutting the fiftieth-anniversary cake. After a while the flashes stopped and the reporters and photographers drifted back over and stood near the door.

Sam came striding across the dance floor, shook hands with the orchestra leader, and came walking back through the crowd. Everyone applauded him. The reporters and photographers were applauding, too. They did not know then that, even as the party was going on, assassination threats were being phoned into the desk of the Methodist House. The would-be assassin had phoned Sam, personally, before the party and told him he would kill him if he showed up. But Sam had showed, all right, and without any police escort. The next morning's newspaper had a photo of Sam and Margaret kissing. Or rather, pecking. They did it tentatively, like people on an electrified rug. Maybe once they would have called the FBI, but now, for all they knew, the FBI had just called them.

Chapter 10

Hᴇ ʜᴀᴅ ʜᴏᴘᴇᴅ to take her past Yellowstone, out to California. But he hadn't enough money to do that. Besides he was hot to get back to Morganton, too. It was a funny thing. When he was working hard he would meditate on the felicity of those who went fishing, played golf, or just generally loafed around. But when he took off from work he couldn't enjoy himself for long. He found that most fun-lovers he knew, in Morganton and elsewhere, were "driftwood." That was a term he'd learned from his father. It was the juror who had no special aims of his own, therefore no special mind of his own. A fellow easily swayed and lacking inner momentum. But to Sam's mind, lolling around in nature, pursuing fun, was boring. So he was glad to get back to Morganton, back to work.

His parents threw a party for the new couple, with his mother in a long, flowing evening gown, his father stiff and formal in a white piqué vest and white cravat; and the two hundred guests wading in the mud of Lenoir Street, which was being readied for concrete paving. Then Sam went back to work. He was putting in long hours, toiling deep into the cricket-throbbing Morganton nights, content within himself and at home, so long as the light shone and the pencils were sharp. They were living in one room, or a room and a half, at her aunt's place. When he got an unexpected fee, he was more likely to spend it on more books.

Meanwhile, his house was rising out of the baseball diamond. He would study nights, work long days, and when the week ended, on Friday nights at six-thirty, instead of collapsing into the love nest, he went to the Kiwanis Club. More often than not, he worked Saturdays, too, and Saturday evenings were given over to preparing the lessons he taught to the Men's Bible Class, working from Tarbell's, or Snowden's, or maybe reading the learned commentaries of G. Campbell Morgan. One evening, as he was drifting off to sleep, his wife said to him, "You know, I didn't think it would be like this."

"Like what?"

"Somehow I thought you were more worldly. That we'd go out more."

He took this as a compliment, believing himself to be the least worldly of men. He loved his wife and did not wish her to be unhappy. So he made it a point to get out more. Bridge was the new rage; she'd joined one of the new bridge clubs, and they'd play with other couples a night or two a week.

He kept on about his business, traveling when he had to, taking the train up in the mountains from Morganton to Marion, from there to Clinchfield and on to Johnson City, Tennessee, to catch the Eastern Tennessee & Western North Carolina which he took to Newland, traveling maybe a hundred miles in a crooked line to get forty as the crow flies. He walked everywhere he went in Morganton, the mile to and from the office, and the other places, too.

The spring he got married, the men who ran the local Democratic Party, H. L. Riddle and Charlie Kirksey and the rest, put him up again for the state legislature, in the same spirit they'd bought him a twenty-five-pound sack of flour when he'd returned from Yellowstone: it was something to give him a start, something that was practical.

The fall after his marriage, Sam ran again for the legislature, and won. It was great to be young and a winner. He went next door to the Claywells', to the Democratic victory celebration. They were all there, his own people, Morgantoners. Somebody handed him a little crystal cup with some yellow, orange-juice-looking liquid in it, and Sam swilled it down thirstily and asked for more, and drank that down too. Then wandered out to the kitchen, found a large iced-tea glass, and filled it with the cold yellow stuff and drank that, too. And now, finally, refreshed and very calm, he emerged from the kitchen to borrow (with great dignity) two large yellow scarves, which he took back to the kitchen with him. Tying one around his head, another about his waist, and deftly seizing two large bread knives — one to be jammed into the waist sash, one to clamp between his teeth — Sam emerged through the door, fingers snapping above his head, hips swiveling, dancing what he announced (around the edges of the bread knife) to be the "SPANISH FANDANGO!" — which was to cause Mrs. Claywell to say, in later years, that if a real Spaniard had seen it, he would have hauled Sam into court for defamation of character. Ah well. They knew him; knew him and were used to him. But these were not Spaniards, and he was not Hemingway, and did not want to be.

When the legislative session began, he took the train across the state to Raleigh, sure in the knowledge that his fellow townsmen wanted more out of him than dancing; they wanted some of the state's road money to come Morganton's way.

This was just after the heyday of Cameron Morrison, "the Good Roads Governor," and North Carolina was still spending millions of dollars for roads of all sorts — concrete, asphalt, sand-clay, gravel — which were articulating themselves into all parts of the state. They went along with the development of the automobile and hydroelectric power. These days power was everywhere in North Carolina, not just at the fall line or where somebody had a steam-generating plant, and when you applied it to inert material you got products and when you got products you had to have the roads to move them out on. This is what Riddle and the rest of Morganton wanted, what Sam wanted, too, and went up to Raleigh to vote for.

But the legislature didn't spend as much time on the roads as they'd planned to that session because of that other thing, which came boiling up over the Smoky Mountains from Tennessee, obliterating other business: that thing about the monkeys. A legislator named Poole had introduced a bill to save North Carolina's children from the teachings of Charles Darwin.

For the first time in decades, intense public interest became centered on the doings of the legislature, and hundreds of North Carolinians came brawling into the gallery to watch the proceedings. Thousands more milled about the Capitol lawn, buying popcorn, balloons, and soft drinks, and listening gap-mouthedly to the assorted exhortations of a score of evangelists.

The fundamentalists, who supported Poole's bill, were the most visible and vocal of the partisans, but behind the scenes the liberals were active, too, and included among them the President of the University of North Carolina, the President of Wake Forest, and Sam's father, whose long, impassioned letter attacking the Poole bill was published by the Raleigh *Times,* under his pen name, Lex.

Sam sided with the liberals, noting in his speech that the only good thing about the bill was "that it will gratify the monkeys to know they are absolved from all responsibility for the conduct of the human race." He was, after all, a Harvard man, and a believer in the First Amendment — and the whole thing was absurd.

When he returned to Morganton, he found his routine was shaping up. There was the law practice, the National Guard drills on Thursday nights (he was a lieutenant again), Kiwanis on Friday, and the gatherings of the various lodges, which met once a month. Walking to work, morning in the office, walking home for lunch, walking back to the office. Maybe in the afternoons he would go over to the Lazarus Brothers' shoe department and swap stories with the dozen other Morganton lawyers gathered there, or visit over in the court house with Dick Michaux, the six-feet-six, rawboned, ham-handed sheriff, a man who had proven himself to be a good friend, who steered much business his way. Or else, if things were slow, he'd walk down the street and drop in on Dr. Jim Kirksey.

Sam was making money now, and so was Jim. It wasn't like when they'd toiled together in the tannery for a dollar a day. But when they were together, they didn't feel that any essential thing had changed. There was a certain watermelon-filching sense of exhilaration about it; two boys together who'd convinced the town they were doctor and lawyer, respectively, and were making good money at it.

By now, Sam and Margaret had moved into the little house he'd had built on the baseball diamond. There wasn't any baseball anymore, but there was tennis, which he played several times a week, and what with that and the four miles he walked every day just getting to and from work, he was trim, moved easily when he walked, breathed deeply and well in spite of the two packs of Camels he smoked each day.

Margaret got pregnant, and throughout that long fall of 1925 Sam would abandon the work he'd brought home and sit with her in the front porch swing, creaking back and forth in the cricket-haunted darkness and watching the headlights probing down Lenoir Street. Time had slid on him. In another year he'd be thirty.

On Sundays he stood at the door of the First Presbyterian Church, greeting the worshippers, showing them to their seats. He was a deacon in the church, locked in, the same way he was locked into the law practice and the National Guard and a dozen other things. If he had anything left that was entirely private, it was his reading.

These were the books by Irvin S. Cobb and Arthur Train. And it may have been that in reading these writers Sam was formulating *who he would seem to be.* Not who he was. Nobody would ever touch that. But the face he'd use, the manners.

The Cobb stories were about a certain Judge Priest, a kindly, courtly, julep-swilling old Confederate veteran who was deeply concerned for the welfare of those who appeared before him, on whichever side. And the Arthur Train stories — maybe half a hundred — concerned Ephraim Tutt, Esq., an aging barrister whose hesitating manner concealed a shrewd wit and brilliant knowledge of his profession. So Sam may have been creating himself.

Other lawyers, who knew how hard he worked, were bringing their cases to him, including corporate cases. And on these he made more money than he did from his own clients, from whom he was never any good at collecting, anyway. So it was easy for him to believe in Progress, because it was providing him with funds, and seemed to be changing Morganton for the better, too, as the smarter, younger black men, the potential malcontents, were emigrating up North, to where Progress created jobs for them in the factories of Detroit, the stockyards of Chicago, and a hundred other places.

That left the good ones at home, such as Essie Tate, the quiet, bespectacled Negro woman who lived in Sam's house, down in the basement, where she had her own room and bath, and from which she issued every day to do the cooking, cleaning, and assorted chores, so that Margaret would have time for the meetings of the Bridge Club, the Book Club, and the various Christian organizations, such as the Missionary Society, which was concerned with bringing the Word to the heathen of Africa.

Nor were Margaret's activities to be dissociated from Sam's own, since it was from her that he learned much of what had happened in Morganton, and what was going to happen. Thus, to the new family, Essie Tate was as necessary, and as quiet-running, as the icebox and the electric lights. When the son, Sam Ervin III, was born the following spring, it was Essie who took over raising him.

Sam felt himself becoming more powerful. He didn't know exactly what that meant yet, but he knew it wasn't like the power of other men in Morganton. They strove among themselves, making of Democratic politics that "fortuitous concourse of unrelated prejudices" it was throughout the South. But when the Kiblers, Gileses, Wilsons, Riddles, and the others had done fighting among themselves, they would, often as not, come to Sam to resolve things. He had that special kind of power.

In 1926, having been unable to agree on a candidate for District Solicitor of the Sixteenth Judicial District, they came to him, several days before the election, and demanded that he run for the post. Which he did, and was defeated, coming in second in a field of six candidates. Which was all right with Sam, because he'd not had time to think about whether he wanted the job in the first place, and besides, he had his law practice.

But it wasn't all right with the old man, his father, who was sure Sam had lost because of ballot-tampering in nearby Caldwell County, and whose first thought was to shoot the malefactors. And who had to be restrained by Sam, who wasn't interested in any political job, unless it was Superior Court judge. Sam knew that, at thirty, he was still mighty young to be thinking about that. He was content to practice law. The only trouble was that, in losing, he'd carried his own county, Burke County, by a larger margin than was ever accorded any candidate for anything, so the requests for him to settle things, serve on committees, and run for things increased.

The following year the Democratic leaders asked him to run for the Board of Trustees of the Morganton Graded School system, and he said no, and they came to him demanding once more, and he said no again. When he went downtown on Monday, he learned that the print shop was putting out the ballots with his name on it. He walked over to the print shop and stood there over the fellow watching as the lead print that was his name was removed from the type case. He stood there, too, while all the new ballots were printed, and left town that afternoon satisfied at having finally had his way, and returned the next day to learn he'd been elected as a write-in candidate.

The only way to avoid power, it appeared, was to exercise it. This was what he did with the 1926 nomination to the state legislature — he managed things so that another man got it, and he was to do the same with the 1928 nomination. But the only way to avoid power altogether was to change that inner, central thing men recognized in him, underneath all the Judge Priest and Lawyer Tutt stuff. They would put all that lovable personality stuff on the posters, but it was that central thing that drew them, that thing which had not been violated because it could not be touched.

Sometimes, when he rode the train across the state to the football games at Chapel Hill — and he did this several Saturdays each fall — he would be reminded of the remoteness and love of study that had been nurtured there. That was a thing he had in common with his friend, Ernest Mackey, the fellow who, more often than not, went to the football games with him. Mackey had been a classmate of Sam's at the University, and was now teaching mathematics at Chapel Hill, enjoying the fullest opportunity for what Edward Kidder Graham had called "the Life of the Mind." And Sam, sitting by the fellow in the stands, watching the Tar Heels play the Cavaliers, maybe, would feel close to Mackey. But Mackey never could do the things he did: Mackey seemed to need the big trees and the lawn and the marble buildings.

Each of Sam's friends could relate to only a part of himself. Ernest Mackey could no more swap stories with Dick Michaux than Dick Michaux could understand a lecture on aleph null. For that reason, neither of them would ever be bothered with power.

Sam was young, healthy, and, when all else failed, could get by on main strength. Thus, when he was offered the position of County attorney, he took that. When he was asked by the decedent's family to take on the job of prosecuting Beau Franklin for the murder of Charlie Smith, he took that on, too; got the fellow convicted and sent to the state penitentiary. Franklin was a great big fellow who lived up in the hills outside Morganton, who was repeatedly involved in acts of violence. He was to be in the penitentiary only for a few years. Then he'd come back.

ANYTHING FOOLISH?

He sat at his desk, hands folded in front of him as if in prayer, face serious and intent. Whenever he sensed I was building up to an important question, he always did this.

"Listen," I said, "did you ever do anything foolish?"

His head jerked around at right angles and I got the profile, eyebrows leaping. He would often look at the wall like this when, in spite of everything, he got caught off guard.

"I suppose so," he said quickly. He stared at the wall for a moment more, his face working. Then he turned head-on and, BANG! *the smile, the great white teeth showing, the eyes squinted up, the chuckles choking up out of his belly.*

"I sure have," he said. "But I'm not so foolish, now, Dick, that I'm going to tell you what it was." He made several attempts to say something more, but it was too much for him and the laughter kept coming on. I changed the subject and, after a time, we began to talk of other foolish matters, such as Ford's pardoning Nixon. When I left him he was still chuckling to himself. He would pull his chair up to his desk and try to work and the laughter would come again and he'd push the chair back and look out the window, out to where the leaves were turning yellow, toward the train station. In the outer office, that morning, Mrs. Spears had said to me that the hardest time was when the pictures came down off the wall. He had pictures of Grandfather Mountain and a meadow near Morganton, things like that.

Chapter 11

WHEN THE national Democratic Party nominated Al Smith for the presidency in 1928, it threatened to put North Carolinians at war with themselves. The Governor of New York was a city man, the voice of his state's vast immigrant population, and a Catholic to boot. This last thing, the Catholicism, was especially disquieting. Indeed, it was the man's practice to get down on one knee to kiss a bishop's ring, and the picture of that gesture, in thousands of Southern minds, intensified the conflict. Because it was hard to believe in a fellow who would bend his knee for another man. Such a gesture, many believed, was the visible manifestation of a lack of self-respect. On the other hand, the Democratic Party had re-established white supremacy in the South, and was the only instrumentality capable of maintaining it, so a vote against Smith could be interpreted as one that would call the Negro forth into politics again.

So Sam supported Smith, because it was necessary to support the Democratic Party, and because the man, in spite of his background, seemed to be a gentleman. That year, when Smith got off the train on North Carolina soil, the first man to push his way through the crowd and shake his hand was Sam himself.

That was at Old Fort, North Carolina, about thirty miles west of Morganton, and Sam got there riding in the back of somebody else's car. He wasn't too venturesome in his own car, yet, which was a Model A he'd bought from the Burke Motor Company.

He'd paid cash for the car, ridden out to the new baseball field with the salesman, and spent all day lurching around the field trying to learn how to use the gear pedals, and other gadgets. The story around Morganton was that in the seven successive days after that Sam had gone back to the motor company and bought a new fender each day. Which wasn't so; actually he'd bought only three or four of the things, and it had taken him two weeks to develop the need for them, as he kept on trying to steer the thing into the new two-car garage he'd had built, and kept hitting the iron pipe that stood in the middle between the bays.

Well, the fenders didn't cost much, and besides, he was making a lot of money — $9000 this year — and the house was paid off, everything was paid off, and he had enough left over to buy more law books. He bought a radio, too, and used it to follow the presidential campaign.

Smith's defeat, when it came, had important implications for North Carolina, and catapulted Sam into politics in a serious way. For the past thirty years, North Carolina had been run by Furnifold Simmons, who hailed from the eastern part of the state, and who represented, essentially, the agricultural interests there. But Simmons had deserted the Democratic Party in favor of Hoover, so now his control of the party was passing over to a coalition headed by O. Max Gardner, who was elected Governor of North Carolina that year.

Sam had known Gardner all his life; the man came from an adjoining county and Sam had appeared in cases with him many times, had traveled the court circuit with him, knew him socially, and was friends, as well, with Gardner's brother-in-law, Clyde Hoey, and with another Gardner intimate, J. C. B. Ehringhaus. These three men were the core of the new group, the so-called Shelby dynasty, which even now was taking over the state. Like Sam himself, they represented the business and industrial interests of the central Piedmont, and regarded Sam as a member of their group — not a coequal yet, but "a promising young man with a fine background." So if Sam wanted to dream, now, of a Superior Court judgeship, he could do so in the name of realism and reasonable expectations.

The future, then, looked promising and Sam put Al Smith out of his

mind, because he wasn't the sort of young man to brood about absolute truth. He believed that the willingness to accept defeat was
necessary when it came to political fights, and that any man who had
lived in a world of men, who wasn't a coddled sissy, knew that.

Although, regrettably, there were idealists in politics, too, men like
his crippled kid brother, Joe, who was practicing law in Charlotte,
steadfastly refusing to take one cent of fee from any corporation, and
threatening to become more successful than Sam himself. Already
Joe, was talking about running for the United States House of
Representatives. But Sam believed that the world should be run by
men more given to compromise. Take the matter of the Negroes. It
was true, as the Northern liberals contended, that the stated system of
things left them poor and defenseless. But what the Northern liberals
couldn't see from their great distance were the private arrangements
that took care of things. For instance, Sam's brother John, the physician, treated them without charge. Hugh Tate, who was just starting
up with a sawmill, gave them free lumber. And Sam himself more
often than not, defended them for nothing. The State of North Carolina was run by Christian gentlemen like himself, and Sam saw no
reason to apologize for it.

In such a world, you could take the unpopular side and not have to
worry about being destroyed for it. This year, for example, Sam
defended two black men accused of raping white women, with no
noticeable diminution of his own popularity in the town. This year,
too, he was elected Secretary of the Burke County Bar Association.
The next year, just before the stock market collapsed, he was named
Chairman of the School Board and President of the Kiwanis Club.
All this happened in spite of his evolution stand and his defense of
the Negro rapists, one of whom had broken into the infirmary at the
state mental hospital and assaulted a retarded twelve-year-old girl.

To be a Christian gentleman, of course, you first had to be a Christian, and many Morganton businessmen might have applauded the
North Carolina real estate tycoon who told Thomas Wolfe that no
man could get along in business who had not given his heart to Jesus
Christ. The "gentleman" part of the formula meant, too, that you
had to have enough money to get by on, because, paying one's debts
was the best proof you loved Jesus.

And Sam was in money trouble. His yearly income dropped from
$9000 in 1928 to less than $2000 in 1930. He was working hard, but

few people could afford to pay him. On top of that Margaret was pregnant again.

At first, he was scarcely aware of the problem, since he was impractical when it came to money, anyway; never knew how much he had, never invested in North Carolina industry or Florida real estate or anything much besides books. Now he cut down on the book-buying, and made himself pay attention to the household budget. He even had a chicken coop built on the tennis court, and planted a vegetable garden out there. And he had a daughter now: Leslie.

He would talk a lot about going fishing, but seldom went, although he could turn half an afternoon on the Catawba into a year's worth of fishing stories. He obeyed the South's unwritten law, that it is all right to work hard as long as you don't seem to. The tales of fishing were metaphors in praise of a leisure he did not dare afford, and could not have enjoyed.

Slowly, his income rose to where the debts were paid. But the margin was scant and he was worried. He did not want to go into debt again and have to live humiliated and vulnerable, no better off than an employee in spite of the years of disciplined toil he'd paid to be free.

He would save the being young for his secret life, the one that came upon him every five years, when, as Permanent Class President, he returned to Chapel Hill for the class reunion. It was at about this time, when he was presiding at the decennial, that a ten-year-old boy was introduced, the son of a classmate who'd been killed in the war. And Sam rose into the silence as the boy stood there, to recite from memory Rupert Brooke's poem to those who

> . . . laid the world away; poured out the red
> Sweet wine of youth; gave up the years to be
>   Of work and joy, and that unhoped serene,
>   That men call age; and those who would have
>   been,
> Their sons, they gave, their immortality.

And, when he was done, walked out, in silence, out across the darkening campus lawn, alone, under the old trees, among the old, wild aroma of spring flowers, of quince apple, jasmine, and boxwood, down the smooth brick walkways glistening with spring rain, under the small, silent mist-haloed street lights, in this, the Chapel Hill of wild intellect, wild promise. And got back in his A Model, drove the hundred and eighty-five miles back across the moonlit state, and next morning returned to his duties.

His son was old enough to talk to now, and Sam would take him driving in the car, or steal ten minutes from the work he'd brought home to lift him up on his knee. Sam III was a gentle little boy with blond hair that was turning red; a shy, intelligent boy with blue eyes like Sam's. He spent a lot of time with the boy, much of it in silence.

But the nastic power he felt developing in himself might be squandered if it were confined to Morganton. Already, the depth of his knowledge and the thoroughness of his preparation went far beyond the demands of local jurisprudence, so that much of his hard work seemed wasted, gratuitous. Perhaps he might have to find some new way of being the thing he was, or risk ending up in the state hospital howling back at the train.

As Sam regarded his fellow North Carolinians and compared his situation with theirs, the thing that distressed him was that many people with mere grub problems seemed willing to overthrow civilization itself to solve them. There was labor unrest throughout the state, as outside organizers were coming in to the mills at Gastonia and other places. And the talk of "rebellion" wasn't limited to the mill workers. No, one heard that word from lots of folks now, from farmers, clerks, and little grocery men all the way up to some of the rich and powerful.

In the spring of 1930, he won the Democratic nomination to the state legislature and won the election against the Republican in the fall. Early the next year, when he arrived in Raleigh, he ran into a lot of lawyers who were up to the same thing he was. Men were looking for political jobs with a desperation that went beyond anything Sam could muster. But he lacked the political credit to get what he wanted — a judgeship on the Superior Court.

Instead, he was offered the post of Assistant Attorney General of North Carolina. He turned that down, first of all because it involved following the orders of another man, something he couldn't do, and secondly because it didn't pay enough. He did not want to be a prosecutor anyway. By now, he had been Special Prosecutor in a few criminal cases, and had done well at it, if "well" meant getting men punished. But it always made him feel bad, and afterward, he found it difficult to purge himself of his discomfiture. His instincts were those of a defender, and he might even have been called a kind man. He even tried to get the North Carolina capital punishment law changed. This law required that anyone convicted of a capital offense be automatically sentenced to death. Sam himself, acting as Special Prosecutor, had sent a man to his death under its provisions, and now he entered into a long, sustained effort to change it, and had no success.

The legislative session plodded on for six months, because of a revenue fight between the east and the west, between the agricultural interests and the industrial ones. Then there were long meetings about consolidating the universities. Meanwhile, his law practice was languishing, and he yearned to get back to Morganton. He studied at night. He loved the law now more than he ever had, its ancient origins, labyrinthine order, human richness. He would go down deep into it for hours, and look up when his reading was done, mildly surprised that he wasn't in Morganton. Then the session was over and he was back in Morganton after all.

One day, driving along a little back-country dirt road near Jonas Ridge, he was stopped by a big man in overalls who stepped out in front of the car. It was Beau Franklin, the man he'd prosecuted and sent to jail for second-degree murder.

"Get on out of the car here," Franklin said. "I got something to show you." There was no one around, no store, no house, nothing.

Sam got out of the car and followed him down a path leading into the pine woods. Presently they came to a tarpaper shack.

"Come on around the back here," Franklin said.

Sam followed him to a cage made of chicken wire.

"I got me some fox cubs," Franklin said. "They are the prettiest things you ever saw." He smiled at Sam, his face shining in the sunlight stabbing down through the silent tarry pines. He was a well-liked man, in spite of his reputation for violence, who was to the mountaineers what Sam was to the town people. There was just that wild thing in him that was three-quarters despair, and that raged out uncontrollably when he drank. He was a large man, larger than the people who loved him, and he seemed to want, all the time, what most folks would have been content to have only occasionally.

Sam stood looking down at the fox cubs. It was very quiet.

"Where did you get them?" he asked, and they stood there talking and looking at the cubs.

There was something that was transforming him, something that grew stronger the more he learned. It would grow now because he had not flinched about going with a murderer into the woods. And it had grown down in Raleigh during the solitary months of studying law alone in the hotel room. He knew that, in order to remain the same, he'd have to have more power. But he didn't look on it as ambition.

That fall, 1931, he was elected Vice President of the North Carolina Bar Association. The following spring, he was named a trustee of the University of North Carolina. Now, when he traveled out of town to the Knights of Pythias lodge meetings (he was regional head of that order) or to the trustees of the University, or the state bar association, he would smile inwardly when he heard himself described as one of the state's young leaders. And would think, driving home through the moonlit North Carolina countryside (often on macadam roads now), that he was an unworldly fellow and didn't want to lead anybody anywhere. He would get out the genealogy books and read about his ancestors. Courage. Nothing was possible without that. Patience was a form of courage, too, he believed. Yesterday, it seemed, he'd bought the radio to listen to the Hoover-Smith campaign, and now he was listening to the '32 Democratic National Convention and his son was old enough to sit with him. The boy was getting known around town, too.

There was even a story going around town about how Essie Tate, their basement-dwelling Negress, had walked into Lazarus Brothers Department Store and said, "I want me a fine pair of socks." Upon being shown a pair, she had said to the clerk, "These ain't going to do, nohow. These socks ain't for your little colored boy. These socks is for Mr. Sam Ervin the Third." Time slid fast. As for the story about Essie, Sam thought it was funny.

In the fall of 1932, Sam campaigned for Franklin D. Roosevelt, and for J. C. B. Ehringhaus, who was running for Governor. He was the campaign manager for Burke County, and when Ehringhaus won, Sam was offered, by way of reward, the post of General Counsel of the North Carolina Highway Commission, and turned it down.

Ehringhaus next offered him the post of associate member of the North Carolina Industrial Commission, which he turned down, too.

A week before Roosevelt's inauguration, Sam's older brother died. You never knew how much time there would be. And Sam, personally, did not want to die before he had left something woven into the permanent fabric of things: elegant, wise judicial decisions, bound up richly in calfskin volumes, which his boy could read when he grew up and got to be a lawyer. But it sometimes seemed to him that he hadn't much more to show for his life than his friends who'd perished in the war at twenty-one. It was the same old round of cases.

One day a mountaineer came to his office and said, "Beau Franklin wants to have a word with you."

"Have him come in," Sam said.

"He can't."

"Oh," Sam said, reached for his hat, and walked over to the court house and into the jail. Franklin was there behind the bars.

"What did they charge you with?" Sam asked him.

"Murder," Franklin said.

"Oh."

"Mr. Ervin, you done put me in the penitentiary one time. I want you to keep me out now. Because I didn't do it."

"All right."

"I swear to God I didn't do it, Mr. Ervin."

"All right," Sam said.

The victim, a mountaineer named McKinney, had been killed the year before. There were tales of the blood-smeared shack, which looked like a butcher's shed, of matted hair on the stairway, bloody clothing, the cadaver half-buried in a thicket out back. Some time later, another mountaineer came staggering drunk into a country store with a check belonging to the dead man and was sent to the penitentiary for forgery, not murder. People had forgotten about the thing. Murders were commonplace up in those mountains.

Then a road-house woman came forward and swore her boy friend had done it, and that Beau Franklin had helped him do it. It was the usual whiskey-soaked narrative — possibly the woman was getting even with her lover, who had refused to leave his wife and children for her — with the usual confusion: the woman put the killing at three in the afternoon, and the other witness said it took place at midnight. And so Sam defended Franklin, and as he expected, won; or rather, got a hung jury at eleven to one for acquittal. Franklin was turned loose, never to be retried.

But Sam was no longer content merely to win a long succession of cases like this. What mattered to him most was his political future, which depended on how he was regarded by the men who ran the Shelby dynasty. Friends of his, lawyers, had written letters to Ehringhaus, recommending that he be appointed to the Superior Court, and had received cordial, noncommittal replies. They had written to Governor Gardner before that, with the same results.

They had recommended him for a Superior Court special judge-ship, one of a half-dozen appointive posts that could be filled by the Governor. Ordinarily, of course, to get on the Superior Court, a man had to run and be elected, but the post for Sam's own district was held by Wilson Warlick of Newton, who was a good friend and, like Sam, a member of the Shelby group. It was unthinkable that Sam would run against him, because to do so would have meant introduc-ing base strife into the peaceful proceedings of that consortium of kindred spirits who ran the state and waited decorously for prefer-ment. Since Warlick showed no sign of stepping down, Sam's only chance of getting on the Superior Court bench was by the Governor's appointment. Which was better, anyway, because he was not much of a campaigner, having been elected to the state legislature simply because the voters had known him all his life, and having been defeated in his one attempt to gain an office representing a wider district. He felt uncomfortable asking strangers to do something for him, although he did not mind giving speeches. He was giving maybe half a dozen of them a week now, if you counted the summations to the juries, the lectures to the Men's Bible Class, the talks on Burke County history to various local groups, and the assorted orations he was obliged to make as district commander of the Knights of Pythias. He was a big shot, and people deferred to him. Even men he sent to the penitentiary did.

Early in 1934, he went up to Washington, D.C., to argue his first case before the United States Supreme Court, and found the city much changed from the sleepy Southern town he'd visited with his father when he was a boy. Whole regiments of busy, intense liberals had invaded the place, and Sam, who had supported Roosevelt, and who had favored most New Deal programs, was disquieted at the thought of what they might be up to. The Agricultural Adjustment Administration and the Federal Land Bank, he knew, were taking mortgages and farm loans out of the hands of the Morganton businessmen, who were friends of his, fellow members of the Kiwanis. The WPA was draining away the laborers his country friends used on their farms. The Department of Labor was trying to fix it so that a man who wanted to go to work for, say, a furniture factory, might be obliged to join a labor union, whether he wanted to or not. And this, too, disturbed Sam, because of the inconvenience it might cause the factory owner. But he didn't think that his opposition to unions smacked of the right wing; no, he was only defending the freedom of the poor factory worker. When there was a textile strike in a nearby town, he led in the National Guard troops — he was a captain, now — got his helmet dented with a rock in the service of freedom.

The week after his Washington trip his third child, Laura, was born.

For some time now, there had been talk of setting up a misdemeanor court in Morganton, to take care of petty criminal cases — drunkenness, fighting, wife-beating, and the like — and early the next year, when it was about to be established, the County commissioners asked him to serve as judge.

The court met every Tuesday morning in the small court room that made up the second story of the Burke County Court House. For the first time, Sam looked down on that room now from the vantage of the bench, down on its eight rows of seats, which rose up behind the green, iron railings set up between the spectator seats and the tables of counsel, at the twelve jury seats over on his left with the white numbers hand-painted on the backs. It seemed that North Carolina's world was divided in three: you were born in the spectator section; if you worked very hard and were healthy and of good character, you could pass through the railing and be admitted to the bar as an officer of the court; and if you were something special, you could come up here, where he was now.

Being a judge in North Carolina was like being a judge in Israel. You were a king, too, in that you were more like the spectators than they were like themselves: human, meaty, and obliged above all things to remember that those who came before you were made of flesh and

blood, not wood or stone. That was the high-flown theory of the
thing, the king part. But you were a judge, too, and the low fact was
that the well-to-do Morganton wanted to comb the Yahoos out of
their hair; and Sam's court was the comb. Well, it would be good
practice for the Superior Court, although the longest sentence he
could dish out was two years in jail or on the chain gang. That, he
supposed, was no worse than a bloody nose to the would-be Beau
Franklins who came before him. He served for a year and a half, with
his law practice still running strong, his children growing, and the
town a nicer place now for the nice people.

He was still a part of the Shelby group, and in 1936 served as Burke
County campaign manager of their candidate for Governor. This was
Clyde Hoey, a courtly lawyer of the old school, a lifelong friend of his
father's, who wore a frock-tailed morning coat with a rose in his lapel,
and who practiced the ancient Southern art of rhetoric with a rich,
orotund style that made him the most listened-to speaker in the state,
the King of Barbecues, the Emperor of the Fourth of July. It was like
music, Hoey's speaking, the empty, lovely, mouth-filling, polysyllabic
effusions to the state's heaven-storming blue mountains and rich
green frothy sea, and Sam was fond of the man even though it was
conceivable that never, ever, could Hoey, on his own, have organized
so much as a picnic lunch. Other people did the organizing, pulled
the wires, hired the hall, and saw to it that the Governor's Mansion
was swept, washed, and furnished, so that men like Hoey could have
their days of service. When his man won, Sam had solid reasons for
expecting a reward.

Sam did a lot of thinking that summer of 1936. He was nearing
forty — half a lifetime for a healthy Ervin, and a mark requiring a
large, handsome achievement. About this time a frowzy Yahoo his
own age came before him on a charge of drunkenness. This wasn't
the first such charge for this man, or even the tenth one.

"I've tried everything I know to help you," Sam said down to the
man.

The defendant didn't reply.

"I can't think of much else," Sam said.

"There is one thing you ain't tried," the man said.

"What is that?"

"A suspended sentence. If you let me walk out of here today, Your
Honor, you will never see me again."

"All right," Sam said.

Later that fall, the fellow was back. He had gone to the Roosevelt-Hoey Victory Day celebration and gotten drunk again. It wasn't permitted for men of his class to get drunk there.

"I thought we had an agreement," Sam said down to him.

"I don't know," the man said. "It was just such a good election. I thought Santa Claus had done come."

And Sam may have thought the same thing.

HOME MOVIES

Senator Ervin was in Richmond, Virginia, visiting the family of his older sister Laura. None of the press knew where he was. He had gotten up early that Saturday morning and walked from his apartment to the garage in the Old Senate Office Building, where he'd fetched out the Chrysler. After picking up his wife at the front door of the Methodist Building, he'd maneuvered the powerful car out onto eight-lane U.S. Interstate 95, and driven the hundred miles to Richmond, a moderate hop for the Senator, and not to be compared with the 440-mile drive to Morganton, which he and Margaret took regularly. On the trip, they'd sat in the front seat together, chatting amiably, as they had been doing for fifty-eight years.

In Richmond there was quietude, good bourbon, the comforting presence of family, and, as the feature of the visit, a color motion picture that had been shot in Morganton in 1937, and that, now, is being projected onto the wall of the darkened living room.

The yaw of years coughs up a gorgeous garden stamped with the exclamation marks of red flowers, and a sandy, pebbly path meandering along among them. Down that path come Sam's mother and father, aged seventy-one and eighty-one. His mother is lissome, smiling, relaxed, picking here a flower, there a flower, and offering them to Sam's father, who neither smiles nor pays much attention to them but who peers fixedly into the camera lens. His eye seems to catch Sam's, and to hold it, here in the darkness of the living room.

Now the scene changes. A young family appears: father, mother, a little girl, a medium-sized girl, and a big boy of eleven. The young father, slim and elegant in a conservative, dark blue business suit, is the ghost of the Senator past. The white-frocked girls play on the lawn, the eleven-year-old boy stares seriously into the camera, the young wife walks, smiling, toward the camera, and then the wall is white where the picture was and the darkened living room rattles with the clatter of the projector.

"Margaret is beautiful, isn't she?" the Senator's voice says. "And I was so young . . ." He does not say anything about his mother and father.

The family voices come into the darkness, commenting, discussing things, remembering what took place that afternoon, thirty-seven years ago. After that, silence again. Then the Senator's voice.

"Please play it again," he says.

They keep running the film, and long after everyone has adjourned into the dining room, the Senator is alone, watching it.

Later that night, driving back to Washington, looking out over the glowing instrument panel at the red corridor of taillights extending for a hundred miles up the concrete trough of Interstate 95, the Senator kept thinking about the movie. There was probably no one along that highway who did not know his name — nor a single one who knew, truly, what his life had been like. When they got back to the apartment, Margaret went to bed and the Senator sat up late into the night, working on the Watergate report. He was used to working hard.

Chapter 12

IN JANUARY of 1937, on the day Clyde Hoey was to be inaugurated as Governor of North Carolina, Sam climbed into his black Ford V-8 and, with Margaret by his side, drove the two hundred miles to Raleigh, wearing his military uniform, with the Sam Browne belt, and the captain's bars glinting on his shoulders. His ceremonial sword now lay glistening on the back seat.

At the Inaugural Parade, he got to stand near Hoey, but he didn't get to talk to him. There wasn't much to talk about, anyway, because it wasn't certain whether there would be any opening on the Superior Court.

Although there was a possibility. One of the Special Superior Court Judges, Lon Folger, was also State Chairman of the Democratic National Committee — something that had been all right in the regimes of Gardner and Ehringhaus, but that was subject to change under the aegis of Clyde Hoey, who believed all that stuff he preached about at the barbecues, and found it repugnant that a Superior Court judge should have anything to do with politics. Still, Sam drove back to Morganton no better off than he'd been when he went down. That was Thursday. On Saturday morning, he was working in his office when a phone call came from Hoey. Folger had resigned, Santa Claus had come.

On Monday morning, over breakfast, Sam was sworn in by a Morganton justice of the peace, Joe Buckley, then set out in the Ford for Charlotte, where they told him the number of the courtroom he had been assigned to, and left him alone. He walked in and went to sit up on the bench; he wasn't even wearing a robe. Superior Court judges in North Carolina didn't do that then.

He found in himself an inherent awkwardness, a desperation; there were whole chasms of opportunities for errors in ruling on motions, in sustaining or not sustaining objections. He worked on his first case far into the night. Counsel for both sides had been studying the case's laws, precedents, and possible pitfalls for weeks, while he, the judge, had heard those things for the first time today. If he handled the case perfectly, he could look forward to another complicated one immediately, with counsel equally well prepared, equally on the hawk for flawed action by a novice judge. And so, that week, all week, Sam scarcely remembered that he had a home, a wife, a civic identity, as he labored far into the night studying the law, filling up page after page of yellow pads as he tried to prepare his charges to the jury.

On Friday afternoon he drove the seventy miles back to Morganton, thinking about the cases every inch of the way, attended the six-thirty Kiwanis dinner in a preoccupied way and returned home to his study. He spent all night there, and the next day and Sunday as well, with time out for nothing but the church service, which he went through as if he'd dreamed it. On Monday he set out for Charlotte again, having passed anonymously through his home as if it had been a train station in Bulgaria. He went through the next week the same way, and the sixteen weeks after that, before his vacation.

What being a Superior Court judge really consisted of, he found out now, was sitting on the ninth floor of the Charlotte Hotel, looking out toward the mountains, where his family's life went on as if he'd died. And he felt sorry for himself for not having his wife around to listen to him, or the boy to go on car rides with, or a little girl crawling over his shoes as he sat reading a book, and if someone had told him that he loved the court house and Kiwanis more than he did his family, he might have sued the man for slander. But he was perhaps better off here resplendent in power above this vast light-dotted city of employees, and if his rise to the bench stole away those old gregarious evenings he'd once spent with fellow lawyers on the firefly-starred front porches of rooming houses, it gave him in return a warm nurturing medium of rich deference in which to enjoy his own conception of himself. He was fond of being catered to, fond of being called "Judge," and could have quit and gone home any time he wanted to.

Occasionally one of his fellow judges would invite him out to dinner. One of these was J. Will Pless, a University classmate of Sam's, who was holding court in Concord, twenty miles away.

"How are you enjoying being on the bench?" Pless asked him.

"I like it pretty well except for the loneliness," Sam said. "But I expect I will get used to that."

"No," Pless said. "The loneliness isn't much now because you are uncertain of yourself and keep thinking about what you have to do tomorrow. Before long you will know what to do without thinking about it, and then the loneliness will get worse."

During summer vacation, Sam went back to Morganton, where everything was the same except that he couldn't practice law. But he didn't have to, because the judgeship paid $8500 a year, a big sum in those days. He read, loafed as he'd not done since summer vacation from the University, and pursued his growing interest in national affairs. Roosevelt, having just been re-elected by the largest plurality in the history of presidential elections, was trying to increase the number of members on the Supreme Court so as to load that institution with judges favorable to his own causes. He was being opposed in this by most southern Senators, Josiah Bailey of North Carolina being prominent among them, and Sam followed the battle. It was troubling that a President would reach out for power like that. It was a very strange thing. Roosevelt had failed to bend the amorphous factionalism of Southern politics to his own purposes, and yet his will was being felt through bureaucrats who'd never been south of Washington, D.C., and whose latitudinarian social beliefs, to Sam's way of thinking, threatened states' rights.

Swiftly, the vacation was over, and Sam went back on the road, only this time not to Charlotte, but traveling all over the state, to wherever the case load was greatest. This time he was dealing mostly with serious criminal cases; it wasn't the drunks now but the embezzlers, armed robbers, rapists, and murderers. They seemed to be concentrated in the cities, in Durham, and Greensboro, where Buck Duke's power, the power of the Catawba, had begun to attract the poor whites and Negroes to the textile and tobacco factories, and to draw out of them the sort of violence that led to death.

During Sam's first week on the bench that fall, he sentenced a man to twenty years in jail. He watched the fellow being led out. He called the next case and the participants came forward, arraying themselves at the counsels' tables as if nothing had happened. That night, Sam could not sleep, and the next morning went to the court house with a burning stomach, taut nerves.

It was a hectic, disjointed life. Some weeks, he would be trying cases in counties bordering on his own and could come home every night, as other men did. Other weeks, he'd be down by the sea, four hundred miles away, or in other distant counties, and again there would be the long nights in lawyers' offices, poring over the books, and the silence of hotel rooms.

If he wanted to, he could lie in his room and read what the local North Carolina newspapers were saying about him: that he was an excellent judge, intelligent and merciful, learned in the law, colorful, a good storyteller, a good man. More often than not, they referred to him as "Judge Sam." But reading these accounts didn't take up much of a long night in a hotel room, and even preparing for the next day didn't take as much time as it used to. He had to find new ways to fill the empty spaces. He took to reading mystery stories, whole suitcases full of them — Sherlock Holmes, Ellery Queen, H. Donald Hunter, and all the others — which the Burke County Library saved for him and which he would stock up on every weekend. Then there was the Bible, and the commentaries. He carried these with him and, instead of preparing the lesson for the Men's Bible Class on Saturday night, he worked on it all week, and overworked it, sitting up at the hotel room desk, the cigarette smoke curling up by his elbow, the messages from the lost Israelites limning themselves out on the long yellow legal pads, just as the law briefs had done.

He found that what he was doing seemed more rational if there were a cigarette to suck, and was smoking two and three packs of Camels every day. When he hadn't slept, the cigarettes tended to take his mind off that burning sensation in his stomach, which had come to be his constant companion, the gut-emblem of his dignity. It became his practice now, in midmornings and a couple of times in the afternoon, to recess court so as to go back to his chambers and smoke. Those cigarettes were the pay he gave himself for doing everything right. The Kiwanis meeting was pay, too, and the first thing he did on arriving back in Morganton on the late Friday afternoons was to go there, to the Kiwanis. He went there before he went home.

He spent little or no time with his daughters, but sometimes he would take the boy out fishing. His son was growing now, was almost thirteen, a good, gentle boy, doggedly loyal to his father. Sometimes it seemed to Sam that he was losing touch with young men, with what they thought about, and, therefore, with his own youth. This, too, he attributed to his service on the Superior Court because, prior to that service, he had kept up with the young men through the weekly National Guard drills and the two-week summer training camps at Fort Bragg or Fort Jackson. But young men now used the same tone in talking to him now that they did in addressing Cary Gregory, the Presbyterian minister only there was more awe in it.

Sam worried about his son. Hated, in a way, to see him growing up because another war was almost ready to break out. What had he and Si Parker and all the rest of them been doing over there the first time? What had his college roommates died for? Sometimes the Superior Court seemed a frail place on which to stand.

Although, of course, a man who sought to become Governor or United States Senator might find this roving judgeship to be a very useful thing, an opportunity to build a wide political base throughout the state. But Sam did not believe he entertained such ambitions, and thought of himself as a scholar. There were plenty of good North Carolinians to be Governor or Senator; plenty of good Southern men. And yet, in spite of all they could do, Roosevelt was having the way with the alphabet-soup agencies, smashing down into the states with what many North Carolinians, including Sam's father, regarded as usurping presidential power.

And Sam, who may have supported more of Roosevelt's programs than his father did, still liked the notion of North Carolina as a wide green democracy capable of handling its own affairs, and one of his more important Superior Court rulings reflected this point of view.

There came before him one day the case of a man and woman who had been jailed on a charge of bigamous cohabitation. They'd been married to other people, met, gone off to Reno, Nevada, obtained divorces, and returned to North Carolina as man and wife. Sam, working that night in his hotel room, alone, decided to instruct the jury that the divorces weren't valid if the couple had gone to Nevada for the sole purpose of circumventing North Carolina law. These instructions, he knew, would oblige a guilty verdict. The next day, one was duly brought in, and Sam sentenced the lovers to the penitentiary. The case, *Williams* v. *North Carolina,* was appealed to the United States Supreme Court, where Felix Frankfurter, in writing the opinion of the majority, upheld Sam, saying that ". . . divorce, like marriage, is of concern not merely to the immediate parties. It affects personal rights of the deepest significance. It also touches the basic interests of society . . ." and that to permit the convenience laws of one state to shred the social fabric of another "would be intolerable."

His first capital case concerned a field worker who ripped the clothes off his boss's wife, tried without much success to rape her, blasted her belly open with a shotgun, leaving her still alive but somewhat too messy to rape, whereupon he bashed in her skull with the shotgun butt. The man was convicted by a jury, and came before Sam for sentencing.

He was an indigent, which meant that Sam, acting as the court, had to appoint and pay counsel. He got the best lawyers he could find, and paid them the highest fee it was in his power to offer, on the condition that an appeal be taken to the state Supreme Court. This was done, not only for the sake of the murderer, but for Sam's sake, because, on this one, he wanted to be certain he had committed no error of law. Because the statute required that he impose the death penalty. Which he did. And it was carried out. The nights in the hotel room got very long, and, beswamped in the billabong of his own ambitions, he found it difficult, sometimes, to pay attention to the Ellery Queen stories.

He was known to his colleagues, and to the lawyers who appeared before him, as a lucid, capable, and fair judge, although it is to be doubted that there was any wide knowledge of how tortured he was; possibly the Judge Priest stuff worked too well. Although it wasn't easy to hide what was happening with his face. When he was under stress his eyebrows would leap upward in circumflexes, and his face would twitch, and there were some who knew, all right. One of them was his brother-in-law, Dr. James K. Hall, the well-known psychiatrist, who was concerned about him, and who told family members that Sam did not belong on the Superior Court bench. On the other hand Sam himself, in those days and even now, would maintain that he was feeling fine, that he was always a happy person, and that nothing, ever, was really wrong.

He was attending a funeral in Morgantown, when sharp pains came to his stomach. He began bleeding from the rectum. It was an ulcer. He was in Grace Hospital for a time and later spent days in his bedroom, flat on his back, being tended by his brother John, the physician. It was very strange to lie there like that, with John coming by in the early mornings and the late afternoons, and with his wife or the Negress fetching the meals in and the empty dishes out, and the rest of the time being alone. He lay there, staring up at the ceiling, not fifty yards away from where he'd lain awake when he was a boy, listening to the wind's murmur in the branches of the old trees. But he could not think himself back into being a boy, into feeling secure as a boy did. All he could think of was the work he was missing, the pending court matters requiring his attention, bills that had to be paid.

"I've got to get out of here," he said to his brother.

"What for?" John wanted to know.

Sam told him what for.

"No," his brother said. "You've got to learn to take it easy."

"Oh yeh," Sam said. He was outraged that his body had betrayed him, and every morning would look out the window and see his father issuing out promptly from the big white house to go down to his law office as always, trim, spry, lively. Eighty-four years old.

He wondered about the difference between the old man and him. The passion for work, intolerance for failure, total intolerance for weakness — his father had tried to instill these qualities in all ten children. And the result had been that some of them were extraordinarily successful (as Joe was getting to be down in Charlotte now) and some were broken. There did not seem to be any middle way and there did not seem to be any getting rid of the ambition once it had been bred in. Acting against John's orders, Sam made himself get out of bed and go back to work.

These were tough days for him, and it wasn't only the hard work on the bench and the normal responsibilities of raising a family. No, besides that, people were bringing him their personal problems, and would talk to him for long hours about their marital, psychological, and financial difficulties. Indeed, the evening before the ulcer began to bleed, he'd been up on his front-porch swing until two in the morning, talking with an employee who was convinced his career would be ruined because of a personality clash with his boss.

So Sam had been operating under a lot of tension, and knew it, and in an effort to help himself, he was reading any psychological or mind-cure book that he thought might help him. By now, he had already read Alfred Adler's *Understanding Human Nature,* Edmund Jacobson's *You Must Relax,* and Alexis Carrel's *Man, the Unknown.* Later he would read many more such books, including Harry Emerson Fosdick's *On Being a Real Person,* Joshua Loth Liebman's *Peace of Mind,* Dale Carnegie's *How to Stop Worrying and Start Living* (his favorite), H. A. Overstreet's *The Mature Mind,* Karin Roon's *The New Way to Relax,* and Bonaro Overstreet's *Understanding Fear.*

If he seemed to relax more, if he spent more time with his children, or sat over on the front porch of the big white house, talking with his father, it was relaxation-with-a-purpose, trickery, really. He was try-ing to fool his body so that he could go on about the main business.

What else was there? Talking to the children didn't seem to be necessary. What they needed, after all, was to be fed (he was doing that) and educated (Essie and Margaret were doing that, as were the schools). Although, for the sake of form, he would talk to them about current events, taking an adversary position on each question that arose, seeking to lure them on to public affairs with his own subtle, gray-templed wit, seeking to be to them what old Horace Williams had been to him during his swift, magic years at Chapel Hill. He gave them quarters for memorizing poems he selected for them out of Kip-ling, Brooke, Noyes, and others among his own preceptors of the spirit. Or he would lay aphorisms on them, such as "A merry heart doeth good like a medicine." But his own shoulders, now, were feeling less broad and less strong, his inner being more in need of medicine.

Nor was he any better at talking to his father. He would go over and sit on the front porch, in the darkness, listening to the old man raging on incessantly into the night against the man in the White House who slaughtered the little pigs and ploughed under the cotton, who could not run his own family and sought to run the country instead, who had imposed the cotton-processing tax and raised the income tax, which was driving him, personally, Sam J. Ervin, Sr., into ruin. Sam had heard these same words from other lips but it made him sad to hear his father saying them. He could not believe an American President would want to be a dictator. He would sit there in the night listening to his father's gentle voice raving on. The old man was getting older. It was not just the little pigs that were going to be slaughtered, or only cotton that would be ploughed under.

Now, another murder case came up, involving a man who had heard that a 103-year-old neighborhood woman carried twenty dollars pinned to her underclothes and who smashed in her skull to get it. Again Sam appointed a lawyer for the man on the understanding that an appeal would be taken; again he sentenced a man to death; again the man was killed.

Meanwhile, as part of his relaxation program, Sam had added on to his schedule picnics, swimming trips with the family, long afternoon naps, all of which stuck to him as unnaturally as bottle caps to a tuxedo. Before long the work had him again, the nervous judge was back, eyebrows leaping, face, working furiously. And time kept sliding. One Sunday afternoon, as he was trying to take a nap in his study, his son came in and told him the Japanese had dropped some bombs on Pearl Harbor. That had come in over the radio he'd bought to follow Progress with.

The next day, Monday, he drove to Charlotte, and stood in line at the army recruiting office.

"What is it?" the sergeant said to him when his turn came at the desk.

Sam told him.

"Listen, buddy. What's your name?"

"Sam Ervin."

"How old are you, Sam?"

"Forty-five."

"Well, we consider you an antique. Next."

He walked from there to the court house, went up on the bench, and called his first case. It seemed now that he would not have another opportunity to face an enemy who could be recognized by a uniform.

His son was almost sixteen years old now and, if the war kept on, surely would be drafted. Then there was his father. One morning, having failed to see the old man go by, Sam went next door and found his mother sweeping the front porch.

"Didn't Daddy go to work today?"

"No," his mother said.

"What is it?"

"He said, 'I don't think I'll go down to the office today.' "

"He'll go down tomorrow."

"No," his mother said.

Behind her shoulder Sam saw the old man sitting in the parlor. He wasn't even trying to read, just sitting there.

"Your father is eighty-five years old," she said.

"Yes."

"Why don't you go in and see him?"

"No mam. I think it will be better some other time," Sam said, and walked back to his car, and drove out on the highway toward the court.

He became more touchy than ever about sentencing anybody to anything, and his sentences, which were already known to be lenient, became more lenient still. The result was that his work load increased, as lawyers clamored to have their clients brought before him. The "nervous tension" increased, and he sought for ways to turn to the past, and to the quietude he'd found there. He walked down to the hardware store, bought a pair of bib overalls, and went out systematically, every morning he was home, to work in his victory garden, remembering, as he did so, how peaceful it had seemed on those dew-dazzled mornings of his childhood when his grandfather had come out here and dug in this black soil, how quiet it had all seemed then.

His brother Joe was talking about running for Congress, and drove up from Charlotte to discuss it with Sam. And Sam, sitting there on the front porch, talking with this crippled, intense, ambitious younger brother, felt sane and relaxed by comparison. Joe, son of the same father, for the past sixteen or seventeen years, had gone to his law offices at five o'clock in the morning, every morning, to study law until the business of the day began, to continue on until nine or ten o'clock at night. Joe was beginning to have success, and listening to him talk, Sam began to realize that he himself was tired of it.

"What do you think, Sam?" Joe asked.

Sam sat there for a long time. He was thinking about his boy more than anything else, who was eighteen and who was getting ready to enlist in the army.

"What?"

"Should I do it?"

"No," Sam said.

"Why not?"

"Because you work too hard. Because you are inflexible. Because you can't compromise."

"That's true of you, too, isn't it, Sam?"

"Maybe so and maybe not. But you don't see me running."

"You're on the court," Joe said. "It's the same thing."

"No I'm not."

"What's that?"

"Not on the court. I just resigned."

SONS OF THE DREAM

On the way to Sam's son's house in Morganton's suburbs, I passed by the old family place, which was empty now and which would continue to be empty until Sam's sister Jean retired from her professorship at the University of Virginia, and came back to Morganton to live.

The garden had been worked; that old garden which had been the silence-domain of John Witherspoon Ervin and Samuel J. Ervin, Sr., now lay lushly turned over in deep browns and blacks, and there was corn growing, and tomatoes, radishes, onions, beets, peppers, eggplants, squash, cantaloupe, watermelon. In the middle of the garden was a lawn chair for an old man to sit in. That would be Hugh Tate, Sam's brother, seventy-five years old, whose serious illnesses had been no more efficacious than his considerable wealth in keeping him away from where he thought he should be, his garden.

Sam III was now a Superior Court judge himself. His red hair, which was brush-cut in old photos, had grown out to ordinary length, his skin was ruddy, his blue eyes lively and intelligent. He was three or four inches shorter than his father.

He led me into the living room. His son, Jimmy, went with us, and sat hunched over on the sofa, his thick, black Sam-like eyebrows working as the boy paid intense attention to what was going on. Jimmy seemed nervous, too, like a needy young man at a job interview, and this was puzzling. He was already a national television celebrity, having appeared on all the national networks at the time of the Watergate hearings, and had seemed, at the time, more cool and self-possessed than he was now. He told me he would be beginning his fresh-man year at Davidson College that fall. He said the prospect made him nervous.

"I don't know whether I can hack it or not," he said.

"That's a curious remark coming from a young fellow who made all A's in high school," his father said. He, too, had gone to Davidson. That was back in World War II, when gas was rationed, and Davidson was closer than Chapel Hill. He had been about to be drafted into the army anyway, and had not been certain he'd ever finish any college.

Sam III was friendly, informal, ready and open in his replies. He'd spent more time with his father than his sisters had, and remembered more. He'd played ball with Sam in the front yard, traveled with him on the judging circuit, ridden with him on a genealogy expedition to an old South Carolina graveyard. He talked about how hard his father had driven himself in the thirties and forties, about the extreme and alarming nervousness Sam displayed in those years. On questioning, he revealed that he himself, after ascending to the Superior Court bench, had begun to drive himself mercilessly, developing high blood pressure and chest pains. And told how Sam had advised him to slow down. And how, after that, the chest pains had disappeared, the blood pressure relented.

Up on the wall, behind him and above him, was an oil painting of Sam Ervin, Sr. — so that now, as I listened to the friendly voice of Sam III, talking on, I sensed all five of them there in the room:

> *1   John Witherspoon Ervin*
> *2   Sam Ervin, Sr.*
> *3   Sam Ervin, Jr.*
> *4   Sam Ervin III*
> *5   Sam Ervin IV (Jimmy)*

I told them that I wanted to discuss the connections: how Number 1 had been an artist and failed at it; how this had embittered Number 2, who learned under the broiling sun in South Carolina's cotton fields to work demoniacally hard, and imposed a contempt for losel dreamery on Number 3, the Senator;

who had passed the same unusually high standards on to his own son, Number 4, who doublèd the ante by his own achievements; who had now passed on the same thing to the boy, Number 5, who would be entering Davidson College that fall.

"I suppose that's about right," Sam III said. "Although I haven't thought much about it. After all, if you have ambition, you just go ahead and work."

"It's true of me," Jimmy said. "I've got it. I always take more courses than I'm supposed to. And I work harder at them than I have to. And try to win every scholarship in sight. And am disappointed if I don't." He paused momentarily, the young black brows working furiously. "Granddad says I am the oldest young man he's ever known."

It was quiet for a long time, and then the sounds of the house came drifting in. There were the others — the wife, sisters, and friends — who were concerned with hikings and outings and loafing and with fixing the dinner, snapping the beans, and talking lazily with one another as they did.

But both these men, father and son, were far away from all that. They would eat the string beans and maybe even go on the outings and maybe even seem to loaf. But they were ten million miles away from the peace of this house and the tranquility the women and girls brought to it. They were always thinking of the next case or the next course assignment, and would never really settle down here, not even when their bones were humus and all that remained of their carnal form was some oil pictures ranged along the wall. Because he, the old man, Sam Sr. — who would be 118 years old if he were living now — was not at peace, and his restless eyes up there on the wall were looking out for something more to do.

Chapter 13

Sam sat in his house staring out gloomily at the wet gray January and wondering what it had all been about, those two decades and more of intense, sustained effort. For seven years he'd sat up on the bench picking his way carefully through the mazes of law, conscientiously seeing that everything ran right, while other men, the lawyers who called him "Your Honor," had gotten rich. They owned mansions, spacious green farmlands, stock in cottonmills, and thick piles of interest-gathering cash — while he himself, the judge, had nothing more than a bunch of law books and a little matchbox of a house that had been too small for a young fool lawyer in the first place.

It was astounding, the changes he'd wrought by resigning. He began to see things he had never seen before. He would stroll down to Collett Parks's barbershop and sit there, watching the faces of the customers, the faces of persons passing in the street, the mottling at the edge of the mirror, the long white folds of the cloths draped chin-to-foot. And watch Parks himself, relaxed and smiling, chatting as he worked, pausing to observe the goings-on out in the street; or listen to the man talk about his lawn, the bass fishing, the weather — and he began to sense a profound difference between the barber and himself.

They had been talking about these things for years, of course, but now it occurred to Sam that Parks knew his lawn intimately, and took deep delight in his fishing and became absorbed down deep in it, and that Parks lived in the weather rather than reading about it in the newspaper. Whereas to him, the judge, lawns and fish and summer showers had been abstractions, names. And now, this January, Sam sat in the barbershop, among the ancient fragrances of tonics. He was forty-seven years old and tired of being a deserving young man. He may have had the notion that Parks could teach him something, that if he could turn and live like the barber, he might be happy.

Of course, all these years, he, Sam, had seemed to be relaxed, as Parks was. But that had all been the Lawyer Tutt business, a mask that was as obligatory in public as trousers were. Now he wanted to learn truly to relax like that, to live in the weather instead of under the clock.

But something in him wouldn't let it happen. The longer he sat around doing nothing, the more ominous inactivity seemed. He would go out fishing on Lake James, trying to shake loose. But it was Parks, still, who did the fishing, and Sam who did the worrying. If word got out that he was spending his time loitering around the lake or the barbershop, he would be ruined, or thought he would be.

That winter of 1944 Joe was laid up in a hospital in Charlotte and Sam went to see him. He walked into the room and Joe was lying there smiling his wide, forced smile.

"You should have saved the gas," Joe said, "because I'll be out of here in no time."

"I heard you were under the weather," Sam said.

"I'm going to be all right. I'm going to run in the primary this year."

"For the Congress?"

"Yes." The smile was very wide and was held there by the will and the muscles and by nothing underneath it. "Say, didn't you have to turn in your *C* card when you left the bench?"

"Yes," Sam said. He saw now there were tears in his brother's eyes. He went over and closed the door leading into the hallway.

"It's all right," Joe said.

"Listen, is there something I can do?"

The smile was still there and the tears were coming now but the smile stayed firm.

"They put maggots in me . . ."

"It'll be all right," Sam said.

"They stick them on my skin in little boxes and they're supposed to eat the diseased bone."

"It will be all right, Joe," Sam said. "It will be all right."

"They are crawling around inside me now. You don't know what it makes a man think about himself, to have those things crawling in him."

"It will be all right," Sam said.

"I mean, how would you like to be a woman and married to a man with those things crawling in him?" The smile was still there when he said this.

Sam pulled up the chair by the bed and sat there for a long time.

"Listen," he said, "why not put off this Congress business a couple more years?"

Joe shook his head.

"You're still a young man," Sam said.

Joe shook his head. "No," he said. "I can't." He was the son of the same father.

Sam returned to Morganton and went back to work. He took fewer of the old, homely, human cases now. He was getting the corporate clients, the big money clients, the ones he'd earned during those years on the bench.

He had thought that when he went back to the law practice it might draw his father out of the house, back down to the office again, but that didn't happen. The old man was eighty-eight now, frail and quiet, nearly blind and nearly deaf, and so Sam practiced alone. He'd not gone fishing enough to ruin his reputation, and what with the Superior Court behind him, and lawyers being away in the armed services, he began to get more clients than ever.

In the middle of this, he had to drive his son down to the railroad station, to see him off for army training camp. Several days later, word came in that Joe had won the Democratic primary for the seat in the United States Congress, which was the same as winning the election. That summer, Sam's father died.

He was sorry that his father would be gone. True, the death had come as no surprise, and Sam was able to say to himself that the old man had had eighty-nine years of living. And there were the old, tried consolations of the Presbyterian Church, the hope that some day they would meet in Heaven. But he was very sorry to be under the sentence of never seeing his father again. All his life he had been, of all the Ervin children, most truly his father's son, in his resolute refusal ever to be obedient to anybody (emotionally the son); in his deep and learned love of the law (intellectually the son); so that now with his father's death he became true heir (spiritually the son); father and patriarch of all the two or three dozen Ervins now constituting the family.

He quit teaching the Men's Bible Class, quit the lodge meetings, cut the Kiwanis down to almost nothing. He was working hard and making a lot of money and putting that into insurance and into the bank. The months passed; the war ended. The boy was in Japan now, in the Occupation Army, and Joe was up in the United States Congress being successful and working long hours.

The first post-war Christmas Day found him presiding at a family dinner at his house in Morganton. Present with him at the table were Margaret, Leslie and Laura, his brother John from across the street, John's wife, Dorothy, and Dorothy's mother, Mrs. Downes. As they were having dinner, the phone in the hallway rang. Essie Tate came in and murmured that it was for him, long distance. He went out in the hallway and took the call.

"This is Lamar Caudle," the voice came over the wire. Caudle was a lawyer from Wadesboro, North Carolina, and Sam had known him for years.

"You know Joe was supposed to have Christmas dinner over at my place," Caudle began. Sam was conscious of the silence coming out of the dining room.

"Are you still there, Sam?"

"How did it happen?" Sam asked.

"We went over to where he lives, in Arlington. He was going to have Christmas dinner with us."

"Yes."

Some of them were trying to talk in the dining room now and Sam was grateful for that. "The screen door was shut," Caudle went on, "and the house door was, too, and he'd left a note in between them saying to be careful going in because of the gas. So we went next door and called the police. They came right away but it was no good. He'd been gone for several hours. He'd dragged all the chairs into one room and was stretched out across them. There was a pistol in one hand and a straight razor in the other."

"Sam, I sure hate to break a thing like this to you."

Sam didn't say anything.

"He left some letters. For his wife."

"All right."

"I will send them down."

"Send them to me," Sam said.

Sam saw to the funeral and to Joe's estate. He looked after the widow, and the mother, and wrote, by hand, responses to the scores of condolence letters that came in, numbering each letter in sequence as it arrived, and answering each one methodically, in that same order, writing neatly on each letter, "Answered," and the date. This meant thirty or forty letters a day, because the Ervins were known throughout the state — indeed, throughout the South — and his mother alone corresponded regularly with more than a hundred persons. Now she had gone up to her room and locked the door. Having finished answering the condolence letters, Sam went back to work. There was nothing else to do. The Democrats, he knew, were meeting to nominate a candidate to take Joe's place, but Sam paid no attention to them. Early in January came a phone call from one of the Democratic leaders.

"We want you to finish out Joe's term."

"No."

The next day there was another phone call, and the day after that, another. Over the weekend the calls started coming in from all over the state. There was even one from Bill Umstead, who was Chairman of the State Democratic Committee now.

"I can't do it, Bill," he said. "This family has had enough trouble from somebody going up to Washington."

The next day he saw his mother crossing the lawn, headed toward his house. She came through the door, walked back into his study where he was working, and stood there looking at him. She was eighty now. He stood up.

"You go ahead and run for Congress," she said.

"Mam?"

"Go ahead and run. Because I want people to find out I have one son who can stand up and face life."

He stood there looking at her.

"You've got to remember I've never been confronted by the discouragement Joe's had," he said.

"Yes," she replied. "Well, people have to know one son of mine can stand up to life regardless of what's in it. People have to know that." Abruptly, she left the room, and in a moment he saw her crossing the lawn toward her own place. The phone calls kept coming in from the state Democratic leaders, urging him to accept the nomination — which, finally, he did.

He went up to Washington with the understanding that he wasn't going to run for re-election. He took his family with him. For living quarters, he selected the Fairfax Hotel, a quiet, genteel old place at the corner of Massachusetts Avenue and 21st Street, N.W., near Embassy Row. In 1946, this neighborhood was the closest thing in Washington to a Southern town. The Church of the Pilgrims, headquarters of the Southern Presbyterians in the nation's capital, was a block and a half away to the west, and a couple of blocks north, on a street that could well have been Morganton's Avery Avenue, was Woodrow Wilson's former home. It was a quiet neighborhood, especially in the evening, after all the commuters had blasted through Massachusetts Avenue on their way to the growing new suburbs, and a man could take quiet walks under the long canopies of leaves.

His old friend, Congressman Bulwinkle, took him in to meet Sam Rayburn, and he was handed the usual minor committee assignments, but, in a sense, he wasn't even a United States Congressman at all; he was the most junior of the 400-odd members, and a lame duck, to boot. And this time, when the calls began coming up from North Carolina urging him to run for re-election, he said no in such a way that the calls didn't come anymore.

His work on Capitol Hill was brisk, businesslike, perfunctory. As for his voting record, it was, probably, a shade more conservative than it might have been if he'd been up there on his own. He voted against exempting eighteen-year-olds from the draft. He voted against what he claimed was the too-rapid demobilization of America's World War II armed services. He voted to appropriate $50,000 for the House Committee on Un-American Activities. But they were actions that, in terms of his personal world, had no past and no future, and when he was alone with himself, on his long nocturnal walks through Northwest Washington, his mind was far away from Capitol Hill. Really, not much thought was required for the job.

He had Joe's old office, and could have had his old house over in Arlington, too. Only he hadn't wanted to go that far; he had wished to avoid associations that were not positive. It was vital to him that he be positive.

Now, it just might be that a way was opening out of everything that went under the heading of "nerves." It all had something to do with the way he had been treated when Joe died. It was strange. Many of the men urging him to take Joe's place had been younger than himself, and some of them, he may have believed, hoped to get something out of having placed themselves on his side. In other words, he was in a position to confer favor, honor, and power.

For seventeen years now, ever since the accession of Max Gardner to the governorship, he had been a young apprentice of older and more powerful politicians. But those men were dying off now, and in some cases, such as that of Gardner himself, leaving the state. (Gardner was in Washington, a lobbyist, making money.) And Sam had told no one of his disgust with politics.

Thus, they hadn't known he was through, none of them had known, and, in the meantime, he'd kept his standing with the Shelby group, gaining in seniority as the older men dropped away. With no sense of work or strife, and with no sense even of wanting it, he had become one of the most powerful men in North Carolina. He was like a man who gives up a rowing race but who is so far ahead that he coasts across the finish line first. Before long, his time in Congress was up, and Joe's estate had been settled for good.

Sam knew, as soon as he got back to Morganton, that things were better. He sensed that important things would be offered him. It was a very strange thing. You crossed over a line and became someone else but it wasn't like a Masonic ceremony of stepping up from degree to degree with the blare of trumpets. No, it was more mysterious than that. All he had to do now was steer.

He was in Raleigh a lot during 1947, spending time with the state leaders as an equal among equals. When the Governor, Gregg Cherry, needed a chairman for the newly formed North Carolina Commission for the Improvement of Justice, he named Sam to the post, and Sam agreed to serve, although this was a minor post, and by now, Sam was the sort of man who could have a chance to be Governor, or United States Senator, if he wanted to. His political base was wide enough. The years of traveling the Superior Court circuit as an able and well-beloved trial judge had assured that. On the other hand, there was some question among his associates as to whether Sam could manage a big elective office, because he wasn't keen on campaigning for himself, and had gotten every important post he'd ever held by appointment.

The first big offering to come his way was a seat on the North Carolina Supreme Court. Of course, it paid a lot less than he was used to — $10,000 a year — and he'd made more than $37,000 the year before in the practice of law. But he took the post; here was his chance for service, the thing Edward Kidder Graham had taught him about; this was what he'd been educated for, he felt.

Besides, the notion of being up there, enrobed, on the high bench appealed to his sense of the fitness of things. He was glad to be elevated to this Platonic Supreme Court, upper world of pure law, in which there were no squabbles over grubby fact, in which the only persons to appear before him were lawyers arguing the law. It was a scholar's world: marble halls, high ceilings, echoing footsteps, quiet, precision. And if it was a political dead end, it was an elevated one.

He rented a house in Raleigh, near the Governor's Mansion, and brought his wife and children there. For the girls, he believed, it would be a good place to complete their growing up, making them more cosmopolitan, more polished than they might have been if they'd stayed in Morganton. Here, they'd have a chance to number among their beaux the sons of some of the most prominent legislators and businessmen in the state. The son, meanwhile, was at the Harvard Law School. And Sam entered into his duties on the high court, happier than he'd been in a long time.

The North Carolina Supreme Court in these years was quiescent and conservative. It did not hear cases that were likely to be controversial or keenly decisive in the ongoing social and economic life of the state. Its meetings somewhat resembled the hushed tea-drinkings of a small English Department in a genteel university. And the decisions, which were returned more rapidly than those of any other state appellate court in the country, were written in the most elegant prose on the most minuscule of matters, and were indistinguishable in spirit and importance from, say, a monograph on the influence of Neo-platonism on the dramatic symbology of Faulkner's *Sartoris*. Only, of course, he, Sam, would not have been interested in Faulkner because he believed that the man wrote about low, degraded people and mad-men. What did Faulkner know of the South? What could anybody know of the South who was not running it?

He enjoyed his cloistered life. Often he would leave his family down in Raleigh to do whatever they were doing — all that dating and socializing business — and drive back across the moonlit, rolling state, to hole up in his beloved law library, write out his opinions in long-hand on the yellow legal pads that had served him all his life, leave them on the hall table for the maid to mail, and go off at dawn, fishing, with his friend the barber.

Back in Raleigh, he smiled in his job, rollicked in it, and with his streak of drollery widening as the years slid by, became known in the state's newspapers as "the Court Jester." He began to reach out for other ways to amuse himself, accepting speaking engagements throughout the state. As a member of the court he was barred from giving political speaches — but there were plenty of other things to talk about. He was, to his own way of thinking, an authentic scholar, and qualified by his years of study to speak on state history, the First Amendment, the Bible.

Yes, he stood for the ideal of the Christian gentleman, as narrowed and refined by men like himself, and if there was a touch of stridency in his advocacy of the old ideals, it was because he may have felt them to be endangered, right here in North Carolina. For the first time in the century, the man who occupied the Governor's Mansion wasn't even a lawyer. He wasn't even a businessman, hadn't gone to the University of North Carolina, and came entirely from outside the freemasonry of the small group of persons who had run the state since Reconstruction. This was Kerr Scott, a farmer, a man who was determined to take the emphasis of state expenditures from the pri-mary roads — which were being built for the businessmen — to the secondary roads, to benefit farmers like himself. And Scott threat-ened to disturb the correct balance between whites and Negroes, not only by his espousal of certain liberal legislative proposals, but also by his appointment of Frank Porter Graham to the United States Senate.

Frank Porter Graham was President of the University of North Carolina, and Sam knew him well and had attended many social functions with him when Graham was courting a Morganton girl. And knew there were those who believed that the notion of putting an academician in the Senate was ludicrous. That is to say, while university professors tended to be a large cut above high school teachers, they were still far removed from being men of affairs; they were supposed to teach people, inspire people, and write a few books, but the people who ran the state had never paid much attention to them. Such men, they believed, had lived with their noses in books, lived measuring themselves against captive nineteen-year-olds, and were unqualified for a man's job of running the world. But Sam maintained solid relations with both Graham and Scott, and, as a member of the Supreme Court, stayed away from any active political role.

Sometimes it seemed to him that the world was getting worse. A certain graciousness was going out of life, and with the new clock-regulated jobs in the cities and mills, something else seemed to be slipping away, too: a man's sense of dignity, of his own worth. It was becoming an employee's world, and he did not always like it very much.

He continued to believe in a world of self-sufficient men, each of whom was responsible for himself. He continued to believe that the old, the Anglo-Saxon, law, was more important than the momentary fates of those who were judged by it. Thus he voted to overturn the murder conviction of John Bridges, because the judge, in his charge to the jury, had neglected to say, specifically, that the jury had the option of declaring the man to be innocent. Sam's opinion went like this:

> The state's testimony tends to show that the prisoner coveted his neighbor's wife and slew his neighbor with rare atrocity that his physical enjoyment of the wife's person might be exclusive. The very sordidness of the evidence strongly tempts us to say that justice and law are not always synonymous, and to vote for affirmance of the judgment of death on the theory that justice has triumphed, however much the law may have suffered . . . And yet, his role on life's stage, like ours, soon ends. But what happens to the law in this case is of the gravest moment. The preservation unimpaired of our basic rules of criminal procedure is an end far more desirable than that of hurrying a single sinner to what may be his merited doom.

He had mellowed, now, and was learning better how to relax. Once, during summer recess, he took the family down to Wrightsville Beach and experienced something new. For the first few weeks, he had

something of the old restlessness, the feeling of time wasted, the sense
he oughtn't to be there. But then the nervousness went out of him, he
fell asleep on the beach, got up relaxed and happy, walked out into
the gentle waves, and swam. He sank down into his vacation, forget-
ting the Supreme Court, and became again the boy who'd lolled on
his back in the Catawba River. Five whole weeks he spent like this,
free from urticant care.

He knew that everything he did was subject to reversal. More and
more, the United States Supreme Court was overturning things. And
when it wasn't the Supreme Court, it was the executive branch, some
bureaucrat with his fingers on federal funds, promulgating codes. Or
the President himself hurling edicts, such as the one desegregating
the armed forces. There was even fear expressed in some quarters
that the Supreme Court, one day, might do to the schools what Harry
Truman had done to the military, might desegregate the schools.

In the 1952 gubernatorial primary, Kerr Scott's hand-picked successor was spurned by the voters in favor of Sam's old friend, Bill Umstead. But Umstead, within forty-eight hours of his inauguration,
was felled by a heart attack and almost totally incapacitated. He
didn't give up the Governor's seat, however, because to do so would
be to surrender the rule of the old boys at a time when the segregation question was before the United States Supreme Court.

In May of 1954, Umstead was still in the Governor's chair, and
Clyde Hoey was up in the Senate. The other Senator, Alton Lennon,
was a lame duck who'd just been defeated by Kerr Scott in the
Democratic primary. And things were happening, were moving,
shifting. The three major trends in North Carolina, then, were stubborn opposition to the civil rights movement, retreat from support of
international involvements, and the rise of a radical right.

All these things were coming to a head. The Army-McCarthy hearings were on television, were continuing, as yet unresolved. Then, on
May 7, the French fortress of Dienbienphu, over in Viet Nam, fell
to the attack of the communist-led natives, and it was thought that
the United States might become involved in a major conflict over
there. On May 12, Clyde Hoey dropped dead. On May 17, the
unanimous United States Supreme Court ruling came down, desegregating all schools in the nation. On May 21, the leading candidate
to replace Hoey — a man named Irving Carlyle — disqualified himself forever by stating, in public, that he believed that Supreme Court

decision ought to be complied with. Shortly thereafter, Sam picked up the phone and heard coming over the wire the weakened voice of his old friend, Umstead, who wanted him to go up to Washington, for good, to help resolve things that seemed, to some, more important than anything the North Carolina Supreme Court was being called on to decide. He wanted him to be Senator now.

A GENTLEMAN, INOUYE

The Senator came in, walking briskly, looking over at me as he moved toward his desk.

"Sit tight," he said.

He stood at the desk, riffling rapidly through notes his secretary had put there, then came over and took the chair next to mine.

"What can I do for you?" he asked.

I told him I was writing a biography of Sam Ervin, and wanted to interview him, but that I didn't want to hear anything more about Watergate.

"Nothing about Watergate," he repeated flatly.

"Right."

"I'm afraid you've come to the wrong place, then. Sam and I don't run in the same circles."

"I'm interested in your impressions of him prior to the time you served with him on the Watergate Committee."

He began to give me The Speech and I watched his eyes as he delivered it — all the stuff about "able Senator"and "distinguished Constitutional scholar" and the rest of the standard, empty things any Senator would have told anybody about Sam. This Senator's eyes were deep brown, hooded, sharp, and I could tell from them I was getting only a small portion of his attention. This was Daniel K. Inouye, the most decorated veteran in the Senate. Sam had once held that honor, but now it belonged to this short, stocky Japanese man, who had lost his right arm in Italy during the Second World War. As he spoke, his eyes told me he didn't believe in these empty things any more than I did.

" . . . and of course, while I have not agreed with the Senator on all the positions he has taken, I regard him, on the whole, as a patriotic man and a very fine representative of his state." He waited now, watching me out of the hooded eyes.

"This is an impressive office," I said to him.

"Thank you."

"Beautiful furniture, nice pictures."

"Thank you."

"You and I both went to George Washington," I said. *"It was a poor university with cinderblock walls and rickety furniture. And I was wondering how it feels to come this far."*

"Well, it is a good office. I like it."

"A lot of the people around here have never known what it is to be poor," I remarked.

Now the eyes, momentarily, widened all the way. *"What do you want of me?"* he said.

"Would one of the things you disagree with Sam about be civil rights?"

"Yes . . . and other matters."

"Would you say he's a windbag?"

"I beg your pardon?"

"To your way of looking at things, is he a windbag . . . a phony . . . a long-winded racist, full of WASP arrogance, hiding behind the Constitution, no more a true scholar than a plate of cornpone is?"

He paused for a long time, looking at me.

"Are you doing a job on Sam?" he asked.

"No."

"I don't think any of those things."

"You were speaking of the circles you run in."

"Yes."

"That would include Kennedy, Tunney, Bayh . . ."

"Yes."

"Doesn't your circle regard Sam as, uh, anachronistic?"

"In what way?" Inouye asked.

"For instance, I think you said he was patriotic."

"Yes."

"Well, a study published in this morning's paper says that less than a fifth of America's college youth think patriotism is an important virtue."

"I read that; I know all that," Inouye said, waving it aside with the back of his large, muscular hand. *"They associate that word, partriotism, with disastrous military adventures in Southeast Asia. But if you asked whether they loved their country you'd get quite a different result. After all, there are ways other than military service to express one's love of country. One might teach, or heal, or seek to change policies which seem to be unwise or unjust. And what-*

ever Sam is, he's no phony, no slicker. You know what a slicker is," he said. "That's a fellow who smiles at you. And smiles and smiles. And all the time, behind his back, is stropping the razor for you." His one, strong arm went through that stropping motion, as the eyes held mine. It occurred to me that I'd been smiling.

"Sam always lets you know where you stand," he said. "Although, of course, he's a gentleman about it."

I nodded.

"This is a gentlemen's club, you know," Inouye went on.

"What about the Presidency?" I asked. "Is that a gentlemen's club?"

"We will have better Presidents."

"What about the notion that we have the Presidents we deserve? And that we're headed for a succession of Nixons?"

"That would be to believe that the American people are fools," he said.

"In a way."

He shook his head. "I can't believe that," he said. "I don't believe that."

Chapter 14

SAM HATED, detested, not being able to get to sleep, and knew that the more he worried, the less likely sleep was to come at all. This, now, was the night before he was to be sworn in as a United States Senator, and he lay there in the blackness, listening to the braying voices of the talkers and drinkers smashing in on him from the next compartment and, underneath them, the rackety-racketing rhythm of train wheels speeding through the black, star-peppered Virginia night. Sometimes, passing a town or house, there'd be a quick smudge of light across the ceiling, then blackness again, relieved only by the thin white line of light in the door crack leading to the compartment where the drinkers roared. They were Morgantoners, a whole carload of them, and this was the Southern Railway he was riding, which he and his father, between them, had represented for more than seventy years. But he did not feel at home tonight, and could not sleep, and his mother's advice, which he tried to recall now, flapped along with him as blackly obscure as the banner on the car hurtling through the anonymous night. "Sam J. Ervin Junior/Senator from Burke County."

It was like riding in a coffin, the blackness of this cramped lower bunk. Hours ago, when he'd first gone to bed, there'd been the aroma of his wife's perfume wafting down from the bunk above, but that had faded as he had gotten used to it, and now there was nothing but the blackness and the voices and his mother's advice: "If you can't sleep, Samuel, make yourself lie down and that will rest you as much as sleep would." In the past half-dozen years, death had claimed nine United States Senators from North Carolina. Before that, there'd been only five of them in thirty-five years. He was already fifty-seven years old. He had seen death on the face of his old friend, Bill Umstead. Certainly the man couldn't have much longer to live. Indeed, it had been the death on Bill Umstead's face, as much as his own vanity, that had moved Sam to take the appointment in the first place.

He'd been nobody's first choice; Umstead had told him that. Brandon Hodges, Irving Carlyle (in spite of the speech), Gregg Cherry, Robert Lassiter: all had significant backing. But Sam had been acceptable to everybody, offensive to none.

He'd gone to see the dying man at the Governor's Mansion. It had been a quiet talk, and much was left unsaid. Together, as students at the University of North Carolina, they'd been warned that destructive, un-American forces would be unleashed on their state, seeking to destroy their culture, their felicity, their homes. Forty years ago they'd acquired together the sense of threatened empire — which was one of the reasons they'd responded so readily to the Rudyard Kipling poems and the Edward Kidder Graham speeches, and why they still lived by those sentiments. The dragon, in the form of the Supreme Court desegregation ruling, had come down at last, putting the pork barrel stuff, the cotton tariff, the national defense questions, even the McCarthyism fracas, to one side. Any of a dozen men might handle those. But this, the Negro business, was an ultimate issue, calling for sustained, resourceful resistance, and it was for this battle Sam had been chosen.

It was all here with him on the train, his life: his wife, son, two daughters, half a hundred home-town supporters who were going up to see him sworn in; all his work, his past, everything he'd ever invested of himself. There wasn't much left back in Morganton; he didn't have any wealth to speak of, or property. But the children were raised, with the boy already practicing law and the girls old enough to get married any time they wanted to. So Sam could pay full attention to being Senator. And he was taking another pay cut to be one; from $16,000 to $12,000 a year.

He lay there now with his heart beating fast as the train slid swiftly through the night, listening for the whistle's roar at whatever cross-roads or madhouse. The next morning, at the train station, he was met by a crowd of three: his sister Jean, a friend she'd brought along, and one reporter. The reporter, as it happened, had a camera, and Sam now fanned out his family to the right and left of him and strode down the empty concrete platform, smiling into the lens. There were worse things than new mornings, new and rational duties. Back in the sidetracked, bannered car, the Senators of the Imagination slept on.

The swearing-in took place after noon. He was escorted down the aisle by Alton Lennon, and came to stand in front of the presiding officer's chair. A young man, maybe two decades younger than Sam, looked down at him, with his big, floppy hand raised as if by a wire, as if it weren't part of the body of this black-browed young Vice President, whose eyes glittered down now over the white smirk. This was the fellow who'd gotten to Congress in the first place by slandering one of the few good friends he'd made in the House, Jerry Voorhis. It was Nixon who made it a Republican Senate, since the head count among the Senators themselves was forty-eight Democrats, forty-seven Republicans, and one independent, who voted with the Republicans.

The trainload of followers was up in the gallery, along with Margaret and the children; as Sam finished the oath cheers came. He looked up and caught sight of his wife. She was in the front row of the balcony, next to the rail, wearing a beige suit with the orange-colored orchid corsage. Her face was surrounded by a broad-brimmed summer straw hat, circleted with an orange sash that matched the flowers. Nothing had changed. First there had been many rivals and then there had been many years. But, in a way, nothing had changed, and now he was here. He took his horn-rimmed glasses out of his coat pocket, put them on, seated himself in the big, leather-covered swivel chair, and signed his name in the Register. When he stood up, the Senators came forward to shake his hand: first Lyndon B. Johnson, the tall, handsome Democratic Minority Leader; followed by bull-like William Knowland, Republican Majority Leader; then his neighbor in the seating arrangements, Olin Johnston of South Carolina; then all the others. Surrounded by well-wishers, Sam took the elevator to the basement and caught the shuttle over to the Old Senate Office Building, where a reception was being held for him. There was plenty to drink, lots of people coming in and his wife and children moving through the room, tanned and talkative.

After a while, he slipped out of the party and walked down to his office alone, went in, and shut the door. This was the room where Clyde Hoey had died. Before Hoey's time, it had been Claude Pepper's, and before that some Florida Senators whose names he didn't know. It had been built in 1909.

Clyde Hoey had died in that big chair, at the desk. Now Sam could have the chair replaced, or sit down. He sat down. He was the Senator now. On the wall behind him was hung a large, colored map of North Carolina, and Sam felt it there, knew the essence of it without having to look at it, having grown up in it, traveled over it, lawyered and judged in it, having known it for fifty-seven years, from the Atlantic Ocean, five hundred miles up to the Blue Ridge Mountains. It was not just that red-headed fellow's state, Wolfe's state, not just flowers and mountains and giants. But a man's state, rational and ordered, a business and industrial state. And Sam, who despised Wolfe and everything he stood for, was its ambassador now, charged with keeping the relations between the races the way they had been since 1898, and charged, too, with seeing that all its industries came off all right in their increasingly obligatory dealings with the national government.

It comforted him, sitting at this massive, old oak desk, to know that Hoey's old staff was still here, working steadily in the rooms behind that tall mahogany door. Chief among them was Jack Spain, who'd been Hoey's administrative assistant ever since 1945, and who knew how to get around on Capitol Hill. Spain was also a wizard at fence-mending back home, a man who, without having to think about it, made sure that every visit by a constituent showed up in a local newspaper, and that the Senator got photographed with all the beauty queens and spelling bee champions from back home.

Sam knew that it wasn't the coastal plain, with its tobacco farms and fishing industry, that ran the state anymore, but the Piedmont. That 200-mile wide strip passed straight through the middle of the state from Virginia to South Carolina — rolling plateau country, ranging in elevation from about 400 feet at Durham to 1500 feet in the rugged hills to the west, a land of red clay (the state supplied almost 100 percent of the nation's kaolin or china clay) and rocks (of which there were none on the coastal plain) — a land where hardwood trees, oak and hickory, began to take over from the omnipresent pines of the coastal plain. It was in the Piedmont that most of the state's manufacturing was done, powered by the electricity old Buck Duke had developed out of the basin of that river, the Catawba, in which Sam had swum as a boy and of whose immense power he was now political mediator.

Since the 1920's the greater part of the state's wealth had come from that power, from factories, and because of the plentiful supply of docile Anglo-Saxon, mostly nonunion labor, North Carolina led the nation in textile manufactures, turning out billions of dollars' worth of cotton and knit goods, silk and rayon products, men's work clothes, woolen goods, cordage and twine. Industrially, the Piedmont was a land of booster superlatives, a golden land of mighty deeds. The Chatham Manufacturing Company, at Elkin, was the world's largest producer of cotton blankets; the Cone Mills, at Greensboro, operated the largest denim and flannel mills in the world. The Blue Bell Company, the nation's largest work-clothing manufacturer, was also in Greensboro, and over at Kannapolis loomed the mighty Cannon Mills, the world's largest producer of towels and other household textiles such as sheets and pillow cases. Sam, alone in his office on this, his first day in the Senate, knew himself to be ambassador of all that mighty industry in a way that left him uniquely free.

Because he wasn't beholden to any of them — the Huffmans, Dukes, Haneses, any of the big manufacturing families in the state. They would not presume to pressure him, or tell him what to do, nor would it ever occur to any of them that they could get him to change his vote by contributing cash to his campaign. For one thing, he would not be needing so very much cash, and for another, they had been watching him for years and knew he believed in business, believed in all that stuff Edward Kidder Graham had preached about the businessman being ipso facto benefactor and patriot. So they would not be pressuring him, because they knew they wouldn't have to.

For the time being, Sam believed, he was secure here, and could do what he pleased. Whether he got to stay or not would depend, in the long run, on the Negro thing and on how well he served the interests of the state's industries.

In terms of "service," Sam would be, primarily, the Senator of North Carolina business and industrial interests. The farmers would have their own Senator in old tobacco-chewing Kerr Scott, who'd be coming up the following January and would look after his own. Sam and Scott could divide the service between them and work together on the ongoing, long-term iterests of North Carolina: the development of the waterways and water power systems, development of highways, and the maintaining of prohibitively high United States import duties on textile imports from foreign countries. And they'd stand together, as all North Carolina Senators had, for a strong national defense, not only because they believed in it for its own sake, but also because of the large complex of military installations in their state, not the least of which was Fort Bragg, near Fayetteville — at the time the largest military installation in the United States — another superlative. In various ways, too, they would seek the federal government's help in developing the other North Carolina industries that were in their infancy now: the electrical-electronic manufacturing; the food producing (notably flour, bread, and butter); the growing chemical industry with its fertilizers, medicines, and cotton-seed oil.

To say nothing of that prime interest of the western third of the state, the forest products industries, which made paper products and lumber, and which was responsible for the state's leading the nation in the production of wooden furniture — another superlative, and one closely tied in with the changing life of Morganton itself, where several furniture plants were in operation, together with a piano factory, a hosiery mill, a shoe factory, an electric lighting fixtures corporation, and a carbon plant — all operating out of the power of the old Catawba. And in the shadow of those blue mountains, which surrounded the town and which still were washed by fresh, clear streams of water, and inhabited still by the white-tailed deer, black bear, wild boar, wildcat, mink, otter, muskrat, skunk, coon, possum, fox rabbit, squirrel, and mountaineers. Sam, guided by Jack Spain and the rest of Hoey's old staff, would be the ambassador in Washington for all these overlapping interests and constituencies: for business, industry, and the military — and for the state's white people.

Of course, a quarter of North Carolina's citizens were not white —

although Sam's office staff, both now and throughout his Senate career, would continue to be all white. And most of the state's citizens were servants of business and industry, rather than proprietors. But Sam believed that the best way to serve North Carolinians was to serve the interests of those who created the wealth that fed them all.

He knew that a position such as his would give rise to charges that he showed favoritism to big business and industry. Indeed, the Raleigh *News and Observer* — which was against him, and would continue to be — had already made such charges. But Sam had expected that, and besides, most of the state's newspapers had been enthusiastic in their approval of his appointment. And there were favorable editorials too — national ones, like the one by Doris Fleeson which said that he, Sam, could be expected to lead the Southerners in the Senate, and inherit the mantle of Walter George, who was seventy-six years old and ill, and at this very moment pacing the office across the hall from Sam and pondering, perhaps, on his retirement.

It was exciting to be the national representative of teeming whole cities, an entire vast busy land. And yet, in all modesty, he could not help feeling that he belonged here. That may have been what he'd had in mind when he said, in his first interview, that the Senate was an honor from which very few men escaped. He may have meant, men like himself. Yes, he thought well enough of himself and there was no one left to put a rein on his self-esteem.

Some would see him as one of a type, in the sense that whooping crane is. The Southern Senator. As William White wrote:

> He has, this archetype one describes here, both a soft voice and manner and underneath a flintlike determination to hang onto power and perquisite. Perpetually he fails utterly to dominate his *national* party at national conventions . . . But almost always he comes near to dominating his party in the Senate — and to a degree the Senate itself — because of the qualities that make him a substantial failure outside the Institution.
>
> While his party has in general maintained a liberal and forward-looking outlook since before the first World War, he has — as has the Senate itself — for the most part kept unchanged his dream of the past.
>
> He has agreed to reforms only slowly and painfully and those who come to him calling for change must carry the most impressive of *bona fides*. He is not effective in any forum (for example, the national convention) of sheer majority rule. For the most part, his whole political life (including his election and re-elections to the Senate) is based upon the choice of *minorities* in position to control the actions of majorities.
>
> He is pre-eminently *the* "Senate man" and this is his great home. It is

not so much that he is so like the Institution as that the Institution is, in fundamentals, so like him. And his degree of at-homeness there, a chamber that he enters from his State with the quiet satisfaction of a man rising from his dinner table to stroll contentedly into his sitting room, is in every way unexampled. He loves what is for this country the center of unaltered traditions. He luxuriates in the dry, underplayed splendor of the place, and in the heavy power that so lightly and casually rests there. He venerates the only place in the country where the South did not lose the war.

Thus Sam, in many ways, was typical of all Senators of that time, from North and South both, in that he was in his late fifties, a WASP, a joiner, a professional man from a small town. But there were ways, too, in which he differed very significantly from even the typical Southern Senator, and these things lay mostly out of sight, glowing with an invisible heat, and fraught with possible future consequences for the nation.

The first difference was that his hatred of tyranny was deeper by far than any Fourth of July oration. This was a hatred that was very extreme in Sam and that, in its genesis, had nothing to do with any theory, Constitutional or otherwise — although he was to become expert in cloaking it with theory. Because his prime directive in life, deeper even than his itch for power, was never, in anything, ever, to allow himself to be violated; and when faced by a man whose prime intention was *to violate,* whether by meddling, or snooping, or malicious bureaucracy, or whatever, he was willing to go to very great lengths to eradicate the source of his displeasure. It went beyond patriotism, or anything so complicated as that. Luckily, perhaps, no tyrant had yet confronted him on what he regarded as an ultimate issue.

The second difference lay in the profundity of his personal isolation — which was beyond that even of Richard Russell, the Georgia Senator, a bachelor who lived alone. Because Sam could express himself, finally, only by his work, and, hence, on important matters was incapable of delegating the research chores that his fellow Senators routinely handed out to someone else to do. Thus, in matters he deemed important he would always be prepared — which is significantly different from merely being briefed.

These two prime differences, taken together, made up the third: he was no good at horse-trading. He was unwilling to squander the hours of work he'd invested in coming to a conclusion, by adopting, for whatever consideration, any other Senator's point of view. And, knowing that he himself could not be lobbied, he was loath to lobby others.

It was unlikely, then, that he would inherit any "mantle" that called for leadership in the Senate. Indeed, in his determination to do work normally delegated to aides, in his unfitness for any sort of lapel-grabbing, in the depth of his contempt for those men he regarded as the tyrants of this world, he was, in a way, unsuited to be a member of the Senate at all, let alone to lead it. In his interior being, he was unique, himself.

It was very quiet in here, quiet.

The door to the hallway opened and Margaret put her head in.

"Are you busy?" she asked.

He stood up, as he always did when she came into the room, as he had always done.

"It's all right," he said.

"I could have gone through the other way."

"No. It's all right."

"Maybe from now on I ought to go through the secretary," she said. She was still, to his eyes, altogether beautiful.

"No," he said. He went over to the big oak desk, picked up a manila folder. "Let's go," he said.

"I thought you wouldn't be bringing work home this first night," she said. Home was a hotel across the park.

"I expect I'd better," he said.

She went with him out into the hall, neither complaining nor asking what was in the folder, mute as always before the everlasting fact of his work. Up ahead of them spectators were spilling out of the Senate Caucus room. A balding head of slicked-back black hair moved sharklike through the crowd while photographers held cameras over their heads and snapped down toward where the head glided.

"There he goes," Margaret said.

"Who?"

"Senator McCarthy. I went in there to watch."

They were at the elevators now. Sam pushed the brass button three times — the signal Senators use — and one appeared. They rode down in the elevator, saying nothing, walked past the guard who said, "Good afternoon, Senator," and out onto the hot, loud sidewalk.

"They had a section reserved for Senators' wives," she said.

"Good." They waited at the curb for the traffic to pass. More of the spectators were thronging out onto the sidewalk behind them.

"I even gave an interview today," she said.

"What did you tell them?"

"Nothing much. That we expected to entertain. Things like that."

Now the traffic stopped and they crossed the street and when they were on the other side began to cut across the vast, smooth lawn under the old trees.

"There are some interesting shindigs at the embassies," he said.

"Really?"

"Oh yes. I expect you could go to a different one just about every night if you wanted to."

In the folder was information about candidates for the U.S. Military Academy appointment that was his gift to give. Thank God for the folder, he thought. Thank God for it. It was inconceivable to him how any man could get through a night without work.

The Senators of the Imagination would be leaving soon, this very evening. All the Morganton people would be leaving soon, going back to the railroad car that had brought them in, and tonight, if he could not sleep, there would be a new ceiling to stare at. Although he thought he could sleep. He thought he could sleep, now.

EMPLOYEES

It was September. Washington's trees were a heavy thick green. It was hot outside, but Sam's reception room here was air-conditioned and pleasant, but there were no windows looking out. Once there had been a window, but then Sam had become famous and they'd built the mail room and blocked it off. I wondered what it must be like for Mrs. Rachel Spears, the receptionist, to sit here all day, every day, lit by nothing except fluorescent lighting, and with no window to look out of. She was sitting at her desk, cutting out clippings, a strikingly good-looking woman in her fifties, who had, by a succession of jobs with North Carolina politicians, put her son through college.

Now the door opened and one of Sam's lawyers came in, a moustachioed young man of twenty-six who had been closest to Sam, closest of all the aides,

*during the past several months. For the past twenty years there had been a
steady procession of eager young men like this.*

*He was jubilant, smiling, hardly able to contain his immense enthusiasm.
So much so that his walk, which was ordinarily a sort of sideways-sliding
Uriah Heep glide, had become a syncopated thing, like a wind-up Confederate
soldier marching to a tin drum.*

"We've beaten the Consumer Protection Bill," he announced.

*Mrs. Spears summoned up an office smile and said, "Well, I know you must
be pleased by that."*

*He juked through the door and into the mail room, and I heard him crowing
it out to the workers in there.*

*Mrs. Spears went on with the newspaper-clipping. She had worked for
Clyde Hoey, Kerr Scott, and Bill Umstead. She had worked for some of the big
ones over in the house, too.*

"It sure is sad, Mr. Dabney," she murmured.

"Leaving?"

*"Yes. You will see what it's like in there," she said, nodding her head toward
Sam's office. "He has all his books down from the shelves, getting ready to move
them to Morganton. He's brought over books from the apartment, too."*

I didn't say anything.

"Sometimes it makes you wonder," she said.

*The clippings she was cutting out had to do with new appointees to various
posts in the North Carolina state government. She was cutting them out for the
case-workers, who needed to know whom to deal with back home. The Republicans were running North Carolina now, and a classmate of mine was
Governor.*

"Do you know what you'll be doing in January?" I asked her.

"Yes," she said. "I was lucky enough to find another position on the Hill."

*I found Sam, as usual, at his desk, working by the excellent natural light
that shone in through the window. For weeks now he'd been leading a
filibuster against the Consumer Protection Bill, giving three- and four-hour
speeches on the floor almost every day. He looked alert; his skin tone was
ruddy, eyes clear. Strewn about his vast office were books, hundreds of them,
on chairs, tables, piled up high on the sofa.*

*During the course of that day's conversation I asked him what he wanted for
his children and he said he wanted them to be happy. He did not say what he
wanted for Mrs. Spears's son, and I did not ask.*

Chapter 15

THE CENTER of the Senate, if it had one, the empyrean bastion of the Christian gentleman, was the cloakroom in back of the floor itself. It was here, at first, that Sam was drawn, the place where his new and insatiable curiosity about his colleagues might begin to be slaked. It was a quiet, marble-solid, high-ceilinged, elegant old place, redolent of stuffed leather chairs, grandfather clocks, and deep, expensive oriental carpets. There were perhaps a dozen phone booths tucked quietly into the walls in woods of rich mahogany. Older pages manned these phones, while younger ones scurried about fetching the Senators. Only you did not notice the pages any more than you did the carpet. Because here, finally, was the refuge for Senators, and only Senators. Here, finally, a man might be alone.

Christian gentlemen, Sam's colleagues were, for the most part — or regarded themselves so — and, indeed, in this cloakroom, with its iced mineral water from Maine and West Virginia, its darkened, faveolate napping rooms off to one side, its quiet authoritative tick of old clocks, one could imagine oneself back in the eighteenth century. Although, in fact, most of these men were, like Sam himself, creatures of the twentieth, Elks, Lions, Rotarians, Moose, Eagles; VFW's elders, deacons, and bar association presidents; 32nd degree Masons, District Attorneys, state legislators, Congressmen, and Governors.

They had served in the war, and could prove it; and if they'd read *Babbitt,* which was unlikely, they hadn't enjoyed it very much, preferring instead patriotic histories or copies of their own speeches.

There were always people outside, in the halls — lobbyists, bureaucrats, and assorted true believers — sending in messages by the pages. But the Senators seldom left this room in response to these summonses; indeed, usually they didn't talk politics among themselves, either, except for the good old stories of days gone by, of other men in ancient times who'd existed expensively in this fine old room as these Senators existed now, retiring to it as a place apart, shut off from staff, tourists, lobbyists, family, and reporters, insulated splendidly from the mad and striving world through which they themselves had striven mightily to reach this eyrie of quiet power.

There were, of course, Senators who did not fit the usual mold, who put out strange, almost disruptive, vibrations. There was, for instance, the young red-headed fellow from Massachusetts, dressed in simple, dark suits costing five hundred or a thousand dollars, and seated in the corner, almost always alone, drumming on his white teeth with the eraser-end of a pencil, absorbed in the *Guardian* or the *Economist* or whatever other foreign paper it was he read, green eyes electric with an intensity that did not come from any county court house or Rotary Club. Startling. A playboy . . . or something else; alien, a being from the future.

Or Carl Hayden, that big, looming old man out of the past, gimlet-eyed and ham-handed, frontier sheriff turned legislator; who'd checked his six-guns back in Tucson before setting out for Capitol Hill in 1912. Who'd been in Congress since then, and whose affinities weren't so much with Dale Carnegie as they were with Wyatt Earp.

Most of the men in this room were comfortable with one another, even when their political differences were very considerable. Take, for instance, that pair standing over by the grandfather clock, swapping stories and basking in a mutuality of good will. The old man, Allen Ellender, squat, curly-haired, crotchety, broad-shouldered and no-necked — a Louisiana confrere of Huey Long's and the last person to talk to him before he was shot — was the most staunch white supremacist from the depths of Dixie. The other fellow, much younger, fresh-faced, and hyperarticulate, was the archliberal, Hubert Humphrey, who was said by some to have succeeded, singlehandedly, in breaking the solid South, which had stood from 1880 to 1948. This man, talking so chummily with Ellender now, had caused the adoption of the civil rights plank that had led to the '48 Dixiecrat bolt of the Democratic Convention. And yet, Ellender liked Humphrey well enough, as many other Southerners did, so that Humphrey was close to being a member of the Inner Club that ran the Senate.

There were three clubs, actually. The Senate itself was one; then there was the Inner Club, which was dominated by, but not limited to, Southerners; and finally there was the Democratic Leader, Lyndon Johnson, a club all to himself, and who would one day run this old place as an autocracy.

The Inner Club was the top of the ziggurat. There was no membership list, no announcement when you made it. But it ran the Senate in those days. It was comprised, by and large, of people with seniority, although that alone didn't qualify a man for membership. Nor did his voting record. No, he had to be the right type, have the right attitudes. It was a mysterious thing, a freemasonry of gentlemen. If you were admitted to the Inner Club, you had immediate access to power: good committee assignments, posh prerogatives, and your opinions were taken into account. Southerners, of course, did tend to be admitted more quickly, and, once in, to dominate the life of all the Senate.

But being a Southerner wasn't enough. For instance, there was the big, tall fellow striding in rapidly now, moving anxiously from Senator to Senator, trying to bum a cigarette, trying to find out what was going on out on the floor: Estes Kefauver of Tennessee. What kept Kefauver out of the Club — and what was going to get Sam in — had something to do with love. You had to love the Senate, its Roman strength, its elegance, traditions, lore, perquisites, order, hauteur, even arrogance; because the Senate, which had been modeled on the House of Lords, was in a way a House of Lords itself. Since its members had to stand for election only once every six years — not every two as on the other side of the Hill — the Senate was not responsive to the shifting raucousnesses of public opinion. It was conservative, tradition-loving; and a man who expected to be taken deep into its workings had to love such a life, with its patrician indifference to the vox populi. Kefauver didn't. He was here running for President, and it didn't matter what he did nor how he voted. He was out of the Club, and would forever remain so.

But Sam was fond of all this; fond of solemnity, slowness, geniality, good will, order. Indeed, he would have been uncomfortable in any place where a gentleman's word wasn't instantly accepted for the absolute truth, where a gentleman's code wasn't in the ascendancy. Forty years ago, at the University of North Carolina, it had seemed to him that this blue marble was a gentleman's world, because everyone he had known then — no matter how rude of manner — had been a gentleman. But he had learned since that it wasn't such a world, that it was, in plain fact, a Yahoo's world (though *run* by gentlemen), and that the places where a gentleman might gather with his own kind were few. So his love of the Senate was genuine, and hence he was clubbable.

Already, now, in 1954, he was close enough to its workings to sense its power. It decided both grand strategy and tone, what would be done on issues of high national importance, and what would be proper procedure within the Senate itself. Recently, it had reached a decision on a matter that had to do with both of these things. Joe McCarthy, and the ism named after him, had gone too far and would be slapped down. There would be no appeal, no chance of discussion. It was settled.

Probably they'd decided it some time early in the spring — men such as Richard Russell, Harry Byrd, Robert Kerr, George Aiken, William Knowland, and John Sparkman. Then, as they so often did those days, they had quietly passed the word to Lyndon Johnson to get the deed done.

Now, Johnson knew that, in this case, some consideration had to be given to public opinion; McCarthy still commanded a vast national constituency, to whom his accusations of communist infiltration in the government seemed reasonable. And so, by applying pressure to Democratic members of McCarthy's Investigating Committee, Johnson had set McCarthy up for the kill. They had seen to it that the Army-McCarthy hearings, that past spring, were televised, and the American public had witnessed the result through its 50,000,000 new television sets, had seen the true McCarthy right down to the sweat on his upper lip. That had whittled down his national constituency enough so that now the Senate might do what it liked; which was to say, what the Club liked. All that was left to do was to pick the firing squad.

Sam stood there in the cloakroom now, talking with William Fulbright of Arkansas, and savoring, as a newcomer, his presence here. He liked Fulbright; whose large, calloused hands were circled at the wrists by soft shirtcuffs elegantly white; whose cosmopolite's purring voice carried in it the plain angularities of the hill country; whose Rhodes Scholar snobberies were rendered less effete by his having been an All-American halfback at his state university.

Now the small shark hove in at a snorkeling walk, glint-eyed, glittering: Bobby Baker, whose brightness of eye announced the advent of the big shark, his master, Minority Leader Lyndon Johnson, who strode in beaming, howdying, shaking hands, pressing shoulders, joking, and guffawing; stopping, falling into sudden seriousnesses, into quick intimate confabs. A moment, just a moment with minuscule Allen Frear of Delaware, his big ham hand grasping down at the little Senator's suit lapel, his other hand flicking a speck of dust away from the jeweled college frat pin Frear always wore there; gorgonizing Frear and moving on . . . going to stand at the edge of a group that was listening to a story told by old Walter George, saying nothing, nodding down deferentially when George looked up at him, and moving on . . . to Thomas Hennings of Missouri, whose raven hair and red face contrasted strikingly with his pressed and spotless white summer suit; standing in close, eyes downcast, listening as Hennings talked, agreeing to whatever it was — standing in closer than anybody else would; Hennings was an alcoholic, and Johnson was always kind to him, and beyond any necessities of partisan politics . . . glancing over at Sam now, sharp-eyed, sizing him up and moving, finally, to Robert Kerr of Oklahoma, a great big man, maybe the smartest man in the Senate, and he and Johnson, both six feet four, standing there face to face a yard apart in serious talk; Kerr the multimillionaire populist, whose coat's lapel also bore a pin, but of no namby-pamby college kid club; it read "Kerr-McGee" — the name of the company he'd made most of the millions with, and no man in his right mind, not even Johnson, would so much as think of reaching out toward that lapel.

Sam was getting ready to leave the cloakroom for the floor when Johnson came over to him and took a position at a sort of middle distance; not so close as he'd stood to Frear or Hennings, not so far as from Kerr; and moving, moving as he talked, in-a-way until the hackles of Sam's resistance rose, out-a-way until he felt his attention wandering; finding, then, exactly the right spot, the place where Sam's aura could be talked through, and settling in there, although still, ever so slightly, moving, in and out, mongooselike, a powerfully handsome man with brown, intelligent eyes. Was the office all right? Sam said it was. Did he have plenty of staff, good staff? Sam said yes. Was there anything he needed? Sam said no.

"I may need you on something" LBJ said to Sam. Then, as quickly as he'd come, he moved away, not saying what it was.

Sam went out on the floor, asked to be recognized, and spoke for a quarter of a minute, in favor of a new shape for peach baskets. It was his first Senate speech, but he wasn't thinking about that anymore.

The next day, he was called to a meeting in the Minority Leader's office, just off the Senate floor. Johnson was there, and Walter George, and Earle Clements of Kentucky, Johnson's Whip. It was a beautiful, quiet old room with arched ceiling, crystal chandeliers, marble fireplace, leather furniture, and a long view down the green Mall to the Washington Monument.

"Walter can't do it and we want you to do it," Johnson said.

"What's that?" Sam said.

"Select Committee — the McCarthy Committee."

"I don't think I am cut out for that," Sam said.

"Why not?"

"For one thing, I don't know anything about it."

"That's all to the good," Johnson said. "Now listen: did you ever make any public statements about McCarthy?"

"Yes. I said I was under the impression that he had been too rough on witnesses. And that I was against taking his chairmanship away from him."

"Is there any reason why you couldn't give him a fair trial?"

"Not that I know of," Sam said.

"We need you to do it," Johnson said. "We've got Edwin Johnson and we've got John Stennis, who was a judge, but we have got to have more judicial experience. And Walter can't do it. He has got too many other things to do."

"All right," Sam said.

But the outcome was already cast; with Johnson having engineered the earlier television exposure; with the censure motion itself having been offered by Ralph Flanders of Vermont, a Republican of impeccable credentials; with the Republican Leader, Knowland, having finally agreed to go ahead with the thing; and with Knowland and LBJ, together, picking the six members, three from each side of the aisle, who would make up the Committee to Investigate the Censure of Senator McCarthy.

It was only the third time in the history of the Senate that such hearings had been held. And if the very fact that the hearings were to take place didn't indicate what was going to happen, the make-up of the committee did. Of the six members, only one, Francis Case of South Dakota, was an outsider; another, Sam himself, was about to be admitted to the Club. The other four — Arthur Watkins of Utah, Edwin Johnson of Colorado, Frank Carlson of Kansas, and John Stennis of Mississippi — were Inner Club members. Though none of them was well known to the American public at large, all four wielded immense power within the Senate itself, and all four were, in point of fact, personally offended by the conduct of McCarthy. So it didn't matter, ultimately, how Sam voted, because there were four Club members in on this one, and the Club was offended. But it wouldn't hurt Sam any if he turned out to be offended, too.

He loved the Senate, loved it. At no other time had life seemed so pleasant. Just to walk around the place, as now, leaving Johnson's office, and moving effortlessly, on legs that seemed young again; walking on color and surrounded by color, with color overhead, too — decorative art creating an entire environment that made it seem that he was walking faster than he actually was; that made him feel, without thinking about it, that what he was doing was vastly important, part of the ages, part of the permanent warp and woof of the Republic. Under his feet, in blue, cream, and red, stretched glazed tiles made in the 1850's by the skilled craftsmen of England's Minton works. On the walls, fanning out from his shoulders as he moved, danced colorful, incredibly varied designs of birds, animals, flowers, and fruits, interlaced with scrollwork, the splendid crop of years of effort by the painter Brumidi, who'd worked in oil and fresco, rendering, amid all the lush scrollery, the medallion portraits of famous Americans, intermingled with battle scenes, landscapes, and panels representing American farming and industry. Overhead, more noble paintings of the history of the Republic. There was no ugly spot, no lacuna; it was like his life up here on this Hill. In deciding on a place to live, Sam had been unable to bear the thought of squandering so many precious, opulent hours steaming through Washington's grimy traffic, and had finally told his wife that they were going to live on Capitol Hill itself. And, indeed they had found a place, an apartment in the Methodist Building, a little one on the second floor, looking out to the Supreme Court, which was just across the narrow side street. It was only five minutes' walk from his office. Ah well. Women were born with broad hips to bear the children of this world, just as men were born with broad shoulders to carry the weight of the world. He had always told his children that, especially the girls. And here, on Capitol Hill itself, in the evening, Sam would muse about these things over the glass of bourbon she brought him. They lived in the Methodist House, from which the church had launched its successful effort, back in the late teens, to get Prohibition passed. Several influential Congressmen had been allowed to make their homes in the Methodist House. It was one of the things the bishops did for Jesus.

A few days later the announcement was made about the membership of the committee. What the newspapers would say was that the members had been chosen by the Vice President, and Nixon was willing to let it seem that way. Immediately after making the announcement from the chair, he led the committee's Senators down the Capitol hallway, grinning and chatting, unctuous, deferential, and accommodating, for all the world like a valet. Nixon took his seat at a table, in the center, with Watkins and Johnson on either side of him, and the rest of them lined up behind him, standing, with Sam on the end, watching. As flash bulbs began popping, the unctuous valet gave way to the decisive executive, the finger shot up from the clumsy hand, admonishing, lecturing. The features became stern. While under it all, the valet's slick little voice nattered on.

In the picture Sam saw on the front page of the New York Times, Nixon looked like a stern father lecturing his children. There had been a lot of North Carolina politicians like that, eager to take credit for everything. What was contemptible, somehow, was the admonishing finger. Because this fellow, Nixon, had no business lecturing anybody on political morality. There was the Voorhis campaign —

slander. Then, the Senate campaign against Helen Gahagan Douglas — slander again. It was the same line of slander McCarthy was going to be censured for now — calling opponents communists, or worse. Nixon was like McCarthy, only smarter, and much more determined. Indeed, it was not unthinkable that he might one day become President. What was it they murmured about Nixon in the cloakroom? Before you enter into a gentleman's agreement with that fellow, just remember you have got to start with two gentlemen.

This was what Joe McCarthy was being tried for — not being a gentleman. Although, of course, it wasn't put like that. Instead, there were five broad categories of charges, ranging from misuse of classified information and a show of contempt in refusing to testify before the Senate Subcommittee on Privileges and Elections on alleged bribes, to bullying a witness, General Zwicker, at the army hearings. But the one that doomed him was the charge that he had abused his colleagues. McCarthy, in his crusade against communists, real and imagined, had charged Senator Guy Gillette with dishonesty, and had called Bill Fulbright "Senator Half-Bright." He had said that Senator Robert C. Hendrickson was "a living miracle — the only human who ever lived so long without brains or guts." And, on more than one occasion, he had referred to Senator Ralph Flanders as "a senile old man," suggesting that someone get a net and take him off someplace.

That was enough right there to get him squashed. In private, you might call a fellow Senator whatever you wished. But in public, you laid off him and you laid off his state, and if you didn't, you were dealt with abruptly. Which is to say, if you uttered such statements on the floor of the Senate, you were gaveled down into your seat; not when you finished your speech, not when you finished your sentence, but then, at once, and it didn't matter how much seniority you had, or whether you were correct in what you said. You were gaveled down, and allowed to continue only when you convinced the chair you would do so "in order," that is, without repeating the violation. You did not question the honor of another Senator.

Sam was especially fond of this rule, because he believed that Congressional debate had to go on, and without such a rule it could not go on. McCarthy, having violated the central injunction, had threatened the dominion of the Christian gentleman. Thus, he would be made to pay.

In the end, it didn't matter that McCarthy brought in an expensive counsel, Edward Bennett Williams. Nor did it matter when McCarthy grabbed the microphone on the first day of the hearings and tried to wrest control of the committee from Watkins, the chairman, who gaveled him down violently into silence. None of it mattered. McCarthy had said those things about his fellow Senators, he did not deny having said them, and that was enough. Sam sat there through the hearings, the junior man at the end of the table, chewing the end of his spectacles, watching mildly as the late summer days passed, watching as McCarthy grew more silent. Only once did Sam question him.

SENATOR ERVIN. In connection with the examination of Senator McCarthy, I may say, as an old cross-examiner myself, that I am very much intrigued by something that occurred very early in the cross-examination of General Zwicker, namely the statement . . . where the Senator made this statement to General Zwicker: "Don't be coy with me, General." Now, I rather admired that, in a way. Personally, I would never have been bold enough to have made that observation on a cross-examination of anybody in the military service, unless perhaps it were a WAVE or a WAC, and I then would have been bold enough to do it only under romantic circumstances, where I was surrounded with soft music, moonlight, and roses; and I am satisfied I never would have been bold enough to give that admonition to either a general or a top sergeant. But I merely want to ask the Senator whether he considered that a proper method of cross-examining a general — that is, General Zwicker.

McCarthy said yes, but Sam was not listening, nor was anybody else, since it was settled now. There were charges, made by McCarthy on "Meet the Press," that Sam had been biased from the start; charges that Sam, on the same program, denied. He found himself somewhat bored with the hearings, in spite of the national notice they brought him. None of the publicity would do him any good, anyway; he wasn't going anywhere in national politics.

The committee report, which was unanimous, recommended that McCarthy be rebuked for contempt of the Privileges and Elections Subcommittee, and for abuse of five fellow Senators and General Zwicker. It said that McCarthy had committed a "grave error" and "manifested a high degree of irresponsibility," and called his actions "contemptuous, contumacious and denunciatory," "highly improper," and "reprehensible." There was to be a full Senate vote, but this was the end of it so far as Sam was concerned.

Chief among the new friends that Sam made at this time was John Stennis of Mississippi, his fellow member of the McCarthy censure committee. Slim, hard, cat-eyed Stennis, like Sam himself, had been a lawyer, state legislator, and superior court judge. Although over-shadowed, as almost everyone else was, by Richard Russell, Stennis enjoyed great respect in the Senate because of his personal integrity, immense charm, and informed devotion to national defense. Like Sam, he considered himself the representative of the business and professional interests back home, and believed that any Negro who wanted to better himself ought to be obliged — as all white men were — to achieve that result by hard work. In short, he had, to Sam's way of thinking, correct views, no small qualification for a friend. Because Sam, while very fond of talk, had no wish for the kind of talk that called into question fundamental philosophical issues. No, he had settled all those to his satisfaction forty years ago.

Then there were the Evanses, Ney and May, North Carolinians who lived up in northwest Washington. Evans, too, was a judge, sitting at the United States Court of Claims, a person who didn't need to in-trude any subtle, greedy pressures into a social relationship. Besides, Sam felt that May Evans, a brisk, cheerful, woman, was good for Margaret. She took her over and kept her busy at all sorts of clubs, got her out of the small apartment.

Henry Gatton, too, one of his aides, was turning out to be as much a friend as anyone else, a companion he often took along when he set out in his 1950 Plymouth to tour the Civil War battlefields of Virginia. He and Gatton had started out below Petersburg and were working their way northward, a battlefield at a time.

This interest was due in part to the influence of Senator Richard Russell, a man whose knowledge of military history was broad, profound, and constant. Russell wasn't exactly Sam's friend, in the sense that Stennis, the Evanses, and Jack Spain were, because the Georgia Senator, for all his amiability, wasn't intimate with anyone, really. Russell lived alone in an apartment downtown, and read a great deal — mostly history and biographies, although he managed, also, to keep up with the state and national news, as well as sports, which gave him useful topics for conversation and helped him keep would-be friends at a comfortable distance. Russell truly was what Sam himself most wished to be: an aristocrat and stoic, a man of immense charm, a kind of king, whose control over himself was absolute and attractive.

So it wasn't exactly a friendship; Russell himself did not desire such a relationship, and, too, Russell's power in the Senate was such as to make such overtures from others seem a trifle suspect. Because Russell could reward whom he wished. Once the Democrats came back to the majority, he would be Chairman of the Armed Services Committee, ranking only behind Carl Hayden on Appropriations. When Walter George retired he would be Chairman of the Southern Caucus. His voice, more than any other, was decisive on matters of national security and on how a hundred billion dollars were to be spent every year. In paramount issues, he would control eighteen Southern votes — Sam's among them — and six of these eighteen belonged to the chairmen of the Senate's most powerful committees.

Sam admired Russell, and believed that of all the men on the national scene it was he who was most qualified to be President. Although, in the fifties, a white Southerner had about as much chance for the presidency as a Negro from Peru. And this permanent exclusion from the highest office gave to Russell an isolated, Byronic aura, which made him, to Sam's taste, very near to a hero.

It was a splendid thing, Sam thought, to be a member of the Senate, a peer of some of the finest men on earth. Very often, it seemed, a certain optimism was justified. A McCarthy could arise, but he could be put down, too. A man could go through dark days, as he himself had, and yet come out of them sound and smiling. And, while some of the younger generation weren't what one hoped they might be, others managed to live up to honorable expectations. Take the boy, Sam III: hadn't he been named, just this month, Chairman of the Democratic Party in Burke County? And couldn't one look with some hope toward a future in which the state, and perhaps even the country, would be run by young men like that? Oh, yes. Life was interesting, various.

Then Bill Umstead died. This happened just a few days before the floor debate on the McCarthy censure motion. And at about this time Sam began to experience a sense of anger toward McCarthy, which, perhaps, was not entirely unrelated to the death of his old friend.

Umstead had been a Christian gentleman in the literal sense; a gentle man who had managed to serve his state and country diligently for many years without indulging in personal abuse. So when Sam took the floor against McCarthy, after coming back from Umstead's North Carolina funeral, he was not in the most charitable of moods, and if he had any hopes besides the desire that the censure vote would be overwhelming, it was that McCarthy would take him on in floor debate. All the Senators came to their desks to sit and listen to Sam's speech — a rare occurrence in the twentieth century. In the end, McCarthy was "condemned," 67 to 22, for abusing the Senate and its committee, the Zwicker count having been trimmed. Thus he was convicted, finally, of not being a gentleman.

When Nixon announced the vote, at 5:03 P.M. on December 3, there was loud laughter from the floor, emanating from a group of McCarthy's supporters, including Senators Jenner, Malone, Welker, and Bridges. McCarthy himself, his arm in a sling, smiled palely.

Bridges, addressing the chair, asked if the word "censure" appeared in the resolution. When told it did not, he said, "Then it is not a censure resolution" and laughter broke out once more from the group.

"The resolution does concern the conduct of the junior Senator from Wisconsin," Nixon said. "The interpretation must be that of the Senator or any other Senator."

Sam held his peace. Now Fulbright was on his feet, reading from a dictionary, while Jenner was bellowing out, amid guffaws, "Let's do a retake."

But there would be no getting around it. McCarthy had become the Senate's equivalent of a nonperson. In the days that followed, when he rose in the Senate to speak, there would be a manifestation of ostentatious disorder; other Senators would shuffle papers, or talk to one another loudly, as if the man were not there. For Sam, however, the censure was enough, and he did not participate in the repeated public humiliations of McCarthy. Instead, he went out of his way to be kind to the fellow.

Sam was at home in the Senate, liked it, and because the Senate liked him, too — at least the Club did — he got some choice committee assignments: Armed Services, Government Operations, and Interstate and Foreign Commerce. He'd wanted a seat on the

Judiciary Committee. It was there, he knew, that the Negro battle would have its storm center. But he could wait for that one. He wasn't in a hurry, and neither was the Senate. He became fond of going into the Senate barbershop for his daily shave, of having a hot towel patted in place about his pink cheeks, of deference. Capitol Hill, even more than Morganton, was his home now. One day he wandered into a meeting of the Armed Services Subcommittee on Civil Defense. It wasn't his subcommittee — his was meeting elsewhere at the time — but he was hungry, and said out loud, to no one in particular, "I think I'll just stay and have my lunch." And, seating himself at the end of the table, he extracted it from the paper bag he was carrying, and sat there munching his cupcake and drinking his chocolate milk shake through a straw. When he was done, he strolled out, casually, to find his own subcommittee. He was at home, everywhere, on the Hill.

THE SMILE OF REASON

There it loomed, a huge, anonymous high-rise perched on a raw hill overlooking twelve-lane U.S. Route 95. This was across the Potomac River on the Virginia side.

There were no stores, children, pedestrians, or dogs, and the sidewalks had that rough, corrugated look of never having been walked on. There were no faces in any of its windows, and the only indication that this was, indeed, the Episcopal Retirement Home was a smudge of red on a small, tin church logo nailed up against its towering wall.

The lobby was vast and empty, except for a woman at a card table working on a jigsaw puzzle. It was a large jigsaw puzzle and she was not quite done with it and did not look up when I came in. Near her, ranged up and down the room, were other tables, also with jigsaw puzzles on them.

Presently May Evans appeared, a comely, smiling woman of seventy-three, dressed in tight-fitting pink silk slacks and a pink jacket and high heels. Her eyes, which were large and blue, looked directly into mine when she spoke. She led me down the corridor to the elevators.

Her apartment was a small, one-bedroom affair, expensively decorated, with many books, and a view from the picture window. We were on the ninth floor and could see for miles: the Washington Monument, the Capitol, the Jefferson

Memorial, and the rest of the Washington skyline, and, between us and it, the flat, snaking brown of the Potomac.

She made me a drink, bourbon in a silver goblet, lots of it, on ice.

"It is a good view, isn't it?" she said.

"Yes." There was a bust on the windowsill. Voltaire.

May Evans, Margaret Ervin's best friend, had earned a master's degree in English and had taught at the Women's College in Greensboro, North Carolina. Becoming bored with that, she'd left the academic life, abruptly, to become active in politics, organizing the Young Democratic Clubs throughout the state. After her marriage to a young lawyer, she'd continued to be active, and had wielded considerable power in North Carolina; had been, while young, the confidante of Ehringhaus, Hoey, and Umstead. Later, she'd come to Washington, and made friends with Mrs. Franklin Delano Roosevelt. After having held high positions in government, most notably with the Department of Health, Education and Welfare, she'd retired a decade ago.

"I suppose you're rather critical of the Senator when it comes to his attitude toward women," she said.

"No mam."

"You know he fought the Equal Rights for Women Amendment."

"Yes." It was good bourbon.

"Sam thinks a woman's place is in the home; that the husband should rule."

"That sounds pretty good to me," I said.

"I'll bet you're against women having the vote, too."

This was true. I devoted my attention to the bourbon, the view, and Voltaire's smile of reason.

"Ask me some questions," she said.

So I did, and got about what I expected: the speech I'd heard from two or three score assorted aides and family. "A great man — Constitutional scholar — good thing for this country — Watergate — because Nixon — potentially a tyrant — of course the position on civil rights — which most people don't understand — really he's been consistent all along — because what he wants is less government — " After a while the words faded and there was only the tune of them.

Ney Evans had died the year before. When she spoke of him, tears came to her eyes. His birthday was the same day as the Ervins' wedding anniversary, and for years the couples had celebrated together. Now May brought out a manila folder and read me some of Ney's poems. Every year he had written a new one for the celebration.

"We moved here about six months before Ney died," she said. "The Ervins didn't want us to do it. We had a lovely house. And they wanted us to wait, at least until they went back to North Carolina. But you know, there comes a time."

I didn't say anything.

"Sam didn't drink when he first came up here," she said.

I told her that was news to me.

"Here you have to," she said.

I didn't say anything.

"You have to here," she repeated. "There has to be some way to relax."

I told her I knew what she meant.

"You know they have condemned some of my property down in North Carolina," she said. "They were running big power lines over the mountains. And they just condemned this whole mountain of mine, cut down the trees, threw the towers up — all without consulting me or even telling me. It's outrageous. I have to go down there and straighten it all out. But I've been so busy. I just got back from Europe, you know."

May walked me back to the elevator. When I got to the lobby it was no longer empty. The old folks had come down from their rooms and apartments and were going, very slowly, into the dining room. Some of them were moving along with the aid of walkers. The woman at the table was still working on the jigsaw puzzle and did not look up.

May Evans was the Ervins' best friend in Washington. Their younger friend.

Chapter 16

Just as he'd expected, the North Carolina Republicans fielded no opponent against him in the '56 election, and Sam was set for another six years. He began to develop a regular routine, but not before he'd pacified the women in the family. The old apartment was good enough for him, with a desk to work at, a place to throw that cone of light on the desk, an overstuffed chair with a lamp behind it, to throw the light over his shoulder. So he got another apartment in the Methodist House. He let his daughters pick out the furniture, and encouraged Margaret to bring up her collection of delicate old glass with its pale tints of rose.

He settled down to the work, enjoying approximately the same standard of living his stenographers did, adhering still, with strong love, to the '50 Plymouth. He didn't even own a television set. At noon, Margaret would come over and have lunch with him in the Senate dining room. Later, for supper, he would take her to the clean, decently run cafeteria in the basement of the Methodist Building, where a good, wholesome dinner could be bought for about a dollar. In the evenings, if she seemed to be restive, there was always an embassy party to take her to, a chance to enjoy a few drinks and to tell some down-home stories, to listen to some words suavely whispered to his private ear by an ambassador or attaché — then a quick, cheap cab ride back to the apartment, where Sam would work on into the night. The work was fascinating, and there was so much to do.

He was getting twenty-five to eighty letters a day. A Greek fellow in Wilmington had some immigration problem and wanted to stay in the United States, so Sam drew up a special bill in the man's behalf — the first of hundreds of bills he'd write — and the thing was passed, and reported in the papers back home. A little North Carolina boy had leukemia and might be helped by being admitted to the National Institutes of Health. Sam made the arrangements. He began recording a weekly radio show, which Spain got aired on most of the state stations. He wrote a regular column for the state newspapers. Or had an aide do it. He accepted whatever speaking invitations came to him from down home, and in the space of a little more than six months gave talks at:

> American-Atlantic Progressive Association
> North Davidson Spring Festival
> Duke Faculty Club
> Davidson Electric Membership Cooperation
> Masonic picnic
> Winston-Salem Executive Club
> Armed Forces Day Celebration at Fort Eustis
> Western Carolina College (where he received an L.L.D.)
> Mocksville Masonic picnic
> Jaycees banquet
> Kiwanis Club
> Moose Association
> Kinston Armory dedication
> Young Democratic Club rally
> Catawba Fair Grounds fish fry
> Convention of State Employees
> Barbers Association of North Carolina
> Gardner Webb College (twice)
> Textile banquet
> Rural Electrification Association
> Bethesda Presbyterian Church Homecoming
> Burke Methodist Church
> North Carolina League of Municipalities
> Knights of Pythias
> First Presbyterian Church
> Veterans of Foreign Wars

Hartnett County Centennial Celebration
State Bar Convention
Duke University Dad's Day
Hendersonville Kiwanis Club
Lions Club
United Daughters of the Confederacy
Morganton Man of the Year banquet

The places he did not speak were notable, too. He did not speak, say, to labor unions, or to the NAACP, or to the Americans for Democratic Action. No, he spoke to his own, and loved it. When he was out of places to speak in North Carolina, or didn't have the time to drive down there in the Plymouth, he headed out across the Potomac, to nearby Arlington or Alexandria, to speak over there. Rarely, anymore, did he have to think very much about the speeches, having learned, long ago, the two prime rules: you speak to your own, and you tell them what they want to hear.

And if there were those who regarded him as an old, kindly, julep-drinking, anecdote-mongering court house lawyer — what was that to him? This was what he'd chosen, long ago, to seem to be. Indeed, the way he looked and acted stood for a certain point of view, and might even prove useful when the Civil Rights fight began to erupt, as it was bound to. Becaue, to Sam's way of thinking, the *Brown v. the Board of Education of Topeka* Supreme Court decision was merely the first salvo of a war. Now, progressing through 1955, this war was quiescent, like that false lull in France in 1940, before the blitzkrieg.

In the meantime, there were the usual Senatorial things to be done: case-work, the routine announcement of the federal government contracts awarded in North Carolina, customary presiding over the Senate, a chore traditionally assigned to freshmen Senators. All this was easy — he could always lean over and have the Senate parliamentarian whisper to him what to do — and looked good to the home-folk tourists in the gallery. Already, editorialists back in North Carolina were suggesting that he ought to be the Democratic vice presidential nominee in '56.

Sam traveled through North Carolina, taking the mild line on the desegregation issue, laying low. The Supreme Court's decision was unconstitutional, he said. It interfered with the most fundamental of human rights, the right to choose one's own associates. It had been made by men of narrow legal background, he told his audiences again and again, and emphasized that no member of the Supreme Court had ever served as a judge of a court of general jurisdiction, either state or federal. Nor had any member of the Supreme Court ever served as an appellate court judge. This was the mild line: throughout North Carolina and the rest of the South, harsher positions were being taken. And on Capitol Hill, too.

Arrangements were made for Sam to go to Nevada, to watch the detonation of the atomic bomb. When, at the last moment, the event was called off, he was able, instead, to drive down to Morganton and pick up the Rotary Club's Man of the Year Award, which was presented at a dinner in the Rainbow Grill, where he spoke to a capacity crowd of 225.

Thus the year passed in speeches and ordinary work. Sam sought, and got, federal relief funds for North Carolina because of the damage done by Hurricane Hazel. He lobbied, successfully, for a federal fish hatchery near Ashville. And when Lyndon Johnson was felled by a heart attack, he was taken into the periphery of Democratic leadership, as Assistant Whip. There were even days when one might believe what the reporter had said about the mantle of Walter George.

One afternoon, that old Senator announced his retirement, and Sam's office was filled with reporters who'd come across the hall, to use his phones, to file the story. The next week Sam announced that he would be a candidate for re-election in 1956. He said it was something he'd promised Umstead, although he needed no urging or sacred promises to the past to confirm his love for the Senate.

But most of all, Sam wanted the federal government to keep its hands out of the state — or, rather, to remove those hands once they'd dropped the money in. There was too much federal government control already, he told his audiences, too much interference by outsider bureaucrats who lived, voteless, in Washington and had never seen the workings of popular government. The Founding Fathers, he was fond of telling those audiences, hadn't intended to set up an efficient government.

He was fond of saying, too, that he didn't need any public opinion poll to tell him how the voters felt back home. "I am from North Carolina," he would say, "and when I want to know what North Carolinians want, I just go in my room and shut the door and try to figure out what I want."

There was no one to challenge him when he said things like this. In North Carolina, unlike New York, the intellectuals of the fifties knew enough to stick to Geoffrey Chaucer and the binomial theorem. And from the point of view of many North Carolina politicians, there wasn't a single Chapel Hill intellectual who had the slightest notion of what was going on in state politics, anyway — although it was true that there were some Kerr Scott supporters in Chapel Hill who'd been stirred up by the young fellow, Terry Sanford, Scott's campaign manager, into "taking an active role." Well, Chapel Hill intellectuals had been muttering like that for years, but they tended to quiet down when the grub was thrown in the trough. Sam saw to it that the University got some federal funds for new dormitories, and continued to express the highest respect for the school and its faculty.

By now, the 1955 Supreme Court decision had come down, defining how the 1954 school desegregation decision was to be implemented. It said that the lower courts must require "a prompt and reasonable start toward full compliance," so that desegregation could proceed "with all deliberate speed."

Bad as this decision was, from Sam's point of view, it was still not so harsh as what Eisenhower wanted: that local school authorities be required to present desegregation plans to the federal district courts. In any case, some sort of struggle was impending, because Eisenhower, whatever he thought about desegregation, wasn't going to tolerate open defiance of any Supreme Court ruling. But when Eisenhower joined Lyndon Johnson as a heart attack victim, it seemed that, for the time being, the fight might be kept out of Congress.

In November 1955, Sam's grandson — Samuel James Ervin IV — was born, and Sam bought him a membership in the Democratic Party. Later he and Margaret went down to Morganton to watch the boy being baptized in the First Presbyterian Church; he was the tenth or eleventh generation Ervin, depending on how you counted, to be a Presbyterian, the sixth or seventh to be a Democrat.

It was about this time that T. Lamar Caudle, who'd found Joe's body in 1945, was getting ready to go to jail, having been convicted, along with Harry Truman's appointments secretary, Matthew Connolly, of "influence peddling." And Sam, upon reviewing the evidence, came to the conclusion that Caudle was innocent. All the man had done, he believed, was what prosecutors frequently do — recommend the commutation of a felon's sentence on the basis of the man's having a heart condition. After all, Sam reasoned, the judge in the case hadn't been obliged to act on the recommendation. And so he wrote to Eisenhower himself, in an effort to get Caudle pardoned. But Caudle was sent to jail anyway. Well, Sam had done his best, and did not brood about the matter.

The month after the birth of Sam Ervin IV, the Negro fight erupted on another front, down in Montgomery, Alabama, where a northern-educated preacher named Martin Luther King, Jr., was causing trouble about riding on the buses. There were arrests, "demonstrations," and early in December, a boycott of the buses began.

All this would be sure to come to the Senate sooner or later. Soon Sam would be defending the old green world he had not been able to escape. And that he had learned to love the way Bobby Jones loved golf or Ty Cobb loved baseball. Because he played it so well, that world; so that his love of the old way was in large part nostalgia for old victories.

About this time, a rookie policeman, patrolling the empty moonlit ribbon of route 70 in North Carolina, saw Sam zooming up the highway in excess of the speed limit, ran him down, rebuked him, and haled him into Iredell County Court for speeding. By the time the hearing was held, however, Sam and the Chrysler were elsewhere. His attorney went into court and paid the fine. Sam himself, to his own way of reckoning, was attorney for the whole state, including the rookie policeman, and could not be spared. Soon now, certainly, the civil rights battle would begin.

Down in Montgomery, the Negroes, operating out of an old red brick Baptist church, which stood right across the street from the state Capitol Mall itself, were continuing their demonstrations, in spite of the fact that their leader, King, had been jailed. At the same time, calls for massive resistance to the desegregation ruling began to arise throughout the South. Virginia, at the behest of Harry Byrd, passed a law that required the closing of any school complying with federal orders to integrate. And now, early in the year, Senator George called together the Southern Caucus in his office. Acting for the last time as the leader of the Southerners, the old man appointed a committee to draw up a statement of the Southern position, a manifesto. This committee would consist of Richard Russell, John Stennis, and Sam Ervin.

It was clear from the start that Russell was going to write the thing. He was to be the new leader of the Southerners, and the position the South took on the Supreme Court's decision would be the one that he, personally, judged to be the most defensible. There were a few pro forma meetings in Russell's office, where he told Stennis and Sam what he was going to say. Sam's contribution, such as it was, consisted of toning down the language, cutting out some of the "maliciously"s and the "tyranny"s.

This Southern Manifesto, signed by nineteen Senators and eighty-two Representatives and made public on March 12, 1956, set the tone for Southern resistance. It called the Supreme Court decisions "contrary to the Constitution," a "clear abuse of power," and spoke of "outside agitators." It said that "the Supreme Court, with no legal basis for such action, undertook to exercise their naked judicial power and substituted their personal political and social ideas for the established law of the land." While steering away from any call to law-breaking or violence, it called for the employment of all means to bring about a reversal of the Supreme Court's decision. The effect of this document was to make the prestige of the Southern Congressional leaders the nucleus around which white resistance to integration might crystallize.

This immediately became an issue in the Democratic primary in North Carolina, where Winston-Salem Mayor Marshall C. Kurfees had announced against Sam. Kurfees chose the manifesto as the focus for his attack, saying that Sam might have put his talents to better use in helping to figure out how the state was going to comply with the orders of the Supreme Court. It was hardly the way to win any election in North Carolina in 1956, and Sam, knowing this, did very little campaigning that spring, preferring to remain in Washington, where the civil rights battle was about to begin.

The Administration's bill came down in April. It called for a Civil Rights Commission, a Civil Rights Division in the Justice Department, and laws protecting Negro voting rights. This measure passed the House, substantially as it had been proposed by the Eisenhower Administration. In the Senate, however, the full Judiciary Committee, which was dominated by a coalition of Southerners and Northern conservatives, refused to report on the bill, and all attempts to bring it directly to the floor failed.

But the debate would not stay quiet for long. The national conventions were coming up soon, and not least among the issues to be settled by them was the question of civil rights planks. By now — late summer of 1956 — Sam had overwhelmed Kurfees in the Democratic primary, beating him in every one of North Carolina's 100 counties. And had been, in effect, re-elected. True, the Republicans were going to field a candidate against him in the November general election, but they had nowhere near the strength to mount a serious threat, not yet.

Then his mother died. She was ninety-one years old. He went to the funeral, accepted the commiserations, answered the condolence letters, and went on about his business. Ninety-one. He remembered her pacing lithely on the front porch, young and crimson-cheeked, waiting for his father to come home from the mountain courts. She'd been born in 1865, the year the War Between the States was supposed to have been ended but hadn't been. Reconstruction was supposed to have been ended, too, and hadn't been. Sam knew how much his mother had suffered because of Reconstruction. And his father, too — his father, even more.

He went to the Democratic Convention in Chicago, served on the Platform Committee, and did what he could to tone down the language of the civil rights plank. But the committee was dominated by Northern liberals, and the plank, while rejecting "all proposals for the use of force" in carrying out the Supreme Court decisions, recognized those decisions as law, and pledged to continue efforts to eliminate illegal discrimination in voting, education, and employment. Indeed, they came close to passing a civil rights plank that would have inserted a pledge to "carry out" the Supreme Court decisions, and would have called for federal legislation to secure and protect civil rights.

Apparently, however, the North Carolina voters felt the way Sam did about the issue. In the May primary, he had spent a bit less than $479 to win the senatorial nomination. Now, in the fall, to get elected over the Republican for another six-year term, he put out just $4,000. In each case, campaign contributions exceeded expenses, and he returned the extra amounts to contributors.

Back in Washington, he became a member of a special five-man Armed Services subcommittee, headed by Stuart Symington, which was studying whether America was strong enough to survive an atomic attack and retaliate against Russia with its own bombs. They

Sam Ervin, about four years old. *Sam J. Ervin, Jr.*

Sam's father, Samuel J. Ervin, Sr.
Sam J. Ervin, Jr.

Sam's mother, Laura Powe Ervin.
Sam J. Ervin, Jr.

Margaret Bell, aged seventeen.
Sam J. Ervin, Jr.

A Morganton outing, summer of 1916. Margaret Bell, perched on the rear fender, is looking down at Sam, who is clinging to the running board. Sam's sister Catherine steers, and another sister, Laura, is behind the hood. *Sam J. Ervin, Jr.*

'17 (AB)

1   "Like Midas, he has that magic touch which makes everyone he meets his friend; and consequently he is liked by all."

From Morganton ... Assistant Editor Magazine ... Class Historian ... Di Society ... President International Polity Club ... Vice-President Class ... German Club, Mu Delta Phi, Sigma Upsilon.

Sam, as he appeared in the 1917 University of North Carolina yearbook. *University of North Carolina Alumni Association Photo*

Sam during the First World War. *Sam J. Ervin, Jr.*

Sam Ervin, as Representative
from Burke County in the 1923
North Carolina Legislature.
Sam J. Ervin, Jr.

Sam Ervin, as a North Carolina Superior
Court Judge, c. 1939.
Sam J. Ervin, Jr.

Ervin and his family at the Union Station train platform on June 11, 1954 —
the day of his swearing-in as a Senator. From left: his daughters, Laura and
Leslie, Sam and Margaret Ervin, Mrs. Sam J. Ervin III, and his son, Sam J.
Ervin III.

Vice President Richard M. Nixon swears in Sam J. Ervin, Jr., as a Senator. The Senior Senator from North Carolina, Alton A. Lennon, center, looks on. *Wide World*

The Vice President sets a publicity photo taken with the just-appointed McCarthy Censure Committee. From left, back row: Francis Case, R-South Dakota; Frank Carlson, R-Kansas; John Stennis, D-Mississippi; Ervin. Front row, left to right: Arthur V. Watkins, R-Utah, Committee Chairman; the Vice President and Edwin Johnson, D-Colorado. *UPI*

Sam, Billy Graham, and Lyndon Johnson, c. 1959. *Sam J. Ervin, Jr.*

Ervin pounds table during battle with Robert F. Kennedy at the Senate Judiciary Committee's civil rights hearings, July 25, 1963. To Kennedy's right is Burke Marshall.   *UPI*

John F. Kennedy and Sam Ervin at the White House in August, 1962. *Sam J. Ervin, Jr.*

Sam and his classmate Herman Baity at the 50th reunion of the Class of 1917.
University of North Carolina Alumni Association Photo

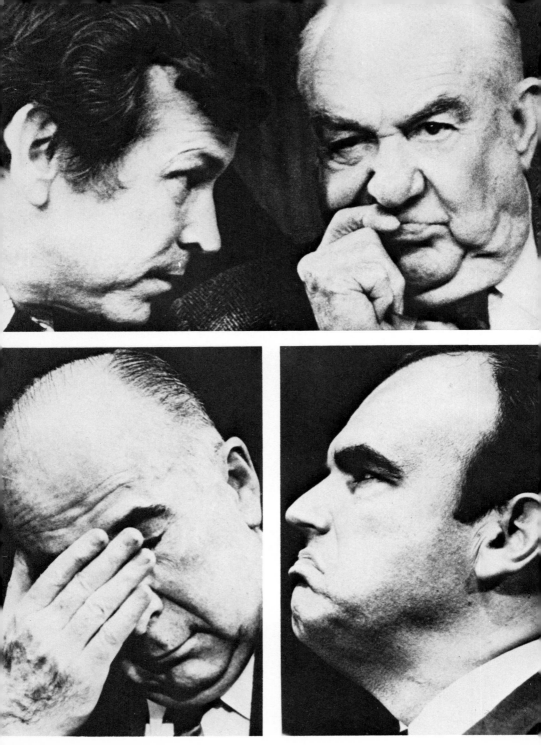

Top: Senator Howard Baker and Sam Ervin confer during the Watergate Hearings, 1973. *Bottom:* John Mitchell and John Ehrlichman on the stand. *UPI (by Frank Cancellare)*

During the Watergate hearings, Sam Ervin checks a Bible quote with his deputy
chief counsel, Rufus Edmisten.   *UPI*

Sam and Margaret Ervin on the campus of the University of North Carolina, March, 1973. *Steve Northup* © TIME

Sam Ervin, in retirement, holds up the shingle that hung outside his office during the years when he practiced law in Morganton. *UPI*

were even discussing the use of missiles that would fire all the way from America to Russia, across the North Pole. A strange world. When Sam had been the age his grandson was now, there had been no airplanes, and the only big explosion you expected to hear was when some moonshiner's still exploded. Things changed fast, and people were willing to pay for some link with the past. Sales of Confederate flags, made in Japan, were up to 140,000 a month.

The new year, 1957, began with the Democrats in control of the Senate, and LBJ, who had recovered from his heart attack, in control of the Democrats, and determined to see to it that some sort of civil rights legislation got through. Some bill, in some form, was almost bound to be passed; everyone knew this. The only question was what kind, and the Southern strategy from the beginning was to water down, as far as possible, whatever bill the liberals succeeded in presenting.

A liberal, to Sam's way of thinking on this issue, was anyone who wanted any civil rights legislation whatsoever, although he knew, as a matter of practical politics, that the Senate was divided in three on the question. There were the Southerners, who wanted no legislation; a small group of liberals — men such as Humphrey and Paul H. Douglas — who insisted on drastic legislation in favor of Negro rights in voting, schools, housing, and public accommodations; and a broad, moderate majority condemned to mediating between the two and resigned to passing a bill that wouldn't offend anybody too much.

This time the Eisenhower Administration introduced a bill designed to enforce the Southern Negroes' right to vote by empowering the Attorney General to seek court injunctions against anyone who had deprived, or was about to deprive, any person of any civil right. Those disobeying such an injunction would be subject to contempt proceedings, under federal law.

Traditionally, of course, there were two kinds of contempt proceedings, civil and criminal. A civil contempt proceeding was one in which the offender, when jailed by the court for refusing to comply with its order, could release himself at any time by doing what the court told him to do. A criminal contempt proceeding, on the other hand, was one in which the offender was punished because he had breached public order by defying the authority of the court. Civil contempt proceedings were always decided by the judge acting alone, without a

jury, and, up until 1957, many criminal contempt cases were, too —
especially those in which the federal government brought the suit
resulting in the court order that was defied.

Much of the 1957 civil rights debate was to center on this: the
question of how contempt proceedings were to be heard. In a civil
contempt case the offender always carried the key in his pocket, and
didn't need a jury of his peers to help him get out. But criminal
contempt cases arising out of civil rights legislation, the Southerners
argued, should be heard by juries, because it would be unconstitutional to subject a man to a jail term without giving him the right
to be tried by a jury of his peers. Before the Senate could get to this
fine point, however, the matter of whether *any* civil rights bill would
be reported out had to be settled first.

One of the leaders of the Senate liberals was Thomas Hennings of
Missouri, whose great-grandfather had been the largest slave-holder
in the State of Missouri, and whose grandfather had served with
distinction in the Army of the Confederacy. Hennings — now that
the Democrats were back in power — was chairman of the Constitutional Rights Subcommittee of the Judiciary Committee. And
Sam, who had been appointed to the Judiciary Committee, just as he
wished, came to take the seat at the end of the table in Hennings' subcommittee. He immediately entered into vigorous clashes with Attorney General Herbert Brownell, who'd come down to testify on the
bill's behalf, and with Hennings himself, who tried, without success, to
make Sam cut short his cross-examination of Brownell, a process that
took three entire days of hearings. The result in Hennings' subcommittee was predecided, Sam knew, because the liberals dominated it.
But for Hennings, who had the white suit, who had the manners and
the Southern gentleman's background, there was no excuse. It was
an ominous spring. Sam took time out from the hearings to go to the
Cherry Blossom Festival, where he crowned his daughter Laura a
Princess of Cherry Blossoms, and returned lugubriously to do battle
with Hennings. It was baffling, strange, that a Southerner would act
like that.

When the civil rights bill was finally reported out to the full Judiciary Committee, which was chaired by James O. Eastland of Mississippi and ruled by a coalition of Southerners and Northern conservatives, Sam took part, along with the others, in blocking it. But

Senate Minority Leader William Knowland of California, working with Douglas of Illinois, managed to by-pass the Judiciary and bring the bill out to the floor. Thus, the full Senate would hear and debate the civil rights bill of 1957. And so the first round of the battle ended, a delaying action in which Sam had done much talking, questioning, and objecting in the committee hearings, but in which the real moves were being worked out, behind the scenes, among Richard Russell, Lyndon Johnson, and Dwight Eisenhower.

Whether Johnson was, as some were saying, deserting the South in order to run for the presidency in 1960, or whether his efforts in behalf of a compromise civil rights bill sprang from a sincere concern for the plight of the Negro, was immaterial to the Southerners. Whatever his motives, he was a powerful and determined man, and had to be dealt with. This was Russell's job. Sam's job, in the overall Southern strategy, was to provide a sophisticated, high-toned Constitutional rationale for rejecting the legislation, so as to drum up enough support, both in and out of the Senate, to force the watering-down of the bill, especially the hated Title III, which empowered the Attorney General to step in and initiate suits in behalf of anyone who had been deprived of his civil rights.

In his research — and, unlike every other Senator, he did most of it himself — Sam happened upon an 1866 federal statute, still on the books, still law (42USC1993), empowering the President to use the army to "aid in the execution of judicial process . . . and force the due execution of the provisions" covered by the statute. He began now, on the Senate floor, to draw a graphic picture of Southern schools being integrated by bayonet-wielding federal troops.

He was aware, all the time, that he was being used by Russell for tactical purposes, but, given the stakes, he was glad to be so used. Besides, what cynics referred to as the "Constitutional gloss" Sam was giving to the Southern argument was, in fact, his true opinion. Any federal legislation about civil rights, he believed, would increase the power of the federal government. Outsiders would be encouraged to come in and vent their moral fervor on the South; Negroes would be stirred up unnecessarily; and the good will between the races, which had been growing since Reconstruction times, would be shattered.

That there were reforms to be made in according greater rights to Negroes, Sam had no doubt. What he was questioning, by participating in the civil rights battle, was whether those reforms ought to be imposed by federal law. What he believed, finally, was that the two races, working together, would settle the questions and keep the good will, too — if let alone. The Northerners who saw Southerners as wishing to keep Negroes down were mistaken, he believed. All Southerners wanted to do was keep Negroes away, and associate with those of their own kind.

In the background, Eisenhower, Russell, and Johnson worked out their compromise: Title III, the part that let the Justice Department step in on behalf of Negro voting rights, would be cut out. The liberals could have a Civil Rights Commission to "study" abuses and an Assistant Attorney General to deal with civil rights cases.

On this basis, the speeches, Sam's included, abruptly stopped. There would be no organized Southern filibuster, only a personal one by Strom Thurmond, a record twenty-four hours and eighteen minutes, and the 1957 civil rights bill passed the Senate. The only thing to be worked out — between its version and the House version — was whether criminal contempt cases arising out of the new statutes would be tried by juries.

On this question, Russell handed over the reins to Sam, to let him do the backstage dealing, and probably to test him, too; to determine whether he was going to be a leader or just another vote. And Sam worked out a complicated compromise in which a judge imposing a penalty of more than $300 or forty-five days was obliged to give the offender a jury trial if he demanded it.

In the process, Sam began to learn a little more about the cost of national leadership. The NAACP researched his old North Carolina Supreme Court decisions, and found he had once ruled that criminal contempt cases did not require jury trials. This was immediately publicized, and became the subject of scathing editorials.

It was at this time, too, that he first began to read references to himself as a "racist." First it was in some of the papers back home, and then it was in the national press. They gave him credit for not cursing the Negroes and calling them apes, as Senator Bilbo had done, but called him a racist all the same.

This annoyed him: racist. To his mind, any man who was any sort of -ist was obsessed with the thing he was an -ist about. Like that fellow from New Jersey, Kasper, who had gone down into Tennessee with a swastika on his arm, stirring up trouble in a place he knew nothing about and had no business being in the first place. Now there was an -ist, all right; a man obsessed. But Sam had never paid much attention to Negroes one way or the other, except to do them good, such as the times when they had come to him, down in Morganton, to be defended, as they had come to his father before him. The Negroes he had known down in Morganton, he believed, preferred to associate with their own kind, just as the whites did, and Sam did not see anything racist about that.

But now the federal government seemed bent on changing the natural pattern of things. The Supreme Court, through the desegregation ruling, was trying to *jam* the races together; the executive branch, by sponsoring this so-called civil rights legislation, was trying to jam the races together — as were the liberals in the legislative branch. All of which was a very fine thing if you were rich, as some of the jammers were, if you dwelt in a marble palace and did not have to be one of those jammed.

What did they think, that he had a plantation and drove them with whips? That he kept a couple of high-yellow wenches in a shed in back of his house? Had they ever sat up night after night, week after week, as he had done, preparing a real Negro's defense, and for nothing? Had they ever gone over to the hospital, as he had done, with money he couldn't really spare, to pay the hospital bill of a real Negro? Had any of them, really, ever done anything for a real Negro?

WATERMELON

I was sitting in Sam's waiting room in the old Senate Office Building. The door opened and a big Negro lumbered in carrying a watermelon. He set the watermelon on the floor in front of the reception desk, and left without saying a word. This was at a time when the assassination threats from Watergate were still coming in.

"I just know it's going to blow up," the girl at the desk said. She picked up a piece of paper the Negro had left, looked at it, put it down on the desk. "This says it's from the Watermelon Growers Association but I just know it's going to

blow up." She got up and went into the next room and I could hear her in there talking to some of the young men about what to do with the watermelon. It was one of the spherical ones, world-shaped, and it lay on the rug about a foot in front of my toe. After a while one of Sam's aides came out of his office and said the Senator would see me now.

He was seated behind the big oak desk, which was clear, except for a red paperback book, the Annotated U.S. Code. His eyes were blue, brooding.

We spent the afternoon discussing his law practice in the twenties and thirties, and while we talked he wrote with a red felt-tip pen on the cover of the book, underlining the title. A few evenings before, he'd said on national television that finishing the Watergate report had made him feel like a boy in Morganton, on the last day of school, when he threw away his shoes for the summer. But he did not look happy now, and I surmised he was sad about the Watergate business being over, about his desk being clean except for the book he was marking with the felt-tip pen. He had less than half a year to go in the Senate.

I started to leave, but he asked me to stay. "I want to see if I can remember some of those old cases," he said. After a time, I let the tape recorder do the listening while I watched him. He got deep into the stories and enjoyed telling them. When he finished I asked him what he thought a good biography was.

"I like the ones that give you the sense of the subject as a living being," he said.

As I was leaving, he got up and came with me to the outer office. There were no phone calls from the national media to be taken, no conferences to attend, no voluminous staff reports to be sifted. Half a dozen aides were sitting around eating bright red slices of watermelon and spitting the seeds into a wastebasket. Sam stood with his back against the dark, mahogany door frame. He was watching the young people eating the watermelon but his eyes were far away.

Chapter 17

Hɪs ᴍᴏᴛʜᴇʀ was dead, his daughter Laura was married, and his son was absorbed in law and politics down in North Carolina. The other daughter, Leslie, who worked for him on Capitol Hill, had her own life, and Margaret had her own life, too — church groups, Senate wives, D.A.R. He, Sam, was still the fixer; when anyone needed anything, when there was a problem, they came to him. When he felt in need of a break, he would go, sometimes, to the Genealogical Research Room of the Library of Congress, and there, as always, trace back through the old records, looking for mention of the ancestors whom he now had catalogued in thick volumes of his own.

But the chief blessing was the work, something interesting to do all day. He loved his work and, having invested his young manhood and middle age in the discipline of law, he began to reap the dividends. His fellow Senators respected his scholarship. This increased his self-respect, and, therefore, his isolation, and he worked long hours. He was fond of saying that, when the day ended, he did not know where the hours had gone. He did not know where the years had gone, either; just that they had slid out from under him, as they had done from all his ancestors and from most of his friends.

When he tired of the legal scholarship, there were always practical things to do. He saw to it that federal monies poured into North

Carolina, for airports, reservoirs, channel-dredging, and a vast program of military construction. When the tobacco interests complained to him of the Surgeon General's trying to get cancer-warning labels affixed on packages of cigarettes, he took to the Senate floor to denounce the practice as smacking of Big Brother. He was, of course, sincere in his opposition to the cigarette labeling, because his basic stance, on everything, was that the federal government ought to stay out of people's lives. And he was sincere about the airports and the channel-dredging and all the other homely practicalities, too. After all, why not? The good old boys from back home, steaming and likable in their simple greed, were an antidote to too much abstraction. Besides, he'd always supported business, although he was no more a businessman than Thomas Jefferson was a hog when he poured swill into the trough.

He had need of good will back home because, like the rest of the Southern Senators who had not filibustered against the Civil Rights Act of 1957, he was under attack. The promise of the Administration (in August '57) never to send troops to enforce school integration, had been followed (in September '57) by battalions of troops pouring into Little Rock, Arkansas, to enforce school integration. And so, like many another Southerner, Sam quit looking for compromises.

Happily, the Administration seemed willing to rest on its 1957 success, and in 1958 Sam decided to take some time off and travel. This time he went with Margaret all the way out to Hawaii, to visit Laura and her new husband. There was the Pacific, the volcanoes, and the unfamiliar thronging Oriental faces. It was a strange world, soon to be stranger, with a dead dog in a space capsule whirling up invisibly over his head every hour and a half, flung up there by the Russians. And here, these yellow and brown faces, soon to be American faces, children's faces, lapping at ice-cream cones, stuck into comic books. He told reporters that the ice-cream cones and the comic books proved they were Americans, that he was impressed with "the industriousness of the native population," and with the willingness with which so many of them had given their lives in the war. "After all," he said, "what higher proof of loyalty is there?" And if he himself knew the answer to that one, he wasn't telling. Shortly afterward he voted to admit Hawaii to the Union — not an easy stand for a Southern Senator, who could be certain that Hawaiian votes would be on the other side in future civil rights showdowns.

He was beginning to become acquainted with Jack Kennedy. They served together on the Senate Rackets Committee. The brother Robert was chief counsel to the committee, and, more often than not, led the questioning of the labor leaders, like Dave Beck and Jimmy Hoffa.

The brothers Kennedy, these days, Sam found, were beginning to make special efforts to be friendly to him, and would invite him to their places in Georgetown and McLean, Virginia. Sam watched all this white-toothed charm with some detachment. John Kennedy, he knew, wanted to be President. If it weren't for that, Kennedy's elegant fastidiousness would have kept more room between himself and Sam's own homely angularities. It was not yet clear whether Kennedy's subtle mind had been lit by the suspicion that there were minds more subtle than his own.

Sam's candidates for the presidency were Richard Russell, who had no chance for the nomination, and Lyndon Johnson, who might win. Sam liked the Texan. Johnson, for all his crudities, was a person who would unhood his eyes for you, however briefly; level with you; make deals; give his word, reluctantly perhaps, and, having given it, live up to it. To Sam's way of looking at it, this was a fine and necessary quality, and it was a good thing that there be at least one gentleman running for the presidency in 1960, although the Republicans, evidently, had something else in mind.

Well, you didn't want a man like Nixon being President, Sam believed, because the country was in bad enough shape without anymore help from the White House. There was, for instance, the matter of organized crime, whose annual income, the Rackets Committee investigators said, exceeded $30 billion a year. There was even evidence of massive interconnection between the organized crime syndicates and some of the labor unions, such as the Teamsters. When Jimmy Hoffa came before the Rackets Committee, Sam asked him why he hadn't fired union officials who'd been convicted of felonies, as was required by the Teamsters' constitution.

HOFFA: I will tell you what it is. I have to bring the executive board of
           that union down to the international or go to New York and
           talk to them. I recognize that under the constitution I don't
           have to do that. I recognize that. But rather than destroy this
           union, this is the procedure I would follow. Then, if there, I
           would go to their membership, if necessary, to have carried

ERVIN: out in orderly fashion the constitution, rather than destroy the union.

ERVIN: In other words, you are telling us that if you follow the constitution, and carry out the powers the constitution gives you to remove from membership or from office convicted criminals, that would destroy the union?

HOFFA: I didn't say that, Senator.

ERVIN: If you said something else, I am unable to understand the English language.

Outside the committee hearing, Hoffa called Sam a "pious speaker telling Aesop's fables about how he wants to protect the worker," and added, "I suggest that Ervin leave his Washington parties and go down to his own home state and spend a day on a picket line, eat from a soup kitchen, and see the National Guard surrounding the picket lines like it was enemy territory."

This, of course, Sam was not going to do, because he'd been suspicious of labor unions all his life, and did not think a man should be obliged to join a union before he could work. Why should a man have to pay tribute to a union for the privilege of supporting himself? This attitude, he knew, endeared him to the business leaders of the state, where over half the working people were employed in textile mills, and where a strong "right-to-work" law was in force. But it was also, genuinely, his own point of view, and he was proud of the fact that North Carolina was the least unionized state in America.

Sam knew the other side had statistics — as always. For instance, the statistic that North Carolina ranked forty-second in the nation in per capita income. But when you came right down to it, he thought the Constitution was more important than all the decimal places of the statistics; and he could quote statistics, too, such as the one that said that North Carolina, in spite of the right-to-work laws, ranked fifteenth in industrial wages. Sometimes it seemed to Sam that many men did not care about freedom anymore, one way or the other, and, instead, wanted mere "job security," a television set to nap in front of, and grub brought to their elbows, out there in the suburbs, by Jimmy Hoffa's trucks.

But he, Sam, would stand up for the old ways, the ways of his ancestors, whose existence, as often as not, was recorded solely in the reliquiae of their public service, whether in the state legislatures of South Carolina, or the military units of the Wars of the Revolution, of 1812, of 1861. These ancestors' private dreams and hungers, their ephemeral quests for grub, had perished with them; just as the purely personal things in his own life, he believed, would perish with him. Who, after all, in a hundred years, would know that he, Sam Ervin, hadn't had enough cash to take his bride to California on their honeymoon? And what did such a thing matter, anyway? But the public things would stand. His war record would stand, for his own children to be proud of. His Distinguished Service Cross would remain, and his Silver Star. These were the things that counted.

Now, another civil rights bill was on its way into the Congress, and Sam knew that when it arrived there would be time for little else. Not for the Rackets Committee, nor for the good old boys from back home wanting federal government contracts or funds.

Fortunately, there would be someone to look after the good old boys now, because his friend Everett Jordan had been named to North Carolina's other Senate seat, replacing Kerr Scott, who had died. Everett Jordan, from Saxaphaw was nineteen days older than Sam, and a lifelong friend. This was the same Everett Jordan Sam had played baseball with, back in Morganton, back in the days when Jordan's father was an itinerant Methodist minister. Jordan was a fair third baseman, a hard worker, and a good old boy himself, a fellow who would look you in the eye; a man, no doubt, who would be called a capitalist by some. But Sam didn't see anything wrong with being a capitalist, and he admired Jordan, because the man had gone to work at twenty-one, as a mill hand in a Gastonia textile plant; and had become, by twenty-seven, the superintendent of one of the largest textile mills in the state; and now owned his own mills. Jordan would become the "service Senator," and Sam would concentrate on the civil rights bills. North Carolina businessmen would understand this as rational division of labor. They would continue to back Sam in spite of the fact that he had seen fit to cosponsor, with Jack Kennedy, a labor reform bill that many of them regarded as liberal.

No, Sam had the trust of the businessmen, and the relationship between them was cordial, relaxed. One evening, at his apartment in the Methodist House, he received a call from a group of them who were at a dinner down in Greensboro, trying out a new toy, direct-distance dialing. They had gotten Honolulu, in nine seconds, to find out the time of day; then reached San Francisco, in seven seconds, to hear a recorded message about lost dogs; and now, they thought, they would call old Sam. Who gave them a little speech. He was determined, as always, to be available to all North Carolinians — of like mind. His telephone was listed in the book.

Now, in 1959, the Eisenhower Administration was sending more civil rights bill to the Congress. Again, Hennings managed to get a bill reported out of the Constitutional Rights Subcommittee, and, again, it was bottled up by the full Judiciary Committee. In the end, the only thing to pass that year was the extension of the Civil Rights Commission, which Sam opposed.

But he cosponsored an antibombing bill, again with Jack Kennedy, in the wake of the Atlanta synagogue bombings, as an expression of his own outrage. He despised the night-riders, the bombers and the murderers, who had nothing whatsoever to do with the South he loved and sought to preserve. Such men only made his job harder, and further imbruted the tooth-picking, beer-swilling, parking-lot Yahoos, whom the South had hitherto kept under pretty good control.

On February 15, 1960, Lyndon Johnson opened a new civil rights debate. The primary thrust of the bills was to provide legislation implementing the voting rights provisions of the '57 bill. That last time, the Southerners had been talked out of a filibuster by assurances that there would be no federal troops sent in to enforce court orders, and were confronted, immediately, by troops in Little Rock. Now they knew, as a matter of practical politics, that they would have to filibuster if they wanted to continue to receive support from back home.

But Sam was sincere about what he was doing. His feelings on the civil rights issue were best summarized, perhaps, by an 1883 Supreme Court ruling that he knew by heart.

> When a man has emerged from slavery, and by the aid of beneficent legislation has shaken off the inseparable concomitants of that state, there must be some stage in the progress of his elevation when he takes the rank of a mere citizen and ceases to be the special favorite of the laws, and when his rights as a citizen are to be protected in the ordinary modes by which other men's rights are protected.

In short, he wanted to treat the Negro as an ordinary citizen. To do otherwise would be to increase the power of the federal government at the expense of all citizens.

"*Salaam, salaam, salaam,*" Richard Russell said, when Johnson brought out the new bill. "*Salaam, salaam,*" raising his arms above his head, and bowing over all the way with his head down near the floor, and raising and bowing again, and rising red-cheeked. "All you have to do is go out and get a piece of paper with the title CIVIL RIGHTS on it, and immediately about half the Senate gets up and says, *salaam, salaam.*" Half the Senate, of course, wouldn't be enough to pass any civil rights bill, because, under Rule 22, it would take two thirds of the Senators to cut off debate. The Southerners, Sam among them, gathered in Russell's office to take their marching orders. They were divided up into three six-man teams, each to hold the floor on successive days.

The filibuster began in the middle of February. There was speculation about whether the Southerners could hold out. They weren't, to begin with, athletic types — that is, most of them weren't — and besides, they were old. Richard Russell himself was sixty-two; Everett Jordan and Olin Johnston were each sixty-three; McClellan was sixty-four; Lister Hill, sixty-five; Allen Ellender and Spessard Holland, each sixty-eight; and Harry Byrd and Willis Robertson, each seventy-three. Sam himself was sixty-three years old now — a couple of years over the average for the eighteen Southern Senators; an average that would have been higher if it hadn't been for three youngsters in their forties: Russell Long, George Smathers, and Herman Talmadge, who had replaced Walter George.

Sixty-three years old, Sam was now, with the old green, slow world changed and forgotten; concrete thoroughfares, acrawl with high-speed glinting automobiles, crisscrossing it; nuclear missiles poised; submarines under the North Pole; dead dogs whirling; and, in Greensboro, North Carolina — of all places, gentle Greensboro — Negroes hunched up at a Woolworth's lunch counter, day after day, demanding to be served.

Lyndon Johnson announced that he was going to put the Senate on round-the-clock sessions, "for the sake of transacting business." He was out to break the old men. Forty army cots were brought into the former Supreme Court chamber, and set up in long rows two or three feet apart, metal folding chairs between them. Some Senators slept in the dim shadows among old marble columns, under the old clock and the bronze eagle flying on outspread nineteenth-century wings, under the big mural of Lincoln, fifteen feet tall, signing the Emancipation Proclamation.

Not all Senators were obliged to sleep on the army cots, however, because many of them, including Sam, had hideaways in the Capitol building, the rewards of seniority. Sam slept, when he could, in the plain surroundings of a small room that was all his own, and that, if he continued to live and gather seniority, would give way in time to yet more opulent surroundings, such as the room Allen Ellender had, with its crystal chandelier, marble fireplace, bar, and private kitchen stocked with shrimp, oysters, ham, eggs, bacon, and fresh vegetables. And a tall window that commanded a view of the Potomac, and, beyond it, Robert E. Lee's mansion. That was for inspiration, Ellender said; who, as a young man, had once held the Senate floor, for six solid days, and who now filled himself with good things and went out on the Senate floor to fight some more.

Actually, it proved not to be so hard. The Southerners, led by Russell, repeatedly called for a quorum, and all talk would cease while the Republicans and Northern liberal Democrats scuttled through the corridors, trying to roust up their own, succeeding finally, but not until the crafty old Southerners had rested. And, as the hours wore on past midnight, there was a lot of heavy drinking, insults on the floor, curses in the corridor; but still the debate wore on, with the Southerners holding their own and, as time passed, seeming to be more fit than their opponents.

Sam would emerge pinkly from the steam bath in the Senate gymnasium, flop down on the table for a massage, and rise refreshed, to go up on the floor and speak for six solid hours against the bill; wait through three or four quorum calls, and, his speaking time having been filled, and the quorum calls done, eat a large dish of vanilla ice cream, packed down by two cups of hot black coffee; and then, instead of going home, relax in the cloakroom, waiting to help his team. Going home to bed at 11 A.M.

On March 10, cloture was rejected by a vote of 42 to 53. Whereupon LBJ, working with Attorney General William Rogers, agreed to delete the bill's two toughest sections — which had been aimed at desegregating schools and jobs — while retaining a system of court-appointed voting referees, a system that would turn out to be unworkable. Sam and his fellow Southerners had won again. A civil rights bill had been passed, but in terms of anything that might issue in concrete results, nothing had been accomplished. Of course, the liberals were determined to try again. Everyone knew that, and, as a result, things at the 1960 Democratic National Convention in San Francisco that summer did not go to Sam's liking, because, in spite of his vigorous opposition, that convention passed the strongest civil rights plank in the history of major American political parties.

The North Carolina delegation to the convention was controlled by Governor Luther Hodges, and was mostly for LBJ, at first, although pressure from incoming Governor Terry Sanford would finally move most of the state's delegates behind the candidacy of John F. Kennedy. Sam backed Lyndon Johnson, something Kennedy would remember.

Still, he was not sufficiently awed by the man to play up to him, and, in the rump session of the Senate called by LBJ after the conventions, Sam opposed the two prime bills Kennedy was trying to get passed: Medicare, and a $1.25-an-hour minimum wage bill. When told by Kennedy in floor debate that the seventy-five-cents-an-hour North Carolina minimum wage was too low, Sam responded angrily by saying he supposed that the legislators down in North Carolina knew more about it than Kennedy, and stood glowering while Kennedy responded, "The difficulty is that people we are helping don't know anything about what we are doing, but the associations, the lobbyists who represent the employers are on top of this, all the time, everywhere." Sam didn't answer, believing the two Kennedy bills would be defeated — as they were.

But when Kennedy's plane touched down at the Greenville airport the next month, Sam was there to greet him, and had his picture taken with him on the speaker's stand out at the stadium — with Terry Sanford between him and the presidential candidate. Sam, riding in a rear car, went along to the airport and rode in the back of the plane as it touched down in Greensboro and Charlotte. He walked by Kennedy's side as they went down the long work-rows in the world's largest tobacco warehouse, stood watching as Kennedy listened, squint-eyed and amused, to the chanting tobacco auctioneers and bought some bright-leaf tobacco, which an aide toted away under his arm. It was all right. Sam was in favor of Kennedy, and knew that, in any case, he wouldn't be overrun by the man, because

Kennedy would need his vote in the Senate on any number of matters. And as for Kennedy's friend Terry Sanford, who, Sam suspected, wanted to run against him for the Senate in 1962, well, let him come on. North Carolina was not as liberal as the rest of the country.

The following January, on a snowy day, Sam stood in front of North Carolinians gathered in Washington for the inaugural dinner, and led them in the ancient state anthem. It pleased him that new throats born up out of the dust should be singing this song he himself had sung, almost fifty years ago, at the University of North Carolina. Of course there would always be men coming along who wanted to change things a bit too quickly. What remained constant — about the national scene, at least — was that there was always a gentleman in the White House, and you could always do business with a gentleman. Kennedy was President now.

A GOOD JOB

Larry Baskir was Chief Counsel of Sam's Constitutional Rights Subcommittee. He was a handsome, dark-haired young lawyer in his middle thirties, and it seemed strange that he should be working for Sam at all. He was too mod; his suits had the latest cut, and his trousers were flared at the cuffs. Then, too, there was the big brush of a mustache. Finally, he was from New York, and called himself a liberal. He made a good salary, in excess of $25,000 a year.

"I'd say that at least half the staff members here were deeply disturbed by the position the Senator took on civil rights," he told me.

"You mean they wish he'd supported civil rights legislation instead of opposing it?"

"Right on."

"I'd imagine they had some pretty good arguments with Sam, then," I said.

"Oh no. You don't just walk up to the Senator and volunteer your personal opinion."

"Did anybody quit?"

"Hunh-uh. Listen. Let me explain to you how it works on Capitol Hill. You learn pretty quickly that there are some things the Senator doesn't want to hear. And if you're smart, you'll see to it he doesn't hear them."

"I notice you always call him 'the Senator.' What about when you're talking to him? Do you call him 'Sam'?"

"No."

"Why not?"

He scratched his head. "It never occurred to me," he said. "You just don't do things like that."

He had done a good job on the Constitutional Rights Subcommittee, and he made a good salary, in excess of $25,000 a year.

Chapter 18

EVERY DAY, now, he went into the Senate barbershop, climbed up in the chair, made himself relax as it was tilted back, and basked in the pleasure of hot, moist towels. He found that having them applied expertly, and replaced immediately, before they'd cooled too much, imparted a healthy, pink color to his complexion. He loved to be treated well in the barbershop, and then to walk down the Senate corridors, surrounded by color, and a bit of the flamingo in the face himself, smiling and howdying. If you'd relax a little, Capitol Hill would nurture you, you'd live longer, and have longer to work.

It was the start of the Kennedy Administration, and Sam was literally in the pink, and he checked in and out of the Bethesda Naval Hospital for a hernia operation without thinking much about it, without being drawn down — as he once might have been — into solemn ponderings about human mortality. It had been the same way, a few years before, when he had a kidney stone attack: one got the best of service, and took advantage of it; one got good treatment, and responded to it; one was not immortal but, by choosing to relax, and letting others — like staff members and barbers — do their jobs, one might thrive.

Sam had more staff members now than ever, because seniority had finally led him up a little hummock of power. Not a full committee;

seven years on the Hill was nowhere near enough for that. But he was named chairman of a good juicy subcommittee, the Constitutional Rights Subcommittee of the Judiciary, the one Hennings had run before his death. The budget wasn't large — $140,000 a year — and the political line-up of the committee was dominated by liberals. But this was to be Sam's point of leverage, the place from which he could begin to initiate legislation, rather than just reacting to the ideas and concerns of others.

It offered him a chance to operate in a new area that was beginning to interest him, namely, the intrusion of the federal government into the lives of private citizens. The new civil rights laws, he thought, were prime examples of such saurian intrusion, and since most of those laws would have to pass through his subcommittee on their way to the floor, he felt in a better position to deal with them. He also wanted to look into wiretapping by government agencies (which he opposed) and freedom of the press (which, he believed, ought to be maintained). He knew, of course, that a chairman on Capitol Hill was a kind of emperor who could hold hearings whenever he wanted to, on whatever he wanted to. He had absolute control over his staff, and any Senator on the committee who, say, wished to have research done in order to oppose him on a substantive matter had to use his people. But Sam — unlike Hennings — assigned an attorney and a secretary to each member of the committee, and instructed the staff to cooperate.

As Chief Counsel of his subcommittee, Sam installed a young North Carolina lawyer named William Creech, a man who had been an aide to Hubert Humphrey, but who seemed, now, to have no difficulty in seeing things the way Sam did. The rest of the staff had been hired by Hennings, and could be expected to be liberals, too, in their private sympathies if not in their public expressions. Two of the employees — one a lawyer, the other a clerk — were Negroes.

About this time, Essie Tate died. She had served Sam's family for thirty-seven years, living in his house, and raising his children as much as anybody else had. And so Sam and Margaret and their daughter Leslie got in the Chrysler and drove the four hundred and forty miles down to the funeral service, which was conducted at the Mission AME Church in Morganton, with a Negro minister presiding and a white minister assisting. Laura came, too, and Sam III, crew-cut and somber, all three of the white children Essie had raised. Then Sam left Essie's grave, a desolate red gash under the blue mountains, and drove back to Washington with Margaret and Leslie.

Leslie, he knew, was uncomfortable with many of the old practices of the South, such as having Negroes come around to the back door. And there were many others who were more discontented than she. This spring, there were bus-burnings and beatings of civil rights demonstrators in Alabama, with federal marshals having to be sent in to keep order, and, finally, martial law. Sam would sit in his apartment looking out across the little side street to where the Supreme Court building stood not fifty yards away, musing on this new and menacing world.

Kennedy was moving away from the Congress, seeking to by-pass it altogether, trying to arrange things down South to suit himself, through executive fiat. On March 6, he established the President's Committee on Equal Employment Opportunity, whose purpose was to "combat racial discrimination in the employment policies of Government agencies and private firms holding Government contracts." It seemed that the government and private employers alike would be obliged to hire Negroes whether they were qualified or not. This committee, headed by the Vice President, Lyndon Johnson, replaced a couple of other committees, with similar names, that had been headed by Nixon during the Eisenhower Administration. But whereas the earlier ones had been obliged to wait for complaints to be filed, this new committee was authorized by Kennedy to make investigations on its own, and to use Labor Department attorneys to help it crack down. There had to be regular compliance reports and, when the committee wasn't satisfied that enough Negroes had been hired, it was authorized to publicize the names of the noncompliers, cancel government contracts, and forbid future contracts.

Not only that, but Robert Kennedy, now Attorney General, petitioned the Interstate Commerce Commission to issue regulations banning segregation in bus terminals. And the Justice Department was moving much more vigorously than Eisenhower's had, enforcing the 1957 and 1960 voting rights acts.

Even so, when the Bay of Pigs disaster struck, Sam lined up cautiously behind Kennedy, as did most other Southerners, some of whom remarked privately that a man who made a mistake of such proportions in foreign policy ought to show more humility at the prospect of disrupting the social patterns of his own nation. The President had too much power; more power than any good man would want, Sam was fond of saying, and far more than any bad man should have. It was a strange world. Down in Morganton, the old church, the First Presbyterian Church had been torn down and moved, ancestors and all, to a plain bare lot in the suburbs of Morganton. The Burke County Building and Loan now, stood stolidly on the spot where he had worshipped for sixty-five years.

But he was ready to fight, did not want to be distracted. Everything was ready. He had the committee he wanted (Constitutional Rights), the staff he wanted (for the most part), the living accommodations he wanted. When it was suggested to him that he take over his parent's home, the old white house down in Morganton, he declined, and gave his share to his wife and two of his sisters. When he was offered a new suite of offices in the New Senate Office Building, he turned that down, too, and like many another man who seems to have everything he wants, he burrowed down into his work as the one best place to keep from brooding over whether he'd wanted the right things in the first place.

When he felt uneasy, there was always the homely row of mother-of-pearl buttons built into his desk, and he knew that pushing any one of them would conjure up, immediately, an aide, with some rational matter requiring his immediate attention. There were the bills providing for more military construction in North Carolina; there was an ongoing hassle with the Interior Department over whether there ought to be any charge for motorists on the Sky Line Drive (he thought there ought not be); there was the question of appropriations for the eradication of witch weed.

If he wanted to see the past anymore, he had to look for it, either in the recesses of his memory, which now seemed to him as labyrinthine and rich as all the colored corridors of Capitol Hill, or down home, at special places, special times. That summer he drove down to North Carolina, to the traditional Fourth of July celebration at Siler City. There was the Saturday night dance at the National Guard Armory (with music furnished by Duke and the Ambassadors) and the bunting-decked patriotic service in the Presbyterian Church the next day; there was handshaking on the streets on Monday, with jocose Sam poking his head in doors, laughing a lot, dropping stories, accepting felicitations. There was a rodeo, with its trick riding, its clowns in barrels, calf-roping, bull-dogging, horse-bucking; and a parade, with its eleven floats got up by the local businessmen, its television person-alities (Captain Five, Old Rebel), and cars that were said to be "antiques" but that to Sam were just plain cars, the way they were supposed to be. And beauty queens regnant on floats. Then, sweat-soaked and healthy feeling, he spoke on the old patriotic themes. There were twenty thousand in attendance, and after his speech there were the foot races and the bicycle races, the pie-eating contest, the greasy-pole walking, tug of war, watermelon fight. Ah. He knew them all down here and they knew him, and were used to him.

Back in Washington, it seemed that his relations with the Kennedys were quicksilvery, ambiguous, not founded on the traditional ways in which politicians did business. He and Margaret were invited out to Hickory Hill, and went, scratched the big black dog behind the ear, watched the young swimmers in the back yard pool, pontificated for the benefit of the svelte, slick young women who always seemed to be about the Kennedys, who were better-looking than all the beribboned beauty queens of Siler City. He and Margaret were invited to the White House, and went, chatted with the President, ate the good French cooking, drank the wines, and emerged for the cab ride back to the Methodist House, having been courted, deferred to. And on the next day, back in his office, it would come to him that yet another federal appointment down in North Carolina had been made — by Jack, or by Bobby — without his knowledge.

Ordinarily, it was he and Jordan who ought to be making all the appointments, in the form of "recommendations," whether for federal judge, or for many other federal positions. And for the most part, they did. But there were disturbing exceptions, with too many recommendations now coming from the President's liberal friend Governor Terry Sanford, who might even be running against Sam in 1962.

Repeatedly, there were blows to Sam's prestige. He wanted a friend of his, Malcolm Seawell, appointed to a North Carolina middle district judgeship. John Kennedy said no. He wanted his old friend, Judge Pless of Marion, appointed to the Fourth Circuit Court of Appeals, but the nomination went instead to State Senator J. Spencer

Bell of Charlotte, a Sanford supporter. On top of that, Robert Kennedy appointed a thirty-year-old Negro as United States Attorney in Greensboro. It was almost as if the Kennedys wanted to reward the Negroes for the lunch counter sit-in business, on the spot where the transgressions were made. And still, the invitations — to the White House, to Hickory Hill — kept coming in. The very presence of the Kennedys quickened things unnaturally, and threatened to obliterate the old, slow human order Sam was used to.

On a cool, brisk October morning that year, Kennedy's DC-6B came snarling in for a perfect landing at the Raleigh-Durham airport, taxied smartly up to the red carpet, stopped precisely on the dot of 10:30 A.M., the moment chosen weeks before for the President to arrive. Out popped Kennedy, perfect, smiling, shaking the hand of Sanford, and waving to the crowd of two thousand assembled, as he approached the speakers rostrum. Behind him the Secretary of Defense, Robert McNamara, also perfect, slim, incisive, slick-haired, smiling, emerged from the plane. Like Kennedy, he belonged to no place, really, and to no time, either, unless it was the future. Then came the former Governor of the state, Secretary of Commerce Luther Hodges, a host of generals and other officials, and a painter of pictures, William Walton, the President's friend. A ten-minute ceremony, perfectly done. Three minutes to get into the limousines and drive off. Perfectly done. Out onto State Route 54, then, in the Lincoln limousine with the transparent plastic top, and along that road, which had been cleared of traffic for the entire fifteen-mile drive to Chapel Hill. It had once taken Sam half the night to walk that fifteen miles, back in the days when he was young, and route 54 was a dirt road.

And this day, with the Kennedy car, surrounded by fifty state patrolmen, hurtling toward him, Sam stood mildly in the sun up on the speakers' stand in Keenan Stadium, waving to friends, reaching down to shake hands, feeling not much different from the way he had at the Fourth of July celebration at Siler City. Kennedy arrived, glowing and triumphant, and Sam, along with Jordan, was shuttled politely, firmly, over to the side, so that the President could sit next to Terry Sanford. Kennedy gave a seventeen-minute speech, with none of the good old comfortable rhetorical rambling, and, after acknowledging the applause, got ready to move. He was always moving.

Sam stopped him as he was moving toward the rear of the platform and engaged him in conversation on a matter of no importance,
watching how Kennedy's green eyes glinted when he spoke. It was
that eagle-eyed look male models had in the advertisements for men's
clothes. There would be a fellow in a new suit, standing next to an
airplane, looking fiercely up at the sky, probably at a cloud or something. Only you couldn't keep from wondering why anyone would
want to look so hard at a plain old cloud. When the fellow got up in
the sky he probably glared down at the ground in the same way. The
eagle-eyed stuff, the motorcade stuff, the fifty-state-patrolmen stuff,
the stopwatch stuff, seemed mindless and vain.

Strange, too, that other moment with Kennedy in Keenan Stadium,
when the President asked the old history professor, the little, neat,
white-haired man, Frank Porter Graham, to step forward. And Graham, former president of the University, former Senator, grinned
and waved into the loud cheers. What Kennedy didn't understand
was that these were college cheers — a whisper of locusts' wings in an
ivory tower, having little to do with the people of North Carolina.
Who had, in effect, recalled Frank Porter Graham from the Senate
for being recklessly liberal on the Negro issue, and who would no
more send Terry Sanford to the Senate than they would Martin Luther King. Not yet.

As the year turned, the Negro issue kept on coming, pushed by the
Kennedys, who now sought to get Congress to pass a Constitutional
amendment outlawing the poll tax, and a bill that would make proof
of a sixth-grade education sufficient to register and vote in any federal election, including the primaries. Sam, of course, was opposed to
both schemes, and helped see to it that the sixth-grade literacy bill was
blocked by a Southern filibuster. But the poll tax bill got through,
over Sam's opposition, and finally became the Twenty-fourth Amendment to the Constitution.

As for the Kennedy Supreme Court appointments, there was nothing to do but oppose them. That fall, Sam voted against seating
Thurgood Marshall on the Supreme Court. It had nothing to do with
the race issue, he said. It was just that Marshall lacked judicial experience and had a tendency to go against the Constitution. But the
nomination was confirmed.

The pace of change was stepping up relentlessly. The University of

Mississippi was integrated, even though there was violence and killing, even though it took 16,000 federal troops to get one Negro into
class. And the murmur of old poems came back.

> The Stranger within my gates.
>   He may be evil or good,
> But I cannot tell what powers control —
>   What reasons sway his mood;
> Nor when the Gods of his far-off land
>   Shall repossess his blood.

Executive orders, too, continued to come down, as Kennedy continued to bypass the Congress. Government-sponsored summer training institutes would be held only at desegregated universities. There
was an effort to cut off all government funds to hospitals that weren't
integrated. There was even an order barring racial discrimination in
federally assisted housing, which put the Southern developer in a
position where he was damned if he did agree to integrate, because
no whites would buy his houses, and damned if he didn't, because he
wouldn't be able to raise the capital to break ground.

Once more, Sam won overwhelmingly in the Democratic primary,
with Terry Sanford staying out of it, and won re-election to the
Senate in the fall of 1962 by a majority of several hundred thousand
votes. In the next six years, he believed, his power was bound to wax.
And Sam loved power, deference, and hot towels.

CONSTITUENT

*I'd spent the afternoon in the air-conditioned office of Robert Bland Smith, an
elegant, handsome young North Carolinian who was Chief Counsel of Sam's
Government Operations Committee. He had just told me the story of how
Senator Keating had denounced Graham County, North Carolina, for not
having any Negroes registered to vote — at a time when there were, in fact, no
Negroes living in that county. And he'd told other anecdotes, too, some of
which tended to suggest that those opposing Sam in civil rights matters were
self-serving or stupid.*

As it happened, the Negro cab driver who picked me up was from Chapel

Hill, North Carolina, and as he drove me out, through Washington's heat and grime, to my all-white neighborhood in Arlington, Virginia, he got to talking about home.

He'd come to Washington in 1949 because life for him in North Carolina was intolerable. Since then, he'd been back only once, in the sixties. That was shortly after his wife died, and he'd taken his two teen-aged sons with him. When the three of them had tried to get served in a restaurant across the street from the University, they'd been turned away.

"Now the thing is," the cab driver said, "that I didn't even know this fellow who was turning us away. For all I know he got into town that day. But my people have been there for two hundred years. Everybody in town knows the Pendergrafts. But don't nobody know him."

He'd been humiliated in the presence of his sons, and was still angry about it. When I asked him what he thought of Sam Ervin, he said, "He ain't never done nothing for my people. He was on the other side."

Chapter 19

IN APRIL, August, and December of every year, he drove back down to Morganton. His house had been enlarged now, extending the dark brick front. In it, he had the kind of study he always wanted: twenty-four feet long, fifteen feet wide, with tall bookcases all around. There were other tall, full bookcases in the hallway and the bedroom, but the house, even as remodeled, did not begin to contain all his books. Most of them were kept in his office in the Ervin Building, which was a mile away, and to which he walked every morning he was in town. As often as not, he left his office door unlocked for the benefit of any local attorney who might want to wander in to clear up some point of law. Or it would be left unlocked because he could not find the key. There were better things to think about in Morganton than keys, and besides, nobody was going to take anything.

This, then, was what he had to show for his life: some books and the quiet, solid house on the lot his father had given him four decades before. He had no secrets, no locked files in his home or office, nor, for that matter, back in Washington. What he said was what he thought, and he was comfortable with anybody.

He liked returning to familiar faces, liked to be in Morganton among them, walking down the street in shirtsleeves in the warm weather, taking his own laundry down to the cleaners', doing the grocery shopping on the way home, walking into Lazarus Brothers Department Store or Kibler's Drug Store to laugh and swap stories and listen to his friends. In the warm weather, he would mow his own lawn, what there was left of it after the driveway had been put in, and he liked to visit around among his friends, or just drive out with Margaret along the old country roads. By now Leslie was married, and Sam and Margaret were alone together again for the first time since the 1920's. There were more grandchildren now, too. Sam III had a new daughter, and Laura and Leslie each had a son.

In the winter, back in Morganton for the Christmas recess, Sam spent much of his time indoors, reading. He did not care for fiction very much anymore, and bothered with it only when the Book-of-the-Month Club, of which he was a member, came up with something exceptional like *Anatomy of a Murder*. There was a shrewd old country lawyer in that one.

He loved to read American history and, drawing on his own genealogical research, was fond of imagining how his ancestors must have responded to past events. Indeed, past history sometimes seemed more real, more substantially founded, than the history in which he himself was now playing a leading part, in which the issues never seemed to be settled, once and for all, but seemed always to recede into the future. And he liked biographies. They gave him pleasure over many a long winter's evening as he sat reading in his quiet, elegant study. Sometimes a biographer could almost capture the inner life of a man, could help you get to know John Marshall or Jeb Stuart.

Biographies, thank God, were often more various than was life itself, where the most fortunate of men often found himself doing the same thing over and over again. As Sam was doing now with the civil rights bills. Maybe Lyndon Johnson had expressed it best when he said, "That's all I ever hear from the liberals: nigra, nigra, nigra." Indeed, one wondered if even the Negroes themselves didn't sometimes weary of the theme.

And now, as he returned to the Congress in January of 1963, he knew it was coming again. He knew, too, that the Senate considering the new civil rights legislation would be more liberal. There were newcomers like Birch Bayh and Ted Kennedy, both of whom landed on Sam's Constitutional Rights Subcommittee.

But the Administration's 1963 civil rights proposals turned out to be surprisingly mild. All they sought to do was broaden the existing voting rights laws, provide technical assistance to schools that were in the process of desegregating, and extend the Civil Rights Commission for another four years. Sam, as usual, set about to block them in committee, to speak against them in the public press, and to vote against them on the Senate floor.

Even as he was doing these things — and he could do them almost by rote now — events themselves seemed to be veering out of control. Early in April, the Birmingham demonstrations began, with the demonstrators using children, and the police using fire hoses, dogs, and cattle prods; with all of this erupting nightly out of the nation's television sets and bringing all sorts of white people into the battle, folks who reacted righteously to the dogs and the fire hoses, white people who did not believe that, in working for what they regarded as the "cause," they were really working for a more powerful federal government, if not totalitarian government. In the hearings of the Constitutional Rights Subcommittee, Sam found himself speaking of "dictatorship," and then, looking down the table, saw Ted Kennedy sitting there, amended himself, and tried to mute his remarks.

In April of 1963 a postman from Baltimore was shot to death as he walked across Alabama in a one-man demonstration for civil rights. Sam issued the appropriate statement, decrying the violence. He had issued many such statements by now. At the same time, he could not help feeling that the moral fervor of those involved seemed to be proportional to their distance from the event demonstrated against. Many of those who came down from the Northern cities to help the Southern Negro seemed to be ignoring what was happening at home. Whites in Chicago, Detroit, and Cleveland were fearful that their own cities would become like Washington, where the end of segregation had caused an exodus of 172,000 white citizens in the 1950's alone, and where 85 percent of the students in the public schools now were black.

On June 11, on national television, George Wallace, Governor of Alabama, stood in one of the doorways of the state university and sought to maintain, against the power of the federal government, the right of a state to control its own educational institutions. And not only failed, but brought on the final onslaught. That evening,

Kennedy took to the air to tell the American people that he was going to send to the Congress the most sweeping civil rights program in history, one that would:

- guarantee Negroes access to public accommodations
- allow the federal government to file suits to desegregate schools
- cut off federal programs in any area where discrimination was practiced in their application
- prohibit discrimination by government contractors
- establish a community relations service to help local communities resolve racial disputes
- encourage the passage of those laws already before Congress calling for Fair Employment Practices Commissions.

At last, then, the battle would be joined. Sam had not been impressed by Kennedy's remarks, which included the inevitable statistics. To wit, that the average Negro born in the United States had half the chance a white man did of completing high school; one-third the chance of becoming a professional man; twice the chance of becoming unemployed; and one-seventh the chance of earning $10,000 a year.

Within a week, the new Kennedy civil rights bill came down, and the next month hearings began, with Robert Kennedy scheduled as the first witness before the full Judiciary Committee. There was a great crowd on hand when he arrived and stood outside the hearing room, posing for the newspaper and television photographers. Sam, walking down the hall with a pencil clamped in his mouth and a tall stack of law books in his arms, plodded by unnoticed.

Kennedy expected to testify that day, and seemed surprised when Sam insisted on speaking instead. But Bobby picked up his briefcase and departed amiably enough, trailed by his aides, who were carrying the charts and other paraphernalia. The spectators, most of them, who'd booed Sam when he disclosed his intentions to speak, followed Kennedy into the hall, watched as he posed for the photographers, and did not return to the hearing room. More than half of the eight hundred seats were empty now as Sam, taking Kennedy's place at the witness table, launched into a point-by-point argument against the new civil rights program, which he called "as drastic and indefensible a proposal as has ever been submitted to this Congress."

He began by saying that he didn't understand what purpose would be served by cutting off federal funds to those states not in perfect compliance with federal desegregation orders; that he failed to see any connection between that and funds for old-age assistance, cancer research, venereal disease control, books for the blind, and other such programs, which, presumably, benefited citizens of both races. Nor could he find sufficient reason to extend the Civil Rights Commission, whose work was duplicated by Congressional committees as well as by the Civil Rights Division of the Department of Justice.

But the heart of the Administration's proposals was the public accommodations bill, which would ban racial discrimination in hotels, motels, restaurants, and stores having any dealings whatsoever in interstate commerce, and it was here that Sam directed his strongest attack. To impose such a standard, he said, would justify federal government regulation of birth, marriage, and death, insofar as brides and grooms wore clothes that had moved in interstate commerce; and babies used diapers and safety pins that had moved in interstate commerce; and corpses were consigned to the grave in coffins that had moved in interstate commerce. By the time he got through making his statement, which cited extensively from legal precedents, he had used up two whole days.

Finally, on the morning of July 18, Robert Kennedy appeared before the Judiciary Committee to begin his testimony. The crowds had returned, and Kennedy sat at the witness table, outlined starkly in the unnatural brightness of the television lights. Sam was up at the committee table with the Senators, looking down, and there were more books in front of him, more sheaves of yellow paper.

He was a couple of seats down from the presiding officer, the Chairman of the Judiciary, James Eastland of Mississippi, a silent man, a hard man to know, although there was no doubt where Eastland stood on the race issue. Eastland was fond of cornering colleagues in the hallways and producing elaborate organizational charts purporting to show how the international communist party, working through cotton cartels, influencing federal judges, and doing God knew what other kinds of undercover business, had set the whole civil rights movement in motion.

Indeed, Eastland's rationale was so complicated that even those on his own side found it difficult to understand what he was talking about. Thus, it had been understood from the beginning that Sam would take the lead in questioning Kennedy. In terms of the ability to argue forcefully, both the Southerners and the Administration would be going with the first team: Sam on one side and Robert Kennedy on the other.

The television cameras were zeroed in, not only because this civil rights bill was newsworthy for its own sake, but also because of the racial unrest and violence that formed the context of the hearings. The ten weeks since Birmingham had seen uprisings in Cambridge, Maryland and Jacksonville, Florida: fights, burnings, shootings, and demonstrators dispersed by tear gas. There had also been violence in Memphis, following the closing of the public swimming pools. Negroes were sitting in at lunch counters in Charlottesville, Virginia, and at the state Capitol in Sacramento, California. In Detroit, Negroes had invaded the city hall and subjected the chief of police to a mock trial. In New York, they had dumped garbage on City Hall Plaza, in Philadelphia, they had clashed with police at construction sites. In Chicago, they'd fought with police at the gates of a cemetery that refused to accept Negro corpses.

Kennedy, said that the demonstrations had created an air of "urgency" that made immediate passage of the civil rights bill imperative. His testimony gave cursory attention to the law precedents, and focused on incidents, statistics. He emphasized to the committee — and to the television cameras — instances of injustice, and statistics to show the effect of discrimination on Negro citizens.

> In Danville, Virginia, there were at least five establishments where a dog, traveling with a white man, was welcome to spend the night. But no places for Negroes to stay.

> In seventy-four of Mississippi's eighty-two counties, less than 15 percent of the eligible Negroes were registered to vote.

> In thirteen Southern counties, not a single Negro was permitted to register and vote.

> In response to a literacy test question in Alabama asking the applicant to name some of the duties and obligations of citizenship, a white salesman wrote, "Support the law vote," and was registered. But a Negro soldier, answering the same question in excellent handwriting, "To vote, obey the laws of Alabama, to obey the laws of the United States. to bear arms against any enemy, to support the constitution of Alabama and the United States," was rejected.

Another white, asked to interpret the provision of the Constitution stating "There shall be no imprisonment for debt," wrote "I think a Negro Should Have 8 years in college Be for voting Be couse He don't under Stand." And was registered.

A Negro woman was rejected for voting because her application bore the misspelling "Louiseana" — in the handwriting of the white registrar.

Less than 20 percent of whites lived below the poverty level. For Negroes, the figure was more than 50 percent.

In the days that were to follow — and Kennedy was to return to the stand on eight different days between July 24 and September 11 — the battle between Sam and Kennedy, and what they represented, was fought out. Kennedy cited tales of injustice, statistics of injustice. Sam sought to show, through painstaking legal precedents, that the federal government had no Constitutional authority to overpower the laws of the states.

Much of the argument between Sam and Kennedy was over the public accommodations law, which would have desegregated just about everything, and which was, of all the Administration's proposals, most odious to Southerners. Sam maintained that the law would cover bootblacks, or hot-dog stand operators, or poor old Mrs. Murphy, the widow who happened to rent out a few rooms to tourists; Kennedy responded that the coverage of the bill's provisions wasn't so wide as it seemed, or so totalitarian in purpose as Sam was painting it.

When they left the public accommodations bill and went on to the voting rights provisions, Kennedy pointed out that now, nine years after the Supreme Court decision in *Brown v. the Board of Education of Topeka*, only 12,800 Negroes out of 2,800,000 in the eleven states of the old Confederacy were actually attending desegregated schools — less than half of 1 percent.

Kennedy was all statistics and change and Sam, stubbornly, was all law, and the television event was coming to be known as the Sam and Bobby Show.

Kennedy was humble, supple, deferential, always boring in, and Sam kept fending him off, trying to nail him down in fine points of law. Once, when Kennedy asked to see the book Sam was citing from, Sam had an aide carry it over to him. Later, when Sam asked for his book back, Kennedy waved the aide aside, got up from the witness table, walked over and delivered it in person, face glowing, eyes large, glittering, amused. Fifteen minutes later, having finished with the book, Sam held it out to Kennedy, asking, "You want to borrow it again?"

Kennedy was deferential, like a good aide; he expressed, again and again, his respect for Sam's scholarship. And yet he kept boring in with his instances and statistics. One evening after the hearings Sam was invited to a dinner at the White House, and went — to be encountered in the hallway by Ethel Kennedy, who said, "What have you been doing to Bobby? He came home and went straight to bed."

Both men were tired now, on edge, and the worst thing, perhaps, from Sam's point of view, was that Kennedy was trying to get him to change his mind, in public. He would appeal to Sam from the witness table: "I hope we can get you to vote with us on this." He would make minor concessions, stating a willingness to redraft the public accommodations sections in order to exempt certain minor businesses, and appeal again, asking Sam to switch his vote. And Sam, embarrassed, said that he loved the Constitution too much to consider doing such a thing.

For the school desegregation arguments, Kennedy had prepared charts showing, in great detail, how Negroes got less schooling than whites, and how the doctrine of separate but equal facilities was only that, a doctrine. He had charts mounted on a board, over to the side, where everybody could see them.

To Sam's way of thinking, of course, all such charts and graphs, in terms of the present argument, were irrelevant, since what the Administration proposed to do was to abolish the Constitution. So Sam, heretofore, had paid very little attention to the charts and graphs. Not only that; he had made it plain to his aides — through the way he spoke to them, the way he bore himself, the silent gravity of his face, the dismissing impatience of his gestures — that he didn't want to see them. And yet now, here these charts were, bathed in the ghastly glow of television lights. Sam was much displeased, but this time there was no aide to glide forward and take them away.

Sam was angry, and he told a bullying story about an illiterate mountaineer who came down to the village to square his account at the store. Whereupon the store's proprietor named an outrageous sum, and, when the mountaineer objected, took out his ledgers and led the mountaineer through complicated columns of figures, which purported to prove that the storekeeper had enormous amounts of money rightfully due him. "Figures don't lie," he said. To which the mountaineer replied, "Yes, but liars sure do figure."

Of course, Sam took the edge off the story; even in anger, he was still smooth enough to do that. He told Kennedy he had no reason to doubt his word. But when Kennedy said, in response, that he was just showing the figures, Sam replied that that was what the storekeeper had said, too.

Sam had always been able to get by with this sort of thing — at least, since he'd been in the Senate. He was fond of intense drollery like this, a form of skewering wit that some would find insulting. His aides, he found, enjoyed such comments, and eagerly took them up. It was like a bonus in their paychecks. It was consoling to be so near the shrine of virtue, and making sure that the Senator never saw what the Senator did not want to see was a small price to pay for such glory.

Still, Kennedy kept on, citing from the charts, showing how massive discrimination against the Negro was rampant throughout the South, and especially in education. Which, of course, also had its effects in other areas — because a Negro who had been afforded no opportunity to go to school could hardly be expected to pass a literacy test. And, of course, if he was voteless, he could not vote money for Negro schools. And still Kennedy kept on. So Sam tried another tack, and, seizing on that small portion of the statistics relating to North Carolina, began to defend his state, saying that it had done a good job in educating the Negro, and that, in fact, it had more Negro school superintendents than several of the northeastern states put together — including Massachusetts. And Kennedy responded by saying that North Carolina had more Negro school superintendents because it had segregated schools.

This argument came to its climax on the last session, September 11, less than two weeks after 200,000 Negroes and whites had shown up for the March on Washington, had thronged up en masse all the way from the Lincoln Memorial to the Washington Monument to hear Martin Luther King give his "I have a dream" speech.

For hours, then, Sam argued with Robert Kennedy about the relative merits of North Carolina and Massachusetts, and maybe even scored a point or two because Kennedy let him, because the statistics did show a clear pattern of racial discrimination in North Carolina schools. But Kennedy, full of lanuginous compromise, was willing to concede inches on this minor front because he was still, incredibly, after the larger gain: he wanted Sam to change his mind.

Finally, Kennedy said, "Senator, with the kind of prestige you have in the United States, you could make a major difference in ending these kinds of practices, as well as bringing the country through a very difficult period of transition. That is all I ask of you, Senator."

ERVIN: The only thing you have a right to ask of me is that I stand and fight for the Constitution, and for the basic rights of Americans. That is what I am doing now. You are not correct in saying I have never spoken out against discrimination . . . All my life I have fought against it. As a member of the North Carolina Legislature many years ago, one of my first acts was to introduce a bill to authorize the issuance of bonds to defray the cost of construction for an adequate school for Negro children in my home town. As a member of the school board in my home town, I fought for equal compensation for all teachers regardless of their respective races. As a member of the Legislature of North Carolina, I have always fought for liberal appropriations for the adequate education of all North Carolina's children. As a citizen, lawyer and judge in North Carolina, I have always stood for the right of all men to stand equal before the law. As a citizen and a public official, I have always stood for the right of every qualified voter to register and vote. So you are not very just to me in saying I have not fought discrimination.

To Kennedy, of course, this had little to do with the issue at hand. Throughout the hearings, he had seen Sam ignore the array of statistics to zero in on small matters in his state or home town, and tried to remind Sam that he was a Senator, not of Morganton, North Carolina, but of the United States. Now Kennedy tried to discuss Mississippi, where the practices of racial discrimination were, perhaps, the most glaring.

"I asked you whether, in your judgment, any discrimination existed in the State of Mississippi against Negroes. You said to your knowledge, it did not. I don't see how you can . . ."

Sam broke in. "I told you the truth, Mr. Attorney General," he said. "I have never been in the State of Mississippi in my life, except on one occasion when I was asleep in a Pullman on a train which passed through the northern portion of Mississippi on the way to Memphis. I said I could not corroborate by personal knowledge any conditions in Mississippi. I said I would accept your statements to the effect that you claim to have and do have some evidence of discrimination. But I can't testify to that."

A few moments later, Kennedy made his final appeal. The hearings were almost at an end now. "I would say, Senator, I have a lawyer here who could take you down into some of these places and maybe your eyes would be opened."

But Sam said, "I have got to stay here and fight the destruction of Constitutional government which this bill contemplates, and haven't the time in this session of Congress . . . "

Kennedy leaned forward, imploring, voice taut. "Senator, it would only take forty-eight hours. Would you be willing to do that?"

It was embarrassing, that a man would try a thing like this, and Sam responded by saying "I do not have even forty-eight hours to spare from my fight to preserve Constitutional principles and the individual freedoms of all citizens of the United States."

The hearings were at an end, after having shown in high relief Sam's most basic attitudes toward civil rights. He had acted as impartially hearing the merits of both sides.

For a time, the 1963 civil rights bill went nowhere, as maneuvering continued behind the scenes. The Judiciary Committee, as expected, did nothing, and although the Commerce Committee reported out a public accommodations bill early in October, that, too, was held in abeyance, because the decisive negotiations were taking place on the other side of Capitol Hill, where civil rights supporters of both parties and the Kennedy men were working together, trying to find a compromise that could override Southern opposition on both houses.

It was into this atmosphere of waiting, of backstage maneuver, that news of the Dallas assassination broke. Sam heard it in his office and, a few minutes later, called in a secretary, dictated a statement. "The assassination of President Kennedy," it said, "is the greatest possible tragedy which could befall the United States and the Free World at the most crucial hour of history." He had put out many statements about murders over the past few years and was running out of things to say.

Now he stood in the doorway of his outer office, leaning up against the tall dark mahogany frame, looking out at the world from behind a face that no barber's towel would redden today. He was sixty-seven years old. Just the previous month, after a lifetime of membership, he had been made a 33rd degree Mason. It was some world. What you worked for all your life could be blown away by a little piece of lead no bigger than your thumb.

"A thing like this makes you sick," he said. For a long time he stood quietly there in the doorway. His aides, now, too, were quiet.

HEADS OR TAILS

Uncle Sam is the obverse of Uncle Tom.

Chapter 20

B<small>Y NOW</small> Sam had been to all the Civil War battlefields from Petersburg, Virginia, to Gettysburg, Pennsylvania, driving out on Sundays, in the Chrysler, with Harry Gatton. As often as not, they'd leave in the morning, at ten or eleven o'clock, missing church services. Anyway, the battlefields were more like church than church was, because his ancestors and relatives had been at the battlefields; their blood was part of the ground he now walked on.

The big battle on civil rights was coming up now, the one they all knew would be conclusive. Once more, the Southerners were divided into three teams, captained by Lister Hill, John Stennis, and Allen Ellender. Sam found himself on Ellender's team, and he prepared himself to speak at length against every portion of John Kennedy's civil rights bill, which the new President, Lyndon Johnson, was determined to ram through Congress. Even as the long Southern filibuster began on March 9, 1964, everybody in Congress knew a strong bill was going to be passed, that only the details remained to be settled, and that this was being handled behind the scenes by a few legislators and Administration officials. Thus, while the aging Southern Senators were prepared to grip on to one another's shoulder straps and plod grimly once more through the muddy black night of filibuster, there were no longer gun flashes lighting up the horizon toward which they marched. No major battle would be joined in their sector, the Senate floor, which was inhabited most of the time by only four Senators, two from each side, watching one another warily for signs of unexpected motions or maneuvers.

This time there were no all-night sessions because, first of all, gross, overpowering tactics weren't the style of the Majority Leader, Mike Mansfield, whose gentlemanly tendency was never to confront anybody openly on anything. Besides, such tactics were unnecessary, because everything was happening, really, down the hall in Everett Dirksen's office, and over on the other side of the Hill. The mood on the Senate floor was like that in a physics lab at olden Chapel Hill, on a Saturday afternoon, on the day the big game was being played on the other side of the campus.

There were the usual statistic-scuffles. The advocates of the civil rights bill, operating under the direction of Hubert Humphrey, pointed out that, ten years after the Supreme Court desegregation decision, less than 2 percent of the Negro children in Virginia went to integrated schools, and less than 1 percent in North Carolina, South Carolina, Georgia, Alabama, Louisiana, and Arkansas. In Mississippi, none.

Sam believed that such statistics had been cooked up to humiliate the South and he, too, could quote statistics. For instance, New York had 300,000 more Negroes than North Carolina, and yet employed only 3700 Negro teachers, as compared with 11,042 in North Carolina. What did that prove? Systematic discrimination against Negroes in New York? Passing a civil rights bill like this, Sam said, might do the job, all right, but the means employed were too severe; it was like curing a man's head cold by blowing out his brains.

But the assassination of John Kennedy had made passage of the bill inevitable. Over in the House, Administration officials, led by Robert Kennedy, were working out a civil rights bill that would overwhelmingly carry the House — including the conservative Republicans. This latter support for the civil rights bill, in turn, put pressure on Everett Dirksen, Minority Leader of the Senate, who was drafting his own version of a civil rights bill — one that would meet various Republican objections on the public accommodations clause. Then, once Dirksen had lined up enough Republican support behind him, he would direct his troops to vote for cloture — an end to the civil rights debate on the floor of the Senate, which droned on now through March, and April, and into May. Once cloture had been invoked, there was no doubt the bill would pass. The question was whether the necessary two-thirds would vote for cloture. This had never been done in a civil rights debate.

But now the decisive power was in the hands of Dirksen, leader of the thirty-three Republicans in the Senate. Dirksen didn't come to listen to Sam's speeches, didn't want to hear them, or see the legal citations, or argue about the Constitution. He was putting the bill together in the back rooms, had made up his mind, and there was nothing Sam or any other Southerner could do about it. On May 26, Dirksen's various proposals were introduced as a clean bill, a substitute for the pending measure. And from there, events moved rapidly to the finish.

Sam offered amendment after amendment, trying to weaken the civil rights bill, and, again and again, was defeated by lopsided votes. He was most strongly opposed, now, to that part of the bill establishing the Equal Employment Opportunity Commission. He argued that "the idea that you can legislate equality among men has been exploded," and that "this bill is going to be used to harass businessmen throughout the United States." But on June 9 his amendment to delete the EEOC was defeated on a 64–33 roll call vote. While Humphrey managed the bill on the floor, Mansfield and Dirksen were working together in the background to build a strong coalition, and on June 10 the two-thirds majority was achieved, and the longest Senate filibuster in history — seventy-five days — was cut off. On June 17, the Senate adopted the Mansfield-Dirksen substitute bill by a vote of 76 to 18, and on June 19, it passed the civil rights bill by a 73 to 27 vote. In the end, only six Republicans — including their presidential nominee, Barry Goldwater — joined the twenty-one Democrats from the Southern and border states in opposition to the bill. There was still some minor jockeying to be done, still some tailoring and fitting between the Senate and House versions, but this consumed only a few days, and on July 2, 1964, Lyndon Johnson, a Southerner, signed the civil rights bill into law.

Sam now was defeated, and for good, on what had been the major effort to date of his Senate career. The 1964 civil rights bill did change things by legislation and, whether for good or ill, changed them permanently. Essentially, it guaranteed Negro voting rights in an authentic and enforceable way, prohibited racial discrimination in hotels, motels, places of amusement, barbershops, and restaurants;

and required that all tax-supported facilities, whether federal, state, county, or municipal — be open on an integrated basis to all races. It gave the Attorney General power to initiate suits to bring about the desegregation of schools. It established the Equal Employment Opportunity Commission, and made it against the law, for employers and unions alike, to discriminate on the basis of race in hiring and firing. It cut off federal funds to any activity that wasn't integrated, and established a Community Relations Agency to shoe-horn in all this integration, to change people's attitudes. From now on, the American taxpayer, the white taxpayer, the Southern taxpayer, would pay the federal government to change the way he thought.

Sam had spent a decade defending the old way — and now the old way wasn't there to defend anymore. It was disappearing, like the past; it was getting so you had to search more and more before you could find it, let alone defend it. But Sam had believed in what he was doing, had fought well enough for them to put the markers up, so that the whole scene would relive itself out into the future like new grass sprouting from Manassas' rusty soil. What he regretted was the bitterness and misunderstanding that had arisen. He had never regarded himself as a racist or "a great mind in chains," as his opponents had done, and was annoyed by that school of thought which saw him sitting around in his Panama hat on his plantation, fulminating against the Negro. Well, he did not have a plantation, only a two-room apartment on Capitol Hill, and a small house, with very little lawn, in Morganton. He didn't own much of anything but books, and was glad, now, of the opportunity to let his mind be in chains to the books once more, to the history, biography, and poetry. He returned to those with relief at not having to spend each night hunched over the lined yellow pads and the endless citations from old constitutional law decisions. He had been the old way's lawyer on the civil rights question, and had lost.

He was sorry about John Kennedy's death, and wanted his opponents to believe that he was a kind man, a good man who had acted from principle, and from no selfish interest. Thus, when the opportunity came to work with Bobby Kennedy on bail reform, he did so, and introduced amendments to existing federal bail laws, and then new bills, designed to lighten the burden placed on indigent defendants. He wanted to fix it so that a man didn't have to stay in jail just because he couldn't come up with the bail or even the bondsman's fee, so that a man could make a modest cash deposit with the court in lieu of the usual surety. And he supported another bill requiring the prosecutor to show good cause why a defendant should be detained. Very many of the defendants whose rights he was thus protecting, he knew, would be Negroes, and he felt that this ought to prove something, and show his good faith.

He held a bail reform hearing with the Constitutional Rights Subcommittee, and had Bobby Kennedy come in and testify. This time, when Kennedy got up to go, he stopped, looked at Sam with that white chipmunk grin, and said, "If I may be permitted a personal remark, I appreciate being here with you, Senator Ervin. And we're all on the same side." Sam smiled back, and, a few minutes later, made a point of taking Kennedy aside in the hallway and talking with him. He had liked both the Kennedys, in spite of the civil rights, in spite of everything and because Bobby Kennedy, now, chose to believe in him as a good man rather than a racist. After all, the whole thing ran on trust: the government, the civilized world. When you had that — men who could take different sides and still get along — good things were possible even in defeat. Although God save the day if one of the weasel-men, the liars, got into power.

Perhaps there was more of the old way left than some people might think, and, unexpectedly, Sam was offered another opportunity to defend it. An offer came from a North Carolina industrialist, Roger Milliken, a textile multimillionaire, who asked that Sam become a lawyer again and try a case in front of the Supreme Court.

Sam knew that Daniel Webster and other United States Senators back in the nineteenth century had appeared as trial attorneys, but that was when Congress met four months in a year and even a Senator's job was part time. In the twentieth century, Spessard Holland of Florida had done it, but the practice was rare. It wasn't that Senators were averse to making some money on the side. But there were easier ways of doing it — for instance, the lecture circuit and the banquet circuit, with their lush honorariums for short speeches. Still, Sam was interested in the case, and agreed to take it. What was at issue — at least to Sam's mind — was whether a man could close up his business if he wanted to, without government interference.

Milliken, who owned a controlling interest in many textile mills (through a corporation, Deering-Milliken), had been having some difficulties at one of his mills down in Darlington, South Carolina. The mill, which had been built during the days of Grover Cleveland's presidency, was an antiquated place and, according to some, hadn't been making very much money. It had been in receivership for a time and was barely breaking even during the Second World War, at a time when most other textile plants were making large profits.

Milliken had called in an engineering consulting firm, which said that, in order for the mill to survive, new machinery had to be put in — which would require that many employees be fired. As Darlington was getting ready to put these recommendations into effect, the union appeared on the scene and told the employees that if they would vote a union shop, the union would see to it that the layoffs didn't take place. An election was held, and the union won. This in spite of Milliken's having warned that he couldn't afford to pay union wages. Faced with the unionization of his workers, he closed the mill.

Thereupon the textile union brought a charge before the NLRB that Milliken had committed an unfair labor practice, and demanded that he be required to keep the mill open. What they said, in effect, was that Milliken had been willing to destroy the economy of the whole town in order to set an example for the would-be unionizers among the 19,000 employees at Milliken's other mills. For several years, then, the proceedings went back and forth between the NLRB and the trial examiners, with the former always ruling for the union, and the latter for Milliken.

Finally the matter was brought before the Supreme Court, which had two issues to decide: whether the Darlington Mill was a separate entity from the other Deering-Milliken enterprises, and, if it was a separate entity, whether Milliken had a legal right to close the mill. It was the second of these two points that Sam was asked to argue.

So now, as 1964 got older, and the national elections were held, and the trouble in Southeast Asia began to look more serious, Sam worked on his law case, his new cause. It was strange and exciting to be a lawyer once more, to be working on a law brief that would be listened to. All his civil rights arguments in the Senate had been law briefs, too, but much of their charm, and all their force, had been eroded by Sam's sure knowledge that they were being presented in a forum where, ultimately, very few men even bothered to listen to legal arguments, where almost everybody had made up his mind in advance, on the basis of political and personal considerations. This had even been true of his allies. But now, preparing the Darlington case, he began to convince himself that, in the Supreme Court, political considerations would disappear, he would be listened to, and the arguments he advanced might have some permanent effect on the right of a man in the United States to dispose of his personal property as he saw fit.

He went into Court that December believing that the thing would be decided much as a proposition in Euclidean geometry might be decided, by rational arguments rationally attached to the axioms, postulates, and corollaries of Constitutional law. There were others, more realistic perhaps, who believed that all cases were decided on political considerations, and who, even now, were bringing political pressure to bear on the Court. Richard Nixon, for instance, was inviting businessmen's close attention to the Darlington case, warning that American industry was about to be taken over by socialism, calling it one of the most important labor relations cases ever to appear before the Supreme Court.

On the morning the case was to be heard, December 9, Sam walked across the street, went into the Court at ten in the morning, and was kept waiting for three hours while the Court heard other cases. But it had been sixteen years since he'd tried a case as a lawyer, and in the meanwhile had never waited for anything other than an occasional red light. He had with him his big brown attaché case and a couple of law books, and now as he sat there waiting, more arguments occurred to him, and he put the attaché case up on his lap, put the brief on it, and began to scribble marginal notes. By the time his case was called he had about twice as much to say as when he'd come in, and he strode across the crimson carpet, up to the raised lectern, and began speaking very fast, taking off his glasses and gesturing emphatically with them, bringing in the Bible quotes, everything, telling the Supreme Court — with the Chief Justice, Earl Warren, sitting bull-like there in the middle of them — that "God judgeth not as man judges; but God looketh upon the heart." He was moving into the heart of his argument, when he looked up, in the middle of a sentence, and realized that Warren had adjourned the Court.

In the end, however, the ruling went his way on the point he argued, and it was decided that a man could close a single enterprise whenever he had a mind to. For Milliken, however, it turned out to be a Pyrrhic victory, because the other point was eventually decided against him — the Darlington Mill was declared to be part of the larger enterprise — and thus he was obliged to pay millions of dollars of interim earnings to Darlington's workers until they could find other jobs. But Sam went back to his Senate chores, proud of having fought for free enterprise, proud of having won. It was very strange, really, that blacks, laborers, and other liberals should accuse him of not fighting for freedom; look what he had done for the freedom of Roger Milliken.

As always, there was the sweet, busy routine of case-work and pork barrel projects to be escaped down into. There were postmasterships to be awarded, cancer research funds — to help the tobacco industry — to be voted for. There was the vitriolic and ongoing struggle with the Federal Trade Commission over whether the cigarette industry was to be destroyed by some bureaucrat stamping a cancer warning on every package. There was the Cape Lookout National Sea Shore Park to be established, and the Environmental Health Center to be put in North Carolina's Research Triangle. There was the new Federal Building in Greensboro. There were the retirement rumors to be discounted, joked at, laughed at. Although, privately (always privately), he did not like to hear people saying he was going to retire. Such a thing would be unnatural, because he was only sixty-seven, eighteen years younger than his father had been when he was still trying cases up in the mountain courts.

But he knew that this pork barrel stuff and the case-work would almost run themselves, if he'd let them, especially since his partner, Everett Jordan, kept watch on such things and liked doing it. There ought to be something else that was more important.

There was Viet Nam, of course, which troubled him even though he was assured by Stennis and Russell that the Gulf of Tonkin Resolution was all right, and that Johnson's sending the troops over there in 1965 was all right, too. Sam still trusted Russell and always would, but he remembered clearly now getting other advice, back in 1954, when he first came to the Senate, from General Matthew Ridgway, a man he also trusted, who'd warned him, in the aftermath of Dienbienphu, that the United States could not win a land war on the Asian mainland. Ridgway had said that the country was ill served by people like Nixon, who was after Eisenhower to send in the troops.

Viet Nam, then, was important business. It wasn't like deciding whether to spend a few million dollars developing a new tank, on which question he could pick up the phone and find the answer from Russell. And so, now, in 1965, Sam closeted himself away for long hours in the cool marble seclusion of his office, methodically going through stacks of books on Viet Nam, its history and present condition, reading the government white papers and the chart-filled intelligence reports on the interlocking organizational infrastructure of the Viet Cong, which seemed to be different from any political party down in North Carolina. Which killed people, murdered them publicly, was hard-bitten, doctrinaire, relentless. Nor did Sam limit himself to the government's publications, but read, as well, the good books by Halberstam and Browne, which said that American involvement was futile and satanic.

The more Sam read, the more he regretted that American troops had been sent over there, the more he despaired of anything good, ever, coming of it. On the other hand, there didn't seem to be anything that could be done about it. So Sam continued to support the President, in spite of his private misgivings. And continued to look for the thing that would interest him.

This year, amazingly, the Johnson Administration came down with yet another voting rights bill, one aimed only at the South. What they proposed was that in states requiring literacy tests federal voting registrars would be sent in when it was shown that less than 50 percent of the population eligible to vote in the 1964 Presidential election had voted. These registrars would stay on the scene until the state could show a record of ten straight years of having more than 50 percent of the people vote. As it was set up, the bill would apply to most of the Southern states, including thirty-four of North Carolina's 100 counties. Sam regarded it as a bill of attainder, whose most outrageous provision was that cases to be decided under the new law would be heard, not in the locality in which they arose, but in Washington, D.C., at the District Court.

This time it was Nicholas Katzenbach who came before Sam's Constitutional Rights Subcommittee advocating the Administration's position, and Sam kept the new Attorney General on the stand, hour after hour, day after day, grilling him. He would pose long, involved questions, detailing to Katzenbach the horrors that would follow passage of the Administration's bill — states' rights violated, individual rights violated, deep and brutal humiliations — and conclude by asking Katzenbach if that weren't so. And Katzenbach said yes.

It wasn't like Bobby Kennedy now, or even Herbert Brownell. There was no longer any pretending that the Administration didn't mean serious business. They knew they had the votes, and they sat there at the committee table and told you to your face that you and your state both could go shove it, and that they would haul you and your state both into Washington, D.C., to be judged.

At this point, perhaps, Sam could have taken over leadership of the Southerners, thus fulfilling the prophecies made when he came to the Senate. There was plenty of opportunity. The old Southern Senators were disappearing, as the old Confederate veterans of Sam's young manhood formerly had done. Richard Russell was desperately ill with emphysema, and returned to the Senate much weakened, to the tail end of the voting rights debate, with some mild remark to the effect that he had his convictions and would vote them, but that the die was cast. Harry Byrd was too ill to participate at all. And South Carolina's Olin Johnston, who'd voted with Sam consistently on the civil rights issues coming up before the Judiciary Committee, was dead.

But Sam was tired of the civil rights battle and was looking for other things to do, things he knew about. He was no longer interested in Viet Nam. Let Stennis handle that one. In the evenings, he stayed up late, watching the newscasts on television and sometimes the shows that came afterward, and he would sleep late in the mornings. His weight was creeping up on him, he was uncomfortable about the middle, and it seemed sometimes that the refrigerator was the only place he could find anything truly satisfying anymore. But he began to skip the noonday lunches with Margaret, and to drink Metrecal alone at his desk.

Some of the things he tried to do brought on more charges of racism. This year, 1965, the Johnson Administration was sponsoring a bill to change America's immigration quotas, which had been set in the twenties according to a "national origins" formula that let in Northern Europeans rather liberally, and severely restricted the numbers of Eastern Europeans. Sam thought the old system was pretty good, and had belonged, for years, to the nativist associations that had lobbied for the legislation in the first place. In the committee hearings, he clashed with Jacob Javits, who favored the Administration's bill. It had nothing to do with race, Sam kept telling him. It was just that immigrants should be admitted on the basis of the good that had been done this country by those of their country. That this would plenteously include Anglo-Saxons (and Irishmen, whom he praised to Teddy Kennedy's smiling face), and exclude Eastern Europe's Jews was coincidental.

Take Abyssinia, he said, "whose King, Haile Selassie, claims to be the direct descendant of King Solomon and the Queen of Sheba. So that Abyssinia has had a long time to contribute something to American development. But I can't think of one contribution the Abyssinians have made to the United States in all these years. Yet this 'reform' would allow twenty-two million Abyssinians to come into this country at the expense of the Irish or English or any of these people who have made the greatest contribution."

When his discussion of Abyssinians resulted in his being called racist again, Sam was aggrieved. "I tried not to say anything about race," he said. "In fact I believe the Abyssinians are Caucasians, of the same race as I am, but I wouldn't know because I never saw an Abyssinian I knew of." Then, the pat on the head. "All I know is that my cousin's son thinks so highly of them that he has gone to be a missionary among them."

He wasn't a racist; he was a Senator, and becoming, through seniority and influence, a powerful one at that. He lived all day, every day, as a member of an institution whose central tradition was never to bring into question the motives of any Senator. He lived surrounded by smooth, bright, well-paid young aides, none of whom had questioned Sam's motives about anything or who'd ever had anything to say except yes. It was well known that the Senator had good motives.

As for the immigration question, Sam saw the danger as coming no longer from Eastern Europe, but from Latin America, whence tantivy whole avalanches of difficult-to-assimilate immigrants came, their numbers having increased by 230 percent in the past five years, and more than 400 percent in the past ten. Finally, aware that here, too, some sort of bill was going to pass, he proposed an amendment which let the administration have its European immigration without the national origins quota, in return for a 120,000 annual quota on all immigrants from the western hemisphere. And this was passed.

He was also working hard to keep the Senate from repealing that section of the Taft-Hartley labor act that enabled the states to have right-to-work laws barring union shops. But he decided he needed some time off.

He took Margaret with him, flew in a jet to Europe, where they spent two days snugly in a Paris hotel. He did not take her venturing out with him to Cantigny and Soissons — whose fields were still pocked from the shellfire he'd endured there almost half a century ago. It would have been much too strange, now, to walk those quiet and peaceful autumn fields, to hear the whistle of birds, scuttle of rabbits, whisk of wind. And she with him there now; she to whom he'd once so madly hoped to return. And now this, the great silence, whisper of their jet high-sailing invisibly above the old battlefield, exclamation mark of contrails in the old blue sky; now this. Old now, old, and she old beside him. And together alone in Europe, with no wish to visit those empty fields where once his strong young legs had dashed for the mere prize of living. And now this. There was no place he could take her that would not remind both of them that most of life was gone. It was only on Capitol Hill, in the Senate, surrounded by the deferential aides, solicited for his vote, his influence, that he could feel that anything, ever, had been worth dashing anywhere for.

He beamed and grinned at the reporters who met him on his return. He told them that he, Sam, had changed more than Europe had. And returned to the Capitol's corridors, where a man who wished to look up could see Brumidi's bright frescoes reassuring him he was part of history, and therefore less mortal than the whispering brown grass on the battlefields of France. It was a funny thing about the modern wars — their monuments were all dedicated to organizations; you didn't see monuments to men anymore. It was almost as if men didn't matter; as if a man were as anonymous, and useless, as brown grass on old battlefields.

But he himself wasn't useless, he was convinced. He still worked long hours, still learned new things, and believed himself to be as able as any man in Washington. And, with the civil rights fights over, he began to see, at last, the cause that could involve him passionately, a thing that, as yet, had no name.

The government, acting on Lyndon Johnson's private say-so, and with no authority from Congress, was establishing quota systems for hiring Negroes, demanding they be hired whether they were qualified or not, seeing to it they were kept on the job and promoted, whether they worked or not — and all this at the expense of qualified white workers. The former government policy — that you hired the best man for the job — had been thrown out, and this, Sam believed, was not only unfair, but weakened the government. During the past three years, he found, Negro employment within the government had increased at a rate three times that of white employment. Letters from whites, complaining about this reverse discrimination, began to come into the Constitutional Rights Subcommittee, and to him, personally, in ever-increasing numbers.

As part of his racial program, Johnson was trying to control the private lives of government employees, and, through them, the lives of citizens throughout the country. In the Federal Maritime Commission, the Treasury Department, and the Commerce Department, memorandums had been put out urging

> . . . employees to participate at the community level with other employees of schools and universities and with other public and private groups in cooperative action to improve the employment opportunities and community conditions that affect the employability of minority group citizens.

Which seemed to add up to, "use your spare time to give the Negro ascendancy over the white man." Not only were the government workers urged on by their bosses to do these things, but the bosses, in turn, were obliged to report back on who complied and who didn't. So a man's promotion might depend on whether he spent his free time pushing the Negro cause. This was being done throughout the government.

But this new thing with no name had to do with more than just civil rights, and government intrusion into private lives was growing ever more extreme. For instance, Sam learned that a woman who applied as a typist in the State Department was required to fill out, in its entirety, a form containing 570 questions. She was to answer these questions, the instructions said, "quickly and without any thinking or deliberation." She was to tell about her family life, whether she hated her mother and father, whether her sex life was satisfactory, whether she believed in God, what she dreamed about, whether thoughts sometimes entered her mind that were too bad to talk about. Was she inhibited sexually? She had to tell. What about her menstrual periods? She had to tell. The State Department told Sam it had to know these things, so as "to provide suitable help to the individual and to protect the interests of the U.S. Government."

The woman's case wasn't unusual, Sam found; the same sort of thing was being done throughout the government. For instance, employees were obliged to tell what part of their income was going to charity, and what part, if any, was being spent on United States Savings Bonds. They were to tell, in writing, whether they were taking part in community activities, and whether, in so doing, they were supporting the social and economic theories of the Administration.

The Treasury Department, for example, sent out a directive saying that managers should "be alert to working with and support of private groups such as the NAACP, the Urban League, Local Human Relations Councils, and Plans for Progress." And when Sam, in the subcommittee hearings, asked the chairman of the Civil Service Commission whether he didn't "think that such organizations as the Hibernian Society, the Anti-Defamation League of B'nai Brith, the Masonic Fraternity, the Women's Christian Temperance Union, and the Knights of Columbus are engaged in worthwhile projects?" he was told that yes, they might be — but they didn't happen to show up in the directive.

And still the reports came in, from the National Security Agency, the Small Business Administration, the Department of Housing and Urban Development (whose very existence Sam had opposed). Employees were required to tell whether they had the night sweats, or wet their beds, or had a parent who'd killed himself, or had a parent who'd had syphilis. From everywhere, more questionnaires. From Andrews Air Force Base Hospital came one that required the employee to check one of three boxes:

1. I am now buying bonds and will buy more.
2. I am not now buying bonds but will begin.
3. I am unwilling to accept my fair share for assisting the President of the United States in making this bond drive a success.

And, throughout the military, the penalties for non-cooperation were: weekend passes denied; extra KP assignments required; forced marches required. There were threats of adverse efficiency reports. And men were threatened with shipment to Viet Nam if they refused to buy bonds.

For years now, Sam had dealt, personally, with many executive branch bosses, on many hundreds of small case-work matters affecting his constituents, and it did not surprise him that these men could be petty and vengeful. What was surprising, and difficult to understand, was their pruriant itch for prying into the lives of their employees. It was almost as if they had no lives themselves and wished to live through other persons.

POTATO FARMER

Stanley Moore had been editor of the Morganton News-Herald *for forty years, and I went to see him at the paper's offices, which were just a couple of blocks from the court house. He was a small, quick-moving little verb of a man, about sixty-five years old, and had just returned to his job after a serious illness. This was his first day back on the job, and his strength hadn't come all the way back, but he was determined to stay on until quitting time. He was interested in Morganton, fascinated by the town, and we spent the morning discussing Morganton politics of the 1930's.*

"You know, Sam came to see me here in Morganton during the Watergate hearings," *Moore said now.* "It was during the break. There must of been a hundred reporters and television cameramen around here. All the networks sent trucks, and everybody was looking for him. They couldn't find him because he was over at my apartment."

"Did they catch up with him?"

"Oh no. He knows the back ways in this town. Anyway, I just said hello to him. You know, I figured he was busy and wasn't even going to sit down. But I gave him some bourbon, and he sat there and talked. I didn't have my strength back so he just kept on talking. And I got him some more of the bourbon. He stayed a right good while."

"I guess he was glad to get away from the reporters."

"I expect so," *Moore said.* "But it wasn't just that. He wanted to know if I needed any money. But he didn't know how to put it. You know, he's shy — you wouldn't think it, a public man and all. But he just went on talking, and he would throw in how he had some extra money and how it plagued him, and how he never could figure out what to do with it, and that he didn't want to put any more in the savings bank, and how he wished he could find somebody to loan it to; how he wouldn't be in any hurry to get it back, if he could find some-

body like that; how the man who borrowed the money would actually be doing him a favor."

Moore rearranged some things on his desk in a businesslike way. As I was leaving the building, he came out of his office, caught me at the door, and lowered his voice.

"Say, did anybody ever tell you about the potatoes?"

"Potatoes?"

"Yes." A secretary walked by and Moore stopped speaking until she'd gone down the hall. When he spoke again it was in a very low tone and I had to lean over to hear him.

"He had this victory garden, see. It was back during the war. And he had him these bib overalls he bought down at Lazarus'. So this fellow went out to Sam's to see him on business, and just as he came around the side of the house he saw Sam walking out in the back yard with a peeled potato on a plate, and, you know, he stood there and watched while Sam diced the thing up into these little bitty cubes, like they do for potato salad. Then he would walk along a ways, and set the plate down on the ground, and walk over in those bib overalls and pick up the hoe. Then he would come back and dig him a little hole in the ground. Then he would walk back and get the plate, and go over to the hole, and drop one of the little cubes down in it, and sort of cover it up with his foot. Then he would do the same thing over again. The fellow got so interested, watching Sam, that he forgot all about his business. It went on for about an hour and a half."

"Didn't anybody ever tell him potatoes won't grow that way?"

Moore shook his head. "You know," he said, "Sam takes notions about things. And the philosophy around here is to leave him alone."

"That is the philosophy up in Washington, too," I said.

"When I asked him about it he said he was trying to raise potato salad. He said he liked potato salad better than mashed potatoes."

Moore followed me to the door, shook hands, and wished me good luck. "I always was more liberal than Sam," he said, "but you know, I've always liked him."

I liked him, too, and was glad to have the potato story. It was a funny story, all right, one for the book. Driving back to Washington that afternoon, I tried to remember whether I knew any funny stories about Sam's opposition to Medicare and the minimum wage, or about his sustained support of the war in South Viet Nam. But I couldn't think of any funny stories about those things.

Chapter 21

THE COLORS of the Capitol's dome changed as weather changed, as times of day changed: grayish blue when clouds scudded in low over the Potomac, glaring white in the sunshine, and, as the sunset roiled away redly over Virginia's hills, a chalky rose. Sam, who often walked over to the Capitol from his office, had seen it thousands of times now, and no two times the same. He had seen it when he was a boy, too, with his father, and in those days this dome had seemed lightsome, airy, as if it had floated down by mere condescension, and could, at any moment it wished, float away again. Since then Sam had learned that the thing was no architectural triumph of balanced arches, but thirty-five tons of cast iron smashing down on the building's fortified supports, threatening to drive it down into the ground and out of sight.

They'd been building the thing when the War Between the States came along, and would have stopped if it hadn't been for Lincoln, who made them keep on, so that the Confederate pickets across Long Bridge, over in Virginia, could see the dome and know the Union meant to endure. Now it had endured and, clustered around the battlefield of Manassas, where that war had begun, was mile after mile of homogeneous suburbs inhabited by thousands upon thousands of government employees, who'd had homogeneous educations, and who'd been taught, somewhere, that the path of virtue was to be bland as milk. Who believed that righteousness was doing what the boss wanted. In a way, it was fitting that these government employees should be so thoroughly obedient, because their ancestors who'd fought on those tourist fields had been obedient, too; had run in the direction they were told to run, shot at whom they were told to shoot. But it was unfortunate that these new Americans were so bland; they looked alike, talked alike, thought alike, and became passionate only when the television set was out of repair.

Sam did not see how day-to-day work for some government agency required the sort of fanatical discipline war called for, where servitude was often the only way to preserve one's life. And so, since no other Senator seemed interested in these people, he began to draw up what he called a Bill of Rights for Government Employees, one that would forbid the government from asking any employee anything about what race he belonged to, or where his people came from, or anything else about his family, or his financial condition, or his sex life. Sam's bill aimed to set up a labor relations board for government employees, one which would free them of petty tyrannies and take them out from under the control of the Civil Service Commission, which had proven itself to be a creature of management.

Suppose a man wanted to wear a frock coat and moustache, and pace up and down his front porch dictating impassioned letters to the newspapers? What business was that of the government? What if a man liked Lithuanian music, or was fond of painting his nose green on Saturdays? What was that to the government? When Sam was a younger man, people had been different from one another, and he did not see why they ought not be different now, if they wanted to be. He would prefer to have them different, prefer to have them active, salty, and contentious, not milky television zombies complacently filling out forms for their employers on whether they attended Parent-Teacher Association meetings or participated in the discussions of the Great Books Clubs. To Sam's way of looking at it, none of that was any of the government's business.

The more he studied such tendencies, the more he became convinced that the totalitarian malaise wasn't limited to the government, but was growing up quickly throughout American society, even down in North Carolina, where the state legislature had recently passed a "radical speakers law," designed to quarantine the Chapel Hill campus, and other campuses of North Carolina, from unorthodox views. Even the University itself, which had taught Sam his Jeffersonian respect for a man's privacy, had changed, and now he discovered, to his incredulity and great anger, that entering freshmen at Chapel Hill were routinely obliged to fill out questionnaires that included such true-false statements as:

> My sex life is satisfactory
> Sexual things disgust me
> I like to flirt
> I have been disappointed in love
> My Mother was a good woman
> I believe in the Second Coming of Christ
> Everything is turning out just like the prophets
>   in the Bible said they would

They were also required to describe, exactly, the color of their bowel movements. Perhaps more shocking than the test itself was another fact: out of 2000 freshmen entering each year, only one or two, at most, objected to answering these questions. This was the truly sinister thing, to Sam's way of looking at it: that people exposed to these invasions of privacy didn't seem to care.

On the one hundred and seventy-seventh anniversary of George Washington's first inauguration, he went with his wife to the American Good Government Society's awards banquet at the Sheraton Park Hotel to receive the medal they'd voted him, and sat there at the head table together with the other fellow being honored, Gerald Ford of Michigan, the new House Minority Leader. He watched the faces of the audience as the speaker warned that the power of the central government was growing, overwhelming individual rights, and went home and brooded about it. Even those who complained of government power had only a vague notion of how severe the threat to individual liberties had already become.

Thus, when Sam introduced his Bill of Rights for Government Employees, he was pleased to find that many Senators wished to cosponsor the thing — including Joseph Montoya, Herman Talmadge, Daniel Inouye, Hugh Scott, John Tower, and Everett Dirksen.

The bill passed the Senate, 79 to 4, with eleven more Senators, who hadn't voted because of absence, saying they would have voted for it if they'd been there. But it was destroyed in a House committee after intensive lobbying by the Federal Bureau of Investigation and the Central Intelligence Agency. This was, to Sam's way of thinking, *strange*, because the these agencies had been exempted from the bill's provisions, and *illegal*, because they were barred by law from lobbying. Sam even chased a couple of CIA lobbyists down the hall one day, reading to them, from the open law book, the words of the statute they were violating. But the FBI, CIA, and NSA (National Student Association) continued to lobby on Capitol Hill. And the Congress seemed more and more anxious to give these people whatever they wanted, such as the new Wiggle Seat the CIA wanted to buy this year (1966), an electronic device resembling an ordinary office chair, in which the prospective employee, by answering questions put to him by the interviewer, would be undergoing a lie detector examination without his knowledge. As the Philco Company brochure put it, "Nothing intrudes on the serenity of the setting. The patient does not see, much less wear, electro straps and wires are prominent only by their absence."

By now Sam had announced that he was going to run for re-election in 1968. It seemed wise to get his hat in the ring early this time. Because already supporters of Terry Sanford — a former FBI agent — were circulating the rumor that Sam was too old, that he was going to retire.

But he had more battles to fight, still had his vigor, and was not the pawn of kindless time. He was only seventy when he made the announcement in 1966, and when he finished the next term, if he won, he would be only seventy-eight. Besides, he knew that, inside his face, the eyes looking out at the world were the same ones that had gazed out with passionate love on the old campus of the University of North Carolina, where the greatest men in the world had warned him, half a century ago, that individual freedom would be threatened in America, and that he would have to fight for it. And thus, while he was old in lore, no doubt, and subtle in his disciplined resourcefulness, smoother than any Wiggle Chair could possibly be, his inner eyes burned out at the world with a youthfulness like those of some helmeted warrior in the *Iliad,* forever young. There was going to be a fight and he had been obliged to wait for it longer than he'd expected to, but he was ready for it, had nothing to lose.

With every so-called beneficence of the federal government, Sam believed, there was imposed an increasing measure of federal control. Aid to education meant textbook control, curriculum control; model cities meant the federal government was actually running cities; funds for highways came equipped with a bureaucrat who looked over your shoulder and told you whom you could hire. The government acted as though it had created the money in the first place. The government, he found, wanted to control the citizen but it did not want the citizen controlling it. Now the Health, Education and Welfare Department announced a plan whereby every baby born in America after a certain date would be assigned a number, to be carried with him the rest of his life. There was another plan, too, for a National Data Center, which would keep computerized files on all American citizens.

Even Sam's allies seemed hazy about what was going on. They would talk about the dangers of computers. But Sam found it unrealistic to place the blame on machines alone. Privately, for months, he had been studying computers: how they worked, what they did, what they'd be likely to do in the future. And when a newspaperman found him down at the IBM Center, at the age of seventy-one, learning about computer programming, Sam had this to say:

> On the basis of my study I came to the conclusion that we have nothing to fear from the computer as a machine. Alone, its use does not threaten individual privacy. The threat to privacy comes from men, from the motives of political executives, from the ingenuity of managers, and from careless technicians — and that threat is there whether the data are placed in metal file drawers, storage drums or in electronic computers.

It was men, not computers, who wanted the government to know everything about the private lives of American citizens, and who, on the other hand, wanted those citizens to know nothing whatsoever about the government. Everything was locked up; citizens couldn't see it; there was always a reason. So Sam introduced a freedom-of-information bill, whereby any citizen could walk into any government agency and inspect any records about himself not pertaining to national security. This was passed by the Senate, passed unanimously by the House, and signed into law by Lyndon Johnson, who was very good at arithmetic and knew in advance what the result would be if he vetoed anything that passed unanimously. So the thing became law, and Sam had won a round, although it still seemed to him there were too many things put under the heading of national security that didn't belong there. Government intrusion into citizens' lives seemed to be getting worse all the time, with complaints now coming in by the mail sack-full about the FBI bugging people's phones. It was amazing. It was not the old world. And things seemed to be careening out of control.

Sam had gotten rid of the Plymouth by now and bought himself a Chrysler, a big, heavy car with power steering and automatic shift; he used it mainly for the trips back and forth to Morganton, which he still made frequently, together with Margaret.

He kept the thing in the Senate garage. One Sunday he went and got it, and drove it up to the Methodist Building, where he picked up Margaret and an eighty-three-year-old friend of theirs, and, once they were in, pressed gently on the accelerator, expecting the smooth gliding he'd paid for. Instead, the thing scratched off like a hot-rodder's heap, juggernauted across Maryland Avenue, bashed down a tree, ploughed up the lawn, and came to smash itself into silence against the white marble wall of the Supreme Court, with its steering wheel locked, as it had been throughout the episode, and the brakes not working, and the motor stopped only because it was demolished.

The three of them were taken to the hospital, where Sam, talking with reporters after being treated and released, said, "I have always been accused of trying to run down the Supreme Court." But Margaret's back was hurt, and she spent six weeks over in Arlington at the Anderson Orthopedic Hospital.

Sam went on working. He had more power now than ever before. The Senate had created a new Subcommittee on the Separation of Powers, which was designed to be wholly Sam's own, to do with as he wished. The authorizing resolution said something about "studying the question" of the separation of powers, but everybody who voted for creating it knew Sam had already done the studying, had determined that the executive branch had too much power, and was intent on curbing it. There was a bill before the Senate now, which he had cosponsored, to ban all federal wiretapping except in cases of national security, and he was working on that, too.

And yet, very often it was the side issues which caused the most attention. The year before, for instance, he'd felt himself compelled to oppose Everett Dirksen's effort to get a Constitutional amendment passed permitting prayers in the schools. He had originally inclined toward Dirksen's views on that one, even told jokes in behalf of the bill, such as the one about the teacher who catches some of his students down on their knees, asks them what they're doing, and upon being told that they're shooting craps, says, "That's good; I thought you were praying."

But as Sam began to research the amendment — personally, as always — he came to the conclusion that the Founding Fathers intended the wall between church and state to be absolute. He took to the floor against Dirksen, in what was perhaps his best Senate speech, and singlehandedly caused the thing to be defeated. The "single-handedly" part was no exaggeration because, for some reason, most of the Senators came to hear Sam this time, and enough of them were swayed by what he said to defeat the Dirksen bill.

A biographer, in later years, might find that address contained a good statement of Sam Ervin's religious beliefs. And in any case, it was, perhaps, one of his more eloquent speeches:

> I look at the universe and behold with wonder the life-giving sun, which rises in the east at morn, travels across the sky by day, and sets in the west at eventide; the galaxies of stars, which twinkle in the infinite heavens; the clouds, which bring the soil-refreshing rain; the majestic mountains with hills at their knees; the rivers, which water pleasant valleys and fertile plains and run endlessly to the sea; the tall trees, which lift leafy arms heavenward to pray; the arbutus and dogwood, which brighten springtime, and the marigolds and roses, which ornament summer; the glory of the leaves and ripened crops of autumn; the crystal snowflakes, which descend so gently in winter; and the other beautiful things past remembering, which adorn the earth.
>
> I note with awe the order and regularity of the processes of life and nature as the tide ebbs and flows, as the harvest succeeds the seedtime, and as the heavenly bodies move in their orbits without mishap in conformity with natural laws. I observe with reverence that, despite the feet of clay on which he makes his earthly rounds, man is endowed with the capacity to obey conscience, exercise reason, study holy writings, and aspire to righteous conduct in obedience to spiritual laws.
>
> On the basis of these things, I affirm with complete conviction that the universe and man are not the haphazard products of blind atoms wandering aimlessly about in chaos, but, on the contrary, are the creations of God, the Maker of the universe and man.

Religion adds hope to man's desire for immortality. This desire is not to be attributed simply to the egotism of men, or their fear of the unknown beyond the grave, or their repugnance to the thought of their nothingness after death.

The pessimistic philosopher Schopenhauer was sadly in error in his caustic comment that "to desire immortality is to desire the eternal perpetuation of a great mistake." The longing for immortality is prompted by the most meritorious motives.

Life on earth at best is all too short and unfinished. Man entertains high hopes for an abundant life with his loved ones, and undertakes worthwhile things for them and his generation. His high hopes vanish as he is robbed of those he loves by death, and his hands drop the working tools of life while his undertakings are incomplete.

As a consequence of these things, our hearts cry out that there must be some place after life's fitful fever is over where tears never flow and rainbows never fade, where high hopes are realized and worthy tasks are accomplished, and where those we "have loved long since and lost awhile" stay with us forever.

I revere religion. I revere religion because it gives us these promises and this hope. I would preserve and protect the right of freedom of religion for all men.

Sam's opposition to the school prayer amendment was all the more reason for him to start his '68 re-election campaign early. What he had done may not have brought him popularity, but it made him feel better than many another such action had; it tended to show that he would go against his constituency when it came to a matter of conscience, thereby putting a better light on his ten-year fight against the civil rights bills.

Still, North Carolinians in ever-increasing numbers were speaking up and saying that he wasn't sincere; and now, as opposition to the Viet Nam War intensified, there were letters to the North Carolina newspapers, and letters to Sam himself, protesting his stand and questioning his motives. There were even delegations coming to his office — as often as not led by preachers — to protest to his face what he was doing, to hint, if not actually say, that his motives were sinister.

He had studied Viet Nam and the reasons for United States involvement there, and come to the conclusion that it was unwise for Johnson to have gone in with troops; but, since there didn't seem to be anything the Congress could do, Johnson ought to be supported.

Those who opposed him on this issue pointed out that his stand amounted to saying that Americans ought to support Johnson because he had acted unconstitutionally, and Sam, listening to them, oscillated between inattention and rage: inattention, because he counted on Stennis and Russell to tell him what was right; rage, because of the very presence of the clergymen in the political arena. These gallinaceous preachers had moved his church away from where he thought it ought to be — the calm and unmoving center of spiritual solace, whose true temporal power depended in large degree on its political indifference. It was very difficult, then, for Sam to discuss with a clergyman the merits of any political question. It was so very different from the way it had been when he was a boy, when the biggest honor a preacher could get was to be invited to dinner at the home of the elder who hired and fired him.

These were the sorts of things — the prayer debate, the confrontation with war objectors — that made news. Whereas the important thing, fighting the government's efforts to pry into and control the private lives of citizens, remained on the back page.

He brooded on the daily evidence of the government's enormous appetite for power. He would support the President on the Viet Nam thing, because he didn't see any other way, and because Stennis and Russell, whom he trusted, said it was all right; but the invasions of citizens' rights, which took place with Johnson's blessing — that was something else again; and Sam found it increasingly difficult, in his contacts with the President, to be polite. He was invited up to New York for the signing of the immigration act, and didn't go. He was invited out for a cruise on the presidential yacht, and declined. He became brusque, almost rude, in his dealings with LBJ. Then he ran head-on into him over a matter of patronage.

In 1966, there was an opening for a new judge on the federal Fourth Circuit Court of Appeals, and Sam recommended a Morganton neighbor, J. Braxton Craven, Jr., for the post, which was just one step down from the United States Supreme Court. Johnson, after a little delay, appointed Craven, who was sworn in by the Chief Judge of the Fourth Circuit, Clement Haynsworth.

This meant that a lesser federal judgeship fell vacant, because Craven, prior to his elevation to the Fourth Circuit bench, had been chief judge of the federal District Court for the western part of North Carolina. And, since Everett Jordan, the other North Carolina Senator, was from the eastern part of the state, it was assumed that Sam would, in effect, make the appointment to fill the vacancy, in the form of a recommendation to Lyndon Johnson.

But it didn't work out that way, and Sam, after having recommended Woodrow Wilson Jones, of Rutherfordton, heard nothing, except some rumors to the effect that the recommendation was being opposed by some Negroes in Charlotte, who had come to the conclusion that the man was a segregationist. Sam made the nomination in July, and by October, having heard nothing, sent a letter to Johnson suggesting that Jones, at the least, be given a recess appointment. Again he heard nothing. In January, Sam phoned Ramsey Clark, Johnson's Attorney General, and asked what was happening with the appointment, and got some unclear answer that left him feeling as if he'd just been through a swift revolving door and come out the same place.

Sam called back, and Clark told him the FBI had not yet filed its report on Jones. When Sam asked if the FBI been told to make the investigation in the first place, he got the answer, no. Besides, Clark said, there was a question as to whether the American Bar Association would say that Jones was qualified, because the man hadn't had any judicial experience to speak of.

One day, with Everett Jordan in tow, he took a cab up Pennsylvania Avenue to see Johnson. He was angry at being made to cool his heels, at being jerked around by Clark, and, most of all, at being publicly humiliated at a time when he was about to come up for re-election.

It ended up with Johnson shouting at Sam that everybody was after him, and with Sam, who'd not been shouted at since he was eleven, standing up and yelling back that if Jones's nomination didn't go through he wouldn't give fifteen cents for Johnson's chances of carrying North Carolina in the next presidential election. But when he left the White House, there was still no commitment from the President.

A few weeks later, Johnson phoned him, complaining that the Negroes were still after him, and wondering out loud how long it would take the nomination to get through the Senate if he sent it down. He didn't want any publicity, didn't want to give opposition time to form. Sam, who was at the center of the Inner Club by now, was able to tell him it would be dealt with at once.

Thus, Senator McClellan called a special subcommittee meeting at 10:20 in the morning and passed Jones's nomination in less than an hour, sending it on to the full Judiciary, which also passed it that morning. Sam brought it out on the floor and got it approved at 1:16 that afternoon. So it was all right, finally, about the Jones nomination, but during the delay and dispute Sam's attitude toward the President, and toward the presidency itself, had shifted. When he had come to the Senate, it would have been unthinkable that any man in the Oval Office would receive anything but deference. But now it was not that way anymore. It seemed to Sam that the man up there wanted to be a king.

It was strange, this new America, with its slick, expensive political machines. Sam voted against a bill that would have given him $375,000 of federal money to spend on television advertising when he ran for the Senate again. He didn't want the government control, and besides, he knew that when it came to campaign funds he wouldn't need to spend much more than what it cost for gasoline and an occasional bacon, lettuce, and tomato sandwich.

Indeed, he expected to win re-election with no more effort than sending out a couple of thousand personal letters to "friends." He didn't have any political organization to speak of; in point of fact, no organization at all. He would let Sanford do the organizing and poll-taking and barnstorming. Until finally Sanford must have believed his own polls, and once again, he didn't run against Sam.

So Sam won the Democratic primary in '68, beating his opponent by an overwhelming majority, and in the fall election won again, by a plurality of more than 300,000 votes over his Republican opponent. With that kind of victory, it was hard for him to believe that the America he had come up from — even the America of 1954 — had largely ceased to exist, was as irremediably lost in the past as was Martin Luther King, whom he'd never liked, and Robert Kennedy. Sam was sorry about their deaths because he detested gratuitous violence. At the same time, he believed that Kennedy and King had excited the passions of Americans in an unnatural way.

And the ultimate calamity had befallen the American presidency. Nixon was in now. Sam went back to the Senate, in January of 1969, with the wary watchfulness of an emergency room intern on Saturday night. There was no question that bad things were going to come in. The only question was what bad things, and when.

MOTHER-OF-PEARL

I was talking to one of his long-time aides, a Southerner, a friendly, smooth man, a true believer in Sam. Or rather, a true believer in "The Senator," as all the aides called him. I'd just gotten through saying that I'd read, somewhere, that the office of the presidency sometimes changes the men who hold it.

"Did Sam entertain any such notion so far as Nixon was concerned?" I asked him now.

He shook his head, and an amused glimmer came up out of his eyes.

"You know what the Senator had to say about the election of seventy-two?" he asked.

"No," I said.

"He called it a choice between stupidity and duplicity," the aide said, and smiled in a friendly way.

There was a buzzer on his wall attached to one of the little mother-of-pearl buttons on Sam's desk, and when it rang the aide would drop what he was doing and go see what the Senator wanted. He would do that without even thinking. Presumably there weren't any choices so far as he was concerned, not even between stupidity and duplicity.

Chapter 22

THE WEEK OF Sam's seventy-fifth birthday was busy, but not abnormally so. On Monday he excoriated the Justice Department for trying to bring one of Senator Mike Gravel's aides before a grand jury in order to question him about the Senator's public reading of the Pentagon Papers. It was the Senate's business, he said, and the executive branch had no business contemplating any sort of criminal charges against anything said on Capitol Hill. Later that day he introduced a bill under which the President would be forbidden to impound appropriated funds for more than sixty days without the approval of Congress. On Tuesday he presided over hearings on the proposed merger of the two major professional basketball leagues, and said that the merger, if allowed by Congress, would mean the virtual enslavement of all the professional athletes in both leagues. On Wednesday he still had sports on his mind; he denounced the American League for letting the Washington Senators remove themselves to Texas, and proposed that Congress put professional baseball under the antitrust laws. He also got in a couple of licks at professional football while he was at it. Later that day he announced plans for hearings, the following week, on freedom of the press. One of the first witnesses was to be Walter Cronkite, and one of the subjects of the hearings would be the Nixon Administration's recent attempts to subpoena reporters and their notes, especially in regard to the Pentagon Papers. That afternoon he flew up to New York City and delivered before the Association of American Publishers a speech saying that Nixon's recent attempts to strengthen the long-defunct Subversive Activities Control Board indicated a lack of faith in the freedom of speech amendment of the Constitution. On Thursday the basketball hearings continued, with Sam hitting hard at the giant sports trusts and bemoaning the condition of athletes who were the serfs of that system. On Friday he took a plane out to Louisville, Kentucky, and delivered a speech at the University of Louisville, again on the First Amendment, a fresh one. Then he got back on the plane and returned to his office to end the day at his desk, reviewing the week's case-work — which had been considerable, and which he'd kept a close eye on. He would work most of the weekend, too, although, of course, he would not neglect the party that had been planned the next day to celebrate his seventy-fifth birthday.

It was an ordinary week, not nearly so intense as some of those that were to come, nor as desperately embattled as some of those he'd just been through. Because he'd been locked in struggle with Nixon's myrmidons from the moment the new President had come into office two and a half years ago.

It had started off mildly enough, with the new Treasury Department guidelines for dealing with citizens who tried to see (without prior appointments) high government officials, like the President, or the Secretary of the Treasury, or the Secretary of Agriculture. The Secret Service took the position that the mere wish to do such a thing was strong evidence of mental instability, and thus, as a matter of routine, many such persons were taken to St. Elizabeth's Hospital, and confined for thirty days' observation. After that, their names went into the Secret Service files, to be passed around to other government agencies. The names of those who wrote frequent letters of complaint about Administration policies also went into such a file. All of this made Sam uneasy, and he wrote the Secretary of the Treasury, complaining about it, and got no satisfactory response.

Next, he was told that the FBI had taken notes as one of his speeches down in Statesville, North Carolina. He did not see any sense in that, and wrote J. Edgar Hoover about it, and again got no satisfactory response. Then there was the matter of the censored mail, the Post Office Department having taken it upon itself to open and read the overseas letters of American citizens. Sam wrote the Postmaster General about that, and was once more sent whirling through the revolving door. These things had taken place in the quiet, ominous first year of Nixon's reign, before it was clear that it was a reign and not just another presidency. Then, early in 1970, Nixon had sent the Crime Bill for the District of Columbia up to the Senate, and from that moment on Sam had no doubt about the totalitarian intentions of the Administration.

It was a complicated bill, in sheer length longer than an average novel, but its major points were plain. For one thing, there was a "no-knock" provision empowering police to break into a citizen's home at any hour, without announcing themselves, and without a warrant specifically stating what was to be seized; they could take anything they wanted to take, including the citizen himself. It authorized wiretapping and bugging without a court order. It authorized the bugging of confessionals, bedrooms, doctors' offices. It said that if a citizen sued a policeman for unlawful arrest, and won, he was still obliged to pay that policeman's legal fees. It required that sixteen-year-olds be tried as adult offenders, and sentenced as adults. And it empowered the courts to authorize preventive detention, whereby anybody who'd been jailed by the police could be held without bail, and without charges, for thirty days, on the strength of police suspicion.

It would have been bad enough if the D.C. Crime Bill had affected only the 800,000 residents of Washington (most of whom were Negroes), but, in fact, it was intended as a model crime bill for the whole nation. Once again, the bureaucrats came before Sam, giving statistical reasons for violating the Constitution. For instance, they told him that, in 1969, in the forty-odd square miles of the District of Columbia, more than 56,000 felonies had been committed, including 7,071 armed robberies, 287 murders, and 336 forcible rapes. What they seemed to be saying was that the Negro was running amok, and that, in response, they proposed to suspend the Constitution, not only for the Negroes, but for everyone else as well.

It was hard for Sam to believe that serious Americans were seriously considering such things. In North Carolina, a man's home was his castle, the police were supposed to come up to the door and knock like anybody else, and if they wanted to take something from the house they had to have a warrant stating specifically what it was, and have good cause for the warrant, too. But the Nixon crime bill proposed to do away with all that. Where Sam had come from, there had been only one way to put a man in jail, and that was to convict him of a crime; but Nixon wanted the police to take on the powers of juries and judges. Nixon won, too, ramming the bill through the Senate in spite of Sam's determined opposition, ramming it through the House, and signing it into law.

But there was more, enough to suggest a pattern that Sam regarded as sinister. For instance, Nixon had seized on a four-day Christmas recess to pocket-veto a $225 million appropriation to train badly needed general practitioners by establishing family doctor specialty departments in medical schools across the country. The bill had been overwhelmingly passed by both houses of Congress. And, of course, it was unconstitutional for any President to pocket-veto anything just because Congress happened to turn its back for a weekend. But Nixon had gotten away with it.

Worse was the matter of impoundment. Repeatedly, Nixon refused to spend funds authorized by Congress. If he'd vetoed the authorizing bills, Congress would have overridden the vetoes, so Nixon hadn't even bothered doing that; he had just refused to use the money, and had gotten away with that, too.

Nixon was attempting to remove the executive branch from any responsibility to the Congress. The government had been designed in the first place so that the executive branch would have some accountability to the Congress, by requiring that the Senate confirm and continue to support the cabinet officers. Under the Nixon Administration, this was still the requirement, but the cabinet officers did not count anymore, were merely high-paid errand boys of the Administration: rich, smooth spaniels who would endure any abuse, and who would do anything the public relations men in the White House told them to do. The Nixon men in the White House, who really ran the government now, did not have to be confirmed by anybody, were beholden only to their master. On top of that, Nixon had created a supercabinet post, the Office of the Management of the Budget, whose officials did not have to be confirmed, and who controlled spending in all the other departments.

Sam introduced bills that would have made the Nixon pocket-vetoes illegal, required that no funds could be impounded for more than sixty days, and made it obligatory for the two top officials of

OMB to be confirmed by the Senate. This bill passed, but was vetoed by Nixon. Later, Sam introduced a bill requiring that future incumbents of these posts be confirmed by the Senate.

He might well have reason to suspect that if he continued in his opposition to Nixon, North Carolina would have to pay. The federal government now spent something like three and a half billion dollars each year in North Carolina, and the state needed the money; was poor. Or at least, a lot of the people down there were. Due to the low unionization rate, its manufacturing workers (who made up 60 percent of the work force) now earned the lowest weekly wage in all the states. North Carolina's average black family earned about half of what an average white family did. Its public assistance standard was the second lowest in the country, its median of school years completed was three years under the national average, and nearly half of its preschool children were subsisting on diets deficient in vitamins A and C, iron, calcium, and protein. So the federal money was needed.

Sam had recently been found by some pollster to be the most admired man in North Carolina, and he was proud of that. Already he was the fourth oldest man in the Senate. He had seniority, power, and the will to act, and it just may have been that his age made him more dangerous to opponents who thought he couldn't handle himself, who took his tentative, absent-minded manner for senility. The truth was that he had been tentative and absent-minded like this when he was eighteen, and so now, full of cunning and power, and with nothing to lose, he represented a formidable threat to anyone who crossed him in a serious way — which Nixon was doing repeatedly.

Sam had never liked the man. He had despised Nixon ever since learning of the lies he had spread in his first California election against Jerry Voorhis; despised him all the more for the lies he'd told as Vice President; and had become alarmed at the dozen insidious ways in which Nixon was successfully arrogating power to himself.

That was even before the latest, worst thing, the revelation of the Nixon administration's massive spying on United States citizens, and the destructive use of information gained from that spying. Government offices had become great storehouses of secret information on citizens — and the man to whom the citizens had given the key was Nixon.

Sam had conducted investigations on the government files, and knew what was in them. For instance, the Department of Justice, he knew, had a data bank containing detailed personal information on the more than 13,000 people who had been involved in civil disorders since 1968. The Department of Agriculture had folders on more than 500,000 borrowers and 50,000 investors, as well as records on the more than 300,000 farmers who'd bought some federal crop insurance. The Secret Service computer tapes contained the names of about 50,000 persons. The Internal Revenue Service, of course, had in storage, and on instant recall, details of the tax returns of more than seventy-five million citizens. The Pentagon had very detailed files on more than seven million Americans who at one time or another may have applied for a job requiring a security clearance. The Veterans' Administration preserved files on more than 13,500,000 veterans and dependents who now received benefits, or who had received them in the past. The Department of Housing and Urban Development maintained records on more than 4,500,000 Americans who'd gotten FHA loans, and planned to computerize its information file on more than 300,000 builders and other businessmen. The Department of Labor had files on more than two million Americans who'd held jobs in federally financed work and training programs. All that was coded by social security numbers. And of course, the Social Security Administration had detailed files on more than one hundred million Americans, including the earnings records of nine out of ten jobholders in the country, and including detailed information on the 26,200,000 Americans whose crime was getting old enough for social security — and more detailed information on the twenty million who'd come under Medicare. The Department of Transportation, too, was doing its share by keeping on instant tap the names of the 2,600,000 American citizens who'd been denied drivers' licenses or whose permits had been revoked or suspended. And then, of course, as always, there was the Federal Bureau of Investigation, which was in the process of computerizing its fingerprint files on the nineteen million Americans who'd been arrested at one time or another, and its larger set of fingerprint files on the sixty-seven million Americans who'd done nothing except leave their fingerprints somewhere — on a job application, perhaps.

The list went on and on. Presumably, there were more secret files no one knew anything about — or was going to know anything about. What was certain, though, was that these files contained much damaging and false information. Moreover, no individual was permitted to see his own file. If a citizen thought there was false information on him in the files, he could do nothing to set it straight. In addition, of course, government agencies passed these files around among themselves. For instance, the Department of Defense regularly gave to the Bureau of Narcotics the names and personnel folders of servicemen who'd been caught using drugs, or who were suspected of associating with those who used drugs, or who were suspected of associating with those who were suspected of using drugs. And so on. It was even revealed what United States Army intelligence probes had done to satisfy the private wants and needs of friendly businessmen.

Of course, many people had been suspicious. A Washington *Post* poll of Congressmen had showed that more than a quarter of them were willing to admit they thought their phones were bugged by the FBI, or by some government agency. But it was Sam, acting through the Constitutional Rights Subcommittee, who began to gather, and to publicize, some of the hard information on government surveillance. It had been less than a year now since he'd revealed that the United States Army had been spying on high-ranking public officials in Illinois, including well-known political contributors to both parties, two Chicago aldermen, United States Circuit Court Judge Otto Kerner, United States Representative Abner Mikva, and newly elected United States Senator Adlai Stevenson III.

Early this year, 1971, he'd held public hearings, which confirmed these things and began to show the massive police-state tactics the government was now using on its citizens. He proved, in public, that military agents with sophisticated electronic equipment had spied on both the Democratic and the Republican National Conventions — unbeknownst to the national party chairmen, the delegates, or, for that matter, the Secretary of the Army — who was kept from knowing about it on the grounds that he was a civilian. The Attorney General of the United States, who was also a civilian, had also been kept in the dark. Military agents had also been on hand at the funeral of Martin Luther King, taking the names of all who attended, including that of Vice President Humphrey. Military agents had infiltrated the Poor Peoples' Campaign camp-out at the Tidal Basin, and had become members of youth groups, after having been told that they could smoke all the marijuana they wanted if it would help them get in. At Fort Holabird, Maryland, the army maintained an ever-expanding master file of dissenters, protesters, and others who were suspected of not being the kind of Americans the army approved of. The army had secret dossiers on persons active in church groups and persons who were just generally active in communities thought to have a potential for civil disturbances. There were files on political figures, persons writing or speaking for peace in Viet Nam, members of lawyers' associations, members of the American Civil Liberties Union, labor leaders, reporters, members of the Southern Christian Leadership Conference, members of the National Association for the Advancement of Colored People, Unitarians, and those accused of taking part in or watching a civil rights or peace demonstration.

When asked by Sam whether the Federal Bureau of Investigation kept files on Congressmen and Senators, one high Administration official who appeared before his committee had smiled thinly and said, "If I knew, Senator, I wouldn't tell you."

Still the surveillance went on, worse under Nixon than under Johnson. It was even going on in North Carolina, where the military intelligence operatives had spied on Charlie Davis, the Negro basketball star who was Player of the Year in the Atlantic Coast Conference, and therefore suspect because he might thereby have some political influence. They had spied on Louis Brooks, the retired marine colonel who was Director of the Greensboro Human Relations Commission. And Cecil Butler, founder of the Rap Room and Director of Social Services for Winston-Salem's Family Planning Council. And on Ned Garboro, a University of North Carolina student who wanted to end the war in Viet Nam. And on many, many more.

Sam noted that those put under surveillance tended always to be the nonconformists, and he saw the effect of the surveillance, then, as one of encouraging conformity — in a nation where everybody was already too much like everybody else, at least to his own eccentricity-loving, diversity-loving mind. He warned that:

> When the ordinary citizen begins to fear that his presence at a rally, his signature on a petition, his questions at a seminar, will cause him to be watched and put into somebody's file, he refrains from any public contro-

versy and political activity. And that means, silent Americans. And a silent American, whatever his views, is an American who has been frightened out of his great birthright, the right to speak his mind.

But Sam was ready to do a lot more than protest. Direct action, he'd always believed, was preferable to whining. He was only seventy-five, in the prime of health and strength, and craved more action.

POEM

Sam was sometimes forbearing and kindly toward his enemies; a man who often sought for, and found, something worth praising in the lives of men who had disappointed him or treated him unfairly. He'd even been able to say, during the Watergate hearings, that Senator Ed Gurney, by his cross-examination of John Dean, was rendering a service to his country. And if there was irony, sometimes, in such praise of his opponents, there was no doubt, when you were sitting five feet away from Sam and could watch him, that the kindly feelings were real, too. He had an abhorrence for the cutting personal remark, for judging those he called his "fellow travelers to the tomb." He could be an extraordinarily gentle man.

When I asked him how he'd sum up the Nixon presidency, he looked startled, and I watched his face as he cast around for something to say. It was like watching a Technicolor time-study of a rose changing hue, as a hundred things came into that face and were rejected. At last he recited a poem.

> *I made the cross myself,*
> *Whose weight was later laid on me.*
> *This thought is torture, as I toil*
> *Up life's steep Calvary.*
> *To think, my own hands drove the nails!*
> *I sang a merry song,*
> *And chose the heaviest wood I had,*
> *To make it firm and strong.*
> *If I had thought, if I had dreamed,*
> *Its weight was meant for me,*
> *I would have made a lighter cross*
> *To bear up Calvary.*

Chapter 23

IT WAS in his Sunday newspaper, the news of men captured at the Democratic National Headquarters in the Watergate. For a couple of days it didn't seem to amount to much, but shortly, when involvement of a White House employee, Howard Hunt, was established, Sam knew "Watergate" was serious business. But he was able to withstand any itch to become prematurely involved, and kept himself mewed up.

Throughout the summer of 1972, Sam stuck to his business, trying to bring the presidentially appointed Office of the Management of the Budget under legislative control, and seeking to override, by legislation, Nixon's impoundment policies. He was involved, too, in a struggle to enhance the freedom of the press, by his bill declaring that reporters ought not be obliged (as they now were) to reveal the sources of their information, under pain of contempt sentences.

As for Watergate, he watched, read, listened. Five days after the break-in, Nixon denied any White House involvement in the crime, saying that such practices had "no place whatever in our electoral process or in our governmental process." And Sam, who had sufficient reason to question the sincerity of such a statement, went on watching. Three days later Martha Mitchell told a UPI reporter she was being held as a political prisoner, and that she was leaving her husband because of "all those dirty things that go on." Less than a week after that, Mitchell quit his job as Nixon's campaign manager. Eleven days later, McGovern was nominated for the presidency by the Democrats.

Events seemed to be running in Nixon's favor; it was an election year and few politicians had time to spare for investigating burglaries. It even seemed that the thing might die down. Sam went about his usual, busy way: fourteen-hour days, dinner with Margaret, an occasional party, and the usual, satisfying speaking engagements. When questioned about Watergate, he kept his mouth shut. He had other serious projects to attend to and wasn't going to abandon them except under great provocation. On July 1, Kleindienst, Peterson, and Silbert — the Justice Department prosecutors — announced that Maurice Stans, the chairman of finance for the Committee to Re-Elect the President, would be questioned in the comfort of the Department of Justice, rather than being required, as an ordinary citizen certainly would be required, to testify under oath before a grand jury concerning his knowledge of how the campaign funds were spent. The day after that, the Washington *Post* said that a $25,000 check given to Stans as a campaign contribution had been deposited in the account of Bernard Barker, one of the men arrested in the break-in. It was delicious bait, because Sam had the staff to launch an investigation of this. But he was master of himself, and did not bite; he went on about his work.

When the Democratic National Convention was over, some serious curiosity about Watergate began to make itself felt on Capitol Hill, where Representative Wright Patman ordered the staff of his House Banking and Currency Committee to investigate the break-in and the Mexico-laundered money. Patman did this the day before the Republican National Convention convened in Miami. Three days later, that convention renominated Nixon for the presidency, by a vote of 1347 to 1.

The next week, Nixon waxed more bold. "What really hurts," he said about the Watergate affair, "is if you try to cover it up." John Dean, he said, had conducted a thoroughgoing investigation, and "I can state categorically that his investigation indicates that no one in the White House staff, no one in this Administration, presently employed, was involved in this very bizarre incident." Righteous disavowals also came from John Mitchell, who told reporters four days later that he was "in no way involved" in the Watergate affair, and that he could "swear now that he had no advance knowledge" of the break-in. Sam watched. He had his own business to attend to; not enough was known yet.

But more became known when Stans admitted to the Patman committee, on September 5, that he had approved the Mexican laundering of eighty-nine thousand dollars' worth of campaign contributions. As for Sam, he kept on about all business, including getting his own, literal, laundry done; one could see him on the street, a big ball of white shirts under his arm, loping long-leggedly to the Chinese cleaners. He loved to do things like that; was an ordinary man, at a time in history when it cost very much to be one. It was an extraordinary time, a dangerous time for those burdened with too much information and too little wisdom. And the news data about Watergate kept on coming.

September 7 Larry O'Brien, Chairman of the Democratic National Committee, revealed that his office had been bugged once before, in a May break-in.
September 9 The Washington *Post* revealed that the Justice Department investigation of Watergate had been completed, without implicating any present member of the White House staff, or any employee of the Committee to Re-Elect the President.

Sam was glad of the Washington *Post*'s persistence, and felt that the bread he had cast on the waters by battling for the freedom of the press was coming back to him in fresh loaves. Still he stayed out of it, watching the main moves.

Stans, Dean, Mitchell: the data seemed to gather around these men like iron filings on a magnet, and to Sam's mind these three — together with that other fellow, Ehrlichman (who was still in the background) — these four, then, seemed to be more than mere men. They represented certain primal ways of thinking; ways not entirely alien to him — but somehow flawed. Smoking them out on what they had done would merely leave the door open for more men like themselves to come in. The truly hard task would be to bring to the docket what they *represented;* what they were in that swampy, fetid territory of the spirit, where big money, self-serving pragmatism, and captive intellect lay intercoiled and triumphant, blinking gelidly over the ruins of the Republic.

September 15 A Federal grand jury, sitting in Washington, returned an eight-count indictment against Liddy, Hunt, and the five men arrested in the break-in, and the Justice Department, through a spokesman, said, "We have absolutely no evidence to indicate that any others should be involved." The investigation was over, they said.

September 16 The Attorney General and the Chief of the Criminal Division tried to snuff the fire with statistics, asserting that the FBI investigation was carried out by 333 agents from 51 field offices, who developed 1897 leads, conducted 1551 interviews and expended 14,098 man hours, to say nothing of the grand jury, which had met for 125 hours and examined 50 witnesses.

That seemed to stave things off for a couple of weeks. The Washington *Post* was still probing, but the Administration's countermoves seemed to be winning the day.

September 29 The Washington *Post* revealed that, while he was Attorney General, Mitchell controlled a secret fund that was used to gather damaging information about Democrats. Mitchell denies this.

Then Sam got a call from Wright Patman, who was seeking advice on how to conduct the Watergate hearings over in the House. Sam told him what he could, and listened carefully when Patman said that such questions might be moot, anyway, because Administration pressure was being exerted powerfully to block the hearings altogether.

October 4 The Patman committee, by a vote of 20 to 15, decided not to hold hearings on Watergate-related matters.

Nixon was holding up well, timing his public statements to follow close on his tactical victories. At an impromptu press conference on October 5, he praised the diligence of the Justice Department, and, as usual, praised himself.

I wanted every lead to be carried out to the end. And I wanted to be sure that no member of the White House staff and no man or woman in a position of major responsibility in the Committee for Re-Election had anything to do with this kind of reprehensible activity.

By now, Sam was certain that something more needed to be done. He was disgusted by the chasm between the rough seriousness of events, and the smooth, self-serving complacencies of the President.

He was aware that the Administration was making countermoves, seemed to be winning.

But then, on October 10, the Washington *Post* came out with a big story. The Watergate break-in, the *Post* said, was only one small expression of a massive sabotage scheme involving White House officials and CRP employees, financed out of a large secret fund controlled by John Mitchell. Immediately, Ronald Zeigler, the President's press secretary, counterattacked by saying that the article was fundamentally "hearsay, innuendo, and guilt by association."

On the other side of Capitol Hill, in the House of Representatives, Wright Patman announced that he would try once more to reconvene his House Banking and Currency Committee, with an eye to investigating Watergate. But Patman failed at that, this time not only because of Administration pressure on members of his committee, but also because, in an election year, few members had the time to squander on the thing. So any immediate action would have to come from the Senate, where only a third of the members were required, that year, to face the people who had elected them. Thus, on October 12, the day Patman failed to reconvene his committee, Ted Kennedy, chairman of the Senate Judiciary Subcommittee on Administrative Practices and Procedures, ordered a preliminary probe of the Watergate incident. Kennedy consulted with Sam before doing this.

Of course, Kennedy had the Chappaquiddick incident only three years behind him, and knew from the start that any open hearings based on such an investigation would have to be chaired by a Senator other than himself. And it was evident now, too, that nothing could be done prior to the four-weeks-distant presidential elections. What Kennedy hoped to do was gather information that would be useful to George McGovern in the presidential fight, because it was increasingly clear that McGovern, without the aid of provable and sensational revelations, would certainly lose.

When Nixon won the presidency on November 7, with 97 percent of the electoral vote, it seemed possible that the Watergate investigation, like the probes of the Kennedy, King, and Kennedy assassinations, would end in an indelible question mark. For more than a month, Watergate news was small change; some resignations from the CRP, a denial by the White House that any "white paper" on Watergate had been prepared. But behind the scenes, in the Senate,

THE LIFE OF SAM J. ERVIN   261

moves were being contemplated. Several times, Sam and Mike Mansfield discussed the matter and agreed that something ought to be done.

Then, early in December, the news began to have some heft once more. On the sixth, the Washington *Post* reported that McCord had recruited the Cubans for the break-in. The next day, Kathleen Chenow, a former White House secretary, revealed the existence of a White House "plumbers' unit" of secret operatives, and named as its members E. Howard Hunt, G. Gordon Liddy, David Young, and Egil Krogh. The next day, Hunt's wife was killed in a Chicago airplane accident, and it was found that her pocketbook contained a hundred hundred-dollar bills. On the same day, Judge Byrne declared a mistrial in the Pentagon Papers trial. And the Washington *Post* quoted Miss Chenow as saying that the telephone in the plumbers' office was used by Hunt to talk to Barker, and that the bills were forwarded to Ehrlichman's office.

Mansfield and Sam were conferring constantly during these days. Undoubtedly, any hearings on Watergate would bring on an all-out clash with the Administration, which was now at the zenith of its power. Kennedy, having removed himself from consideration as chairman, was willing to hand over to whoever would head the investigation all the material gathered by his own subcommittee.

So Mike Mansfield and Sam talked about what other Senate committees might do the job. There was the Judiciary, on which Sam was the second-ranking Democrat in terms of seniority. Then there was the Government Operations Committee. That was a possibility, too — and Sam was the second-ranking Democratic Senator on that, also. The only trouble was that both committees had members who aspired to the presidency, so any actions by either of them would draw the instantaneous Administration response: the Democrats are playing politics. Sam and Mansfield began to mull over other possibilities, and December passed quietly. Both sides were working behind the scenes, and Washington was awash in rumors. Men close to the action suddenly found themselves rediscovered, as close friends, by acquaintances they'd not heard from in years. It was a winter of treacherous parties and grotesque love affairs.

And yet, somehow, even if one managed to burrow to the Senate's core, where Sam and Mike Mansfield sat talking about the thing, one would not hear anyone express that thing which was the main fear and therefore the prime issue. Which wasn't whether or not Nixon was a crook. Millions had been talking on both sides of that issue for more than a quarter century now. Everyone knew what the prime issue was. A certain thumb moving awkwardly toward a certain red button, a certain question of sanity.

It was that question, unexpressed between them, that made Sam and Mike Mansfield proceed with such meticulous care. Query: if the man who holds the thumb over the button is mad . . . and we began hammering on the Hun-guarded door of his office, threatening to pull him off his golden throne . . . So the real question was whether to proceed at all.

Early in January, Sam, who was spending the holidays down in Morganton, drove to Charlotte, left his car there, and flew up to Washington. It was less than three weeks to the second Nixon inauguration, and a Gallup poll, taken just after the announcement of a "peace settlement" in Viet Nam, showed the President's popularity rated at 68 percent, matching the previous high, which had been recorded in November of '69, when Nixon had announced his peace plan. In Washington Sam and Mansfield, meeting together, decided that the risk must be taken. And Sam flew back to Charlotte and drove the car from there to Morganton. It was the old route — the mountains still there, the same ones he'd been born out of. But no friendly old curves anymore, no more humans walking and talking near the highway. Just a straight, smooth, expensive way, like a jet's power against one's back at takeoff. Then he was with his family again, in the old place. He was due to return to Washington the next week.

It snowed, then rained and froze, then snowed again, this time deeply, and catapulted the mountain town of Morganton back sixty or seventy years, to the time when getting out of town meant abandoning one's wheeled vehicle. So as the week began, and with it the Ninety-first Congress, Sam was obliged to stay at home. The next day he was snowed in, too, when the phone rang.

It was Mansfield, who told him the Democratic Policy Committee had met and decided that the Watergate investigation ought to be conducted by a Select Committee, similar to the McCarthy censure committee, and that he, Sam Ervin, ought to be chairman. The Policy

Committee's recommendation had been taken to the Democratic Caucus, which had endorsed the recommendations unanimously. Would he accept? And Sam, who had seen this coming, said yes. Reluctantly yes, because he had good reasons to believe that extraordinary pressures would be placed on him, and much power spent in trying to discredit him.

With the help of two of his best staffers, lawyers like himself, he drew up the enabling legislation. At first he called for a five-man committee, but the Republicans, who'd been brought into the plans by then, demurred, saying that if they had only two members on the committee, and one of the two was gone off on business, that would put too much pressure on the remaining member. So a compromise was reached, seven, and it was further agreed that all of the members would be lawyers, and that none of them would hold current ambitions to ascend to the presidency. (Or descend, depending on how you thought about it.)

Mansfield, who was to pick the committee, conferred with Sam and said he'd like to have Herman Talmadge and Daniel Inouye. Which was fine with Sam. He liked and respected both of those men.

Talmadge, who was successor to Walter George's Senate seat, was Chairman of the Senate Agriculture and Forestry Commission, son of a former Governor of Georgia, and himself had been Governor of that state when he was thirty-two years old. And it wasn't just Talmadge's political precosity, or even his political beliefs, that made Sam regard him so highly. Talmadge was a decorated and solidly authentic hero of Guadalcanal and Okinawa, a man who had gotten combat duty because he requested it. He had been willing to give his life for his country when he was a younger man, and, even now, he could be counted on to sacrifice ruthlessly his support of Nixon, and his own political well-being, if he believed it was in the nation's interests to do so. And Sam felt the same way about Inouye, whose political persuasion was somewhere to the left of Talmadge's and Sam's both. Inouye, like Sam, had attacked machine-gun nests in defense of his country, had been severely wounded, and had earned the Distinguished Service Cross, the Bronze Star, and three Purple Hearts.

The choice of the fourth Democrat was left up to Sam, and, after considering Gaylord Nelson, who was coming up for re-election and didn't have the time, he settled on Joseph Montoya, a Democrat he respected, and a man of long political experience, who had been continuously in public office since 1936. Montoya, too, had been elected to his state's House of Representatives when in his senior year of law school. He was a man of exceptional stamina, who had built up a successful law practice while pursuing a political career. In addition to that — and once more, singlehandedly — he had become sole owner of Western Van Lines.

The Republican members were chosen by Hugh Scott, the Minority Leader, who picked men remarkably similar to those seated on the other side. Howard Baker of Tennessee had seen action as a PT boat skipper in the Pacific during World War II. Ed Gurney, who was the first Republican since Reconstruction to be elected to the Senate from Florida, had entered that war as a private, seen action overseas as a tank commander, been severely wounded in action. He had emerged from the war as a lieutenant colonel and the holder of the Silver Star and the Purple Heart. Lowell Weicker, who had attended the University of Virginia Law School with Ted Kennedy and John Tunney, Senator from California, had also served on active duty in the Korean War, as first lieutenant, then captain, in the artillery.

None of these men could be called unpatriotic, although calling them that might be the first thing that came to Nixon's mind, if his past performances in politics were any indicator of how he might behave now. So he would have to go on to the second thing, "political opportunism." But that was foreclosed, too. None of these men was on the make, at least not yet.

Of course, Sam knew that it would be impossible to forestall every single Nixon accusation. But the President would be well advised to lay off the charges of wild-eyed liberalism, too. For instance, Sam's most recent rating by the Americans for Constitutional Action was 100 percent, higher than that of Nixon himself. As for the rest of them . . . well, there weren't any liberals on this committee. Montoya, Inouye, and Weicker were moderates, and as for Gurney, Baker, and Talmadge . . . they were the right. So Sam, now, was satisfied with his committee, and ready to work.

The Senate's processes went on with the usual slow majesty. On February 7, 1973, it voted 77 to 0 to establish the Select Committee. Two weeks later, Sam was named Chairman, Howard Baker Vice Chairman, and Sam Dash Chief Counsel and Staff Director. Minority Counsel was Fred D. Thompson, who was new to the Washington scene, but an experienced federal prosecutor in his (and Baker's) home state of Tennessee. Rufus Edmisten was named Deputy Chief Counsel. There would be more than twenty lawyers on the staff of the Select Committee, and more than fifty staff members backing them up.

Throughout the late winter and early spring of 1973, the Select Committee did its work, and Sam did his, toiling late into the night, assimilating and structuring the mass of evidence developed. His only break from this routine came when one of his two remaining brothers died and Sam went down to Morganton for the funeral. This was John, the physician, the one who'd tended him when he was ill from ulcers.

Now Sam was intensely active, assimilating data at an enormous rate, so that he could be above data when the showdown came. Because the true dragon of Watergate was not Stans, Mitchell, Dean, or Ehrlichman. Neither was it their senior associate, Nixon. Instead, Sam believed, it was a certain way of thinking, what this quaternion represented.

Later that month, Sam and Howard Baker went to a secret rendezvous with Ehrlichman at the Blair House. Ehrlichman argued strenuously for executive sessions, where the whole thing would be done behind closed doors. Sam told him the American people didn't need any more closed doors, that there would be none.

In that case, Ehrlichman said, he thought it very likely that the presidential assistants would be obliged to plead executive privilege — as they had done, successfully, on very many things over the past four years. And Sam responded, in his reasonable, gentle voice, that, while such a position was understandable in a way, the Congress was also obliged to take a position, which was that in the event of any claim of executive privilege it would be necessary to put the claimant in the Capitol jail, and keep him there until he talked.

Ehrlichman then appealed to Baker, who said that under the circumstances, he too would jail the claimant of executive privilege and keep him jailed. And this was final.

Sam was pleased with what happened. He knew quite well that there were those who would see Baker as the White House's smooth agent on the committee. But a lot of men in this world were not what they seemed to be.

Of course the press didn't know then, nor was it later to learn, about this private meeting, and Sam didn't see why they should know, because, after all, that was stage-managing, a private matter.

ASSESSMENT

We were sitting in his study and I asked him what he thought of Nixon's role in Watergate.

"It has been my experience," he said, "that the madam of a whorehouse is very seldom a virgin." And he laughed out loud like Santa Claus.

Chapter 24

WHEN HE BANGED DOWN the gavel to open the Watergate hearings, Sam Ervin was the most modern man in the room, and the most prepared. His suit, blue, tie, blue, and shirt, also blue, had been selected by him with an eye to the necessities of the new color television sets. And, although he would have used the Indian gavel in any case, he was not above thinking that its bright scrollery would show up well on the tube, and mean something too — the old calling the new to account. But he didn't enter the cross examination, actively, right away. Instead, he lay back, waiting for the big fish, and what they represented.

On Tuesday of the fourth week of hearings, Maurice Stans stood at the witness table and took the oath, and Sam, who by now was a national celebrity, was ready to enter the case more actively. During the testimony and questioning of the preliminary witnesses, he had managed the proceedings with the practiced ease of an experienced driver maneuvering in traffic. There was plenty of stopping and starting, many turns to be made, but nothing calling upon the resources of his inner being. His experience with legislative hearings went back fifty years, and he operated smoothly and well. The television lights did not bother him, nor did the cameras, and he would forget for hours at a time that they were there. He was, indeed, the most modern man in the room; the most experienced in the ways of television, and besides that, something of a computer expert, having devoted considerable time since his seventieth birthday to studying computers.

Thus, the fresh stacks of print-outs at his left elbow were no more unfamiliar to him than was the worn black Bible now resting on top of them. Indeed, the print-outs were there because Sam had ordered them to be, so that immediate and elaborate cross-checks could be made on the interweaving testimonies of a score of witnesses.

A large computer was in the wings now, one of the IBM 7000 series, whose language Sam alone, of all the committee, knew how to speak. He knew, as few moderns do, that humans were very bright and very slow, computers very stupid and very fast. So he was being practical. At the same time, he was wise in the ways of television directors, and knew it was the Bible they would zoom in on. He kept the computer in another room.

He would indulge in four major confrontations, the first of which would be with Maurice Stans. No one except Sam knew what was coming, and no one, including Sam, knew how they would turn out.

Stans was already under indictment in New York in the Vesco cases (where he would be acquitted), and, on the basis of that, had asked to be excused from testifying — a request Sam turned down.

Like Sam himself, Stans was a man who had made himself by hard work, and who still worked hard beyond that time when simple need would have required it.

At seventeen, Stans had been on his own, in Chicago, away from home, working as a stenographer by day and paying his own way for accountancy training at night, at Northwestern University. By the time he was nineteen, he'd learned enough to go to New York and join an accounting firm there. At twenty-three, he was a certified public accountant, and by thirty, a senior partner of the firm he'd joined. He had been in public life for many years, starting as Director of the Bureau of the Budget during the Eisenhower presidency, and he went back and forth with ease between government and private work. Since 1961, he'd been senior partner in a New York investment banking company, and had served two years as Nixon's Secretary of Commerce, before resigning to become finance chairman of the Committee to Re-Elect the President.

Of course, to some observers, Stans wasn't like Sam at all, for whereas Sam believed that money was to buy one's freedom with, Stans seemed to think it bought respect, and he was fond of saying that his proudest boast was having raised the largest amount of money ever spent in a political campaign, more than $50 million.

Looking at Stans out there at the witness table, it was hard to believe that he had ever been poor. Everything about him — his face, voice, gestures, suit — seemed Rolls-Royce expensive and solid. And his opening statement was smooth, too. He denied that he had committed any intentional violations of campaign financing laws, denied that he'd been aware of the break-in or cover-up, and seemed puzzled as to why he had been dragged into this hearing. It had nothing to do with him, he said, in a tone that declared that his good suit would provide his excuse. It was all a mistake.

Sam began by discussing CRP records Stans had caused to be destroyed.

ERVIN: Rather a suspicious coincidence that the records which showed these matters were destroyed six days after the break-in at the Watergate.

STANS: Mr. Chairman, the adjectives are yours.

ERVIN: Sir?

STANS: The adjectives that you are using, queer coincidence and suspicion.

ERVIN: Don't you think it is rather suspicious?

STANS: No, I do not think so, Senator.

ERVIN: Do you think it is kind of normal . . .to expect people who had records concerning outlays of campaign funds to destroy those records after five men are caught in an act of burglary with money from the committee in their pockets?

STANS: On April 6 I asked Mr. Sloan to build up the records of all the contributors and he did so. I asked him on April 10, before I left on my vacation, to balance out his cash account. He did both these things pursuant to my requests. Now, the fact that they came to me after the Watergate was pure and innocent coincidence.

ERVIN: Well, why did you destroy the records?

STANS: For the reason I have already said, Mr. Chairman . . . We have kept some records to reconstruct what has happened.

ERVIN: Well, why destroy your previous records and why destroy your subsequent records and reduce yourself to the necessity of reconstructing something that you already had and destroyed?

STANS: Very simple, for the reason —
ERVIN: It is too simple for me to understand, really.

Gone was the deferential tone Stans was accustomed to hearing.
Sam bore in on him.

ERVIN: In other words, you decided that the right of the contributors
            to have their contributions concealed was superior to the right
            of American citizens to know who was making contributions
            to influence the election of the President of the United
            States? Mr. Stans, do you not think that men who have been
            honored by the American people, as you have, ought to have
            their course of action guided by ethical principles which are
            superior to the minimum requirements of the criminal laws?

A bit more of that, and Ed Gurney entered the action.

GURNEY: Mr. Chairman . . . I for one have not appreciated the harass-
            ment of this witness by the chairman in the questioning that
            was just finished. I think this Senate committee ought to act
            in fairness.
ERVIN: Well, I have not questioned the veracity of the witness. I have
            asked the witness questions to find out what the truth is.
GURNEY: I didn't use the word "veracity." I used the word "harass-
            ment."
ERVIN: Well, I am sorry that my distinguished friend from Florida
            does not approve of my method of examining the witness. I
            am an old country lawyer and I don't know the finer ways to
            do it. I just have to do it my way.

By now Sam had accomplished what he'd set out to do, anyway, by
raising the question of whether respectability and virtue were the
same thing.

Stans, in his closing statement, said this: "All I ask, Mr. Chairman
and members of the committee, is that when you write your report
you give me back my good name." Where Sam came from, of course,
a good name was something no man could take from any other man.
You either earned one for yourself or you didn't.

Gurney's defense of Stans had come as a surprise. Indeed, the seating arrangements were such as to make Sam almost forget that
Gurney was there at all. To Sam's right was Howard Baker, who
would whisper a pleasantry every hour or so; or even pass to Sam the

dirty poem that had originated at the reporters' table and been passed on to Weicker, Gurney, Baker, and finally to Sam. Who read it, laughed, and whispered to Baker something even more ribald than that. To Sam's left, when Dash wasn't in the way, was Talmadge, a disciplined man who got up at 3:30 A.M. every morning, cooked his own eggs and ham, donned a marine fatigue suit and combat boots, and ran for a mile on the narrow forest trail of Glover-Archbold Park. Talmadge was a conservatively dressed man, usually, who'd taken to wearing a nifty sports coat after having been accosted and kissed by some Yankee beauty in the hallway of the Old Senate Office Building. All seven of these Senators were national celebrities now. Already, there were Sam Ervin T-shirts and Sam Ervin fan clubs throughout the country. There was even a Sam Ervin wristwatch. And he was receiving about 5000 letters a day, some of them with proposals of marriage, and some threatening to kill him. Once or twice he had given in to the Capitol Police, and let them detail a man to meet him in front of the Methodist Building, to walk with him to his office. But he tried to dissuade them from that, and usually succeeded, although it made him uncomfortable to realize that an assassin could strike at any instant.

When asked about assassins, Sam would blush deep crimson, in his body's shock at the possibility. But his mind was dominant in that body; he was master of himself, and he knew that it was exhilarating, even profitable, to feel fear; because after you faced it, endured it, and learned what it was about, you were better off, and you felt better. No man was going to get out of this world alive — every good soldier knew that — and at the final extremity there was the consolation of his Southern Presbyterian heritage. That was part of him now, bones and marrow.

It wasn't until two weeks later, the week of June 25 to July 1, that Sam once more entered the interrogation in other than a perfunctory way. This time the witness was John Dean, whose lengthy testimony would directly implicate the President. Dean, too, was already a national celebrity. The build-up had continued during one week in which he had been bargaining for immunity, and another in which the hearings had been suspended during the state visit of Soviet leader Leonid Brezhnev. Dean's testimony, which he read in a low, careful voice, was 245 pages long, and it took him an entire day to get through it. Sam, who already knew most of what he was going to say, let his eyes wander around the hearing room.

All the seats were taken, and there were several rows of people standing in the back. Often Sam's eyes would light on the face of a friend, and sometimes there would be a celebrity. There was Ben Cartwright, or, rather, the fellow who played that role in "Bonanza" on television; there was Norman Mailer, the novelist; there was even Dick Cavett, who in some ways was reminiscent of the man now reading this lengthy statement. And there was an outstandingly gorgeous blonde in hot pants and a see-through blouse.

John Dean had entered upon his adult years well connected. His first wife was Karla Hennings, daughter of Sam's old political foe, Senator Tom Hennings of Missouri. His first job as an attorney had been obtained by that connection, just as a later job on the Hill had been secured by exploiting an old college tie. Dean, like Sam himself, managed to be soft-spoken without behaving like a puppy. He respected himself, and his voice showed it.

Sam's cross-examination of Dean was designed to bring strong pressure on Nixon, and it was carried out in a cooperative spirit, because there was no longer anything in John Dean that needed to be confronted. No, Dean was proof that a man could change.

Sam engaged Dean in a Socratic dialogue, which showed that the President of the United States had approved of a scheme whereby government agencies were to be empowered to employ electronic surveillance, the interception and reading of mail, surreptitious entry, and campus infiltration by United States military agents, in dealing with "subversive elements" and "selected targets of internal security interests." What all this meant, essentially, was that Mr. Nixon had authorized the executive branch to violate the Constitutional rights of anybody he didn't like. What was in the air, now, was the ozone whiff of impeachment.

ERVIN: Just one other matter. Article II of the Constitution says, in defining the power of the President, Section 3 of Article II, — "He" — that is the President — "shall take care that the laws be faithfully executed." Do you know of anything that the President did or said at any time between June 17 and the present moment to perform his duty to see that the laws are faithfully executed in respect to what is called the Watergate affair?

DEAN: Mr. Chairman, I have given the facts as I know them and I
          don't — I would rather be excused from drawing my own
          conclusion on that at this point in time.
ERVIN: I will ask you as a lawyer if the experience of the English-
          speaking race, both in its legislative bodies and in its courts,
          has not demonstrated that the only reliable way in which the
          credibility of a witness can be tested is for that witness to be
          interrogated upon oath and have his credibility determined
          not only by what he says but by his conduct and demeanor
          while he is saying it and also by whether his testimony is
          corroborated or not corroborated by other witnesses?
DEAN: That is correct.

In a way, Dean's personal situation, that of having no roots, no
home, was common to all the leading figures in the Watergate
scandal, including Nixon himself. He was intelligent, likable, hardworking, and fundamentally honest, and if he'd had a community to
come from instead of just connections to profit from, his story might
have been different. Everyone kept moving, moving — so there were
no old friends to know it when you got better or got worse. For very
many Americans, the only game left was *success,* which was about as
satisfying as playing Monopoly in an automobile. Even when you
won.

Nor were any of these men coming before the committee especially
happy. John Dean had not been able to make himself happy with the
town house overlooking the Potomac, or the closetful of $200 suits, or
the maroon Porsche 911 that he drove to the White House each
morning. But he was the sort of fellow who might acquire some
depth later on.

As the hearings progressed, Sam was somewhat astonished that the
Nixon Administration made no moves to discredit him, beyond a perfunctory inquiry or two among North Carolina's Republicans, and he
waited for the attack to come, curious as to what form it would take.
It would be interesting to see them try to work this one out. What
would they do? Call him a liberal? Say that he was young and brash?
Accuse him of presidential ambitions? In fact, he was way to the right
of Nixon himself, and had always been; had fought civil rights legislation for almost two decades now; had consistently voted on the side
of big business and against many welfare programs. He had been one
of the few Senate members who was still hawk enough to vote against

the repeal of the Gulf of Tonkin Resolution. And he had been the fellow to campaign for Mendel Rivers because, by his standards, the fellow was a good solid moderate. What could Nixon do to him now?

So there was no effort to discredit him, and no one stepped up to blow out his brains, either. Mildly then, for the most part, he presided over the hearings, taking his moral counsel from the Bible and advice of another sort from the IBM 7000.

As he'd expected, there was public criticism of him by lawyers who said that he did not know, or had forgotten, how to conduct a courtroom cross-examination. But this was not a court room, and his purpose from the beginning — once Ehrlichman and the others had seen the light about showing up in the first place — had nothing to do with sending anybody to jail.

No, it was more like the McCarthy hearings, on a larger scale. You made sure those people got on television, and then you asked them the kind of questions that would let them be, in public, the same kind of persons they were in private. Then you let the American people decide what they were.

Beneath that place where words were, however, Sam was able to sympathize with many of the men who came before him. Especially John Mitchell, who had one outstanding quality that never came across in photographs, or even got through the television tube. Mitchell — again, as Sam was, and as Dwight Eisenhower had been — was a physically beautiful man. There were no reservations to his movements, no self-protecting tendencies. He moved as one who would rather have his face smashed than wince. This grace and courage had served him well in sports, and in earlier years he had been a semiprofessional hockey player and a no-handicap golfer.

In a way, this rapport Mitchell had with his own body had disserved him, because he had learned so much, over the years, about handling himself, that others were quick to assume that he knew how to handle other things as well. Which wasn't always the case. Thus, during Mitchell's tenure as Attorney General, Nixon had suffered significant reverses as a result of placing too much confidence in him.

Mitchell's suit to block the publication of the Pentagon Papers had failed; his recommendation of Haynsworth for the Supreme Court had failed; his recommendation of Carswell for the Supreme Court had failed; his prosecution of the Chicago Seven had

failed; of the Harrisburg Seven, failed; of Daniel Ellsberg, failed; of
the antiwar demonstrators in Washington, likewise failed. Indeed,
outside his narrow legal specialty — municipal bonds — John Mitchell was not a very practical man, but Nixon had relied on him to be
one, and much of the "teamwork" metaphor of the Nixon Administration sprang from the special relationship between the President
and his Attorney General; between the awkward scrub who made it
big and longed to ease old aches by association with a champion
athlete. Nixon had been willing to overlook many mistakes if in
return he could have the feeling, finally, of making the varsity; and
John Mitchell, a lonely man whose genuine teams had broken up long
ago, had fallen in with this.

> ERVIN: Mr. Mitchell, on yesterday, when Senator Talmadge asked
> you concerning your political activities in respect to the Com-
> mittee to Re-Elect the President while you were still serving as
> Attorney General, you pointed out that it was not illegal for
> you to do that.
>
> MITCHELL: Yes sir, that is correct, Mr. Chairman.
>
> ERVIN: Yes. Now I think we might meditate just a minute on what St.
> Paul said. He said, "All things are lawful unto me but some
> things are not expedient." Don't you think it is rather
> inexpedient for the chief law enforcement officer of the
> United States to be engaging in, directly or indirectly, in man-
> aging political activities?
>
> MITCHELL: I do, Senator.

Mitchell was a man's man — other men sensed his physical bravery
and liked him. And Sam sensed this, because he himself was a man
like that, capable of engendering this sort of response from other
men. But because of Margaret Ervin, because of the solidity of his
home life, Sam had been able to stand back from being too friendly
with the wrong sort of person, and thus had been able to avert life's
debilitating camaraderies. Mitchell, on the other hand, had capital-
ized on his physical qualities, because the "team" was all he had. And
Sam's job, as he saw it now, was to lay bare this way of thinking.

> ERVIN: . . . Now, twice while you were still Attorney General of the
> United States and the chief law enforcement officer of the
> United States, and the chief legal advisor to the President of
> the United States, meetings were held in your office in the

Department of Justice in which such matters were discussed as to bug the opposition political party and to burglarize the headquarters of the opposition party and to employ prostitutes to induce members of the opposition party to disclose secrets, weren't they?

MITCHELL: They were so discussed and, of course, disapproved.

ERVIN: But the burglary and the bugging were discussed in the second?

MITCHELL: That is correct.

ERVIN: Then on the third occasion, namely the 30th of March, Mr. Magruder, who was your deputy director of the committee, visited Key Biscayne where you were and discussed these matters, at least the bugging and the break-in, a third time with you, didn't he?

MITCHELL: I wouldn't use the term "discussed." They were presented —

ERVIN: And you declined to do that on three occasions.

MITCHELL: That is correct, sir.

ERVIN: Can you explain to me why it was, after you declined on the first occasion, that you had a second discussion on the matter and after you declined on the second occasion, that you had a third discussion of the matter or presentation of the matter?

MITCHELL: I cannot for the life of me understand as to why this matter was constantly brought back, except for the point that somebody obviously was very interested in the subject matter.

That was it, of course; when you played on a team you played with the team and you did not penalize your own players as long as they played with you. And of course, approaching a referee to point out a team member's infraction of the rules was out of the question. Because the glue that held it all together was camaraderie, not the ground rules spectators mistook for ethics.

ERVIN: You . . . were informed by Magruder that he . . . was prepared to commit perjury when he went before the grand jury . . . rather than to reveal what he knew about these matters?

MITCHELL: That was correct, sir.

ERVIN: Now, did you agree that this was the proper action to take?

MITCHELL: It was a very expedient one, Senator.

After Mitchell's testimony came that of Alexander Butterfield who disclosed that, all along, Nixon had been transcribing the conversations that took place in the Oval Room and his hideaway in the Executive Office Building, as well as many phone conversations. When Sam's early efforts to obtain the tapes failed, it was decided, at a meeting of the full Watergate Committee, that he and Howard Baker ought to talk to the President in person. Nixon wasn't receptive to that, and so it was suggested, instead, that they talk to him on the telephone. And Nixon, by that time, didn't want to talk to Baker at all.

So Sam left his own office, where the Watergate Committee was meeting, and went into an aide's office to talk to the President of the United States. When Nixon came on the line, there was no small talk. Sam told him the committee wanted the tapes.

"I'm not well," Nixon said.

"I'm sorry to hear that, Mr. President," Sam said.

"I'm going in the hospital today," Nixon said.

"Well, I certainly wish you a speedy recovery."

"I have pneumonia."

"Well, I hope they will fix you up out there, Mr. President," Sam said. He waited. He wanted the tapes so that Nixon could be Nixon in public.

"You guys are out to get me," Nixon said. His voice was husky.

Sam, of course, assured him that they were only out to get the truth. But he could not help thinking, in the privacy of his mind, that it probably amounted to the same thing.

But he understood Nixon, and knew what it was to want loyalty. It was very hard to survive in this world without someone who would be loyal, and all his life, he believed, he had been lucky in that. His grandson, Jimmy, was there in the hearing room, and behind him in more ways than one. His wife, as always, was there. He knew what it was to want to give loyalty, too. He had been loyal to his parents, his family, his church, his political party, and his community. But he knew, too, that he'd never been as severely tested as Mitchell had been. And he had no way of ensuring that Jimmy might not likewise be tested that way.

In the meantime, all that could be done for Jimmy, or for the country, was to show how men like Mitchell thought, and let people take their choice. There could be no certain safeguards, because having had vigilant ancestors did not ensure that a man, or a country, would remain vigilant. None of the good things could be defended by dead ancestors. Not even the Constitution could be defended that way. And there were many Americans now who believed that the Constitution was just one more instrument in the hands of the President, to be interpreted as he saw fit. Such a man was John Ehrlichman.

Who was a genius, as was Sam. Of course, Sam had never applied that term to himself, since it seemed to him at best a very low honor, like being a corporal. Actually, he thought, it wasn't even that good, being a genius; it was like being six feet one; it had nothing to do with one's own efforts, and he believed, out of a lifetime of personal experience, that many geniuses were in jail, and deserved to be. What counted was what your motives were.

Cynics might say of Ehrlichman that he had become the third most powerful man in America by having been a college chum of H. R. Haldeman's at UCLA, but those who knew him believed that, wherever he'd been born, or whomever he'd known, the man might have risen because of his intelligence and his sharp, graceful wit. In earlier days, he'd been more likable, and still was liked by many who found themselves in disagreement with the political policies of the Nixon Administration. Because Ehrlichman wanted to be a truth-teller, and was plainly annoyed on those occasions when the interests of the Adminstration — and, now, his own self-interest — seemed to require that he be less than candid.

When he came before the committee, during the eighth week of testimony, he was the first witness who did not bother to feign deference and cooperativeness. He scowled, he snapped, he banged the brown-felt witness table with karate chops, he jabbed his finger angrily at his interrogators, and denied everything. He hadn't told Dean to "deep six" sensitive documents, hadn't asked Nixon to provide clemency for Hunt, hadn't briefed Mitchell on the doings of the plumbers, hadn't reassured Herbert W. Kalmbach about the legitimacy of the hush money, hadn't gotten Gray to burn evidence.

Sam, of course, wasn't as interested in the things Ehrlichman had done as he was about the motives from which the man had acted. Thus, when he entered into the questioning of Ehrlichman, the nominal questions had to do with paying money to burglars and authorizing the break-in of Ellsberg's psychiatrist's office. But the real questions had to do with the power of the presidency.

ERVIN: Mr. Ehrlichman, do I understand that you are testifying that the Committee to Re-Elect the President and those associated with them constituted an eleemosynary institution that gave $50,000 to some burglars and their lawyers merely because they felt sorry for them?

EHRLICHMAN: I am afraid I am not your best witness on that, Mr. Chairman. I do not know what their motives were. I think those will appear in the course of this proceeding.

ERVIN: You stated this was a defense fund just like that given to Angela Davis and to Daniel Ellsberg, did you not?

EHRLICHMAN: I stated that was my understanding of it.

ERVIN: Yes, well, Daniel Ellsberg and the Angela Davis defense funds were raised in public meetings and the newspapers carried news items about it, did they not?

But Ehrlichman was not like the other witnesses. He was smarter than any of those who had preceded him.

EHRLICHMAN: I am not sure we know who the donors to those funds were. I dare say there are many people in this country who contributed to those funds who would not want it known.

Nothing — he'd moved away, and Sam kept after him.

ERVIN: Yes. But do you not think most of the people contributed to these funds because they believed in the causes they stood for?

EHRLICHMAN: I assume that.

Now to move in. The television lights were very bright.

ERVIN: Well, certainly, the Committee to Re-Elect the President and White House aides like yourself did not believe in the cause of burglars or wiretappers, did you?

EHRLICHMAN: No.

ERVIN: Can you —

EHRLICHMAN: I didn't contribute a nickel, Mr. Chairman.

One point for Ehrlichman. The television lights were very bright and there were many people in the room. Sam kept after the man, and Ehrlichman kept slipping away, not sneakily, but with demonstrations of defiance. He was not going to be made a fool of, was not going to wilt, and Sam knew why: the man stood for something, and it was that thing he stood for that Sam was trying to bring out for the camera.

He felt himself coming closer to the essence of Ehrlichman's position when he asked the man whether he believed the President had the Constitutional right to order the burglary of Dr. Fielding's office. Ehrlichman responded by saying that such a thing was authorized under the Constitution, and he sat there arguing Constitutional law with Sam, on that point.

ERVIN: Is there a single thing in there which says the President can authorize burglaries?
EHRLICHMAN: Well, let us read it, Mr. Chairman —

Sam was very angry now, close to rage.

ERVIN: I can ask about it without reading. It says [in the statute under discussion] that this shall not interfere with the Constitutional power of the President to —
EHRLICHMAN: *To do anything.* [Italics added.]
ERVIN: — To do anything necessary to protect the country against five things. The first says actual or potential attacks of a foreign power. You do not claim that burglarizing Dr. Ellsberg's psychiatrist's office to get his opinion, his recorded opinion, of the intellectual or psychological state of his patient is an attack by a foreign power, do you?

Now John Wilson, Ehrlichman's attorney, spoke up.

WILSON: May I get into this, may I get into this legal debate?
ERVIN: Well, yes. You claim that, Mr. Wilson, do you?

Sam himself had participated in drawing up the statute under discussion, and now Ehrlichman and Wilson were telling him that it superseded the Constitution and put in its place arbitrary presidential power.

WILSON: Then, you read into that sentence which says, "or to protect national security information against foreign intelligence activities."
ERVIN: Against foreign intelligence activities. The foreign intelli-

gence activities had nothing to do with the opinion of Ellsberg's psychiatrist about his intellectual or emotional or psychological state.

WILSON: How do you know that, Mr. Chairman?

ERVIN: [shouting now] Because I can understand the English language. It is my mother tongue.

It was Talmadge, a few minutes later, who finally brought Ehrlichman to the point of summerizing the very essence of Watergate.

TALMADGE: Now, if the President could authorize a covert break-in;
and you do not know exactly what that power would be
limited to — You do not think it would include murder or
other crimes beyond covert break-ins, do you?

EHRLICHMAN: *I do not know where the line is, Senator.* [Italics added]

That was the whole point. The country had many intelligent,
educated men, and fewer of them seemed to know where the line was
anymore, or to care. It had been a long time since Sam had floated on
his back in the gentle-gliding Catawba River, looking up at the bridge
where the automobile toiled, and knowing that his responsibilities
waited for him up here. It had been a long time since he'd pulled on
his clothes and climbed up that steep bank to accept his responsibilities. There was a war going on, and Edward Kidder Graham had
warned him about it fifty-five years ago. It was a war to the death,
between men like Sam and men like Nixon and Ehrlichman, and
though they would lose this round, it was no longer clear who would
win.

TREE

*It was a bright, clear November morning. The wind was blowing up from the
Potomac and scuttling brown leaves across the sidewalk, rasping. Sam had
only a couple weeks left in the Senate, and today they were planting a tree on
the grounds of Capitol Hill, to be dedicated in his honor. I arrived early.
None of the other spectators was there. The tree was ten feet tall. A few
clusters of brown leaves still clung to its branches. Two Negroes were digging
a circle around the base of it, shoveling the dirt up into a mound.*

I walked over there and sat on the stone wall, watching them work. The little Negro was about sixty, and the big, darker one maybe twenty years younger. They shoveled steadily, not talking, and when the O around the tree was a few inches deep, they took their long-handled wooden shovels over to a black pickup truck and returned with the little man carrying the ceremonial shovel, which shone, handle and all, glinting in the sunlight. He made a few mock shoveling passes at the low mound of dirt. The big man laughed loudly at this, white teeth shining beneath his bushy black moustache. Presently, they sauntered over to talk to me, leaving the silver shovel stuck in the mound.

The day before, the wind from the Potomac had been rougher than it was now, and the Capitol grounds, this morning, were littered with tree branches and fallen trees, and they talked about that.

"I expect we'll be sawing wood all day," the big man told me. "Reminds me of the day I come up to Washington to get away from wood-sawing. I disremember what year. There was a hurricane."

"Where did you come up from?" I asked him.

"North Carolina," he said. "The minute I got here they put a saw in my hand and I been sawing ever since."

"They plant a lot of trees like this one," the little Negro said. "They leave town and the next week the tree is down and they don't know the difference. Last week they done planted a tree to the Indians and today we got to saw it up. Funny what folks do. They even made us take some green paint and spray around the thing, to look like grass."

"There wasn't a man there who didn't know it was paint," the big Negro said. He was wearing a khaki shirt with his name over one pocket and the Shell Oil symbol over the other.

"Some of them trees last a long time," the little one explained. He pointed past a line of yellow and black school buses toward a tree in the middle distance. "That one there is George Washington's," he said.

"I though we done sawed his up last year," the big one said. His pea jacket was unbuttoned and under the Shell shirt were other shirts.

"That was Martha's," the big one said.

The children, sixth-graders, I judged, were coming down out of the buses now — Caucasian, Negro, Oriental. "Who is this one for?" the big Negro asked me.

"Sam Ervin," I said.

He scratched his head. "Is that a Senator?"

"Yes."

"You can't know them all," the little one said. "Up here, everybody is a big cheese."

A young woman came up to us now, pushing a baby in a stroller. She wore glasses and had a serious look on her face, like a person who reads many books and is disliking what she's learning.

"It's disgusting," she said. "Choking him with concrete like this." The tree was in a six-feet-wide strip of earth, between the street and the sidewalk. Beyond her, near George Washington's tree, the school children were lining up serpentinely along the undulating gray stone wall. Finding no one willing to talk to her, she went away, walking angrily. The Negroes, who were calmer, moseyed over to an ancient elm, fifty yards away, and took up a position, watching. Now I was alone with the tree.

Bigger leaves from bigger trees had already been caught in the depressed ○ and lay still in there, undisturbed by the brisk wind. Above all this, the Capitol dome glared dazzlingly white against a sky of cloudless blue. The jabber of children's voices came tumbling down the sidewalk. Presently, two men came and stood near me: a reporter and a photographer, as I judged from their conversation. They talked about the tree, which was a dogwood.

"That's about the hardest wood there is," the photographer ventured.

"Yeh," the reporter said. "It makes good firewood. I got some out at my house. We burn it in the fireplace all the time."

"Rots quick, though," the photographer said. "It's either good or it's nothing."

"Here we go," the reporter said, nodding his head toward where a cluster of a couple of dozen persons came toward us now along the curving sidewalk. When they were nearer I recognized Pat Shore, Bill Pursley, Hall Smith, Rachael Spears, Marcia McNaughten, Bill McEwen, and other members of Sam's staff.

"The Senator was delayed," Pat Shore said to me. "He's arguing a bill on the floor."

After the howdys were done I walked over to where the Negroes were watching and stood with them, also watching.

Presently, across the broad esplanade, Sam came striding, trailed by two aides doing a little skip-run to keep up with him. Sam's hair, in the sun, was as white as the dome soaring above him, and he had on one of his blue suits. He loved blue, slate blue, University blue, like the ink he wrote with, like the lettering on his stationery.

"How old is that fellow?" the big Negro asked me.

"Seventy-eight," I said. "He holds up pretty good, doesn't he?"

"I reckon so," he replied. He burst out laughing. "I reckon I'd be holding up pretty good, too, if I sat on my ass all the time. Yeh. He's been sitting on his while I've been busting mine." And he laughed some more.

"Where did you say you're from?" I asked.

"North Carolina," he said.

Afterword

IN DECEMBER OF 1973, Sam announced that he would not run for re-election to the Senate. He pointed out that he would be eighty-four years old before his next term ended and added that the tolls of time were such that he could not reasonably expect to continue for so long with vigor unabated and intellect undimmed. This meant, then, that he had a year left to work, and in 1974 he introduced and piloted through the Senate three important pieces of legislation: the Congressional Budgetary and Impoundment Control Act, the Privacy Act, and the Speedy Trial Act.

The first of these was perhaps the major landmark in the legislative branch's effort to wrest control back from the executive. It curbed sharply the President's ability to refuse to spend monies that Congress had authorized to be spent. Moreover, and more importantly, it set up a Congressional Office of the Budget which was heavily funded for research. This would mean that in the future, the Congress would not be obliged to react passively (and often ignorantly) to the budget requests of the Chief Executive. The Privacy Act underscored and tended to make absolute that provision of the Constitution which made citizens free from unwarranted snooping into their personal affairs. And the Speedy Trial Act provided the machinery whereby the constitutional guarantee of a trial within a reasonable length of time could begin to be carried out once more.

It was a fine year for Sam; his health was good, his prestige and power had never been higher, and he was accomplishing, legislatively, things he had long wanted to accomplish. Then there was the biographer. Sam talked a lot to me that year. After all, having a good biography was not the least of the things Sam wanted; he believed in biographies, in monuments, and it was not for nothing that the entry under his name — consisting mostly of a long list of honors he'd won — was by far the largest of the more than 500 in the Congressional Biographical Directory.

So he finished out his year, carried his own suitcases down to the car, hefted them up into the trunk, opened the door as always for his wife, then got behind the wheel and drove the 440 miles to Morganton with Margaret by his side. He was looking forward to a new career: traveling, speaking, writing, and hopefully practicing a little law.

The rest of that winter and the spring of 1975 were unusually sweet. He traveled to twenty-two or twenty-three states, picking up honorary degrees, citations, laudatory speeches. He spoke to college commencements, bar association meetings. He was on the Dinah Shore show. His house back in Morganton was the same good old home base, solid and interesting, and Margaret was there supervising what little painting needed to be done. His books were there and, when he was home he would read them every day — the good stuff, Shakespeare and the Victorian poets, and Kipling, whom he still loved, and of course the Bible. He kept up with current events, too; was a subscriber to the Winston-Salem *Journal,* Washington *Post,* Charlotte *Observer, National Observer,* Morganton *News Herald, Newsweek, Time, Congressional Quarterly, U.S. Law Week,* and other publications.

He had said in his retirement announcement that he intended to do some fishing, but he did not, in fact, go fishing, nor want to, especially. There were too many absorbing things to be done. He spent a couple weeks in New York City, holed up in a hotel room, writing Bicentennial television scripts at night, memorizing them, and performing them for motion picture and television cameras the next day. And, when he was in Morganton, he walked daily the mile to work, and the mile back, in all kinds of weather, delighted at being among the old familiar faces he'd known all his life. He loved Morganton and he loved hard work; he wrote the *Encyclopedia Brittanica's* article on the Bicentennial; he took a law case defending a man who'd been sentenced to life for first degree murder, whose appeal was to be heard by the North Carolina State Supreme Court. There was a lot of research to do on that one, and he had the books to do it and loved the research, as he always had.

For his father had been right in the things he'd taught Sam. Work wasn't a curse, but a blessing, a deep blessing and perhaps the chief one of all his life. He did not brood about the future, or about getting senile; he was seventy-eight years old and in the prime of life, and although he made a resolution now to work only eight hours a day, six days a week, he was having trouble sticking to it because all his life he had worked seven days a week, twelve or fourteen hours a day. His old law office on the court house square was set up and working now, and he'd brought his old secretary, Mary McBride, down with him from Washington. As for the Senate, he was glad to be out of it, and missed it not at all.

Then, in June, catastrophe moved in on him — this book. His sister, Jean, came walking across Ervin Street carrying the thick manuscript in her arms. I had asked her to deliver it to Sam, who long before had agreed to read it with an eye to correcting errors of fact. He was afterwards to say that the biography was the worst thing that ever happened to him.

It seemed to Sam that I had done a "hatchet job" on him similar to the one Thomas Wolfe had done on the University of North Carolina; it seemed that I was trying to picture him as a "degraded being" not unlike the contemptibly unreal monsters that inhabited the sewery works of that chief of all Southern traitors, William Faulkner. He demanded that an extensive rewriting be done, one that would entirely change the interpretation, as well as correcting the errors of fact. And there were plenty of errors of fact.

Which I changed. But the "errors of interpretation," from Sam's point of view, remained. Specifically, I believe he would say that his father was not so tough and domineering as he's pictured here; that he himself, during the period of his service on the Superior Court, was not so brooding a person as he's pictured here; he would insist that he has always been a happy, cheerful man all his life — except for the seven months when he was doing battle with a stubborn biographer. And he might add that he has had suspicions as to whether the title *A Good Man* was meant ironically.

Well, it wasn't — but that brings up the question mark looming behind the whole of this book and the entirety of American civilization during this Bicentennial year; whether a person we disagree with on fundamental issues can be truly regarded as a good man.

Because I disagree with Sam on many things. To be specific, I do believe that he was arrogantly uninformed on the abuses suffered by our Negro citizens — however current he may have been on his Constitutional law. I believe, too, that he was irresponsibly passive in letting Stennis and Russell do his thinking for him on Armed Services matters, and that as a result his votes on our involvement helped to kill and maim a lot of people — Americans and Vietnamese alike. To make matters worse on that score, Sam believed the Viet Nam war was unconstitutional, and in refusing to confront Lyndon Johnson on that basis, he was being untrue to himself. Finally, it seems to me that his entire voting record regarding rich vs. poor, corporations vs. individuals, sick vs. healthy, and old vs. young was hard-heartedly insensitive, on the whole, and failed to reflect the deep sense of human compassion that he did in fact exhibit in his personal life.

On the other hand, he made admirable, sustained, and on the whole, successful efforts to protect the individual American citizen in his rights to privacy and freedom of speech, and, finally, during the Watergate hearings, he scored what may turn out to be Old America's last victory over New America; maybe that was the last time humans would win out over once-humans who, being rootless, turned themselves into machines that could be plugged into the most convenient power outlet.

In the world of those machine-humans — which is upon us, no matter what the outcome of Watergate — one's political opponents are to be regarded as utterly evil, and are to be harmed and thwarted at whatever cost. In the world of machine-humans, freedom of speech means merely freedom to say what the boss tells you to say. In the world of machine-humans, there is no such thing as a good man.

But Sam Ervin is a good man: a truth-teller, even when he's wrong; a hard worker; a true scholar and lover of good books; a kind man, in his personal relationships; a man with a sense of humor, who laughs more in one day than a platoon of Wasteland-denizens does in a year; a believer in God. I'd not like to think that he's the last of his kind.

And I'd like to believe that his work on behalf of individual freedom hasn't been wasted. There are higher virtues in this world than employees' virtues, and if we don't start practicing them, the machine-humans will certainly win, and there won't be any more good men.

DICK DABNEY

Arlington, Virginia
January 24, 1976

Appendix
Notes
Index

Appendix

Statement on civil rights bills and activities
sent to author by Sam J. Ervin, Jr.

1) Racial problems cannot be satisfactorily solved by the coercive power of law. They can be solved satisfactorily only by goodwill, tolerance, and understanding among the people of the communities where such problems arise.

2) Civil rights legislation is in essence thought-control legislation. In any sound system, the law makes acts illegal because they are externally evil. Not so with civil rights legislation. The acts such legislation condemns are in themselves entirely innocent. They become illegal only if they are accompanied by a discriminatory state of mind. As a general rule, civil rights legislation does not permit the existence of the alleged discriminatory state of mind to be ascertained in trials in courts of law as other issues of fact are determined. On the contrary, such legislation provides for a determination in the first instance by bureaucrats and erects devices to prevent a fair and full review of the determination of the bureaucrats by courts of law. It is extremely hazardous to justice to make legal rights and responsibilities hinge solely on one man's decision respecting the state of another man's mind because people are not clairvoyant.

3) After the ratification of the Fourteenth Amendment, Congress enacted laws sufficient to secure to every member of a minority race voting rights and other basic rights identical with those of white people. These laws make it possible for every member of a minority race to enjoy exactly the same rights enjoyed by white people, and established the sound principle that all Americans stand equal before the law. To be sure, these laws are enforceable in the customary manner in the courts where every litigant has his day in court and is permitted to establish his claim or defense by tested and tried rules of evidence.

4) Civil rights legislation is repugnant to the principle that all men of all races, religions, and national origins stand equal before the law and are entitled to have their rights adjudged in accordance by uniform and constant rules of law with what Edmund Burke so well called "the cold neutrality of the impartial judge."

5) This is true because civil rights legislation robs all Americans of basic rights by

conferring specially created rights upon minorities and by subordinating the rights of all to the demands of these minorities. This assertion is illustrated by the so-called open occupancy provisions of civil rights laws, which declare, in substance, that every American has the right to sell or lease his private property to persons of his choosing unless a member of another race, religion, or national origin desires to purchase or lease it, and that in that event his freedom ends and he becomes obligated to sell or lease his private property to a member of another race, religion, or national origin designated by the government.

6) The voting rights provisions of civil rights legislation were totally unnecessary because pre-existing federal statutes established civil and criminal proceedings by which the right of every qualified American of any race to vote in any election could be made secure, and by which any election official who willfully denied any qualified voter the right to register or vote could be punished by imprisonment and fine. During hearings on such proposed legislation, Attorneys General Brownell, Rogers, Kennedy, Katzenbach, and Clark admitted that they had never had the Department of Justice institute any criminal prosecutions against any election official under these criminal statutes because they assumed that Southern jurors would not convict Southern election officials, thus indicating that their bias against Southerners was as deeply rooted as the supposed bias they were endeavoring to eliminate from Southern minds. In their testimony, they ignored the fact that the civil proceedings for vindicating the right to vote could be tried by federal court judges in suits in equity where the right to trial by jury does not exist.

7) Being unwilling to have the voting rights of minorities adjudged by procedures harmonizing with the judicial process, civil rights advocates persuaded Congress to enact the Voting Rights Act of 1965, which is totally incompatible with the interpretation placed upon the Constitution by Chief Justice Chase in *Texas* v. *White,* 7 Wall. 700, 19 L.Ed. 227: "The Constitution, in all its provisions, looks to an indestructible union composed of indestructible states."

8) The Voting Rights Act of 1965 condemned the entire states of Alabama, Georgia, Louisiana, Mississippi, and South Carolina, and certain counties in North Carolina and Virginia, by a bill of attainder declaring, in substance, that they and their election officials had violated the voting rights of blacks in violation of the Fifteenth Amendment, and on that basis suspended for five years the constitutional power of these states and counties under Article I, section 2, Article II, section 1, and the Seventeenth Amendment to employ a literacy test as a qualification for voting. Even if any of these states or counties had registered without discrimination every person of voting age residing in them, it would nevertheless have been covered by this strange bill if 50 percent of its registered voters had voluntarily failed to vote in the presidential election of 1964, and if all the registered voters so failing to vote had been members of the white race. Inasmuch as the Voting Rights Act covered various counties in which no racial discrimination in voting had been practiced within the memory of any living person, and was, therefore, known to all informed people to be unjust as applied to such counties, it had the tragic effect of tending to destroy all respect for law in the minds of many people in these counties and elsewhere.

9) The most unspeakable tyranny practiced by Parliament on Englishmen was passing bills of attainder declaring them guilty of offenses without judicial hearings, and on that basis punishing them or depriving them of rights. The Founding Fathers were determined that such tyrannies should not be practiced in America, and, for that reason, stipulated in Article I, sections 9 and 10, of the Constitution that neither

Congress nor the states should pass any bill of attainder. The constitutionality of the
Voting Rights Act of 1965 was challenged by the State of South Carolina in *South
Carolina* v. *Katzenbach,* 383 U.S. 301, 15 L.Ed. 2d 769, on the ground that it consti-
tuted an unconstitutional bill of attainder and deprived the state, its officials, and its
people of their constitutional rights without due process of law in violation of the Fifth
Amendment.

10) The Supreme Court avoided invalidating the Voting Rights Act of 1965 by
drastic rulings to the effect that neither the prohibition upon congressional bills of
attainder nor the due process clause apply to states, their public officals, or their people
when Congress robs them of governmental powers vested in them or reserved to them
by the Constitution. This ruling cannot be reconciled with the prior decision of the
Supreme Court in *United States* v. *Lovett,* 328 U.S. 303, 90 L.Ed. 1252, where it was
rightly held that the prohibition on congressional bills of attainder protects federal
officials, or the ruling of the Supreme Court in the *Communist Party* v. *Subversive Activities Control Board,* 367 U.S. 1, 6 L.Ed. 2d 625, where it was rightly held that the
prohibition on bills of attainder protects communists.

11) The Voting Rights Act of 1965 nullified the constitutional authority conferred
upon the State of New York by Article I, section 2, Article II, section 1, and the
Seventeenth Amendment to prescribe literacy in the English language as a qualification
for voting, and substituted for it a newly created federal qualification for voting, which
no syllable whatever in the Constitution authorized the Congress to prescribe. In
upholding this provision in *Katzenbach* v. *Morgan,* 384 U.S. 641, 16 L.Ed. 2d 828, a
divided Supreme Court made this startling decision: first, that section 5 of the
Fourteenth Amendment, which merely authorizes the Congress to enforce by appropriate legislation the provisions of the amendment, empowered the Congress to enact a
statute nullifying a state voting qualification in perfect harmony with the equal protection clause embodied in the amendment, and to substitute for it a congressionally
prescribed voting qualification absolutely inconsistent with the powers expressly conferred upon the states by Article I, section 2, Article II, section 1, and the Seventeenth
Amendment; and second, that the Supreme Court would not even inquire into the
question whether or not the annulled state voting qualification was in perfect harmony
with the equal protection clause if the Court can reach the conclusion that Congress
acted "rationally" in nullifying the state voting qualification. How the Supreme Court
can ever conclude that Congress acts rationally when it enacts a statute incompatible
with the express words of the Constitution is something which beggars the understanding of the most powerful intellect. If this illogical decision is carried to its logical
conclusion, it sustains the queer proposition that Congress may supplant the states in
respect to all matters covered by the equal protection clause, which means in practical
effect all state legislation.

12) The decisions of the Supreme Court in the South Carolina and Morgan Cases
repudiated in effect the essentially sound doctrine that the provisions of the Constitution are to be construed as one harmonious instrument rather than a set of mutually
destructive clauses. These decisions do this by holding that under the enforcement
clauses of the Fourteenth and Fifteenth Amendments, Congress can nullify or suspend
powers expressly granted or reserved to the states by other provisions of the Constitution.

13) In suspending the constitutional powers of the states in the methods previously
indicated, the Voting Rights Act of 1965 is repugnant to the sound decision of the
Supreme Court in Ex Parte Milligan, 4 Wall. 2, 18 L.Ed. 281, where the Supreme Court

held that the Constitution is a law for public officials and people alike at all times and under all circumstances, and that no notion involving more pernicious consequences was ever invented by the wit of man than that any of its provisions can be suspended in any emergency.

14) Having adopted a bill of attainder suspending the rights of the covered states and counties to exercise their constitutional rights under Article I, section 2, Article II, section 1, and the Seventeenth Amendment to prescribe literacy tests, the Voting Rights Act of 1965 stipulates that none of them can recover the right to exercise such constitutional powers during the period of suspension unless they prove that they have not practiced discrimination on racial grounds during the preceding five years, and that the only court on earth which is open to them for making such proof is the United States District Court for the District of Columbia. Manifestly, the covered states or counties would have to transport witnesses for distances ranging anywhere from 100 to over 1000 miles to Washington, D.C., to establish nondiscrimination on their part if they sought to regain the right to exercise their constitutional powers under the provisions which have been specified. This is a strange law for a supposedly free republic, which gave as one of the reasons for severing its political bonds with England on July 4, 1776, the complaint that the British King and Parliament had transported colonists "beyond the seas to be tried for pretended offenses." Notwithstanding the declaration of the Supreme Court in the South Carolina case that the due process clause does not apply to states or their election officials or their people, it may be rightly asserted that the provision of the voting rights act giving exclusive jurisdiction to a court sitting in Washington, D.C., is a rank denial of procedural due process, and for that reason is irreconcilable with basic justice.

15) Notwithstanding the provisions of Article I, section 2, Article II, section 1, and the Seventeenth Amendment, which confer upon the states the power of prescribing qualifications for voting, and notwithstanding Article I, section 4, which expressly confers upon the states the power to prescribe "the times, places, and manner of holding elections for Senators and Representatives," and notwithstanding the Tenth Amendment, which reserves to the states the power to regulate the elections of state and local officials, the Voting Rights Act of 1965 expressly provides that none of the covered states or counties can make effective any change in any election law without first obtaining the approval of the Attorney General of the United States, who holds an office not created by the Constitution, or the approval of the United States District Court for the District of Columbia. Notwithstanding the fact that a majority of the Supreme Court has upheld the validity of this strange provision, it may be rightly asserted that any reasonable interpretation of the Constitution requires the conclusion that this peculiar provision is repugnant to the structure of government created by the Constitution for the reasons so clearly stated by Justice Black in his dissent in the South Carolina case.

16) Every decision from the *Civil Rights Cases of 1883*, 109 U.S. 3, 27 L.Ed. 835, down to the date of the introduction of the bill which became the Civil Rights Act of 1964 held that the Constitution reserved to the states the power to regulate places of public accommodation within their borders, and denied such power to the Congress. These decisions were manifestly sound because a place of public accommodation is a local commercial enterprise requiring the rendition of personal services within the borders of a state, and has no real connection with interstate commerce, which is the movement of persons, goods, or communications across state lines. Notwithstanding these obvious facts, Title II of the Civil Rights Act of 1964 regulates public accommodations within

the borders of the states on the specious theory that they use in their operations goods which may have moved in interstate commerce at some time before they came to rest within the borders of the state. In upholding the validity of this title, the Supreme Court effectively destroyed the distinction which the commerce clause itself established between commerce "among the several states" and the internal concerns of a state — a distinction which is vital to the maintenance of our federal system.

17) Title VI of the Civil Rights Act of 1964, which undertakes to prohibit racial discrimination in programs which are financially assisted by the federal government, does extreme violence to the concept that every person is entitled to have his cause adjudged by uniform and constant laws rather than by the arbitrary and inconstant wills of men. Under the provision of this title, a federal department or agency administering a program which is financially assisted by the federal government is authorized to make regulations, investigate alleged violations of such regulations, prosecute charges of such alleged violations, enact the role of judge and jury in passing on the issues of fact arising out of such charges, and penalize those it adjudges guilty of offending by depriving them as well as the innocent beneficiaries of federal financial assistance. It is contrary to every principle of fair play and due process to combine the roles of lawmaker, prosecutor, judge, and jury in one department or agency, or for any department or agency to be the judge in its own case. Despite the protest of its supporters that they abhor discrimination in federally assisted programs, this Title provides, in substance, that such discrimination is permissible if it is done on religious grounds.

18) Under the free enterprise system, any American who invests his capital or his talents in any business enterprise is entitled to liberty of determining for himself who he should employ, promote, or discharge to make his enterprise a success. Title VII of the Civil Rights Act of 1964 robs American employers of this right, denies them access to the courts to disprove charges of discrimination, and provides that charges of discrimination against them are to be determined by an Equal Employment Opportunity Commission, whose members as a rule have been crusaders for this particular cause. Under the Thirteenth Amendment, it is slavery for A to compel B to work for him against B's will, but under Title VII it is the civil right of B to have the EEOC subordinate A's right to B's and make A employ B against A's will. As is the case with federal departments and agencies administering federally assisted programs, the findings of fact of the EEOC are binding upon the courts in any subsequent judicial review of its decision if such findings are supported by any of the evidence taken by it, no matter how incredible such evidence may be. This requirement effectively handicaps courts in their effort to do justice because it denies them the right to pass on the credibility of the testimony and for that reason virtually restricts them to the power to correct legal errors only.

19) The action of federal courts and of the Department of Health, Education, and Welfare in attempting to usurp the power of the states to assign children to public schools has created much divisiveness and turmoil in our land, especially the South, which these courts and this department insist on treating as a separate region to which the laws which prevail in other regions of the nation do not apply. When it handed down its decision in *Brown* v. *Board of Education of Topeka*, 347 U.S. 483, 98 L.Ed. 873, on May 17, 1954, the Supreme Court adjudged unconstitutional the separate but equal doctrine which had been invented by the courts of Massachusetts years before Lincoln became President, and which had been adjudged to be the law of the land ever since, and adjudged for the first time in our nation's history that a state violates the equal

protection clause of the Fourteenth Amendment if it denies a child admission to any of its public schools solely on the basis of race. In all of its subsequent decisions, the Supreme Court has professed to adhere to this original ruling, and in so doing has asserted that the equal protection clause requires a state to conduct its public schools "as unitary school systems within which no person is to be effectively excluded from any school because of race or color." The quotation originated in the Supreme Court opinion in *Alexander* v. *Holmes County Board of Education,* 396 U.S. 19, 24 L.Ed. 2d 447, and has been repeated by the court in later opinions. Nevertheless, applications of this general principle in some of its decisions afford some support to the notions of judges of inferior federal courts and to bureaucrats in the Department of Health, Education, and Welfare that they have an obligation to compel states — particularly those in the South — to mix the races in their public shools in undefined proportions pleasing to such judges or department.

20) The true interpretation of the Brown case and of the equal protection clause itself are set forth with clarity by one of America's greatest jurist of all times, the late Chief Judge John J. Parker of the United States Court of Appeals for the Fourth Circuit, in a per curiam opinion he wrote for the three-judge United States District Court in one of the cases which was argued with the Brown case, i.e., *Briggs* v. *Elliott,* 132 F. Supp. 776, on its remand. In so doing, Chief Judge Parker said:

> This Court in its prior decisions in this case, 98 F. Supp. 529; 103 F. Supp. 920, followed what it conceived to be the law as laid down in prior decisions of the Supreme Court, *Plessy* v. *Ferguson,* 163 U.S. 537, 16 S.Ct. 1138, 41 L.Ed. 256; *Gong Lum* v. *Rice,* 275 U.S. 78, 48 S.Ct. 91, 72 L.Ed. 172, that nothing in the Fourteenth Amendment to the Constitution of the United States forbids segregation of the races in the public schools provided equal facilities are accorded the children of all races. Our decision has been reversed by the Supreme Court, *Brown* v. *Board of Education of Topeka,* 349 U.S. 294, 75 S.Ct. 753, 757, which has remanded the case to us with direction "to take such proceedings and enter such orders and decrees consistent with this opinion as are necessary and proper to admit to public schools on a racially non-discriminatory basis with all deliberate speed the parties to these cases."
>
> Whatever may have been the views of this court as to the law when the case was originally before us, it is our duty now to accept the law as declared by the Supreme Court.
>
> Having said this, it is important that we point out exactly what the Supreme Court has decided and what it has not decided in this case. It has not decided that the federal courts are to take over or regulate the public schools of the states. It has not decided that the states must mix persons of different races in the schools or must require them to attend schools or must deprive them of the right of choosing the schools they attend. What it has decided, and all that it has decided, is that a state may not deny to any person on account of race the right to attend any school that it maintains. This, under the decision of the Supreme Court, the state may not do directly or indirectly; but if the schools which it maintains are open to children of all races, no violation of the Constitution is involved even though the children of different races voluntarily attend different schools, as they attend different churches. Nothing in the Constitution or in the decision of the Supreme Court takes away from the people freedom to choose the schools they attend. The Constitution, in other words, does not require integration. It merely forbids discrimination. It does not forbid such segregation as occurs as the result of voluntary action. It merely forbids the use of governmental power to enforce segregation. The Fourteenth Amendment is a limitation upon the exercise of power by the state or state agencies, not a limitation upon the freedom of individuals.
>
> The Supreme Court has pointed out that the solution of the problem in accord with its decisions is the primary responsibility of school authorities and that the function of the courts is to determine whether action of the school authorities constitutes "good faith implementation of the governing constitutional principles."

21) Notwithstanding the true interpretation of the Brown case and the equal protection clause of the Fourteenth Amendment, some judges of inferior federal courts and some officers of the Department of Health, Education, and Welfare insist that public schools must be integrated in undefined racial proportions pleasing to them, and that the equal protection clause, which merely prohibits states from treating in a different manner persons similarly situated, robs the states of the power to maintain "freedom of choice" school systems, and robs school children of the right to attend the public schools which they wish to attend or which their parents wish them to attend. Manifestly it is just as reprehensible and tyrannical for a judge or an agency of the federal government to compel a child to attend a particular school against his will solely on account of his race as it is for a state to deny a child admission to a public school he desires to attend solely on the basis of his race.

22) Notwithstanding these considerations, the judges of inferior federal courts and officials of the Department of Health, Education, and Welfare are compelling thousands of school children, some of them of very tender age, to attend public schools they do not wish to attend instead of their neighborhood schools, which they wish to attend, solely because of their race. This is being done under multitudes of school assignment plans imposed upon state officials by these judges and officials, and by the forced busing decrees of federal judges. Under any proper interpretation of it, the equal protection clause of the Fourteenth Amendment actually forbids instead of justifying the entry of forced busing decrees, and such decrees actually violate the equal protection clause in two respects. When he enters a forced busing decree, a federal judge orders the school board, which acts for the state, to divide the school children in a particular school district or school attendance zone into two groups. He authorizes the school board to permit the first group to attend the neighborhood schools in the school district or attendance zone in which they reside, and orders the school board to deny to the second group the right to attend such neighborhood schools. Since the two groups of children reside in the same district or attendance zone, they are clearly similarly situated, and the order of the judge compels the school board to violate the equal protection clause by requiring it to treat in a different manner two groups of children similarly situated. The forced busing order of the District Judge then compels the school board to place the second group of children in buses and to transport them to public schools elsewhere either to decrease the number of children of their race in their neighborhood schools or to increase the number of their race in the schools elsewhere. Oceans of bureaucratic and judicial tyranny cannot wash out the plain truth that the children who are forcibly bused under the court decree are being denied their right to attend their neighborhood schools solely on the basis of their race, which is precisely what the Supreme Court held in the Brown case violates the equal protection clause.

23) The tragedy is that every American denied equality of right by the action of any state or its officers could have had the denial of his rights redressed and the vindication of his rights assured by patient legislators, patient bureaucrats, and patient judges by the execution of laws in perfect harmony with our constitutional, our governmental, and our legal systems. To be sure, every qualified voter is entitled to have his vote cast and counted, and any election official who willfully denies him this right ought to be severely punished. But under laws existing at the time of the Voting Rights Act, the right of every qualified voter residing anywhere in the United States could have been enforced in equitable proceedings, including class actions, where the federal judge acting either in person or through special masters could have determined all of the facts necessary to vindicate the right within a relatively short period of time. Instead of

resorting to actions consistent with our constitutional, governmental, and legal systems, impatient federal officials sought to emulate the example of Samson, who in his blindness undertook to destroy the pillars upon which the temple rested.

As a Senator, Sam Ervin opposed civil rights bills because their benign titles covered what he considered to be many constitutional and legal iniquities, proposed in vain many amendments which would have robbed such bills of what he contemplated to be their constitutional and legal iniquities, sought vainly to secure the enactment of freedom of choice laws and laws securing to each child the right to attend his neighborhood school, and supported the Stennis amendment, which undertook to make the federal courts and the federal departments and agencies enforce federal civil rights statutes with equality of operation in the North as well as the South. On April 14, 1967, Sam Ervin wrote a letter to his Congressman, Basil L. Whitener, which reveals his views in the area of civil rights. This letter reads as follows:

Dear Basil:

I am deeply grateful to you for suggesting the desirability of placing in the Congressional Record the feature article entitled "Sam J. Ervin Just Won't Fit in a Mold," which appeared in the Charlotte Observer on April 2, 1967. As you know, the author, James K. Batten, is one of Washington's ablest young reporters. I would be glad to have you place this item in the Record together with this letter.

The article was exceptionally well-researched and typically well-written, and I am flattered by the time and trouble he devoted to the project. Nevertheless, he makes one point which deserves an answer — a point which has particular significance as Congress begins its annual consideration of an Administration civil rights bill.

It is implicit in the article that my opposition to so-called civil rights bills is inconsistent with my defense of individual liberty. Unfortunately, the view that civil rights legislation is synonymous with freedom is a common attitude, and, in my view, a common mistake.

For the record — and I do not think Mr. Batten has indicated otherwise — I have never said an unkind word about any race or about any man because of his race. My stand is unequivocal: No man should be denied the right to vote on account of race; no man should be denied the right to seek and hold any job, the right to live by the sweat of his own brow; no man should be denied the right to have a fair and impartial trial by a jury of his peers; no man should be denied the right to a decent education or to enjoy any other basic human right. I have publicly and privately deplored violence or threats of violence against any man because of his creed or color; and, where necessary, I have supported Federal remedies for such violence.

But we will not fool history as we fool ourselves when we steal freedom from one man to confer it on another. When freedom for one citizen is diminished, it is in the end diminished for all. Nor can we preserve liberty by making one branch of the Federal government its protector, for, though defense of liberty be the purpose, the perversion of it will be the effect. The whole fabric of our Constitution — the Federal system and the separation of powers doctrine — is designed to protect us from such centralization; but even the language and lessons of the Constitution cannot stop a people who are hell-bent on twisting the document to the will of a temporary majority. In the words of Madison: " . . . a mere demarcation on parchment of the constitutional limits of the several departments, is not a sufficient guard against those encroachments which lead to a tyrannical concentration of all the powers of government in the same hands."

Yet, we have ignored all of this American political philosophy in considering civil rights legislation. We have stolen the freedom of one man to hire and serve whom he wishes in order to give another the false freedom to work in the first man's business or buy in his store. We would rob a man of his freedom to sell or rent his own home in order that another have a choice of locations. Every recent voting rights bill, every current Federal proposal concerning alleged discrimination in State Courts, represents an effort to centralize, with a loss of liberty the end result.

It is particularly sad that encroachments come in the area of the right to vote and to have an impartial jury, because effective and constitutional remedies for discrimination have existed for almost 100 years in the form of federal criminal and civil statutes prohibiting a denial of rights. Each year for over a decade the representatives of three Administrations have come to the Congress seeking new tools. Each year I asked them what they had done with the old ones; and always the answer was "Nothing." Not one prosecution brought for denying the right to vote, yet wholesale denials were claimed! In the face of this, Congress is asked to substitute its wisdom for that of the States and set up new systems for voter registration and juror qualification. My answer remains that constitutional innovations are unthinkable answers for a Justice Department that is either lazy in its enforcement or untruthful in its pronouncements.

The preservation of liberty is tedious work, and we must not be distracted from it by the civil rights side shows which rob us in their own name's sake.

Civil rights legislation has been urged in Congress by sincere men, and I attribute to them only the loftiest of motives. However, as Justice Brandeis said:

> Experience should teach us to be most on our guard to protect liberty when government's purposes are beneficent. Men born to freedom are naturally alert to repel invasion of their liberty by evil-minded rulers. The greatest dangers to liberty lurk in insidious encroachment by men of zeal, well-meaning, but without understanding.

It is not the "civil rights"of some, but the civil liberty of all on which I take my stand.
With all kind wishes, I am,
    Sincerely yours,
    Sam J. Ervin, Jr.

Notes

Knob, halfway to Asheville, when she was ten or eleven. Mrs. Samuel J. Ervin, Sr., *Reminiscences;* manuscript lent to author by Jean Ervin.

3   9   *Journal* of John Witherspoon Ervin (Sam's grandfather), n.p.; manuscript lent to author by Jean Ervin.

3   *11*   JWE *Journal,* n.p.

3   *14*   The grandfather had been born in Cheraw, South Carolina, on March 27, 1823, and would die in Morganton April 15, 1902. Ervin bluebacked genealogy, lent to me by Sam.

3   *24–27* SJE, Jr., letters to the author.

4   *3–5*   Jean Conyers Ervin interview; SJE, Jr., interview.

4   *9–11* Jean Ervin interview.

4   *21*   SJE, Jr., interview. Interviews with Jean Ervin, Eunice Ervin, Stanley Moore, Hugh Tate Ervin, and Harry Riddle also established the way Sam's father dressed. It was the one thing everybody seemed to remember of him.

4   *26–27* Aug. 1897 letter from Sam Ervin, Sr., to his wife.

4   *32–33* JWE *Journal,* p. 71.

4–5   *34 ff.* Hugh Tate Ervin interview; also Clancy, p. 36. Many of the letters of Sam's father to his mother render detailed instructions for the care of the garden.

5   *6–7*   Jean Ervin interview.

5   *8–11* SJE, Jr., letter to the author.

5   *11–14* Jean Ervin interview; SJE, Jr., letter to author.

5   *14–18* Jean Ervin interview; also Clancy, p. 39.

5   *18–19* Jean Ervin interview.

5   *20–25* Interviews with SJE, Jr., Hugh Tate Ervin, Eunice Ervin, and Jean Ervin.

5   *25–26* SJE, Jr., interview.

5   *27–29* SJE, Jr., interview.

5   *29–31* JWE *Journal,* entry for July 27, 1899.

5   *32–34* Jean Conyers Ervin allowed the author to read the manuscripts of most of John Witherspoon Ervin's published works.

5–6   *35 ff.* SJE, Jr. interview; Jean Ervin interview; JWE *Journal,* throughout.

6   *15–19* Sam says that his father always had the greatest affection and respect for his (Sam Sr.'s) father. Eunice Ervin, however, stated in an interview that her father — who had once written a novel himself — had contempt for any signs of artistic dreamery in his children, and sought to keep their attention on practical business. Furthermore, the father was fond of repeating the stories about how he took care of his mother when his father would not. See, for instance, Sam Ervin, Sr., *Reminiscences,* 1944; manuscript furnished author by Jean Ervin. And if the grandfather's *Journal* may be believed — and I think it can — Sam's father would not allow the old man to have any pocket money. Sam also asserts that the father was self-sufficient after coming to Morganton, but Eunice, Jean, and Stanley Moore contradict this, saying that the school never had any success. So the father was dependent on the youngest son from 1877 or earlier.

6   *15*   John Witherspoon Ervin had three daughters: Susan, Louise, and

Page	Line	
		Annie; and six sons: Lawrence, Erasmus, John, Donald, Henry, and Samuel. Blue-backed genealogy.
6	*20–25*	Jean Ervin interview.
6	*30–33*	Jean Ervin interview; Eunice Ervin interview; Hugh Tate Ervin interview.
6	*33–36*	Perhaps he was in some way typical of very many white Southern men of his time, not just novelists. For instance, W. J. Cash, in *The Mind of the South* (New York: Vintage Books, n.d. First published by Alfred A. Knopf in 1941.) writes: "Best with difficulties beyond his control and comprehension and increasingly taken in his vanity, puzzled, angered, frightened, the common white tended like his fathers before him . . . to retreat himself to his lot in this world as of no more moment than a passing shadow cast on the sun by a cloud."
7	*1–4*	JWE *Journal,* throughout.
7	*8–14*	JWE *Journal,* throughout.
7	*19–21*	JWE *Journal,* p. 71. Politics was always personal in Burke County. In the Revolutionary War, John Bowman, Burke County's first sheriff, started out for Ramseur's Mill to fight for the Tories. On his way he met a neighbor who was going out to fight for the Whigs. They decided not to wait for the battle, and Bowman killed his neighbor. Then went on to the battle and was himself killed. SJE, Jr., interview.
7	*28–34*	JWE *Journal,* throughout; also Hugh T. Lefler and Patricia Stanford, *North Carolina,* 2nd edition (New York: Harcourt Brace Jovanovich, 1972), pp. 305 ff.
7	*34–37*	Sam Ervin, Sr., to his wife, letter, 1898.
8	*8–23*	JWE *Journal,* pp. 57–59.
8	*26–28*	Lefler, pp. 331 ff.
8–9	*31 ff.*	JWE *Journal,* p. 9.
9	*6–8*	Lefler, pp. 331 ff.
9	*9–10*	JWE *Journal,* entry for November 3, 1898.
9–10	*35 ff.*	Lefler, p. 16.
10	*3–7*	JWE *Journal,* p. 9.
10	*8–11*	JWE *Journal,* p. 10, cites instances of Negroes being turned away from polling place during this election. That amendment was passed in Aug. 1900, and applied *only* to Negroes, not to whites. Clancy, p. 19.
10	*12–17*	Hugh Tate Ervin interview. Clancy, p. 27, quotes Sam's sister Eunice as saying that her father confronted Felix Fleming, a Negro who was leading other Negroes to the polling place, and telling him he would be killed if he attempted to vote.
10	*18–21*	JWE *Journal,* p. 10.
10	*28–34*	Letter from SJE, Jr., to the author.
10	*32*	Sam's father frequently said, in later years, speaking of Sam: "They respect me, but they love my son." Jean Ervin interview.
10–11	*35 ff.*	Hugh Tate Ervin interview; Eunice Ervin interview; Jean Ervin interview.
11	*4–10*	SJE, Jr., interview.

Chapter 2

15	*1–17*	Jean Ervin interview. She has in her possession the gold wire Ben Franklin glasses. Author has seen them and worn them.
15	8	Among the books in the Ervin house were Stoddard's *Lectures, The Library of Southern Literature,* the complete novels of Sir Walter Scott, the complete works of Charles Dickens, an encyclopedia, *The Winning of the West* (in leather binding), a volume of North Carolina history, and the complete works of Shakespeare, with each play bound individually. Jean Ervin interview; Eunice Ervin interview.
15	*21 ff.*	Sam Ervin, Sr., *Reminiscences;* 1944 manuscript as dictated to Jean Ervin.
16	9	Mrs. Samuel J. Ervin, Sr., *Reminiscences,* 1945 unpublished manuscript, as dictated to Jean Ervin.
16	*13–14*	Clancy, p. 26, quoting the Morganton *News Herald.*
16–17	*19 ff.*	Eunice Ervin interview; Hugh Tate Ervin interview.
17	*3–7*	SJE, Jr., letter to the author.
17	*10–12*	Sam J. Ervin, Sr., *Reminiscences.* According to his recollections, he argued between 300 and 340 cases before Supreme Court.
17	*16–23*	Sam J. Ervin, Sr., *Reminiscences.*
17	*24–38*	Eunice Ervin interview; SJE, Jr., interview; Jean Ervin interview.
18	*3–6*	Jean Ervin interview.
18	*13–14*	SJE, Jr., interview.
18	*21–27*	Clancy, p. 24; SJE, Jr., interview.
18	*31–34*	Morganton *News Herald,* Nov. 16, 1972 quoting SJE, Jr., speech to Burke County Historical Association; SJE, Jr., letter to the author.
19	*17–19*	Eunice Ervin interview.
19	*21–26*	Eunice Ervin interview.
19	36	Some of these old Bible Memory Cards are on display in the historical room of the First Presbyterian Church of Morganton, together with the hexagonal marble baptismal font, which held the blessed Catawba water with which Sam was baptized. The room also contains the old lectern, the three chairs the minister and assistants sat in, and the organ from the old church.
19–20	*39 ff.*	SJE, Jr., interview. Large-scale hydroelectric development may be dated from 1904, when Duke met William S. Lee, an engineer who interested him in power development. They organized the Southern Power Co., which was later the Duke Power Co., in 1905, and began by acquiring a local plant near Charlotte and setting out to develop the entire Catawba-Wateree river system. They built a plant at Great Falls, South Carolina, in 1907; it was the first link in the chain of dams and plants extending from the upper reaches of the Catawba at Bridgewater, North Carolina, all the way down to Camden, South Carolina, on the Wateree. By 1925, 10 hydroelectric stations had a total capacity of 483,000 horsepower and this energy was used to operate 300 cotton mills. George F. Tindall, *The Emergence of the New South, 1913–1945* (Baton Rouge: Louisiana State University Press, 1967), p. 72.
20	*26–27*	Thad Stem, Jr., and Alan Butler, *Senator Sam Ervin's Best Stories* (Durham: Moore Publishing Co., 1973).

Page	Line	
21–22	*18 ff.*	E. K. Brown, ed., *Victorian Poetry* (New York: Ronald Press, 1942), pp. 265–66.
24	*26–27*	Dale Carnegie, *How to Stop Worrying and Start Living* (New York: Simon & Schuster, 1948); also Cash, pp. 43 ff., who says that "the body of businessmen, including those of high rank, read no books heavier than Dale Carnegie's manuals on how to make more money by false geniality."

Chapter 3

25	*5–21*	SJE, Jr., interview.
26	*11–14*	SJE, Jr., interview.
26	*14*	Piedmont settlers found gold in 1799 near what is now Concord. Between then and 1860, at least $50,000 worth of gold was mined in North Carolina, so it was called the Golden State. Lefler, p. 10.
26	*15–18*	SJE, Jr., interview.
26	*20–23*	SJE, Jr., letter to the author.
26	*24–30*	SJE, Jr., interview.
26–27	*32 ff.*	Hugh Tate Ervin interview; SJE, Jr., interview.
27	*7–15*	Jean Ervin interview.
27	*16–20*	Eunice Ervin interview. Dixon was expressing sentiments held by many white North Carolinians of the time when he wrote:

> Since the dawn of history the negro has owned the continent of Africa — rich beyond the dream of poet's fancy, crunching acres of diamonds beneath his bare black feet. Yet he never picked one up from the dust until a white man showed him its glittering light. His land swarmed with a thousand powerful and docile animals, yet he never dreamed a harness, cart, or sled. A hunter by necessity, he never made an axe, spear, or arrowhead worth preserving beyond the moment of its use. He lived as an ox, content to graze for an hour. In a land of stone and timber he never sawed a foot of lumber, carved a block, or built a house save of broken sticks and mud. With league on league of ocean strand and miles of inland seas, for four thousand years he watched their surface ripple under the wind, heard the thunder of surf on his beach, the howl of the storm over his head, gazed on the dim blue horizon calling him to worlds that lie beyond, and yet he never dreamed a sail! He lived as his fathers lived — stole his food, worked his wife, sold his children, ate his brother, content to drink, sing, dance, and sport as the ape! *The Clansman* (New York: Triangle Books, 1941. First published, 1905), p. 292.

27	*23–29*	SJE, Jr., interview.
27	*30–37*	Eunice Ervin interview; Jean Ervin interview.
27–28	*38 ff.*	SJE, Jr., interview.
28	*8–23*	SJE, Jr., letter to the author.
28–29	*37 ff.*	SJE, Jr., letter to the author.
29	*2–9*	Stanley Moore interview.
29	*8–9*	Eunice Ervin interview.

Chapter 4

30	*1–4*	In addition to the regular meetings of the Superior Court, Morganton was also the place where the North Carolina State Supreme Court held

summer sessions for two decades prior to the War between the States, and, because the law library in Morganton was meager compared to the one in Raleigh, the decisions handed down in Morganton were referred to as "Morganton law," which was considered to be of inferior quality to Raleigh law. Morganton *News Herald,* Nov. 16, 1972, quoting speech SJE, Jr., made to Burke County Historical Association.

30	*5–13*	SJE, Jr., interview.
30	*13–15*	Stanley Moore, interview.
30–31	*18 ff.*	Jean Ervin, interview.
31	*9–15*	SJE, Jr., letter to the author.
31	*16–21*	Jean Ervin interview; Mrs. Sam J. Ervin, Sr., *Reminiscences.*
31–32	*22 ff.*	Jean Ervin interview; Eunice Ervin interview.
32	*17–25*	SJE, Jr., interview.
32	*27–30*	SJE, Jr., letter to the author.
32–33	*32 ff.*	SJE, Jr., interview.
33	*10–29*	SJE, Jr., interview.
34	*17–21*	SJE, Jr., interview.
35	*17–27*	SJE, Jr., interview.
36	*10–14*	SJE, Jr., interview.
36–37	*38 ff.*	SJE, Jr., interview.
37	*8–21*	Tindall pp. 1–3, 22.
38	*3–22*	SJE, Jr., interview.
38	*25–29*	Sam's sister Eunice recalls that before leaving for Chapel Hill he was to walk her to her first day at the first grade and that he read a book all the way to school. Eunice Ervin interview.
38	*30 ff.*	Herman Baity footnotes. Mr. Baity's picture appears in the photo section in this book. It was taken with Sam at the 50th reunion.

Chapter 5

41	*1–6*	SJE, Jr., interview.
41	*7–8*	Thomas Wolfe's description of the campus at about this time: "The central campus sloped back and up over a broad area of rich turf, groved with magnificent ancient trees. A quadrangle of post-Revolutionary buildings of weathered brick bounded the upper end: other newer buildings, in the modern bad manner (the Pedagogic Neo-Greeky), were scattered around beyond the central design: beyond, there was a thickly forested wilderness. There was still a good flavor of the wilderness about the place — one felt its remoteness, its isolated charm." *Look Homeward, Angel* (New York: Modern Library, n.d.), p. 329. Original edition, Scribner's, 1929. Also Agatha Boyd Adams, *Thomas Wolfe: Carolina Student* (Chapel Hill: University of North Carolina Library, 1950), p. 22. Wolfe writes, "The countryside was raw, powerful, and ugly, a rolling land of field, wood, and hollow; but the university itself was buried in a pastoral wilderness, on a long tabling butte, which rose steeply above the country. One burst suddenly, at the hill-top, on the end of the straggling village street, flanked by

Page	Line	
		faculty houses, and winding a mile to the town centre and the university." *Look Homeward, Angel,* p. 329.
41	*12–13*	SJE, Jr., interview.
41	*14*	SJE, Jr., interview.
41–42	*21ff.*	SJE, Jr., interview.
42	*4–7*	*New Yorker,* Oct. 15, 1973.
42	*11*	SJE, Jr., interview.
42	*12–23*	*Rudyard Kipling's Verse* (Garden City: Doubleday, 1940), p. 549. The poem is entitled "The Stranger."
42	*24ff.*	Wolfe again: "The vast champaign of the world stretched out its limitless wonder, but few were seduced away from the fortress of the State, few ever heard but the distant reverberation of an idea. They could get no greater glory for themselves than a seat in the Senate, and the way to glory — the way to all power, highness, and distinction whatsoever — was through the law, a string tie, and a hat. Hence, politics, law schools, debating societies, and speechmaking. The applause of listening Senates to command." *Look Homeward, Angel,* p. 406.
42	*31–39*	Adams, pp. 22–23.
43	*11–14*	Adams, p. 24, says that "sloppy dress has been somewhat of a campus tradition, and the average student of his [Wolfe's] day wore sweaters, and no caps or hats, and seldom shined his shoes or had his suits pressed." Herman Baity, who worked in the laundry, vigorously denied this.
43	*19–22*	1913 University of North Carolina catalogue.
43	*23–24*	Clancy, p. 47.
43	*28–30*	1913 University of North Carolina catalogue, p. 11.
44	*14–16*	Thomas Wolfe, *The Web and the Rock* (New York: New American Library, 1966), p. 203.
44–45	*31ff.*	SJE, Jr., interview. Adams, p. 25, says that the dorms were very plain, that there was only cold water, and lots of noise, broken beds, and no good place for study, and that fewer than half the students lived in the dorms.
44	*31ff.*	At Chapel Hill Sam roomed in town the first year, and his roomate was John Pierce, who has been dead for several years. The second year he roomed with a boy from Morganton named Louis Beach, who was killed fighting with the Marines in World War I. The third year he roomed in New East, which was mostly labs and classrooms, and he was given the big room on the top floor, where he roomed with Herman Kirksey of Morganton, his brother Joe, Jim Younger, and Grady Goode. The fourth year he roomed in the Vance Building with Grady Goode and his brother, Joe. SJE, Jr., interview.
45	*5–8*	S. I. Parker interview; SJE, Jr., interview.
45	*11–18*	Julian Harris (a classmate of Sam's, and the only other one currently in *Who's Who*) in letter to the author; also SJE, Jr., interview.
45	*19–24*	SJE, Jr., interview.
45	*25–26*	Albert Coates interview.
45	*30–35*	SJE, Jr., interview; also Adams, pp. 25–26.
45	*35–37*	David Ewen, ed., *American Popular Songs from the Revolutionary War to the Present* (New York: Random House, 1966).

Page   *Line*

45-46   *38 ff.*   Cash, p. 113: "Southerners in 1900 would see the world in much the same terms in which their fathers had seen it in 1830, as in its last aspect a simple solution, an aggregation of self-contained and self-sufficient monads, each of whom was ultimately and completely responsible for himself." Cash, p. 237, says that "by 1914 it was an absolute maxim in the South that whoever built a factory or organized a business was ipso facto a social benefactor, and a patriot of the first order."

46   *14-17*   Sam looks on Thomas Wolfe as having done a "hatchet job" on the University of North Carolina. SJE, Jr., letter to the author.

46   *18-22*   Wolfe, *The Web and the Rock*, pp. 202–03; also Andrew Turnbull, *Thomas Wolfe* (New York: Scribner's, 1967), p. 29.

46   *23-33*   SJE, Jr., interview.

46-47   *34 ff.*   SJE, Jr., interview, also Clancy, p. 47.

47   *2-4*   Julian Harris letter to the author; SJE, Jr., interview.

47   *18 ff.*   Julian Harris letter to the author; SJE, Jr., interview. There are two campus literary societies "for those who aspired to leadership." The Dialectical Literary Society, or "Di," recruited from those who came from the western half of the state, and the Philanthropic, or "Phi," from the eastern half. Albert Coates interview; also Turnbull, p. 21.

47   *20-22*   Sam's papers on the state's early history won the Colonial Dames History Prizes in his freshman, sophomore, and senior years. Two of these, "A Colonial History of Rowan County, North Carolina" and "The Provincial Agents of North Carolina," were published by the History Department of the University of North Carolina and the James Sprunt Historical Publications, and are available at the Southern Historical Collection in Chapel Hill.

47   *27-28*   Wolfe, in *Look Homeward, Angel*, p. 329, writes: "Its great poverty, its century-long struggle in the forest, had given the university a sweetness and a beauty it was later to forfeit. It had the fine authority of provincialism — the provincialism of an older South. Nothing mattered but the State: the State was a mighty empire, a rich kingdom — there was, beyond, a remote and semi-barbaric world."

Chapter 6

51   *1 ff.*   SJE, Jr., interview. Cash, pp. 239–40, points out "that in many of the small towns of the up-country it was the custom for the young sons of business and professional people, including the executives of the mills, to do a summer's turn in the factories."

51   *10-13*   Jean Ervin interview.

51-52   *13 ff.*   SJE, Jr., interview.

52   *14*   Wolfe, in *Look Homeward, Angel*, p. 350, writes:

He had seen them, happy and idle, on the wide verandahs of their chapter houses — those temples where the last and awful rites of initiation were administered. He had seen them, always together, and from the herd of the uninitiated always apart, laughing over their mail at the post-office, or gambling for 'black cows' at the drug store. And, with a stab of failure, with regret, with pain at his social deficiency, he had watched their hot campaigns for the favor of some desirable freshman, someone vastly more elegant than himself, someone with blood and with money. They were only the sons of the little rich men, the lords of the village and county, but as he saw them go so surely, with such laughing unconstraint, in well-cut clothes, well-groomed, well-brushed, among the crowd of humbler students, who stiffened awkwardly with peasant hostility and constraint, — they were the flower of chivalry, the sons of the mansion house, they were Sydney, Raleigh, Nash.

So Sam, by not joining a social fraternity, was not so snobbish as he might have been.

52	*17–23*	Tindall, p. 42.
52	*28–39*	Wolfe, *The Web and the Rock*, p. 179
53	*1–6*	SJE, Jr., interview.
53	*6–14*	SJE, Jr., letter to the author; also Clancy, p. 55.
53	*14–17*	SJE, Jr., interview.
53	*19–32*	Wolfe, *Look Homeward, Angel*, p. 330.
54	*1–4*	Quoted by Clancy, p. 49.
54	*6–12*	Tindall, p. 186.

54   *22–25*   The *Tar Heel* said of those North Carolina students who would soon go into battle, "Their quest is like that of the Knights of the Round Table. They go to preserve Democracy and its attendant blessings, to secure the rights of small nations, to make straight the ways of peace, and to protect Civilization. These are the noblest and purest causes, most free from selfish motives and narrow prejudices."

54	*27–34*	SJE, Jr., interview.
54–55	*35ff.*	SJE, Jr., letter to his mother, 1916; also Clancy, p. 51.

55   *11–20*   For a good discussion of this movement, see F. Digby Baltzell, *The Protestant Establishment* (New York: Vintage Books, 1964) and John Higham, *Strangers in the Land: Patterns of American Nativism 1860–1925* (New York: Atheneum, 1965).

55	*20–24*	SJE, Jr., interview.
55	*27–30*	SJE, Jr., interview.

55–56   *31ff.*   Sam has written an article on the Brown Mountain Lights for the Morganton *News Herald*, May 25, 1971.

56	*3–23*	SJE, Jr., interview.
56	*24–33*	Jean Ervin interview.
56	*34–38*	SJE, Jr., interview.

57   *30–32*   The attitude of Southern men toward Southern women in those days is perhaps difficult for those who live in other times and places to imagine. Cash, p. 339, quotes Carl Carmer, from *Stars Fell on Alabama:*

One of the rituals of the university's dances [here speaking of the University of Alabama] is that of a fraternity of young blades entitled key-ice. During an intermission the lights are turned out and these young men march in carrying flaming brands. At the end of the procession, four acolytes attend a long cake of ice. Then a leader, mounted on a table in the center of the big gymnasium, lifts a glass cup of water and begins a toast that runs, "To woman, lovely woman of the Southland, as pure and chaste as this sparkling water, as cold as this gleaming ice, we lift this cup and we pledge our hearts and our lives to the protection of her virtue and chastity." Frequently the young man is slightly inebriated and the probability is that he and his cohorts are among the better-known seducers of the campus. But no one sees any incongruity in this.

57   *33–36*   Jean Ervin interview; blue-backed genealogy.

58   *9–16*   SJE, Jr., interview.

58   *18–26*   Adams, p. 23.

58   *29–36*   SJE, Jr., interview.

59   *10–14*   S. I. Parker interview; SJE, Jr., interview.

59   *10–14*   Sam was his class historian and wrote in the yearbook that it was an average class in scholarship "but it is in athletic prowess that the class surpasses all its predecessors." He was also assistant editor of the university magazine, voted most popular in his class, "the best egg," and lost out the editorship of the *Tar Heel* by only one vote — his own. It would be the last time he would ever vote against himself. Clancy, p. 55. Perhaps the biggest campus hero of his senior year was Bill Folger, a halfback who "could play a mandolin and quote Kipling, and who scored the winning touchdown against the University of Virginia." Turnbull, pp. 21–22.

59   *25–29*   Eunice Ervin interview.

59   *30–31*   This paper is available at the Southern Historical Collection at Chapel Hill.

59   *32–36*   SJE, Jr., interview.

59–60   *38 ff.*   S. I. Parker interview.

60   *17*   Wolfe, in *Look Homeward, Angel,* p. 406, said university dignities went to "some industrious hack who had shown a satisfactory mediocrity in all directions . . . He was safe, sound, and reliable. He would never get notions . . . He was a university Two Man. He always got Two on everything except Moral Character, where he shone with a superlative Oneness. If he did not go into the law or the ministry, he was appointed a Rhodes Scholar."

The yearbook says of Sam that "everything he meets responds, and at once a sympathetic friendship ensues. Like Midas, he has that magic touch which makes everyone he meets his friend, and consequently he is liked by all." Clancy, p. 47, quoting yearbook.

60   *17 ff.*   The University of North Carolina in Sam's senior year had 1137 students. Turnbull, p. 19.

60   *18–19*   Sam says he believes that his was the first class at the University of North Carolina to graduate as many as a hundred with the bachelor's degree. SJE, Jr., interview.

60   *22–26*   SJE, Jr., interview.

Chapter 7

64   *1*   SJE, Jr., letter to the author; also Clancy, p. 62.

64   *1–5*   Heywood Broun, *Our Army at the Front* (New York: Scribner's, 1919), p. 30.

64   *6–9*   About four million men served in the American Army in 1917–1918.

Page	Line	
Page	*Line*	
		Two million were sent to France, and more than a million engaged in combat. The Big Red One was the first of 42 divisions to get overseas, and 29 of these fought in the front lines. Harvey A. DeWeerd, *President Wilson Fights His War* (New York: Macmillan, 1968), p. 233.
64	*9–11*	Broun, p. 147.
64	*14–20*	Broun, p. 171.
64	*18–20*	The sense of unity and mission was far beyond that of recent American wars. DeWeerd, p. 242, writes: "So well organized was the draft program, and so strong were the patriotic sentiments aroused, that out of the 24 million men involved there were only 337,649 deserters from the draft, of whom 163,738 were apprehended and punished after some fashion. Of some 4000 men who sought exemption from combat duty on grounds of conscientious objection, 1500 were furloughed to farms and factories, 1300 were accepted for noncombat service, and 371 were sentenced to average terms of ten years' confinement."
64–65	*21 ff.*	Broun, p. 170.
65	*4–5*	The 28th Regiment, together with the 26th, made up the Second Infantry Brigade. Henry Russell Miller, *The First Division* (Pittsburgh: Crescent Press, 1924), p. 2.
65	*6–12*	Broun, p. 54.
65	*13–17*	SJE, Jr., speech to VFW in Durham, June 12, 1955.
65	*27–30*	S. L. A. Marshall, *World War I* (New York: American Heritage Press, 1964), p. 300; Broun, p. 62.
65–66	*34 ff.*	Broun, p. 87.
66	*8–10*	Miller, p. 5.
66	*10–15*	Broun, p. 86.
66	*18–20*	SJE, Jr., letter to the author.
66	*20–21*	Religion and nationalism were closely identified in those days, and on the eve of a battle a priest said to Sam's unit, "I see before me a cross-section of America. I see before me Protestants, Catholics, Gentiles and Jews. You stand on the eve of one of the great battles of history, and before tomorrow's sun goes down many of you will have paid the supreme sacrifice for our country. But I have a conviction that any man who is willing to die for his country will be saved." Clancy, p. 69.
66	*22*	SJE, Jr., letter to the author.
66	*29–31*	Jean Ervin interview; also Clancy, p. 65.
66	*32*	SJE, Jr., letter to the author.
66	*32–36*	A preliminary tour of the trenches had taken place from Oct. 15 to Nov. 15, but Sam had somehow missed that. Miller, p. 6; also SJE, Jr., letter to the author.
67	*1–7*	SJE, Jr., letter to the author; also S. I. Parker interview.
67	*7–14*	Broun, p. 181.
67	*15–32*	SJE, Jr., letter to the author.
67–68	*33 ff.*	SJE, Jr., statement sent to the author. Now in archives of Southern Historical Collection. It was S. I. Parker, in an interview with the author, who first indicated to me that Sam's official version of the WW I incident involving his demotion was not a correct one.
68	*21–24*	The official version is to be found in Clancy, pp. 64 ff., and in an

earlier hand-written statement Sam gave to me, which is now at the Southern Historical Collection, as well as in the literature put out by his Senate office in Washington. The official version also may be found in numerous newspaper articles and speeches made about Sam, and in his presence — including a speech by LBJ. For instance, see the article by Fred Hardesty in the Asheville *Citizen-Times* for Aug. 25, 1963. The papers detailing what happened are on file at the National Archives in Washington, D.C., and may be obtained through Timothy Ninninger there, providing Sam waives the seventy-five-year seal on these papers. He did not give his consent for me to see these files. When I asked him to release the papers to me, he said that if he did it for me he would have to do it for everyone else. However, private sources within the Archives have led me to believe that the statement Sam gave me is, in its essentials, correct.

68   *25–28*   Sam's war records were lost until 1932. SJE, Jr., interview.

68   *29 ff.*   After the demotion, Sam wrote to Margaret, telling her that perhaps she had better forget about him because he was just a private. Clancy, pp. 64–65.

68–69   *30 ff.*   Miller, pp. 7–10.

69   *33–38*   SJE, Jr., interview.

70   *1–15*   SJE, Jr., letter to his mother dated May 12, 1918.

70   *16–28*   Jean Ervin interview; Eunice Ervin interview.

70   *29–33*   A good photo of that rehearsal, including pictures of the French tanks, is to be found in S. L. A. Marshall, p. 369.

70   *34–40*   Robert Lee Bullard, *American Soldiers Also Fought* (New York: Longmans, Green & Co., 1936), p. 31.

70   *38–40*   French morale at the time of Cantigny was low, and few there were who believed that the Americans could fight, or fight well. See Miller, pp. 12 ff.

71   *1–10*   SJE, Jr., interview; also Clancy, p. 66.

71   *10–19*   Miller, p. 14.

71   *12 ff.*   Clancy, pp. 66–67.

71   *16–26*   Miller, pp. 14–15.

71–72   *33 ff.*   SJE, Jr., interview.

72   *21–23*   This may have been the first battle in which Americans used flame throwers. There were long tunnels in the town and they burned the Germans in the tunnels — or burned them out. For the caves they used hand grenades. On May 28, 15 died of wounds, 151 were killed, and 3 were wounded. The ratio of killed to wounded is somewhat astounding. In modern battle, there are 5 wounded for every 1 killed. Also see Broun, pp. 231 ff. Among those participating in the battle were Maj. Theodore Roosevelt and Pierre Teilhard du Chardin. Clancy, p. 74, and *American Soldiers Also Fought*, p. 32.

72–73   *24 ff.*   SJE, Jr., interview.

72   *38*   A good photo of the 40 & 8's is in S. L. A. Marshall, p. 345.

73   *19–28*   Miller, pp. 20 ff.

73   *28–31*   S. L. A. Marshall, pp. 398 ff.

73–74   *32 ff.*   Clancy, pp. 69 ff.

74   *4 ff.*   DeWeerd, p. 323.

Page	Line	
74	*8–10*	S. I. Parker interview.
74	*11–18*	SJE, Jr., interview; also Miller, p. 23.
74	*19–25*	SJE, Jr., interview.

WHAT IT TAKES TO WIN

75–77	*30 ff.*	In 1932, Major General Hanson E. Ely, who commanded the 28th Infantry at Cantigny and Soissons, and whose action was approved by Colonel Redmond C. Stewart and two of the wartime commanders of the First Divison, Major General Charles P. Summerall and Major General Frank Parker, recommended that Sam be awarded the Distinguished Service Cross for his activities at Soissons. This recommendation was supported by Lieutenant Samuel I. Parker; as well as by Corporal Arlie C. Oppenheim and Private Dewey Price, who had participated in the attack on the German machine gun at Soissons. The War Department awarded the DSC to Sam under this official citation:

> Samuel J. Ervin, Jr., formerly private, Company I, 28th Infantry, 1st Division, American Expeditionary Forces. For extraordinary heroism in action near Soissons, France, July 18, 1918. During the attack, when the leaders of the other two platoons of his company had become casualties, Pvt. Ervin displayed marked courage and leadership in assisting his platoon commander in reorganizing those platoons and in fearlessly leading one of the platoons through heavy enemy artillery and machine-gun fire to the capture of the objective. Upon arriving at the objective they were swept by terrific fire from an enemy machine-gun nest which inflicted heavy casualties. Pvt. Ervin called for volunteers and led them in the face of direct fire in a charge upon the machine-gun nest until he fell severely wounded in front of the gun pit, but two members of the party reached the machine gun, killed the crew and seized the gun. After being wounded he crawled back to the firing line and organized an automatic-rifle post and refused to be evacuated until danger of counter attack had passed. Pvt. Ervin's gallant conduct in this action exemplified exceptional courage and leadership, and was an inspiration to his comrades.

In congratulating Sam on the award General Parker wrote:

> I am conversant with your case and have been ever since the days of your war service. I wish that I might take credit to myself for having been instrumental in some degree in your getting the decoration which you so thoroughly deserve and should have had long ago . . . I am sending to you my warmest congratulations and my expression of my admiration for a man who typifies the spirit of the 1st Divison, A.E.F., in its highest degree.

Sam was also awarded the Purple Heart with one Oak-Leaf Cluster on account of wounds suffered in combat, and the French Fourragère as an individual decoration on account of his presence with the 28th on the occasion for which it was cited in French Orders of the Army.

Chapter 8

78	*1–11*	SJE, Jr., interview.
78–79	*12 ff.*	Miller, p. 24.

Page	*Line*	
79	*5–12*	Clancy, p. 72.
79	*13–16*	Blue-backed genealogy.
79	*17–21*	SJE, Jr., interview.
79–80	*31 ff.*	Clancy, p. 76.
80	*5–6*	This knife is now in the possession of Jean Ervin.
80	*20–27*	Jean Ervin interview.
80–81	*30 ff.*	Sam says he had a lot of rivals up until about 1923, although he and Margaret had come to an "arrangement" in 1922. SJE, Jr., interview.
81	*7–8*	Eunice Ervin says that Sam's response to familial questioning about the war was "nervous laughter," and that he told a story about the murderous gunfire that had trapped some wounded men out in no man's land and about how he and another soldier had gone out after the men with a stretcher. And that the other soldier was later killed, and Sam went to see his father in South Carolina after the war. Clancy, p. 62.
81	*17–21*	Hugh Tate Ervin interview. Margaret Ervin says, "For a while he was terribly nervous. He smoked excessively. You could tell he had been through a ravaging sort of thing, but gradually seemed to get over it. You could certainly tell it was nothing you would want anybody to have to go through if you could help it." Quoted in Clancy, p. 77.
81–82	*22 ff.*	SJE, Jr., interview.
82	*27 ff.*	Sam, like Richard Nixon, went to law school far away from home. For Nixon, far away from home was North Carolina.
82–83	*29 ff.*	SJE, Jr., interview.
83	*2–5*	Sam says he never put her into the shadows of his mind, but the fact is that there was no understanding between them until he had finished studying at Harvard. And he knew there were plenty of rivals. And he stayed up North, studying law.
83	*7–11*	Albert Coates, *What the University of North Carolina Meant to Me* (Richmond, Va.: William Byrd Press, 1966), p. 119.
83	*12–29*	SJE, Jr., interview.
83	*25*	Sam evidently disliked Wolfe for the way he portrayed North Carolina in his writings. And, in our interviews, he was close-mouthed about his relationship with him. However, Turnbull, p. 51, says that Wolfe's chief companions

> were a group of North Carolina law students (three of them his roommates) who thought of him as a card, as "a long old boy from Asheville who can really write." They would take him to dinner just to get him started on affairs back home, after which they might go to the theatre where they sat in the cheap top balcony, or to the burlesque at the raucous, smoke-filled Old Howard. At the end of one such evening, during which large quantities of alcohol had been consumed, Wolfe's comrades — these were North Carolineans who roomed elsewhere — walked him home from the subway for fear he would topple in the gutter.

I believe that Sam was one of these.

Thomas Wolfe, Albert Coates, and Billy Polk were roommates at Harvard. (Albert Coates interview.)

83	*30*	Coates, p. 121.
83	*31–33*	SJE, Jr., interview; also Coates, p. 125.
83	*33 ff.*	Coates, pp. 120–23.

Page   *Line*

Chapter 9

87   *1–14*   SJE, Jr., interview; also Harry Riddle interview.

87–88   *15 ff.*   SJE, Jr., interview; Jean Ervin interview.

88   *8–14*   Jean Ervin interview.

88   *14–18*   Clancy, p. 101.

88   *19–26*   SJE, Jr., interview. Jean Ervin interview.

88–89   *27 ff.*   1962 Senate Scrapbooks; Morganton *News Herald* clipping on 40th anniversary of Kiwanis founding.

89   *13–35*   SJE, Jr., interview.

89   *34–35*   Back in Morganton, he got a reputation as a man who went to the dances and danced with the wallflowers. Jean Ervin interview; Eunice Ervin interview.

90   *9–14*   Most of these organizations were fairly new, but Masonry in Morganton dated back to 1797. Morganton *News Herald,* Oct. 28, 1959. Sam was a charter member of the American Legion Post #21, which was formed in 1920.

90   *9–16*   Lefler, p. 304, shows Morganton as being a conservative county, dominated by Democrats, and the Ku Klux Klan as being active there. Sam denies that it was active. Also see Tindall, pp. 99–100. William S. White, in *Citadel,* (New York: Harper & Bros., 1956), p. 20, writes that in the 1920s the Klan held control over as many as 26 American states.

90–91   *17 ff.*   In 1922, at the first meeting of the Morganton Kiwanis Club, Harry Riddle was chosen president, Charles Lane vice-president, and Sam secretary-treasurer. Harry Riddle, interview. See Cash, pp. 265 ff., for a treatment of post–World War I Southern boosterism. Sam was one of 62 charter members of the Morganton Kiwanis Club. At the meetings, a singing session was always held, with either Rev. Norman C. Duncan, rector of Grace Episcopal Church, or Rev. Fred A. Bower, pastor of the First Baptist Church, walking between tables and leading the singing with much gusto. Cash called this "the grafting of Yankee backslapping upon the normal Southern geniality."

90   *28–29*   Ewen, *American Popular Songs.*

91   *2–15*   Sam's father continued to be active in the church, and, because the minister was ill, he would often take the Wednesday night services. Besides, he was Superintendent of the Sunday School for many years. SJE, Jr., letter to author.

Cash writes "The old-fashioned Southern minister was gradually giving ground to men who had the stamp of Babbitt upon them as clearly as any of their parishoners. Brisk, unctuous, and greatly given to grandiose schemes for the creation of an always more elaborate organization and ever-larger plants. Men as obsessed with the passion for large fixtures as any factory builder." He goes on to say, "On every hand, men of business, position, and aspiration were showing a continually more rigorous zeal for going to church and having everybody else go to church, passing the collection plate, teaching Sunday School, and leading the multiplying prayer meetings. Terms like 'salvation' and 'grace' and 'soul-winning' occupied their grave lips on Sundays

		and Wednesday nights as absolutely as talk of making money occupied them the rest of the week."
91	25	SJE, Jr., interview.
91	26–29	SJE, Jr., interview; also Clancy, p. 87.
91–92	31 ff.	Cash, pp. 224–25.
92	5–11	Tindall, p. 99.
92	13–19	Cash, pp. 52–53.
92	20–24	Cash, p. 114, speaking of the politicians of the New South, writes:

> They were more set in the custom of command, much more perfectly schooled in the art of it, knew better how to handle the commoner, to steer expertly about his recalcitrance, to manipulate him without ever arousing his jealous independence. They had observed more intimately the irresponsibility with which the conditions of the Old South had imprinted on the commoner, and were certain now that he was inherently a child, requiring to be looked after. And as the issue of it, they were decidedly more imbued with the imperious conviction of their own right, and not only their right but their duty, to tell the masses what to think and do.

> Cash, p. 271, describing the Southern ruling class in the 1920s, writes: "The class would remain a whole in the broad sense, but particularly in the states where Progress was making the greatest gains, a small group of industrial and commercial barons, who had far outstripped the rest at making money, bankers, the larger manufacturers, utility magnates, would wield an increasingly great share of actual power. In the smaller towns, the ubiquitous Great Lawyer was still around with his familiar hand and warm greeting, but even he was not always certain these days to remember your name."

92	20–24	Sam is fond of quoting De Tocqueville to the effect that the profession of law is the only aristocracy that can exist in a democracy without doing violence to its nature. That is, in Sam's opinion it did not do violence to its nature in North Carolina.
92	25–30	Tindall, pp. 99 ff. It was either Tindall or Clark who said that the mill village was the parent of suburbia.
92	29–30	For a discussion of child labor in North Carolina and throughout the South at this time, see Tindall, p. 322, he points out that "the constitutional amendment authorizing federal child labor legislation, which passed Congress in 1924, was never ratified, and as late as 1937, only three Southern legislatures had approved it. The rest had rejected it, and in the struggle against it the textile interests joined forces with the National Association of Manufacturers and the American Farm Bureau Federation. The amendment would take away parental control of children, they argued. It was part of a hellish scheme laid in foreign countries to destroy our government . . ."
92–93	25 ff.	There was an abundant supply of labor in North Carolina, and it was advertised as being labor of the purest Anglo-Saxon stock; it was asserted that strikes were unknown among the workers. Thus, Anglo-Saxonism and political docility were equated in the ads of those who sought to lure Northern money down South.
93	3–5	Clancy, p. 88.

Page	Line	
93	*14–28*	Lefler, pp. 548, 555, 557, 558, 561, 565, 570–574, 605, 607, 609. Also see Richard L. Watson, Jr., "Furnifold M. Simmons: Jehovah of the Tar Heels," *North Carolina Historical Review,* No. 44, April 1967, pp. 166–87.
94	*4–10*	SJE, Jr., letter to the author.
94	*8–10*	Jean Ervin interview.
94	*11–20*	Stem, throughout.
94	*21–17*	SJE, Jr., interview.
94	*28–33*	Stanley Moore interview; Judge J. Braxton Craven, Jr., letter to author.
94–95	*39ff.*	Jean Ervin interview.
95	*13–32*	This is a constructed scene based on facts supplied by SJE, Jr., in an interview.
95–96	*33 ff.*	Jean Ervin interview.

Chapter 10

98	*1–2*	SJE, Jr., interview.
98	*3–11*	No one whom I interviewed had ever seen Sam going fishing. All whom I interviewed noted his passion for hard work.
98	*13–22*	SJE, Jr., letter to the author; Jean Ervin interview.
99	*1–8*	SJE, Jr., interview.
99	*8–12*	This is a constructed scene, based on facts given me by SJE, Jr., in an interview.
99	*14–17*	Eunice Ervin interview.
99	*18–24*	SJE, Jr., letter to the author; also see Johnson City (Tenn.) *Press-Chronicle,* Jan. 25, 1964.
99	*25–30*	Harry Riddle interview.
99–100	*29 ff.*	Grace Clagwell interview; SJE, Jr., interview and letters to the author.
100	*16–17*	For a discussion of the state's road-building program in the twenties, see Tindall, pp. 226 ff.
100	*21–26*	For a discussion of the hydroelectric power development of the Catawba basin, see Clark, pp. 245 ff.
100	*26–28*	Harry Riddle interview.
100–01	*29ff.*	SJE, Jr., interview.
101	*7–9*	The letters to the editors of various North Carolina newspapers written by Sam J. Ervin, Sr., under the name "Lex" and other pen names, are in the possession of SJE, Jr., and will eventually be donated to the Southern Historical Collection at Chapel Hill.
101	*9–12*	SJE, Jr., interview; also Clancy, p. 94.
101	*14–25*	SJE, Jr., interview.
101	*15–16*	Sam served as a First Lt. in B Company of the 105th Engineers of the North Carolina National Guard from Jan. 3, 1924, to May 3, 1926, and was a First Lt., Engineer Corps, North Carolina National Guard Reserve, May 4, 1926, to July 5, 1934. He was a Capt. in the Engineer Corps, North Carolina National Guard from July 6, 1934, until Au-

gust 31, 1938. He commanded Company B of the 105th Engineers from July 6, 1934, to Feb. 4, 1937. He was aide-de-camp on the staff of Governor J. C. B. Ehringhaus. Blue-backed genealogy.

102   6–9   Sam was a Deacon in the First Presbyterian Church of Morganton from 1928 to 1935. He has been an Elder there since 1935, and has been at times Superintendent of the Sunday School and teacher of the men's Bible class. Blue-backed genealogy.

102   22–25   SJE, Jr., interview.

102   22–28   The name of the slain classmate was Oliver Ransom. Clancy, p. 111.

102   28   Sam denies there was ever any Negro discontent in Morganton. The last major riot of the post–WW I era took place in 1921 in Tulsa, Oklahoma. See Tindall, pp. 154 ff.

102   31–38   Jean Ervin interview; SJE, Jr., interview.

103   9–11   Tindall, p. 25, quoting from John Hay. Quoted in same source, H. L. Mencken called the Democratic Party "two gangs of natural enemies in a precarious state of symbiosis."

103   15–21   SJE, Jr., interview.

103   22–25   Harry Riddle interview. Sam denies part about the gun.

103–04   32 ff.   SJE, Jr., interview.

Chapter 11

106   1–3   One of the benefits gained by Republicans in North Carolina in the years when they couldn't get elected locally was that they got the federal patronage when a Republican was President. Such people were often said to belong to the "federal pie brigade." There was a lot of Republican strength in Morganton.

106   1–14   According to Cash, p. 378, it was the Protestant ministers who took the lead in getting the South to abandon its historical allegiance to the Democratic Party in 1928.

106   3–14   Tindall, pp. 253 ff.; also p. 246.

106   15–19   SJE, Jr., interview. SJE, Jr., letter to the author.

107   3–8   Jean Ervin interview.

107   8–12   SJE, Jr., interview.

107   13–17   SJE, Jr., interview.

107   18 ff.   Smith lost North Carolina in 1928, Humphrey lost it in 1968, and McGovern lost it in '72. Otherwise, the state has gone Democratic in presidential elections. The last Republican U.S. Senator, Jeter Pritchard, was replaced by a Democrat, Lee S. Oberman, in 1903. Between 1911 and 1929, and again between 1931 and 1953, no Republican Congressmen were included in the state's delegation, although as of 1972, 4 were serving. Also, there is now a Republican Governor, and a Republican Senator as well.

107   22–25   See Clark, pp. 269 ff. The Simmons machine controlled North Carolina politics from 1901 through 1928. The Shelby dynasty ruled for the next twelve years, until 1940. But no enduring organization devel-

Page	Line	

oped between 1949 and the present to replace these machines. There was factionalism, but no dominant authority. And the Republican party was gaining strength. The factions were no longer east and west, but there were three factions: east, west, and the increasingly powerful Piedmont industrial section. See William C. Havard, *The Changing Politics of the South* (Baton Rouge: Louisiana State University Press, 1972).

107   26–30   SJE, Jr., interview.

107   30–35   For a discussion of the Shelby group, see Tindall, pp. 645 ff. Also see F. M. Simmons, *Memoirs*, pp. 66 ff.

107   31   Its friends referred to it as the "gentleman of the first water." Judge Wilson Warlick, U.S. District Judge, Western District of North Carolina, in letter to the author, dated Nov. 24, 1975.

108   5–20   Jean Ervin interview.

108   22–30   SJE, Jr., interview.

108   31–35   Thomas Wolfe, *The Notebooks of Thomas Wolfe*, eds. Richard S. Kennedy and Paschal Reeves (Chapel Hill: University of North Carolina Press, 1970), p. 11.

108–09 38 ff.   SJE, Jr., interview; also Clancy, pp. 111–12.

109   6–10   Jean Ervin interview.

109   22–28   Mrs. Albert Coates interview.

109   29–34   Rupert Brooke, "The Dead."

110   2–4   Albert Coates interview; SJE, Jr., letter to the author.

110   5–9   Sam seems to have spent more time with his son than he did with his daughters. Sam Ervin III interview; Laura Ervin Smith interview; Leslie Ervin Hansler interview. He would play catch with his son out in the front yard, take walks with him, talk with him. But life was mostly all business for Sam.

110   20–22   There was a bloody, brutal strike at Gastonia in 1929, which was brutally put down. The strikers were led by organizers sent in by the National Textile Workers' Union, which was a communist-controlled rival of the UTW.

110   22–25   Cash, p. 361.

110   26–28   SJE, Jr., interview.

110–11 37 ff.   For instance, he assisted in the prosecution of Dwight Beard, the murderer of Augustus Benuse. SJE, Jr., interview.

111   10–13   Jean Ervin interview.

111   11–15   SJE, Jr., letter to the author, and SJE, Jr., interview.

111–12 20 ff.   SJE, Jr., interview. This scene is constructed on facts given me by him. Also, Clancy, pp. 114 ff. See also Charlotte *Observer*, Nov. 4, 1956.

112   22–25   Jean Ervin interview.

112   27–33   Jean Ervin interview.

112–13 34 ff.   SJE, Jr., interview.

113–14 11 ff.   This scene is constructed on facts given me by SJE, Jr., in interviews.

114   7–10   SJE, Jr., interview.

114   11–31   SJE, Jr., interview.

114   34–37   SJE, Jr., interview.

Page	Line	
Page	*Line*	
115	*13–15*	Jean Ervin interview.
115	*23–29*	That courtroom today is about the same as it was then.
115	*29–34*	Apropos of this point of view, Clancy, p. 122, tells the story of a day of a heat wave, when Sam was presiding in Superior Court. The first day, he told the spectators to take their coats off. The second day, he told the lawyers to take their coats off. The third day, he took off his own coat.
116	*3*	Sam objects to my use of the term "Yahoo." He says that it has never been in his vocabulary, in his mind, or heart, and that he has always loved all people. Note that I do not put it in his vocabulary.
116	*11–26*	Sam contends that this paragraph tends to heap contempt on Governor Hoey. I base this paragraph largely on an interview with Stanley Moore, editor of the Morganton *News Herald,* who had heard Hoey speak many times, and on an interview with Sam himself, who told me that Hoey was no good at organizing things but that Gardner was. It seems to me there's nothing inherently contemptible about the old style of Southern rhetoric. Cash wrote: "Thus rhetoric flourished here far beyond even its American average. It early became a passion, and not only a passion but a primary standard of judgment, the sine qua non of leadership. The greatest man would be the man who could best wield it."
116–17	*27ff.*	This scene is constructed on facts given me in an interview with SJE, Jr.

HOME MOVIES

117	*20ff.*	This film was lent to the author by Jean Ervin.

Chapter 12

119	*1–20*	SJE, Jr., interview; SJE, Jr., letter to the author.
119	*21*	V.O. Key, Jr., in *Southern Politics in State and Nation* (New York: Vintage Books, 1949), p. 213, writes that "whereas the Simmons strength had rested primarily on a personal network of followers extending from county to county over the state, the Gardner-Ehringhaus-Hoey power rested chiefly on the elective and appointive offices of the state administration. Particularly important, by common repute, have been the highway and revenue departments in their political activity and significance."
120	*1–6*	SJE, Jr., letter to the author. There were 20 Superior Court districts in the state, and 6 Special Judges, 3 in the eastern half and three in the western. These Special Judges were used for emergencies when there was a case overload. They were appointed by the Governor. The other 20 were elected.
120	*7–28*	SJE, Jr., interview.
120–21	*29ff.*	SJE, Jr., interview.
121	*7–16*	SJE, Jr., interview.

Page	Line	
121	*17–33*	SJE, Jr., interview; also Clancy, p. 122.
121	*19*	His salary didn't include expenses. These cut deeply into his income, since he was on the road most of the time.
121–22	*34 ff.*	SJE, Jr., interview. Eventually Sam was to hold court in 46 or 47 of North Carolina's 100 counties. Later this would be of enormous political benefit to him, because he was a popular judge. He was away 5 days a week, 40 weeks a year. But in all his years as a judge, missed going home on a weekend only once, when he was ice-bound in the far western corner of North Carolina. Clancy, pp. 121–22.
122	*8–10*	Sam, in his criticism of this manuscript, says that he was not nervous when he was on the bench. But the fact was that he smoked two or three packs of cigarettes a day during most of that time; that his official biographer, Clancy, pictures him as nervous then; that his sister Jean so characterizes him; as does Stanley Moore, the editor of the Morganton *News Herald* and his son, Sam J. Ervin III. According to Dr. J. K. Hall, the noted psychiatrist, who was Sam's brother-in-law, Sam was "unsuited" for the Superior Court bench because it troubled him to sentence people to jail. According to Sam himself, in an interview with me, he said that he was made very unhappy by having to sentence those he called "his fellow travelers to the tomb." And according to a letter from a man who admires him — Judge J. Braxton Craven, Jr., of the U.S. Fourth Circuit Court of Appeals — Sam was more temperamentally suited to the North Carolina Supreme Court, where things were quieter and where there was no gory sentencing, than he was to the daily grind of the Superior Court. I have corresponded with a number of notable members of the North Carolina bar, including Wilson Warlick, U.S. District Judge for the Western District of North Carolina (formerly a judge on the North Carolina Superior Court); former Chief Justice William H. Bobbitt, Chief Justice of the North Carolina State Supreme Court; J. Braxton Craven, U.S. Judge for the Fourth Circuit Court of Appeals; Don A. Walser, attorney; Susie Sharp, the present Chief Justice of the North Carolina Supreme Court; Frank C. Patton, attorney (Sam's old Morganton adversary); Fred B. Helms, attorney; Bailey Patrick, attorney. And these persons are unanimous in saying that Sam was an able Superior Court judge — learned, fair, decisive, strong, kindly to first offenders, stern to habitual criminals. The question at issue between Sam and me is not the quality of his performance on the Superior Court bench, but his temperamental suitability for this post. And the evidence indicates that Dr. J. K. Hall was right.
122	*11–16*	SJE, Jr., interview.
122–23	*21 ff.*	SJE, Jr., interview.
123	*14–16*	SJE, Jr., interview.
123–24	*38 ff.*	SJE, Jr., letter to the author.
124	*16–21*	Clancy, p. 133.
124	*22–32*	SJE, Jr., interview; SJE, Jr., letter to the author.
124	*36*	Shortly after Sam came to the Senate, Doris Fleeson wrote an article comparing him to Judge Priest.

Page	Line	
Page	*Line*	
125	*8–12*	SJE, Jr., letter to the author.
125	*21–25*	This short scene is constructed on facts given me by SJE, Jr., in an interview.
125–26	*38ff.*	SJE, Jr., letter to the author.
126	*10–17*	SJE, Jr., letter to the author.
126	*22ff.*	My interviews with each of Sam's three children tend to confirm this. Also see Clancy, pp. 128–129, 131. Sam was usually preoccupied with his work. Once his daughter Leslie saw him walking toward her on a Morganton street. He walked right on past. She was too shy to call out to him. He was a Superior Court judge at the time.
126	*25–29*	SJE, Jr., interview.
126	*29–33*	Laura Ervin Smith interview; Sam Ervin III interview; Leslie Ervin Hansler interview; also Clancy, p. 129.
126–27	*36ff.*	Jean Ervin interview, also Tindall, pp. 30–31. Moreover, the "Lex" letters reflect these concerns and attitudes. Sam's father was a remarkable man. At the age of 82 he was still quoting love poetry to his wife in his letters. "The night hath a thousand eyes, the day but one, but the light of the whole world dies at set of sun. The mind has a thousand eyes, the heart but one, but the light of the whole life dies when love is done."
127	*16ff.*	Sam laughed a lot, too. Once when he was presiding at a first-degree murder trial he had a special jury summoned in from another county, and he asked one of the jurors if he could give the defendant a fair trial. The juror responded, "I think he is guilty of murder in the first degree, and he ought to be sent to the gas chamber, but I can give him a fair trial." Clancy, pp. 120–21.
127	*16–24*	SJE, Jr., interview; Harry Riddle interview.
127	*25–38*	This scene is constructed on facts given me by SJE, Jr., in an interview.
128	*1–17*	A constructed scene based on facts given me by Jean Ervin in an interview.
128	*18–23*	SJE, Jr., interview.
128	*23–25*	Stanley Moore interview.
128	*32–36*	Clancy, p. 136.
128–29	*38ff.*	A constructed scene based on facts given me by SJE, Jr., in an interview. Sam told me that his service on the Superior Court made him lose his taste for public service, and that he was through with politics at that time. "I thought that would be the end of my public life. I saw practicing law as offering more satisfaction than anything I've ever done, and I still say that."

Chapter 13

132	*9–10*	Jean Ervin, interview.
133	*15–16*	SJE, Jr., interview.
133–34	*20ff.*	This is a scene constructed from facts given me in an interview by SJE, Jr.

Page	Line	
Page	*Line*	
134	*20–22*	He was on retainers from the Southern Railway Corporation and the Drexel Furniture Company, among other firms. Jean Ervin interview.
134	*26–29*	SJE, Jr., interview; SJE, Jr., letter to the author.
134	*30–34*	SJE, Jr., interview; Jean Ervin interview.
135	*9–14*	SJE, Jr., interview.
135–36	*15 ff.*	The scene is constructed from facts given me by SJE, Jr., in an interview; Jean Ervin interview; Eunice Ervin interview; and a detailed account in the *New York Times* of Dec. 26, 1945, p. 30.
136	*10–13*	I have read all these letters. They are in the possession of Jean Ervin.
136	*15–16*	Jean Ervin interview.
136	*22–30*	This scene is based on facts given me by SJE, Jr., in an interview.
136–37	*31 ff.*	Scene is built on facts given me by SJE, Jr., interview and Jean Ervin interview.
137	*7–9*	SJE, Jr., interview.
137	*10–14*	SJE, Jr., interview.
137	*23–29*	SJE, Jr., interview.
137	*30–36*	SJE, Jr., interview; also Clancy, pp. 139 ff.
138	*18–19*	SJE, Jr., interview.
138–39	*34 ff.*	SJE, Jr., interview.
139	*9–14*	SJE, Jr., interview; also Clancy, p. 144. Sam was appointed to the North Carolina Supreme Court on Feb. 3, 1948; won a special election later that year, and another election in 1950. Supreme Court Justices in North Carolina are elected for eight-year terms.
139	*11–12*	SJE, Jr., letter to the author.
139	*22–30*	Laura Ervin Smith interview.
139–40	*31 ff.*	The North Carolina State Supreme Court during the years of Sam's service (1948–1954) apparently made no decisions of wide social importance. Indeed, many of the members of the North Carolina bar would take pride in this, saying that the court ought not to act as a legislature. My view — that the court made no decisions of wide social importance during these years — is shared by former Chief Justice William H. Bobbitt (letter to the author) and Judge Wilson Warlick (letter to the author). The question of social significance aside, however, Sam's opinions tend to be lucid, often humorous, literate, and well written, and are to be found beginning in Vol. 228 of the North Carolina Reports and Vol. 44 of Southeastern 2nd, and ending in Vol. 240 of the North Carolina Reports and Vol. 81 of Southeastern 2nd. Among the more interesting of the opinions written by Sam are: *NC Highway Commission* v. *Black* 239NC198; 79SE2d778 *Garrett* v. *Rose* 236NC299; 72SE2d686 *State* v. *Bridges* 231NC163; 56SE2d397 *State* v. *Scoggin* 236 NC1; 72SE2d97 *State* v. *Ballance* 229NC764; 51SE2d731 *Freeman* v. *Ponder* 234NC294; 67SE2d292 *State* v. *Speller* 230NC345; 53SE2d294 *State* v. *Hart* 239NC709; 80SE2d901 *Dixie Lines* v. *Grannick* 238NC552; 78SE2d410
140	*2–5*	SJE, Jr., interview; SJE, Jr., letter to the author.

Page	Line	
Page	*Line*	
140	*7–13*	His personal law library, by this time, was almost as extensive as that of the North Carolina Supreme Court — and was reputedly the largest private law library in the state. Clancy, p. 147.
140	*15–16*	Clancy, p. 147.
140	*23–26*	Narrowed, in that it applied, apparently, only to white, solvent men of similar political convictions; refined, in its freemasonry of genteel manners.
140	*26–31*	"We had right good control of the state government from that time [Gardner governorship] on up until [Kerr Scott was elected in 1948]..." SJE, Jr., interview; also Havard, p. 370.
141	*13–17*	SJE, Jr., interview.
141	*26–36*	23NC 163.
141–42	*37ff.*	Leslie Ervin Hansler interview; Laura Ervin Smith interview; SJE, Jr., letter to the author.
142	*16–18*	There was a mild gubernatorial boom for Sam in that year, which he discouraged in favor of Olmstead. SJE, Jr., interview; also Clancy, pp. 150–51.
143	*1–6*	SJE, Jr., interview.

Chapter 14

146	*1 ff.*	"Sam didn't sleep much on the train that took him to Washington in 1954, but remembered his mother's advice that he could rest up by lying still and relaxing." Clancy, p. 154.
146	*11–12*	Morganton *News Herald,* June 10, 1954.
146	*17–18*	June 1954 Senate Scrapbooks.
147	*15–29*	SJE, Jr., interview.
147	*37–38*	SJE, Jr., interview.
148	*5–7*	A prescient remark was made by a letter writer to the Washington *Star* about this time (June 10, 1954). T. N. Sandifer wrote: "From his picture, the judge is a man who never monitored another's conversation on the telephone or otherwise..."
148	*11 ff.*	June 1954 Senate Scrapbooks.
148	*16–18*	SJE, Jr., interview; also Clancy, p. 155.
148	*21*	Wayne Morse was the lone independent.
148–49	*23 ff.*	Charlotte *Observer,* June 12, 1954.
149	*7–9*	U.S. Capitol architect's office interview.
149	*10 ff.*	In case you're interested, here are my notes on what Sam's office looked like in 1974, when he was gone and the staff let me work in there. Large red leather chair with soft comfortable cushions in front of it, a red sofa piled high with books on one side, *The History of the State of North Carolina, Ballots and Bandwagons, The Law as Literature;* straight ahead from the desk a big tall wooden door and above it an electric clock with an elaborate system of lights and buzzers that show what's going on on the Senate floor; pictures, one on the left above the marble fireplace is of Table Rock Mountain near Morganton. Ivy growing on mantlepiece. Picture was given him as Morganton Man of

the Year Award in 1955 in Morganton (he still lists that as the chief of his accomplishments). The other picture to the left of the door is of farmland, probably near Morganton, clouds above it, haystacks in the field. To the right of the door, another scene of mountains with purple mountain flowers. Many plaques all over the walls. The Army-Navy Legion of Valor with four medals on it, a Doctor of Laws degree from Wake Forest University, a plaque from the Masons with red and blue trimmed sash hung over it with two medals (maybe it's an Indian sash of some sort). Right under those another red leather armchair and by it is another phone. It's comfortable in here; quiet, too. There are nine upholstered chairs. The phone on the desk has twelve outgoing lines and six buzzers; a battered, comfortable, old-looking wood desk with papers and photos and Congressional Records, paper clips, stapler, ink, and a much-used staple-biter; back of the desk a television set, photos, bookcases, lots of cluttered things on top of it. Sam's Watergate photo. Four gavels, briefcases. View out the window is of Union Station. Flag flying above trees above green Capital grounds. Beige curtains with U.S. eagle woven into it. High windows. Mahogany frames, dark wood. Eight shelves of books, ten feet high. Mostly law books, with maroon bindings, dark green bindings; 62 volumes of *American Jurisprudence*, very few paperbacks. Books look as if they've been read. Among the titles are *Durry's Senate Journal 1944–45, Biography of Zeb Vance, Who's Who, French Portrait of a People* by DeGraumont, *Federal Tax Regulations, Air Force, Nine Lives for Labor.* Carpet is green with dark blue woven into it. On either side of the red sofa there are lamps with American eagles on them; motif in brass and black; an old 1890s wood coatrack, homely; out the window one can also see the Teamsters' Union Building; construction going on in streets out there but jackhammer hardly audible up here. Behind the desk to Sam's right as he would sit here, a U.S. flag, to his left a North Carolina flag with "May 20, 1775" on it. Also a whole bunch of framed cartoons on the wall to either side of the window. Some of them are not favorable to Sam. One has him kicking a dead horse marked "Watergate Caper." Another showing him driving spike through heart of Civil Rights Bill. More gavels I hadn't seen. On desk, also; an ink blotter, some memo paper, a black single phone in addition to the green one; an almost used-up bottle of permanent blue-black Schaeffer Scrip ink (he writes often with a fountain pen; also with felt-tip); a little ovoid-shaped leather box full of envelopes, letter openers, and scissors and a little wooden box with some Pentel pens, a Cross pen and pencil, some wooden pencils with erasers worn down somewhat; Scotch tape dispenser and a little round glass container full of paper clips and a rubber band or two; a U.S. Senate memorandum pad, and much stacked correspondence. On the wall also: framed Great Seal of North Carolina, a picture of the Old Well at the University in Chapel Hill; a doctoral degree from Davidson College; a plaque of recognition from the University of North Carolina; plaque from the Sons of the American Revolution; a certificate of merit from the John Jay College of

Criminal Justice of CCNY; a citation from the Democratic party of Forsythe County; photos of Sam and LBJ, signed by LBJ (Everett Jordan also in photo); a beautiful honorary Doctor of Laws degree from Boston University; also color picture of Senate in session with JFK as President addressing same; above that, photo of State Capitol at Raleigh. More plaques on wall include resolution of tribute and honor from the Board of Trustees of the American Good Government Society; a religious liberty citation from the Americans United for the Separation of Church and State; a plaque of appreciation from the U.S. Jaycees, yellow against dark wood; a Sleppy Creek Pork Barbeque citation; commission to U.S. Senate; certificate of appreciation from Eliose Stone; certificate of recognition from National Association of Broadcasters. A notepad holder beside phone contains clover image of 4H Club.

149   27–34   Hall Smith interview; May Davidson interview; Pat Shore interview.

149–51 35 ff.   For this long section see Lefler, throughout, especially pp. 3, 4, 7, 12, 17, 346–51.

150–51 38 ff.   I asked Sam whether, at the time of his interview with Umstead, the recent Supreme Court desegregation ruling must have been foremost in Umstead's mind and a large factor in dictating his final selection. To which Sam replied, "Yes." SJE, Jr., interview.

151   3–6   Scott was somewhat more liberal than Sam. Whereas Sam's opposition to civil rights bills would be based on constitutional grounds, Scott's reluctance would be based on gradualism.

151   11–17   The military establishment in North Carolina is sizable; major federal military-industrial commitments have been made by the government there. The state includes Fort Bragg, near Fayetteville, the largest Army base in the world; a Marine Corps base and Naval Hospital at Camp LeJeune, and several Air Force stations and Air Force facilities around the state. Major Department of Defense contractors these days include the Western Electric Division of A T & T, which is working on the ABM; Condec Corporation in Charlotte, working on cargo trucks; and Athey Products in Wake Forest, working on fork-lift trucks. R. J. Reynolds in Winston-Salem and Burlington Industries are receiving federal monies for unspecified projects. Stephen Klitzman, Ralph Nader Congress Project, *Citizens Look at Congress* (Washington, D.C.: Grossman Publishers, 1972), p. 8. (Henceforth referred to as "Nader.")

151   37   When I say that Sam was the ambassador for the state's white people, I am speaking primarily of the civil rights question. He worked hard to help individual Negroes in need. There was, for instance, a Negro short-order cook by the name of Peterkin, who came up from North Carolina in June 1964 and in October was shot in the back on the Washington streets. He was ineligible for District of Columbia vocational therapy, and North Carolina authorities ruled that he lost his residency in that state. Sam wrote the District Commissioners, saying that people shouldn't have to wait a year to be eligible for benefits, and he and his aides sought a variety of ways to obtain vocational assistance for Peterkin. Finally, Sam wrote a letter to North Carolina's Dan

Moore, who saw to it that Peterkin was accepted for treatment at the North Carolina Rehabilitation Hospital in Charlotte. Then Sam went on to try to change D.C. residency laws. Washington *Star,* March 6, 1966. There would always, of course, continue to be divided opinion about him down in North Carolina on account of the race issue. Some would call him the last of the Founding Fathers. Others would refer to him as the Claghorns' Hammurabi.

152   *6–9*   June 1954 Senate Scrapbooks.

152   *12–16*   New York *Post,* Feb. 22, 1957. Also, as Harry McPherson wrote in *A Political Education* (Boston: Little Brown, 1972), p. 34, "At first, many people thought he would be Russell's heir as leader of the Southern caucus, but he had little knack for the political business of the Senate, the negotiating; he was an ideologue with a lawyer's devotion to the 'truth' of rigid Constitutional formulas."

152–53   *26ff.*   White, *Citadel,* pp. 71–72.

153   *10–12*   Donald R. Matthews, *U.S. Senators and Their World* (New York: Norton, 1973), p. 44. Matthews' work is a good scholarly sociological profile of U.S. Senators at the very time Sam came to the Senate.

153   *33–37*   Hall Smith interview.

153–54   *38ff.*   SJE, Jr., interview.

154–55   *12ff.*   This scene is constructed from what I believe to be facts. Namely, that Margaret did stay at the reception while Sam went down to his office alone, that she did come down and meet him, that they did go from there to the Raleigh Hotel, that she had been at the McCarthy hearings, that she did give an interview saying she expected to entertain while she was in Washington, that she did hope to have a house while they were in Washington, and that he was working on the U.S. Military Academy appointment.

155   *14–17*   Sam's first act as a Senator was to choose Joseph P. Hales of Fayetteville, North Carolina, as principal candidate for West Point. 1954 Senate Scrapbooks.

Chapter 15

157–62   *1ff.*   For a good picture of the Senate at this time, see McPherson, pp. 36–45. Some of this material comes from that book.

157–58   *18ff.*   Matthews, pp. 11–46.

159   *8–12*   "In the Eighty-fourth Congress, *seven* of the nine truly powerful committees of the Senate had as their chairmen men from the Deep South and thus substantially in command of all legislation in these great committees. On the other two, Southerners were dominant on the Democratic side, although the actual chairmanships were in non-Southern hands." White, *Citadel,* pp. 70–71.

160   *28–38*   Rowland Evans and Robert Novak, *Lyndon Johnson: The Exercise of Power* (New York: New American Library, 1966), pp. 81–82.

161   *26*   McPherson, p. 36.

162   *12–14*   June 1954 Senate Scrapbooks.

162   *21–38*   SJE, Jr., interview.

Page	Line	
163	*9–21*	White, p. 127. He also wrote, pp. 128–31, "What was not generally understood then was the important fact that on the day that the Senate made provision for this select committe it made all but inevitable the eventual condemnation of Senator McCarthy. This moral certainty lay in a number of complicated reasons." To wit, White says (1) most of those who would ultimately try him knew how they were going to vote; (2) "the decision to proceed with the establishment of the select committee in itself amounted to a general unspoken acceptance that a prima facie case had been made against McCarthy"; (3) the Inner Club had already decided that McCarthy "had gone too far"; (4) most conclusive, the nature of the select committee indicated what was going to happen.
164	*14–19*	SJE, Jr., interview.
164	*21–33*	Aug. 1954 Senate Scrapbooks.
164–65	*38 ff.*	Sam told me that he had come into the Senate distrusting Nixon because of his treatment of Voorhis and Douglas.
165	*18–23*	It was Sam himself who made a much-noted speech against McCarthy when Watkins did not show up to do so. In that speech he said that McCarthy should be expelled for moral incapacity if he made the charges against the other Senators, and for mental incapacity if he believed the charges to be true. Congressional Record, Nov. 16, 1954. There was an earlier floor debate between Sam and McCarthy regarding the censure charges. See Greensboro *Daily News,* Nov. 11, 1954. Also see Congressional Record, Nov. 10, 1954.
165	*24–34*	I may be wrong about this. It may be that upon occasion senior Senators were allowed to denounce junior Senators — and that what took place depended very much on who was presiding.
166	*12–25*	U.S. Senate, *Hearings on Resolution 301* (1954), 640.
166–67	*33 ff.*	See *Time,* Oct. 4, 1954.
167	*3–15*	SJE, Jr., interview.
167	*15–17*	May Evans interview.
167	*21–24*	Jean Ervin interview.
167	*25–29*	SJE, Jr., letter to the author.
167–68	*30 ff.*	SJE, Jr., interview.
168	*5–7*	SJE, Jr., interview.
168	*29–31*	Nov. 1954 Senate Scrapbooks.
168	*35–36*	Nov. 1954 Senate Scrapbooks.
169	*13–26*	Dec. 3, 1954 Congressional Record.
169	*27–31*	White *Citadel,* p. 133.
169	*31–34*	When McCarthy died three years later, Sam was asked by the family to be one of the three Senate Democrats to appear at the funeral. But he was in bed with the flu and couldn't attend. Clancy, p. 164.
170	*3–4*	Patricia Shore interview.
170	*6–14*	Washington *Star,* March 12, 1955.

THE SMILE OF REASON

171	*19*	He fought it consistently for years. Indeed, he took the lead in fighting it when Carl Hayden left the Senate. He was fond of saying

that he wished to protect women "from their fool friends and from themselves."

Chapter 16

173	*1–3*	The growing strength of Republicans in modern North Carolina can perhaps best be illustrated by the percentage of the votes their gubernatorial candidates received. 1948: 27 percent. 1952: 32 percent. 1956: 33 percent. 1960: 45 percent. 1964: 42 percent. 1968: 47 percent. And in 1972, they won.
173	*3–10*	Jean Ervin interview.
173	*13*	Nov. 16, 1954, Congressional Record.
174	*4–7*	Wilmington (N.C.) *Star*, Jan. 15, 1955.
174	*8–10*	Aug. 4, 1956, United Press story.
174	*10–13*	Hall Smith interview.
174–75	*16ff.*	1955 Senate Scrapbooks.
175	*32–34*	1955 Senate Scrapbooks.
175–76	*36ff.*	An April 1955 speech to the New York Harvard Law School Alumni Association.
176	*8–13*	1955 Senate Scrapbooks; also SJE, Jr., letter to the author; J. D. Fitz interview.
176	*14–17*	1955 Senate Scrapbooks.
176	*17–20*	Sam, interestingly enough, says that he was never Assistant Whip. However, newspaper clippings for July 12, 1955, in his Senate Scrapbooks say that he was. Perhaps it was just an honorific title and he wasn't even told about it.
176	*21–24*	1954 Senate Scrapbooks.
176	*24–26*	SJE, Jr., interview.
176	*32–34*	1954 Senate Scrapbooks.
176	*35–39*	1954 Senate Scrapbooks, also SJE, Jr., interview.
177	*1–11*	The information about the political quiescence of Chapel Hill intellectuals was given me by quiescent Chapel Hill intellectuals who did not wish to be quoted.
177	*11–13*	Greensboro *Daily News*, July 25, 1956; SJE, Jr., letter to the author.
177	*27–29*	Morganton *News Herald*, Sept. 13, 1956.
177	*29–30*	Wilmington (N.C.) *News*, May 29, 1956.
177	*30–32*	Blue-backed genealogy.
177–78	*37ff.*	Charlotte *Observer*, May 3, 1960; SJE, Jr., letter to author.
178	*18–26*	Charlotte *Observer*, Dec. 14, 1955; Morganton *News Herald*, Dec. 8, 1955; SJE, Jr., letter to the author.
178	*34–39*	1956 Senate Scrapbooks.
179	*1–8*	SJE, Jr., interview.
179	*9–21*	March 1956 Senate Scrapbooks. The theme of outside agitators was a favorite one with Sam. A typical remark was, "North Carolina has a fine school system, with able teachers of both races. I have great faith that people can cope with this problem if outside influences would let them alone. These outsiders have been trying to reconstruct North Carolina for a long time, but we have been able to withstand such efforts." Charlotte *Observer*, June 3, 1955.

Page	Line	
Page	*Line*	
179	*23–30*	1956 Senate Scrapbooks.
180	*2–5*	In the Democratic primary, Sam received contributions of $300.00 and had expenditures of $478.57. Twin City *Sentinal,* May 16, 1956. Also SJE, Jr., letter to the author.
180	*9–11*	Morganton *News Herald,* June 18, 1956.
180	*19–28*	1956 Senate Scrapbooks.
180	*30–34*	1956 Senate Scrapbooks.
180–81	*35 ff.*	Raleigh *News and Observer,* April 16, 1956. He said at the time that this was the most important committee he had ever served on in the Senate.
181	*6–7*	Greensboro *Daily News,* June 13, 1956.
181	*16–24*	Sam was fond of saying that "all civil rights bills are politically inspired." For instance, see Winston-Salem *Journal,* Feb. 1, 1960.
181–82	*25 ff.*	1957 Senate Scrapbooks.
182	*14–33*	When Hennings tried to cut off Sam, Sam responded by saying that "justice delayed is justice denied, but justice hurried is justice murdered." He said that for three days of cross-examination he had been trying to get a simple answer from Brownell, to wit, whether the proposed provision wouldn't give the federal government opportunity to avoid proceedings in which the grand jury indictment and petit jury trials are mandatory. Brownell, in a loud voice, said it would take him only two letters to answer: *N-O.* Feb. 1957 Senate Scrapbook.

Sam said to Brownell, in the midst of this hassle, "I have lived in North Carolina — the best place this side of Heaven — for sixty years and I have never heard of a single individual that's ever been denied his right to register and vote." Feb. 14, 1957, Senate Scrapbook.

Sam maintains that his relationships with Hennings were always cordial, but a reading of the hearing transcript indicates something different. At one point, fed up with Sam's long testimony and questioning, Hennings said, "Will the Senator from North Carolina change his mind if he reads the record? He has made most of it, anyway. He made most of it with his own testimony. Will rereading it change his position even an inch? Is he like Joseph Smith, waiting to receive the word from the angel Moroni? I've learned Aesop's Fables by heart, I've heard the Senator extol the virtues of Nicodemus. I am quite sure he was a great man, but he has been dead for many years and it is time to take up the present." 1959 Senate Scrapbooks.

182	*20*	At that time he was serving on five subcommittees of the Judiciary: Constitutional Rights, Immigration and Naturalization, Juvenile Delinquency, Internal Security, and Revision of Codification. He said that he could pick out any one of these and make a full-time job of it. Jan. 22, 1957 Senate Scrapbook.
182	*30–33*	Washington *Post,* March 31, 1957.
182–83	*35 ff.*	Greensboro *Daily News,* March 26, 1957.
183	*14–20*	SJE, Jr., interview.
183	*21–27*	Professor Philip Kurland, a law professor at the University of Chicago who has often worked with Sam on matters relating to constitutional rights, has frequently testified before Sam's committees, and knows

Page *Line*

him well, said, "He is not a scholar. But in terms of Senators, you'd be hard-pressed to name anybody since Daniel Webster and Henry Clay who is as well grounded as Ervin on the Constitution. A sizable block of Senators regard Ervin as a constitutional expert, whether he is or not." Charlotte *Observer,* Apr. 2, 1967. Profile by James K. Batten.

183   *25–27*   1957 Senate Scrapbooks.

184   *4–7*   In a widely printed interview, Sam had said,

> It should be borne in mind that, in the South, public schools are social as well as educational institutions. I disagree with those who seek to abolish the social segregation of the races by judicial decree or legal fiat. Every day they thunder at us that racial segregation is merely the product of racial prejudice. I do not believe this. In my opinion men segregate themselves in society according to race in obedience to a basic natural law which decrees that like shall seek like. Whenever and wherever people are free to choose their associates, they choose as associates members of their own race.

Charlotte *Observer,* Nov. 15, 1955. Interview was originally done for the *U.S. News and World Report.*

184   *8–12*   LBJ's role in getting the 1957 voting rights bill through the Senate made him a national figure and had much to do with Kennedy's selection of him as a running mate in 1960.

184   *13–25*   July 24, 1957, Senate Scrapbook. A couple of weeks later, Sam was offered a life membership in the Ku Klux Klan and turned it down. Aug. 10, 1957, Senate Scrapbook.

184   *26–30*   Charlotte *Observer,* April 5, 1957.

184   *31–35*   1957 Senate Scrapbooks.

184–85 *36ff.*   Hall Smith interview; Jean Ervin interview. Mary McGrory, writing in the Newark *Evening News,* April 11, 1962, had this to say of Sam: "He can tell stories by the dozens, quote Scripture by the yard, and talk about the Constitution, it seems, forever. He never touches on the heart of the matter, never loses his temper, never makes a racist argument."

Chapter 17

187   *6–10*   Sam J. Ervin IV interview.

187–88 *20ff.*   1958 Senate Scrapbooks.

188   *2–5*   He also used the occasion to quote Kipling to the effect that "A woman is only a woman, But a good cigar is a smoke."

188   *15–26*   1958 Senate Scrapbooks.

188   *31–39*   Aug. 1958 Senate Scrapbooks.

189   *1–2*   For an interesting discussion of this period, see Robert F. Kennedy, *The Enemy Within* (New York: Harper, 1960).

189   *6–23*   SJE, Jr., interview.

189–90 *34ff.*   1958 Senate Scrapbooks.

190   *10–15*   Twin City *Sentinal,* May 25, 1959.

190   *34–35*   Theodore H. White, *Making of the President 1960* (New York: New American Library, 1967), p. 251.

Page	Line	
Page	*Line*	
191	*13–16*	Charlotte *Observer,* April 20, 1958.
191	*16–29*	SJE, Jr., interview.
191	*29–31*	Sam would also see fit to go before a Senate Labor subcommittee and testify against certain provisions of his own labor bill. By so doing, he threw a sop to his big business critics in North Carolina. To his liberal friends, he said that weakening the bill would allow it to pass. Washington *Post,* Feb. 6, 1959.
191	*33–39*	Charlotte *Observer,* June 23, 1959.
192	*3–8*	Winston-Salem *Journal,* Jan. 22, 1959.
192	*29–34*	Wilmington *News,* June 11, 1959.
193	*1–12*	Feb. 15, 1960 Senate Scrapbook.
193	*28–31*	*New York Times,* Feb. 2, 1960.
193–94	*2 ff.*	Richmond *News Leader* of March 5, 1966: "Here is the world's greatest deliberative body with a third of its members sprawled on cots in the cloakrooms, some of its most able spokesmen groaning on methodically to an almost-empty chamber, and the legislative process reduced to the level of a seven-day bicycle race or a marathon dance."
194	*25–32*	March 3, 1960, Senate Scrapbook.
195	*8–13*	SJE, Jr., letter to the author.
195	*14–26*	Congressional Record, Aug. 14, 1960. When Kennedy became President, however, Sam ended up voting for the administration's $1.25 per hour minimum wage bill — with reservations, he said. Charlotte *Observer,* April 21, 1961.
195	*27–37*	Sept. 17, 1960 Senate Scrapbook.
196	*5–7*	Jan. 1961 Senate Scrapbooks.

A GOOD JOB

196	*23–24*	Baskir, in an interview, told me this: "And of course I had to sort of make my peace with that conflict when I came here. Because I'm not a Southerner, and I have strong feelings on civil rights, as I do on civil liberties. In coming to work for a Southern Senator — his feelings on civil liberties are the same as mine, but his feelings on civil rights are opposite. It caused me some difficulty, as I think it causes most of the young people who come to work up here. But it was less difficult for me because I came after the session in which it was really critical. I came in sixty-five or sixty-six."
196	*32–34*	"Most of the people who worked for him did so with really divided loyalties." Larry Baskir interview. An attitude typical among Sam's aides was perhaps expressed best by Rufus Edmiston when he told Nader's interviewers that "North Carolina is no utopia. These other problems — low wages and hunger — just aren't burning issues or we would have heard more about them. But this busing business does concern a lot of people in North Carolina."

Page   Line

Chapter 18

198   *10–14*   Charlotte *Observer,* Feb. 20, 1961.
198   *14–15*   Charlotte *Observer,* April 11, 1957.
198–99 *20 ff.*   Sam was frugal in his office expenditures, and as of this year, 1960, when Senators were allowed $150 annually for long-distance phone calls and telegrams, Sam drew $8.14. 1960 Senate Scrapbooks.
199   *4–5*   Feb. 1961 Senate Scrapbooks.
199   *25–28*   George Autry interview; William Creech interview.
199   *28–31*   SJE, Jr., letter to the author.
199–200 *32 ff.*   Morganton *News Herald,* March 27, 1961.
200   *1–3*   He had paid Essie's hospital expenses. He was more willing to help individual old people than he was willing to act as a Senator to help old people in general. For instance, he voted to kill Kennedy's Social Security health care plan. Washington *Post,* July 18, 1962. A few days after that, he pronounced himself elated over the success of the test of the Nike Zeus antimissile missile, which had been developed by Western Electric Corp., a prime contractor with several plants in North Carolina. July 1962 Senate Scrapbooks. Sam also voted against the administration's Social Security–Medicare bill. Washington *Post,* July 11, 1965. The vote was 68–21, and Sam was 1 of only 7 Democrats who opposed the bill at that time. Charlotte *Observer,* July 27, 1965. A couple of days after that, he entered vigorously into a fight to save the American alligator from extinction. Washington *Post,* July 29, 1965.
200   *4–5*   Leslie, Sam's daughter, was on his staff in the Senate, and a nepotism charge was leveled against him when the Washington *Daily News* in Jan. 1959 named him as one of 92 Congressmen from 32 states who had relatives on their payroll. Sam defended himself against the nepotism charge by saying, "I hired my daughter, not because she is my daughter, but because she is the best-qualified person I know for the particular work she is doing, namely, research. Everybody in Washington and Morganton knows she has been working for me for the past two years, and that nobody in government service works any harder than she does. If I could find anybody as diligent as she is, I'd get them on my payroll, too." Winston-Salem *Journal,* Jan. 6, 1959.
200   *13–30*   Anthony Lewis and the *New York Times, Portrait of a Decade* (New York: Random House, 1964), pp. 120 ff.
200   *31–35*   May 1961 Senate Scrapbooks.
201   *5–9*   SJE, Jr., letter to the author.
201   *13–15*   Jean Ervin interview.
201   *15–29*   1961 Senate Scrapbooks.
201–2   *30 ff.*   1961 Senate Scrapbooks.
202   *13–26*   SJE, Jr., interview.
202–3   *34 ff.*   Sept. 1961 Senate Scrapbooks.
203–4   *9 ff.*   The date was Oct. 12, 1961. Many accounts of this appear in the Senate Scrapbooks.

Page   *Line*

204–5   *23 ff.*   1962 Senate Scrapbooks.

205   *4–9*   Rudyard Kipling, "The Stranger."

205   *19–22*   Sam spent a total of $1241.03 on his 1962 Senate campaign. Items include 42¢ for lunch in a Raleigh drugstore; 50¢ for lunch in a Fayetteville cafeteria; $1.18 for the most expensive meal, in Winston-Salem; 25¢ parking in Greensboro; and $1.50 to fix a punctured tire in Newton.

205   *22*   Sam says I put this thought in his mind, and, indeed, it is a surmise on my part. But certainly, as a practical matter, he must have known that as his seniority increased his power would increase — as does the power of every Senator.

Chapter 19

207   *2–13*   SJE, Jr., letter to the author.

207   *16–18*   SJE, Jr., interview.

207–8   *19 ff.*   Stanley Moore interview.

208   *1–6*   J. D. Fitz interview.

208   *6–9*   Leslie Ervin Hansler interview.

208   *10–15*   1959 Senate Scrapbooks.

208   *16–26*   SJE, Jr., interview.

208   *24–26*   These are two of his favorite biographies. SJE, Jr., interview.

208   *31*   Evans and Novak, p. 119.

208–9   *34 ff.*   1963 Senate Scrapbooks.

209   *34–38*   Sam was critical of Wallace's attempts to block school desegregation in Alabama. He said, "Governor Wallace's actions in the past few days have made him the chief aider and abettor of those who would attempt to pass foolish laws like this." Washington *Post*, Sept. 11, 1963.

210   *4–12*   John F. Kennedy Address to Nation, June 11, 1963.

210   *13*   Prior to the opening of the hearings, Sam was presented with a petition signed by 435 Southern Presbyterians supporting the civil rights bill. The names of 52 North Carolinians were on the list.

210   *15–19*   John F. Kennedy Address to Nation, June 11, 1963. The *New York Times* of Aug. 4, 1963, carried charts based on a study released by the Census Bureau the week before, showing that (1) non-whites were concentrated in the low-paying occupations; (2) non-whites earned less than whites with the same schooling; (3) non-whites are paid less when they do the same work as whites; (4) income differential between the two groups remains large.

210   *20–26*   *Time,* July 26, 1963.

211   *1–21*   U.S. Senate Judiciary Committee. Civil Rights — The President's Program, 1963. Hearings on S. 1731 and S. 1750. July 16, 17, 18, 24, 25, 30, 31; Aug. 1, 8, 23; and Sept. 11, 1963; pp. 1—91.

212–13   *20 ff.*   1963 Civil Rights hearings, pp. 93 ff.

213–14   *33 ff.*   1963 Senate Scrapbooks.

214   *6–9*   SJE, Jr., interview.

Page	Line	
Page	*Line*	
214	*10–23*	1963 Civil Rights hearings, pp. 93 ff.
214	*24–33*	Larry Baskir interview.
214–15	*34 ff.*	1963 Civil Rights hearings, pp. 321—22.
215	*9–15*	I base this opinion on many hearings transcripts and voluminous correspondence with Sam, as well as on interviews with a score of his aides.
216–17	*4 ff.*	1963 Civil Rights hearings, pp. 416—18. It would seem to me that Sam lost this bout. Of course, there are others who think otherwise, and the Charleston (S.C.) *News and Courier* of Aug. 4, 1963, carried a column by James Gregoire de Roulihac Hamilton — Sam's old history prof, then in his nineties — praising him for his handling of RFK.
217	*32–35*	Charlotte *Observer,* Nov. 23, 1963.
218	*3–4*	Oct. 23, 1963 Senate Scrapbook.
219	*7–8*	Charlotte *Observer,* Nov. 23, 1963.

Chapter 20

219	*1–7*	SJE, Jr., interview; Hall Smith interview; SJE, Jr., letter to the author.
219–20	*8 ff.*	1964 Senate Scrapbooks.
220–21	*28 ff.*	"The *facts* of the case . . . were that while support of the Civil Rights Bill undoubtedly was professed by a majority, the true majority was made up between those openly opposed and those secretly opposed and filled with the secret hope that somehow the issue could be put aside. The chief difference between the vehemently articulate Southern opposition to civil rights and a good deal of the rest of the Senate, in short, was the difference between harsh candor and no candor at all." White, *Citadel,* p. 61.
221	*13–33*	1964 Senate Scrapbooks.
221–22	*34 ff.*	The earlier bills had brought changes, although as late as 1961 only a quarter of the five million Negroes of voting age in the South were registered, by the middle of 1964, 40 percent were. And yet one might call in question whether it was on the Constitution and only on the Constitution that Sam based his opposition to civil rights bills. In a speech given to the United Daughters of the Confederacy of the District of Columbia on Jan. 23, 1957, and in talking about Robert E. Lee, Stonewall Jackson, and Matthew Maury and their decision to go with the Confederacy, he said that these men had faced no simple choice between good and evil, and that in such a conflict of loyalties, a citizen's best recourse was to "his heritage."
222–23	*32 ff.*	SJE, Jr., interview.
223	*7–20*	1964 Senate Scrapbooks. The amendments introduced by Sam to the existing federal bail laws provided that (1) no person should be denied bail solely because of financial insufficiency; (2) a defendant jailed because of his inability to make bail received credit toward his sentence for the time spent in confinement; (3) the defendants

Page   Line

who were financially able were permitted to make a cash deposit with the court in lieu of the usual surety, thus avoiding the bondsman's fee. Washington *Post,* May 16, 1964.

223 *23–25* Wilmington (N.C.) *Star,* Oct. 31, 1964.

223–24 *33 ff.* SJE, Jr., letter to the author.

225 *14–18* Nov. 1964 Senate Scrapbooks.

225 *19–36* Washington *Post,* Dec. 10, 1964.

225–26 *37 ff.* SJE, Jr., letter to the author. Since the Darlington case, Sam has been involved as amicus curiae in three Supreme Court cases. *Flast* v. *Cohen,* 1967; *Tatum* v. *Laird,* 1972; and *Gravel* v. *the United States,* 1972. He received no fees for these latter three appearences; took them as public-interest cases. They involved, respectively, judicial review of federal aid to religious institutions; army surveillance of private citizens; and congressional immunity.

226 *17–20* Asheville *Citizen,* Jan. 13, 1965; Greensboro *Daily News,* Jan. 7, 1965.

226 *30–33* Hall Smith interview.

226 *33–39* SJE, Jr., interview.

227 *1–14* As of this time, he was saying he regretted the U.S. involvement in Vietnam, but knew of no suitable alternative to the policy being pursued by Johnson. Charlotte *Observer,* Aug. 3, 1965. The next year he said that the Vietnam War was unconstitutional, but there was only one way to end it — to fight to win. Dec. 23, 1966 Senate Scrapbook. He made the same statement about the constitutionality of the war the following month. Charlotte *Observer,* Jan. 6, 1967. He contended in a telephone interview to a Charlotte *Observer* reporter that the Vietnam War was unconstitutional. He said that offensive wars had to be approved by Congress, and that, in spite of that, Johnson and two other Presidents before him sent American troops to Vietnam without any such declaration of war, thus violating the Constitution. But he said it was a metaphysical discussion, like the one about how many angels could dance on the head of a pin, and that he saw nothing to do as a practical matter except to fight and win, or to fight harder to bring the enemy to the conference table. In recent days, in letters to me, he has said that the war was constitutional, after all, because the Gulf of Tonkin Resolution amounted to a declaration of war. He was all for letting the generals and admirals run this unconstitutional war. Speaking to the North Carolina Association of Professionals on the Wednesday prior to April 13, 1967, he said, "The politicians should take a back seat and let the admirals and generals decide how the war should be fought."

227 *15–20* SJE, Jr., interview.

227 *21–33* 1965 Senate Scrapbooks.

227–28 *34 ff.* Washington *Star,* March 24, 1965: a Mary McGrory article. "The Senator would ask a long involved three-part question based on a horrible hypothesis, ending up with a lurid picture of states rights abridged, Southern states humiliated. 'Is that what the bill would do?' 'Yes,' said the Attorney General, simply."

Page	Line	
228	*5–8*	Sam was fond of saying that the U.S. had forgiven every country they had ever been at war with, except the South. Winston-Salem *Journal,* May 15, 1965.
228	*13–17*	May 24, 1965 Senate Scrapbook.
228	*23–30*	SJE, Jr., interview.
228–29	*31 ff.*	SJE, Jr., interview. Sam's nativist proclivities date as least as far back as the 1920s, as this book has shown, and continue throughout his Senate career. For instance, in 1955, in a speech to the Junior Order of United American Mechanics and its auxiliary, The Daughters of America — two nativist groups — Sam decried any legislation that would favor the foreign-born. "Some people go to ridiculous lengths to deprive native Americans of their fundamental rights to the benefit of those who are not American-born Americans." He cited at this time the fair employment laws of New York State, which made it unlawful to ask a man what name he was born under. If the original name had a foreign sound, Sam said, "that might lead to employing some good American in his place." Asheville *Citizen,* Aug. 6, 1955. Feb. 1965 Senate Scrapbooks.
229	*7–21*	1965 Senate Scrapbooks.
229	*29–37*	1965 Senate Scrapbooks.
230	*3–20*	This trip took place in Oct. and Nov. of 1965.
230	*21–23*	Nov. 1965 Senate Scrapbooks.
230–31	*36 ff.*	1966 hearings, p. 143.
231	*16–20*	1966 hearings transcripts, p. 140.
231	*21–27*	Robert Bland Smith, Jr., interview.
231–32	*28 ff.*	Greensboro *Daily News,* Jan. 11, 1965; also Washington *Star,* Jan. 6, 1967.
232	*11–21*	U.S. Senate, Privacy and the Rights of Federal Employees. Hearings before the Subcommittee on Constitutional Rights of the Committee on the Judiciary. Washington, G.P.O., 1967, pp. 140, 152. This hearing was held Oct. 3, 1966.
232	*22–27*	1966 and 1967 Senate Scrapbooks.
232	*27–33*	Asheville *Citizen,* March 3, 1967.
232	*34–38*	Clancy, p. 297.

Chapter 21

235–36	*18 ff.*	SJE, Jr., interview.
236	*13–21*	Raleigh *News and Observer,* Feb. 22, 1967. Government employees were becoming a larger proportion of our population. As of 1970, 1 out of every 7 Americans who worked, worked for local, state, or federal government.
236–37	*35 ff.*	Thomas D. Clark and Gilbert D. Kirwan, *The South Since Appomattox* (New York: Oxford University Press, 1967), pp. 200–201.
237	*3–21*	Charlotte *Observer,* Jan. 30, 1967.
237	*22–32*	May 1, 1966 Senate Scrapbook.
237–38	*33 ff.*	1966 Senate Scrapbooks.
238	*6–8*	Hall Smith interview. Sam says he didn't chase them down the hall.

Page	Line	
238	*9–18*	Detroit *Free Press,* Sept. 21, 1967; also Houston *Chronicle,* Sept. 24, 1967.
238	*19–23*	Sam's original strategy against Terry Sanford was to ward off opposition by a show of strength and by making it clear he had every intention of running. He shored up his support with the state's tobacco farmers and manufacturers by holding a news conference to blast the anti-smoking report of the Surgeon General and to insist that there was no proof that smoking caused cancer or heart disease. It was the second news conference of his Senate career. Then Richard Russell made a public statement praising Sam's skill in promoting the industrial development of North Carolina and in securing federal monies for the state. Sam also became unusually active on the speaking circuit, averaging more than one speech back home each week. Winston-Salem *Journal,* Dec. 7, 1967. While he had no organization as such, Sam himself was organized, and in the corner of his office was a small map of North Carolina at about this time, with 49 red pins stuck around it, representing speeches he had made or was scheduled to make in the state during 1967. Hardly a section of the state was without a red pin. He was also, at this time, mailing 6000 personal letters to his "friends," asking if they would send him the names of 20 people who would help him in his campaign. And he told a reporter that if he did have opposition he could assemble a campaign organization in every county of the state within a week. Winston-Salem *Journal,* Aug. 20, 1967. He ran things very plainly. He made little use of federally financed service — a state office. His was located in Morganton across from the courthouse in a two-story office building owned by himself. It was the same office he used as a practicing lawyer and later as a judge. A visitor found an open door and no one in the rooms, which were filled with law books. Apparently the place was used only during congressional recess. The office had no campaign material or information on things such as Sam's voting record. It did disperse campaign materials in election years.
238	*24–25*	"I find myself working without great difficulty for ten or twelve hours a day. I've done that all my life." Morganton *News Herald,* July 25, 1967.
239	*1–14*	1967 Senate Scrapbooks.
239	*15–21*	Newark *News,* Oct. 10, 1967.
239	*22–27*	March 1967 Senate Scrapbooks.
239–40	*32 ff.*	1967 Senate Scrapbooks.
240	*9–12*	SJE, Jr., letter to the author.
240	*13–27*	Charlotte *Observer,* Feb. 27, 1967; also SJE, Jr., interview; Jean Ervin interview.
240–41	*28 ff.*	1967 Senate Scrapbooks.
241	*13–16*	Bill McEwen interview.
241–42	*20 ff.*	Congressional Record, Sept. 20, 1966.
242	*29–30*	Part of this incipient opposition may have had to do with the demographic patterns. North Carolina urbanization as of 1960 was 34

percent; as of 1970, 45 percent; by 1980, it will probably be 50 percent.

242   *36–39*   SJE, Jr., interview. Speaking at Wake Forest University, on April 30, 1966, Sam said, "The right of clergymen and civil rights agitators to disobey laws they deem unjust is exactly the same as the right of the arsonist, the burglar, the murderer, the rapist, and the thief to disobey the laws forbidding arson, burglary, murder, rape, and theft." See the article on Sam's quietist position regarding political activities by ministers in *Presbyterian Outlook,* June 6, 1966. Also see Sam's speech of May 3, 1967, on Law Day at Chapel Hill, in which he once more blasted clergymen for becoming involved in politics. Morganton *News Herald,* May 3, 1967.

243   *4–11*   Sam was asked by the *Presbyterian Survey* of July 1960 whether official church bodies and local bodies should take a public stand on political issues. He said no, because (1) it would violate the Westminster Confession of Faith; (2) it would violate the doctrine of the separation of powers; (3) "while such bodies do possess a special competence to instruct their members as to how they should render to God the things that are God's, they do not possess any special competence to instruct their members as to how they should render unto Caesar the things which are Caesar's." Also see Salisbury *Post,* Nov. 3, 1969.

243   *16–21*   Hall Smith interview; George Autry interview.

243   *21–26*   Sam said on numerous occasions, "You know what's wrong with Lyndon Johnson? I bet you Johnson has never read a book unless it was written about him."

243   *23–24*   Pat Shore interview; also Clancy, p. 193; Charlotte *Observer,* Oct. 4, 1965.

243   *27–39*   June 14, 1966 Senate Scrapbook.

244   *1–5*   June 1966 Senate Scrapbooks.

244–45 *5ff.*   SJE, Jr., interview. At about this time, Sam, in an interview, said, "Johnson is not as popular in North Carolina now as he was the first time he ran. But candor does compel me to say that will reflect to some degree on the Democratic vote for all of us." Morganton *News Herald,* July 25, 1967.

244–45 *36ff.*   This took place on June 29, 1967.

245   *10–12*   Greensboro *Daily News,* Sept. 17, 1967.

245   *16–19*   SJE, Jr., interview.

245   *22–24*   In his fall campaign against the Republican, Sam had contributions of $20,931.92 and expenditures of $17,076.32 — and returned the surplus on a pro-rated basis to his contributors. Nader, p. 16.

245   *28*   April 6, 1968 Senate Scrapbook. Sam said, "I would not deny that I have disagreed with his methods [speaking of King] and the disruptive forces they set in motion."

245   *33–36*   Hall Smith interview.

MOTHER OF PEARL

246   *1–19*   In private conversations with me, Sam always spoke well of McGovern, and it is a fact that McGovern leaned heavily on Sam's work in compiling a list of examples of Nixon Administration flauntings of basic American constitutional rights. With only one major exception, McGovern's White Paper on civil liberties, issued on Sept. 2, 1972, echoed arguments that Sam had developed over the few years preceding. *New York Times,* Sept. 3, 1972.

Chapter 22

247–48   *1 ff.*   For this account of his activities on the week of his seventy-fifth birthday, see Winston-Salem *Journal,* Jan. 2, 1972.

248   *17–34*   1969 Senate Scrapbooks.

248   *35–38*   SJE, Jr., letter to the author.

248–49   *38 ff.*   1970 Senate Scrapbooks.

249   *9–23*   1970 Senate Scrapbooks. Also see New Orleans *States Item,* Jan. 3, 1967. Sam said on the Senate floor that "the pretrial detention authorized by the Nixon bill is unconstitutional and smacks of a police state rather than a democracy under law. It repudiates centuries of Anglo-American concepts of fairness, due process, and common standards of justice. The Administration bill protects no one. All it does is conflict and imprison without due process. Judges are not gifted with the prophetic power necessary for accurate judgments as to which individuals represent a danger to the community. This law will result in the imprisonment of many innocent persons." Congressional Record, July 26, 1969. Also see Sam's article on preventive detention in the *New York Times,* Aug. 19, 1972.

249   *24–34*   1970 Senate Scrapbooks.

250   *5–7*   After the House passed the crime bill for Washington, Sam called it "an affront to the Bill of Rights," and said "it is as full of unconstitutional, unjust, and unwise provisions as a mangy hound dog is full of fleas." He told a special Senate District Committee hearing that the Omnibus Crime Bill was "a garbage pail of some of the most repressive, near-sighted, intolerant, unfair, and vindictive legislation that the Senate has ever been presented."

250   *9–36*   *New York Times,* Jan. 10, 1971.

250–51   *37 ff.*   Washington *Post,* March 17, 1971; April 26, 1971; September 28, 1971.

251   *5–17*   Nader, p. 7.

251   *18–19*   Raleigh *News and Observer,* Aug. 28, 1971.

251   *29–33*   SJE, Jr., interview; also Hall Smith interview.

252–53   *1 ff.*   1971 Senate Scrapbooks.

253   *12–14*   July 21, 1971, Senate Scrapbook. For instance, one such probe was ordered by the assistant operations officer of the 771st Military Intelligence detachment at San Juan, Puerto Rico.

Page	*Line*	
253	*15–18*	Reported in Winston-Salem *Journal,* April 11, 1971.
253	*18–26*	Hearings of Feb. 24, 1971.
253	*29 ff.*	Dec. 1970 testimony. It was also revealed at this time that the Army had collected personal data on Whitney Young, Joan Baez, Arlo Guthrie, Julian Bond, Benjamin Spock, William Sloan Coffin, and Jesse Jackson.
253–54	*38 ff.*	See Jack Anderson's column of March 22, 1971 in the Washington *Post.*
254	*4–15*	March 1971 hearings.
254	*16–19*	This statement was made by Nicholas Katzenbach on March 9, 1971. The army was uniformly uncooperative during these hearings and in other attempts by the Constitutional Rights Subcommittee to look into army surveillance of civilians. Larry Baskir said, "They have given us as little help as they thought they could get by with. Time and again, we catch them giving us incomplete information. We'd ask them about it, and they would reply, oh yes, we forgot about that. It seems they were always forgetting. We don't know in detail how the snooping was conceived. We want to know who ordered it, we want to assign responsibility. But it doesn't look as if we will be able to." Greensboro *Daily News,* Sept. 1, 1972.
254	*21–30*	April 1971 hearings.
254	*29–35*	See the Constitutional Rights Subcommittee report issued Aug. 30, 1972.
254–55	*36 ff.*	Asheville *Citizen,* March 1, 1971.

Chapter 23

256	*1–6*	SJE, Jr., interview. Clancy, pp. 11–12, says that Sam had been slaving away in the Senate for two decades on precisely the issues that were raised by Watergate. "It seemed uncanny, but he was standing, by virtue of his seniority, of his committee positions, his knowledge of the Constitution and love of history, his judicial experience and reputation for fairness, his disdain for political pressure, his old-fashioned ideas of morality, right in Richard Nixon's path."
256	*7–13*	SJE, Jr., interview.
256	*14 ff.*	The chronology of Watergate events that follows throughout this chapter and the next is taken from Sam's Senate Scrapbooks and, extensively, from The *New York Times, The End of a Presidency* (New York: Bantam Books, 1974).
256	*14–17*	June 22, 1972. *The End of a Presidency,* p. 136.
256	*19–21*	June 25, 1972. The reporter was Helen Thomas. *The End of a Presidency,* p. 140.
256–57	*21 ff.*	July 1, 1972. *The End of a Presidency,* p. 143.
257	*1–3*	July 12, 1972. *The End of a Presidency,* p. 146.
257	*6–11*	SJE, Jr., interview.
257	*28–29*	August 20, 1972. *The End of a Presidency,* p. 149.
257	*29–31*	August 23, 1972. *The End of a Presidency,* p. 150.

Page *Line*

257 *32–37* Richard M. Nixon, August 29, 1972 press conference. *The End of a Presidency*, pp. 150–151.

257–58 *37ff.* September 2, 1972. *The End of a Presidency*, p. 151.

258 *8–11* Hall Smith interview.

258 *16–18* *The End of a Presidency*, pp. 151–52.

258 *19–22* *The End of a Presidency*, p. 152.

258 *23–26* SJE, Jr., interview.

259 *1–5* *The End of a Presidency*, p. 153.

259 *6–11* *The End of a Presidency*, p. 154.

259 *18–23* SJE, Jr., interview.

259 *30–33* *The End of a Presidency*, p. 156.

259–66 *34ff.* SJE, Jr., interview. George Douth, *Leaders in Profile: The United States Senate* (New York: Spess and Douth, 1972).

ASSESSMENT

266 *3–7* Sam says that he did not make this statement until after the Senate issued its Watergate report; that he would never have done such a thing while the investigation was going on. But it is my clear memory that he said this during our second interview. See "The Character of Americans," pp. 20–24.

Chapter 24

267 *1–3* Sam alone, of all the Watergate Committee, went in cold each day without having read the staff summaries of interviews — the daily crib sheet. He had read it *all*, the transcripts of those interviews, and didn't need the crib sheet. Clancy, p. 272.

268 *4–8* SJE, Jr., interview. *The Watergate Hearings: Break-in and Cover-up*, published by the *New York Times*, pp. 867–70.

269–70 *16ff.* *The Watergate Hearings*, pp. 242, 243.

270 *5–12* *The Watergate Hearings*, p. 243.

270 *14–25* *The Watergate Hearings*, p. 244.

270 *29–31* *The Watergate Hearings*, p. 246.

270–71 *36ff.* Douglas Kiker, *Washingtonian*, Sept. 1973.

271 *14–20* Patricia Shore interview; SJE, Jr., interview.

272–73 *32ff.* *Watergate Hearings*, pp. 352–53.

274 *1–3* Charlotte *Observer*, April 16, 1969.

274 *8–18* SJE, Jr., interview.

275 *13–25* *Watergate Hearings*, p. 395.

275–76 *35ff.* *Watergate Hearings*, p. 396.

276 *32–37* *Watergate Hearings*, p. 398.

277 *1–23* SJE, Jr., interview.

277 *28* Sam said of Margaret at about this time,

It is very hard to describe the traits of a person who is perfect. Margaret has an excellent mind, a wonderful mind and a wonderful spirit, and an almost uncanny ability to distinguish between things that are important and things that are not important, things that are right and things that are wrong, and things that are wise and things that are foolish. Love me? She must, she has put up with me for so long. I would think there are rough corners in my personality that require a good deal of forbearance from a wife. If I have done anything that is worthwhile it is due to the fact that she has always stood beside me in shadow as well as in sunshine.

Eugene (Ore.) *Register-Guardian,* Aug. 19, 1973.

When interviewed several years before regarding Sam's implacable opposition to the Equal Rights Amendment for Women, Margaret had this to say: "I think Sam is exactly right. I suppose you would like for me to say I disagree with my husband on this, but I think Sam is exactly right. I think he is trying to help women. I can't say he is right for sure because I haven't talked to any younger, more militant women." She went on to say that she saw her role as wife, mother, and participant in church and community affairs. She acknowledged that there had been changes in women's roles over the years, and admitted that other women might not share her views or appreciate Sam's stand. "My daughter is a little unhappy herself." September 18, 1970 Senate Scrapbook.

277–78	*34 ff.*	SJE, Jr., interview.
279	*1–15*	*Watergate Hearings,* p. 515.
279	*18–20*	*Watergate Hearings,* p. 515.
279	*22–25*	*Watergate Hearings,* p. 515.
279	*27–32*	*Watergate Hearings,* p. 515.
280	*10–12*	*Watergate Hearings,* p. 518.
280	*14–24*	*Watergate Hearings,* p. 518.
280	*26–27*	*Watergate Hearings,* p. 518.
280–81	*32 ff.*	*Watergate Hearings,* p. 518.
281	*9–12*	*Watergate Hearings,* p. 521.

Index